Graphic Classics:
ARTHUR CONAN DOYLE

Graphic Classics Volume Two
Second Edition
2005

Edited by Tom Pomplun

EUREKA PRODUCTIONS
8778 Oak Grove Road, Mount Horeb, Wisconsin 53572
www.graphicclassics.com

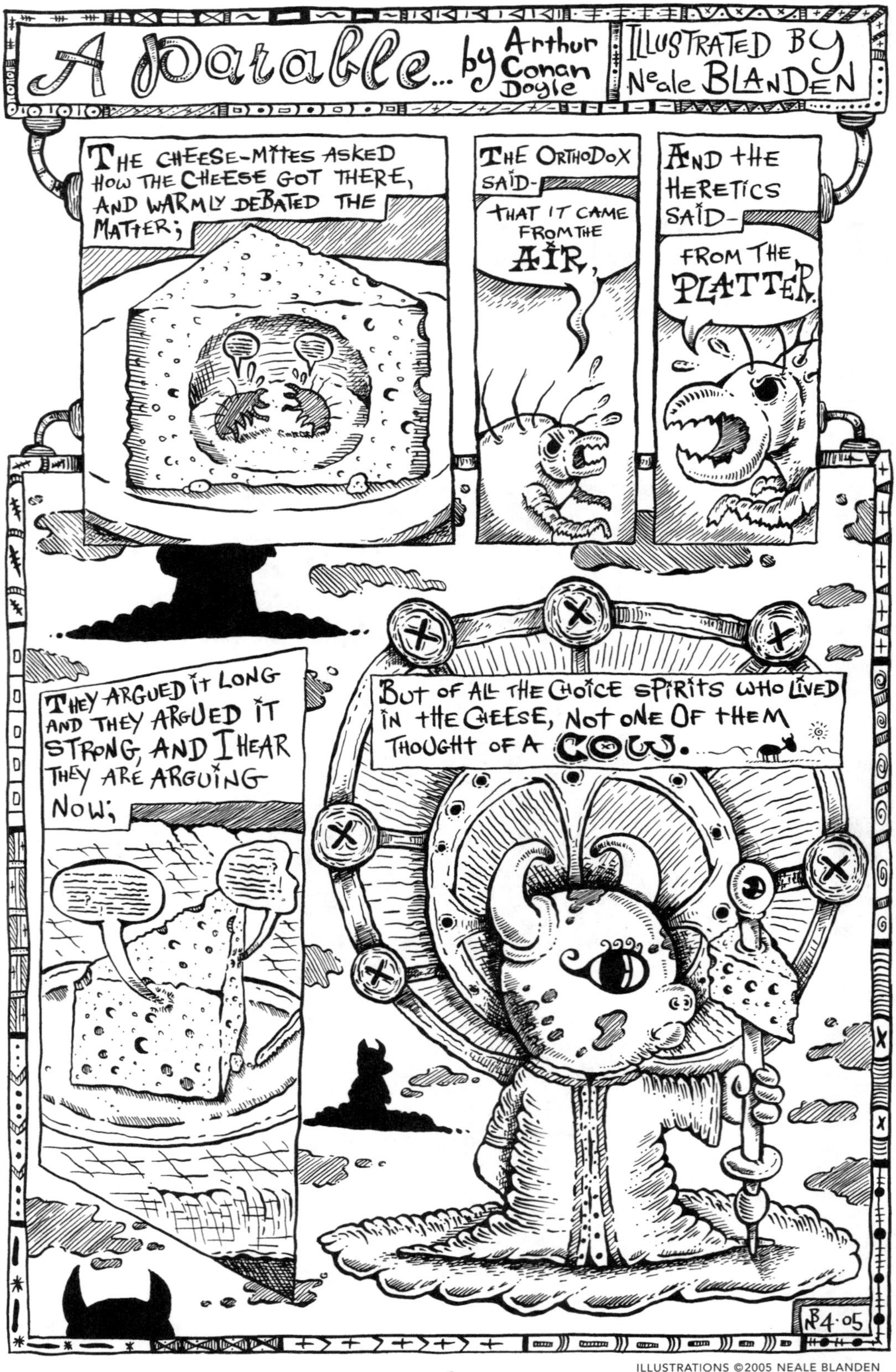
A Parable... by Arthur Conan Doyle
Illustrated by Neale Blanden
The cheese-mites asked how the cheese got there, and warmly debated the matter;
The Orthodox said-
that it came from the AIR,
And the Heretics said-
from the PLATTER.
They argued it long and they argued it strong, and I hear they are arguing now;
But of all the choice spirits who lived in the cheese, not one of them thought of a COW.
NB 4·05

CONTENTS

Graphic Classics:
ARTHUR CONAN DOYLE

ILLUSTRATION ©2005 TEAM SPUTNIK

Cover illustration by Rick Geary
Back cover illustration by J.B. Bonivert

Graphic Classics: Arthur Conan Doyle is published by Eureka Productions. ISBN:13 #978-0-9746648-5-9 / ISBN:10 #0-9746648-5-5. Price US $11.95. Available from Eureka Productions, 8778 Oak Grove Road, Mount Horeb, WI 53572. Tom Pomplun, designer and publisher, tom@graphicclassics.com. Eileen Fitzgerald, editorial assistant. Compilation and all original works ©2005 Eureka Productions. All rights revert to creators after publication. Graphic Classics is a trademark of Eureka Productions. For ordering information and previews of upcoming volumes visit the Graphic Classics website at http://www.graphicclassics.com. Printed in Canada.

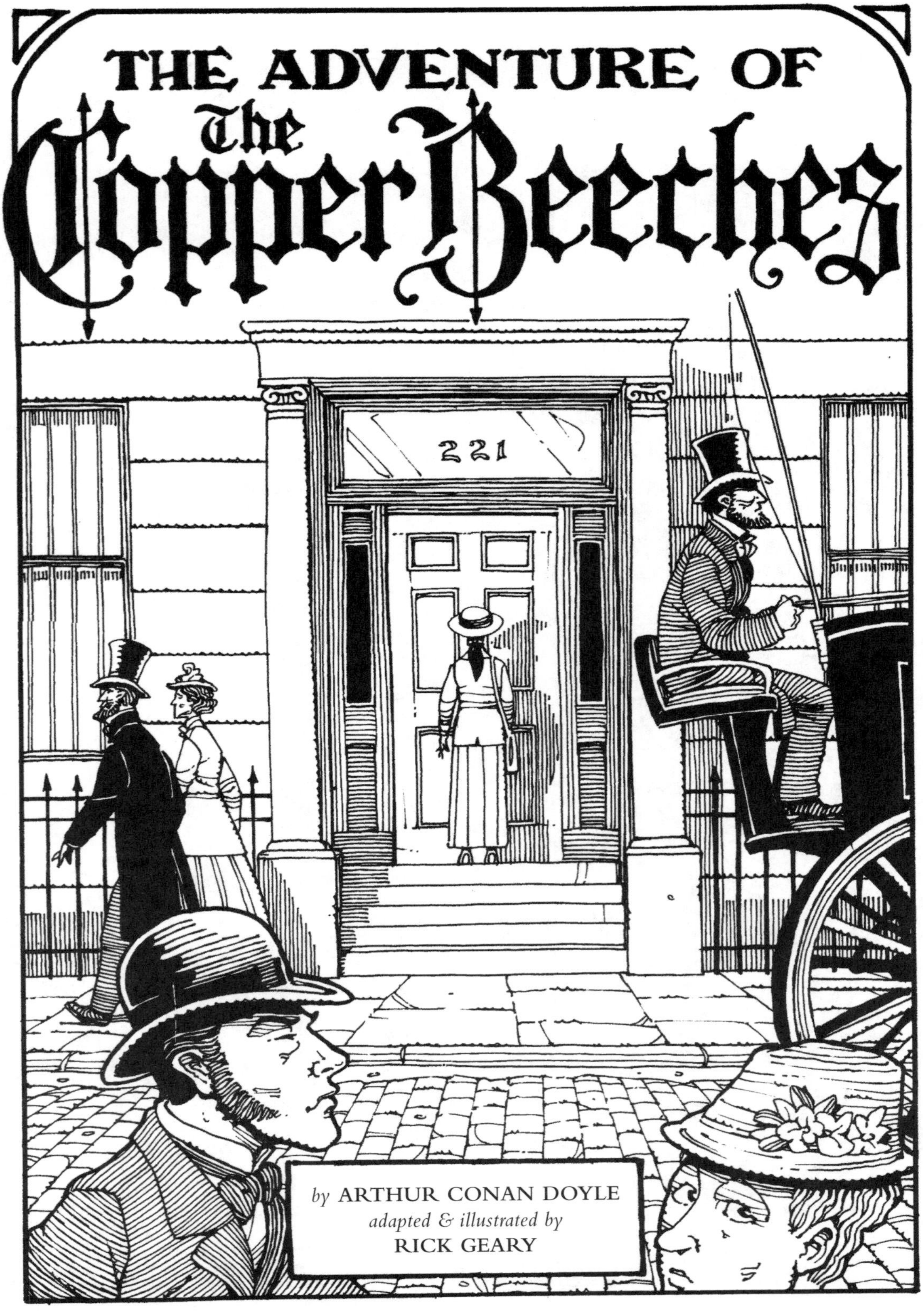
THE ADVENTURE OF
The Copper Beeches
221
by ARTHUR CONAN DOYLE
adapted & illustrated by
RICK GEARY

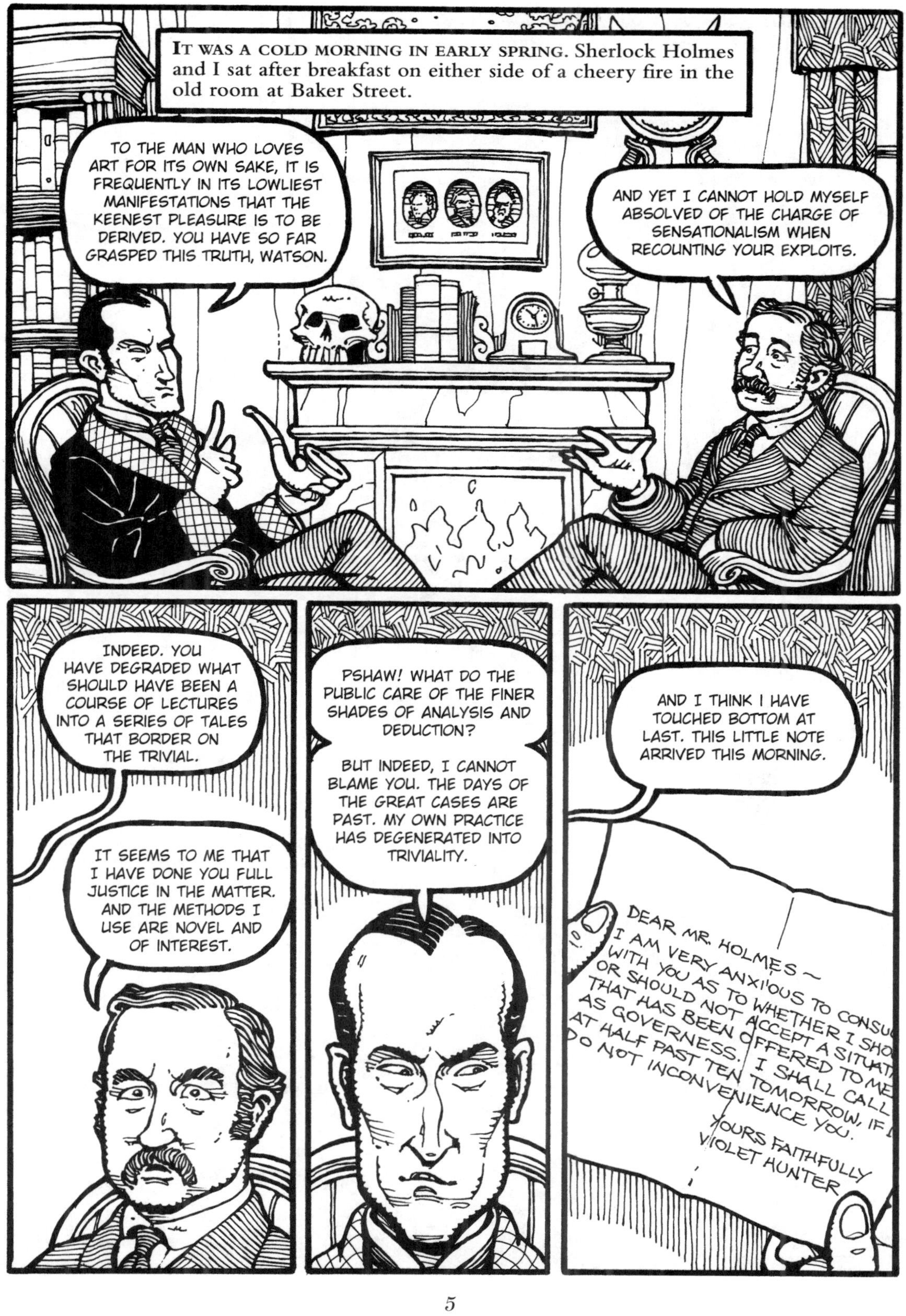
IT WAS A COLD MORNING IN EARLY SPRING. Sherlock Holmes and I sat after breakfast on either side of a cheery fire in the old room at Baker Street.
TO THE MAN WHO LOVES ART FOR ITS OWN SAKE, IT IS FREQUENTLY IN ITS LOWLIEST MANIFESTATIONS THAT THE KEENEST PLEASURE IS TO BE DERIVED. YOU HAVE SO FAR GRASPED THIS TRUTH, WATSON.
AND YET I CANNOT HOLD MYSELF ABSOLVED OF THE CHARGE OF SENSATIONALISM WHEN RECOUNTING YOUR EXPLOITS.
INDEED. YOU HAVE DEGRADED WHAT SHOULD HAVE BEEN A COURSE OF LECTURES INTO A SERIES OF TALES THAT BORDER ON THE TRIVIAL.
IT SEEMS TO ME THAT I HAVE DONE YOU FULL JUSTICE IN THE MATTER. AND THE METHODS I USE ARE NOVEL AND OF INTEREST.
PSHAW! WHAT DO THE PUBLIC CARE OF THE FINER SHADES OF ANALYSIS AND DEDUCTION?
BUT INDEED, I CANNOT BLAME YOU. THE DAYS OF THE GREAT CASES ARE PAST. MY OWN PRACTICE HAS DEGENERATED INTO TRIVIALITY.
AND I THINK I HAVE TOUCHED BOTTOM AT LAST. THIS LITTLE NOTE ARRIVED THIS MORNING.
DEAR MR. HOLMES ~
I AM VERY ANXIOUS TO
WITH YOU AS TO WHETHER I
OR SHOULD NOT ACCEPT A
THAT HAS BEEN OFFERED TO
AS GOVERNESS. I SHALL
AT HALF PAST TEN TOMORROW,
DO NOT INCONVENIENCE YOU.
YOURS FAITHFULLY
VIOLET HUNTER

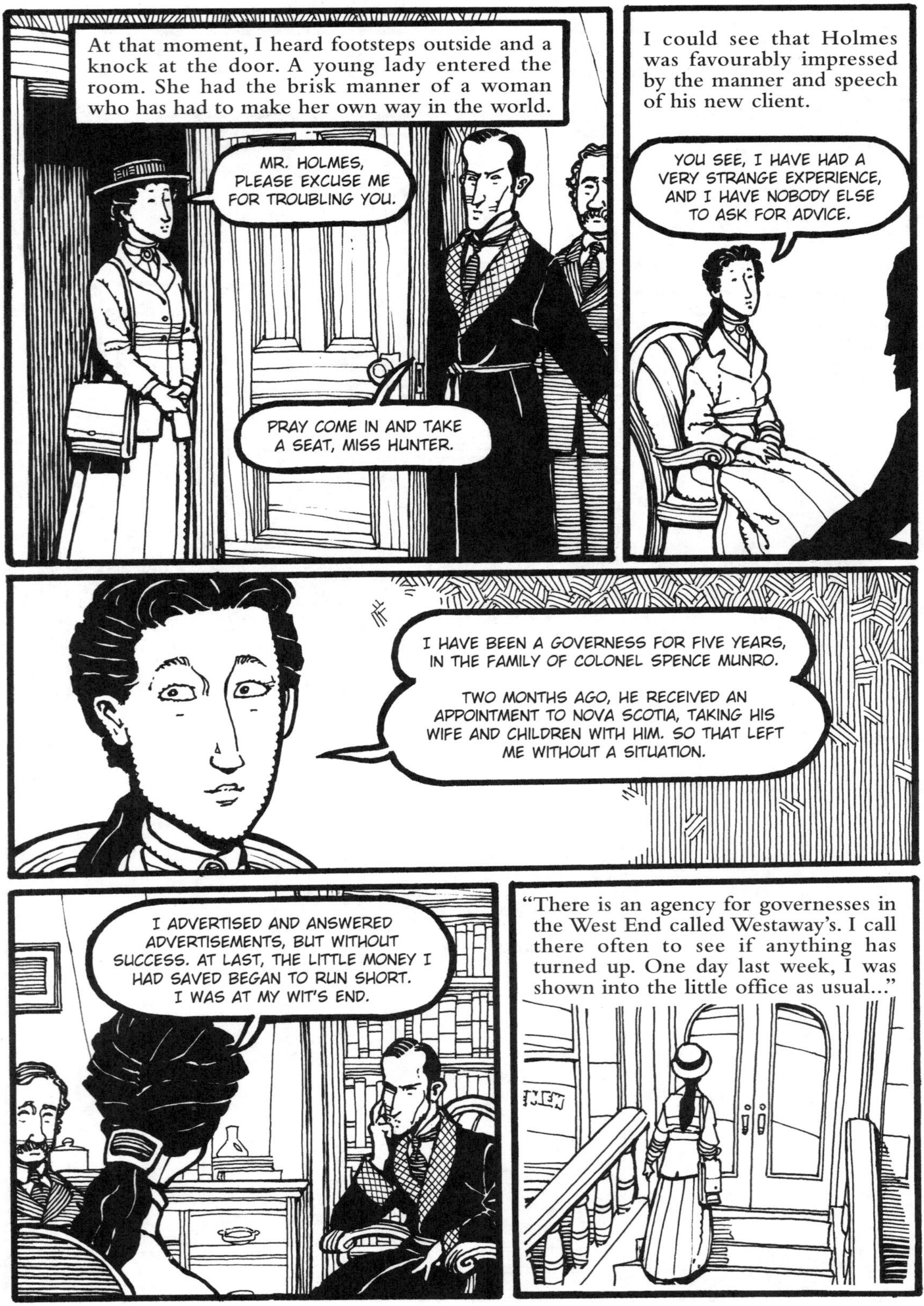
At that moment, I heard footsteps outside and a knock at the door. A young lady entered the room. She had the brisk manner of a woman who has had to make her own way in the world.
MR. HOLMES, PLEASE EXCUSE ME FOR TROUBLING YOU.
PRAY COME IN AND TAKE A SEAT, MISS HUNTER.
I could see that Holmes was favourably impressed by the manner and speech of his new client.
YOU SEE, I HAVE HAD A VERY STRANGE EXPERIENCE, AND I HAVE NOBODY ELSE TO ASK FOR ADVICE.
I HAVE BEEN A GOVERNESS FOR FIVE YEARS, IN THE FAMILY OF COLONEL SPENCE MUNRO.
TWO MONTHS AGO, HE RECEIVED AN APPOINTMENT TO NOVA SCOTIA, TAKING HIS WIFE AND CHILDREN WITH HIM. SO THAT LEFT ME WITHOUT A SITUATION.
I ADVERTISED AND ANSWERED ADVERTISEMENTS, BUT WITHOUT SUCCESS. AT LAST, THE LITTLE MONEY I HAD SAVED BEGAN TO RUN SHORT. I WAS AT MY WIT'S END.
"There is an agency for governesses in the West End called Westaway's. I call there often to see if anything has turned up. One day last week, I was shown into the little office as usual..."

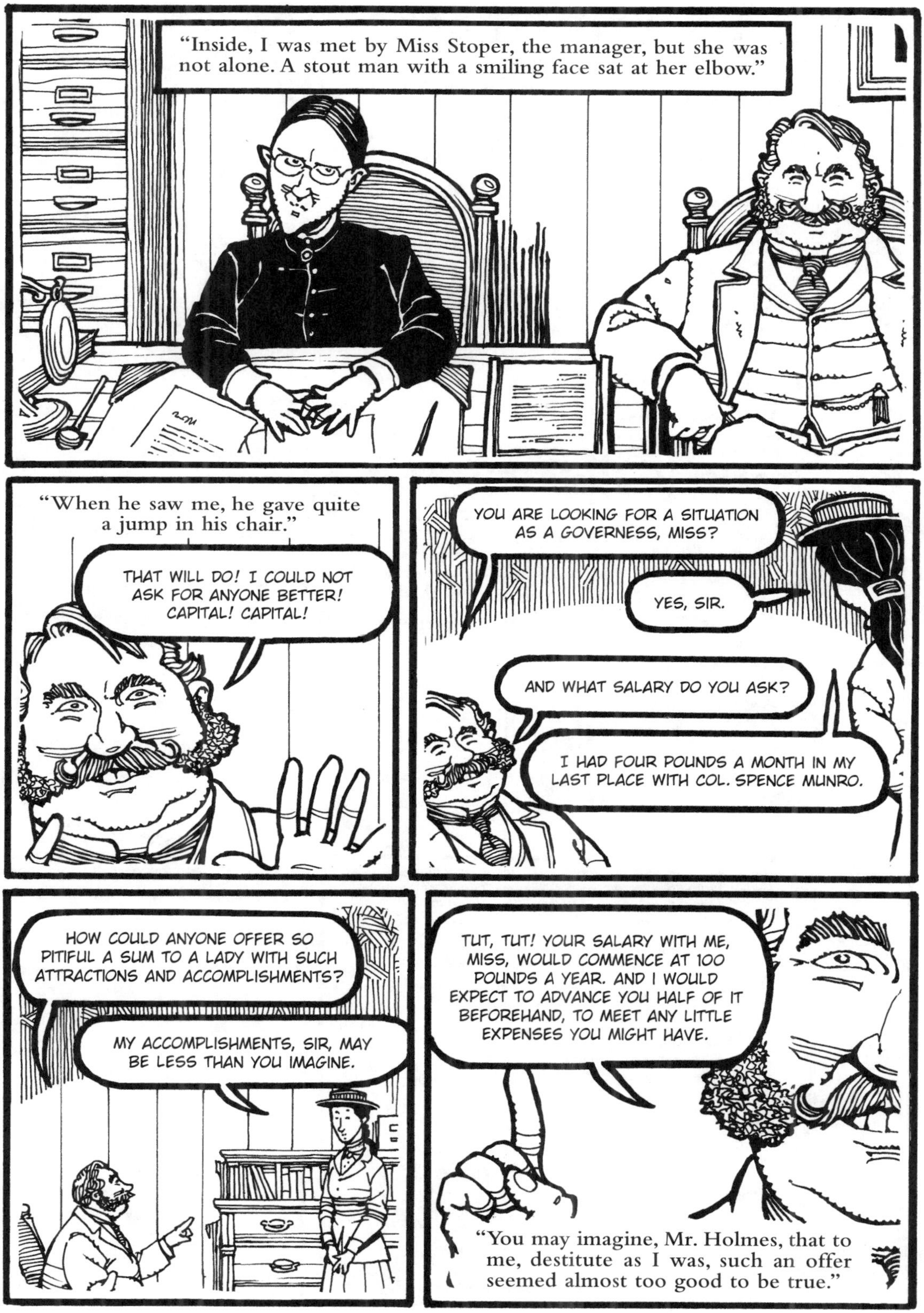
"Inside, I was met by Miss Stoper, the manager, but she was not alone. A stout man with a smiling face sat at her elbow."
"When he saw me, he gave quite a jump in his chair."
THAT WILL DO! I COULD NOT ASK FOR ANYONE BETTER! CAPITAL! CAPITAL!
YOU ARE LOOKING FOR A SITUATION AS A GOVERNESS, MISS?
YES, SIR.
AND WHAT SALARY DO YOU ASK?
I HAD FOUR POUNDS A MONTH IN MY LAST PLACE WITH COL. SPENCE MUNRO.
HOW COULD ANYONE OFFER SO PITIFUL A SUM TO A LADY WITH SUCH ATTRACTIONS AND ACCOMPLISHMENTS?
MY ACCOMPLISHMENTS, SIR, MAY BE LESS THAN YOU IMAGINE.
TUT, TUT! YOUR SALARY WITH ME, MISS, WOULD COMMENCE AT 100 POUNDS A YEAR. AND I WOULD EXPECT TO ADVANCE YOU HALF OF IT BEFOREHAND, TO MEET ANY LITTLE EXPENSES YOU MIGHT HAVE.
"You may imagine, Mr. Holmes, that to me, destitute as I was, such an offer seemed almost too good to be true."

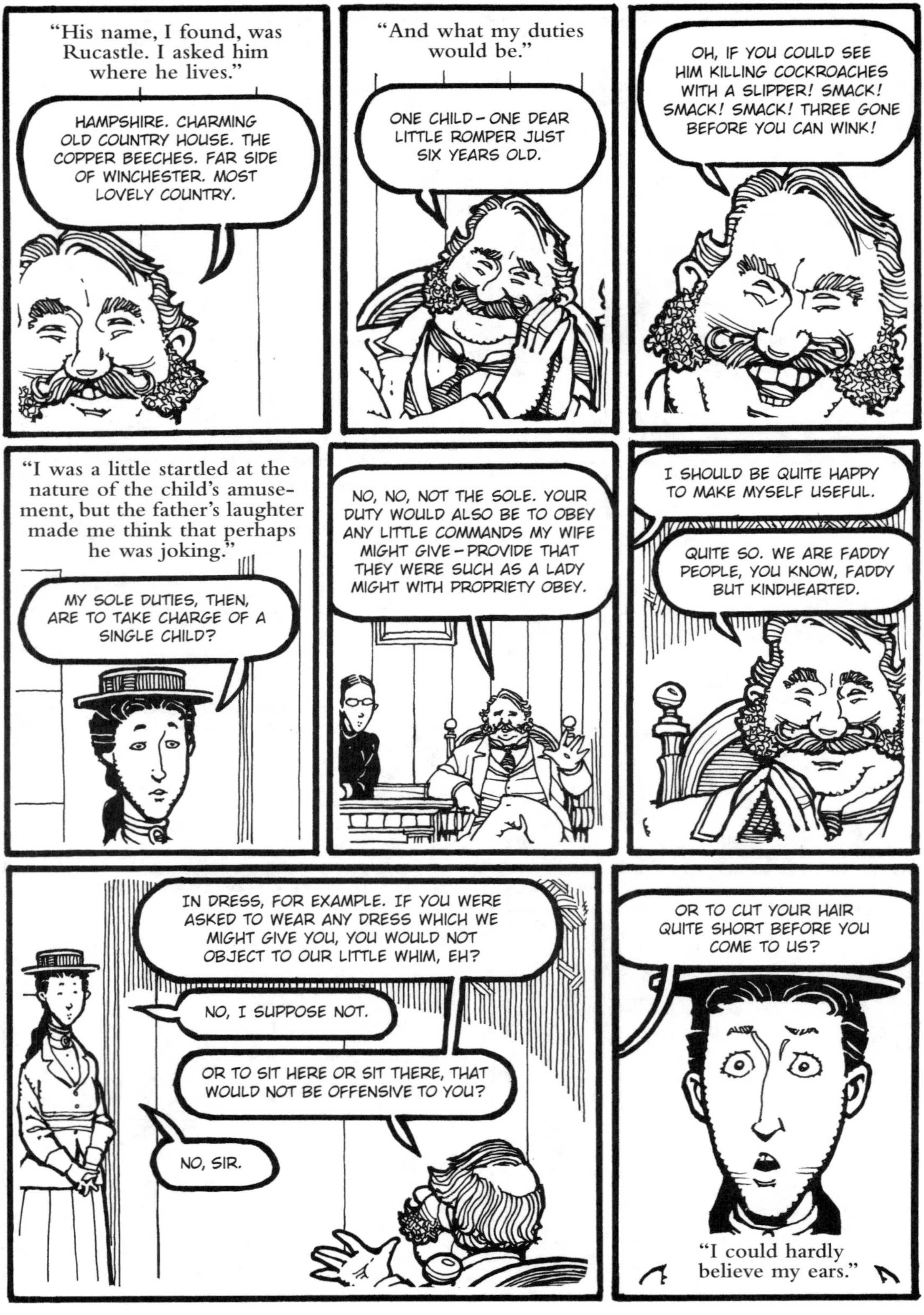
"His name, I found, was Rucastle. I asked him where he lives."
HAMPSHIRE. CHARMING OLD COUNTRY HOUSE. THE COPPER BEECHES. FAR SIDE OF WINCHESTER. MOST LOVELY COUNTRY.
"And what my duties would be."
ONE CHILD – ONE DEAR LITTLE ROMPER JUST SIX YEARS OLD.
OH, IF YOU COULD SEE HIM KILLING COCKROACHES WITH A SLIPPER! SMACK! SMACK! SMACK! THREE GONE BEFORE YOU CAN WINK!
"I was a little startled at the nature of the child's amusement, but the father's laughter made me think that perhaps he was joking."
MY SOLE DUTIES, THEN, ARE TO TAKE CHARGE OF A SINGLE CHILD?
NO, NO, NOT THE SOLE. YOUR DUTY WOULD ALSO BE TO OBEY ANY LITTLE COMMANDS MY WIFE MIGHT GIVE – PROVIDE THAT THEY WERE SUCH AS A LADY MIGHT WITH PROPRIETY OBEY.
I SHOULD BE QUITE HAPPY TO MAKE MYSELF USEFUL.
QUITE SO. WE ARE FADDY PEOPLE, YOU KNOW, FADDY BUT KINDHEARTED.
IN DRESS, FOR EXAMPLE. IF YOU WERE ASKED TO WEAR ANY DRESS WHICH WE MIGHT GIVE YOU, YOU WOULD NOT OBJECT TO OUR LITTLE WHIM, EH?
NO, I SUPPOSE NOT.
OR TO SIT HERE OR SIT THERE, THAT WOULD NOT BE OFFENSIVE TO YOU?
NO, SIR.
OR TO CUT YOUR HAIR QUITE SHORT BEFORE YOU COME TO US?
"I could hardly believe my ears."

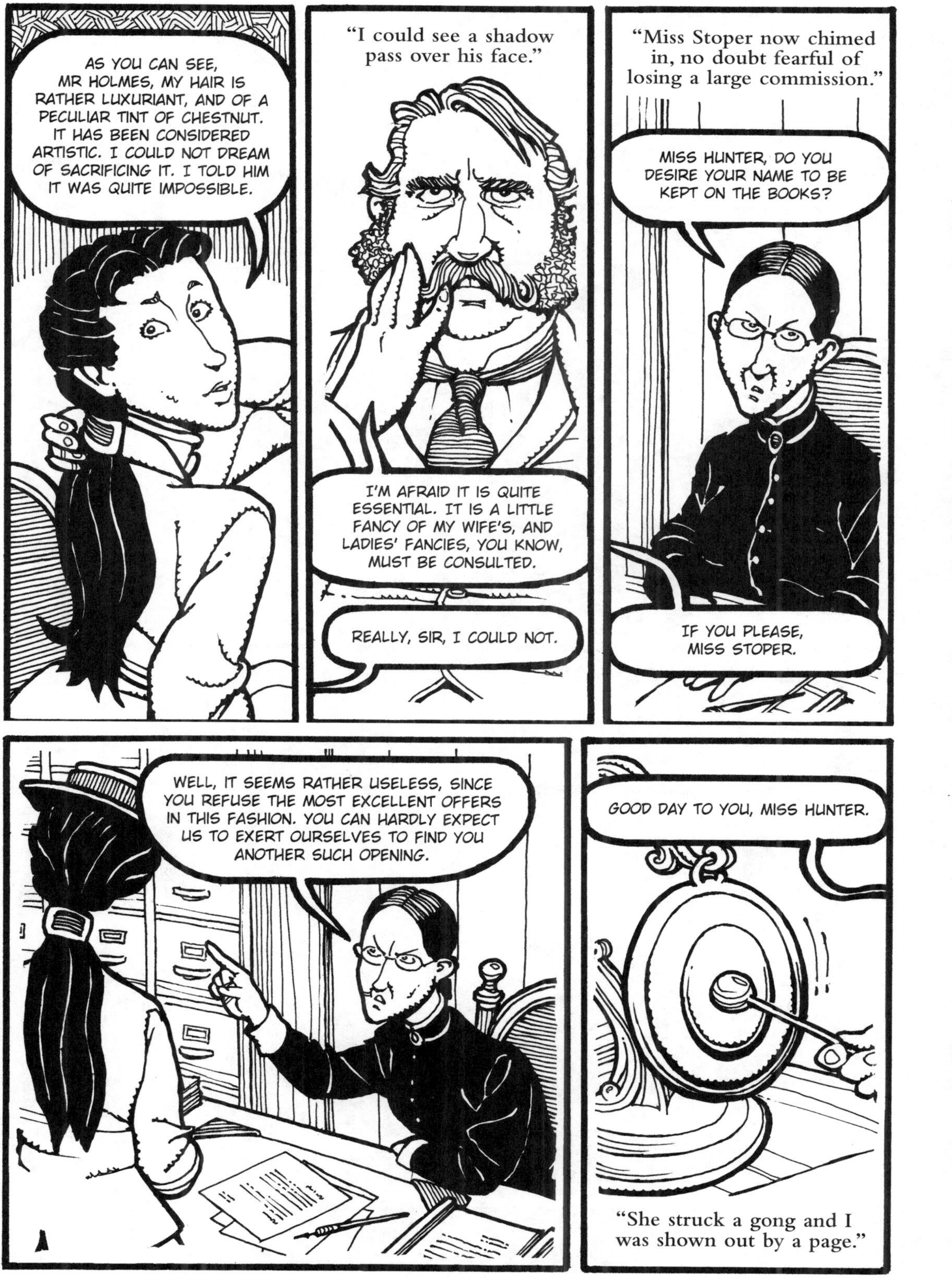
AS YOU CAN SEE, MR HOLMES, MY HAIR IS RATHER LUXURIANT, AND OF A PECULIAR TINT OF CHESTNUT. IT HAS BEEN CONSIDERED ARTISTIC. I COULD NOT DREAM OF SACRIFICING IT. I TOLD HIM IT WAS QUITE IMPOSSIBLE.
"I could see a shadow pass over his face."
I'M AFRAID IT IS QUITE ESSENTIAL. IT IS A LITTLE FANCY OF MY WIFE'S, AND LADIES' FANCIES, YOU KNOW, MUST BE CONSULTED.
REALLY, SIR, I COULD NOT.
"Miss Stoper now chimed in, no doubt fearful of losing a large commission."
MISS HUNTER, DO YOU DESIRE YOUR NAME TO BE KEPT ON THE BOOKS?
IF YOU PLEASE, MISS STOPER.
WELL, IT SEEMS RATHER USELESS, SINCE YOU REFUSE THE MOST EXCELLENT OFFERS IN THIS FASHION. YOU CAN HARDLY EXPECT US TO EXERT OURSELVES TO FIND YOU ANOTHER SUCH OPENING.
GOOD DAY TO YOU, MISS HUNTER.
"She struck a gong and I was shown out by a page."

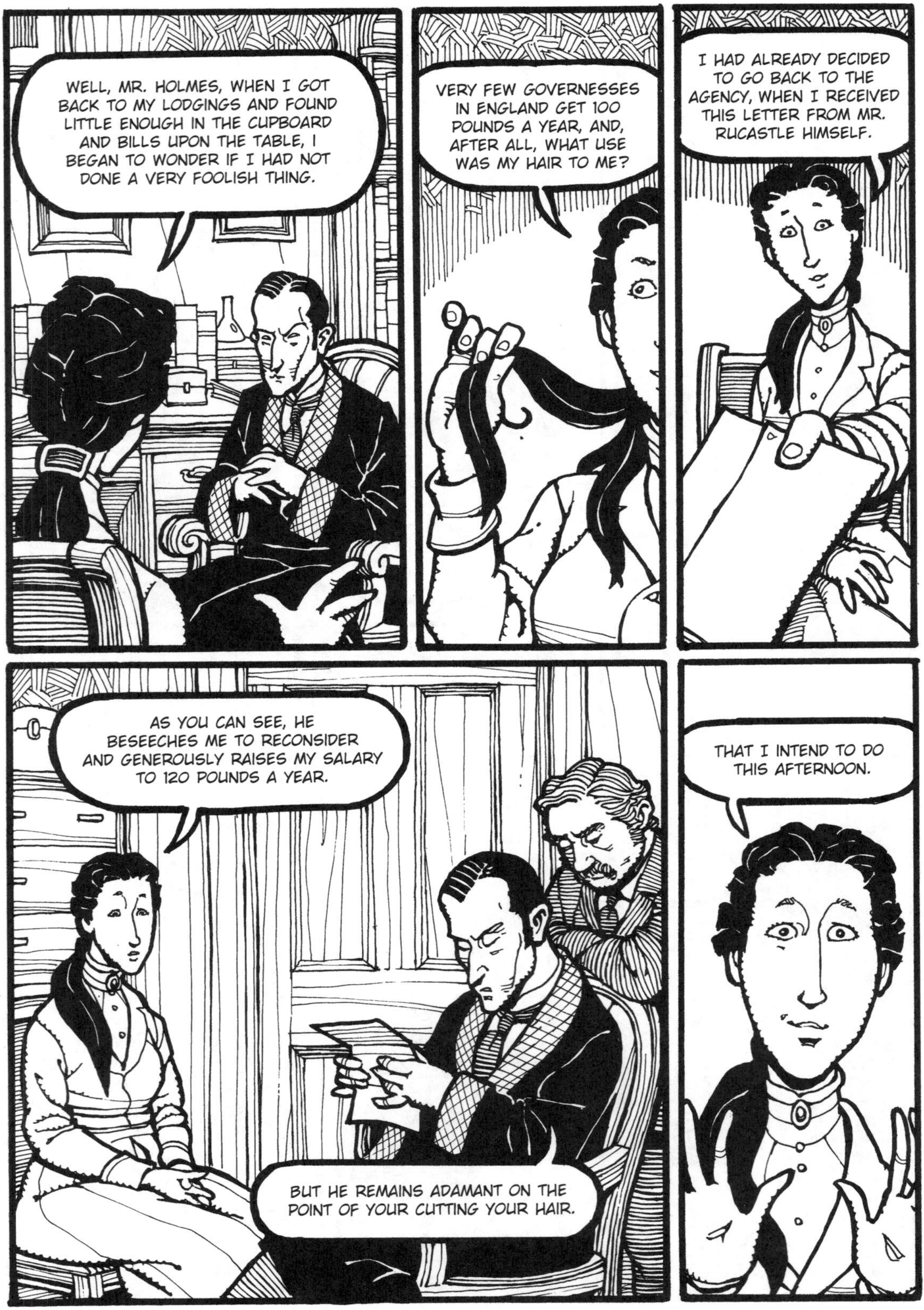
WELL, MR. HOLMES, WHEN I GOT BACK TO MY LODGINGS AND FOUND LITTLE ENOUGH IN THE CUPBOARD AND BILLS UPON THE TABLE, I BEGAN TO WONDER IF I HAD NOT DONE A VERY FOOLISH THING.
VERY FEW GOVERNESSES IN ENGLAND GET 100 POUNDS A YEAR, AND, AFTER ALL, WHAT USE WAS MY HAIR TO ME?
I HAD ALREADY DECIDED TO GO BACK TO THE AGENCY, WHEN I RECEIVED THIS LETTER FROM MR. RUCASTLE HIMSELF.
AS YOU CAN SEE, HE BESEECHES ME TO RECONSIDER AND GENEROUSLY RAISES MY SALARY TO 120 POUNDS A YEAR.
BUT HE REMAINS ADAMANT ON THE POINT OF YOUR CUTTING YOUR HAIR.
THAT I INTEND TO DO THIS AFTERNOON.

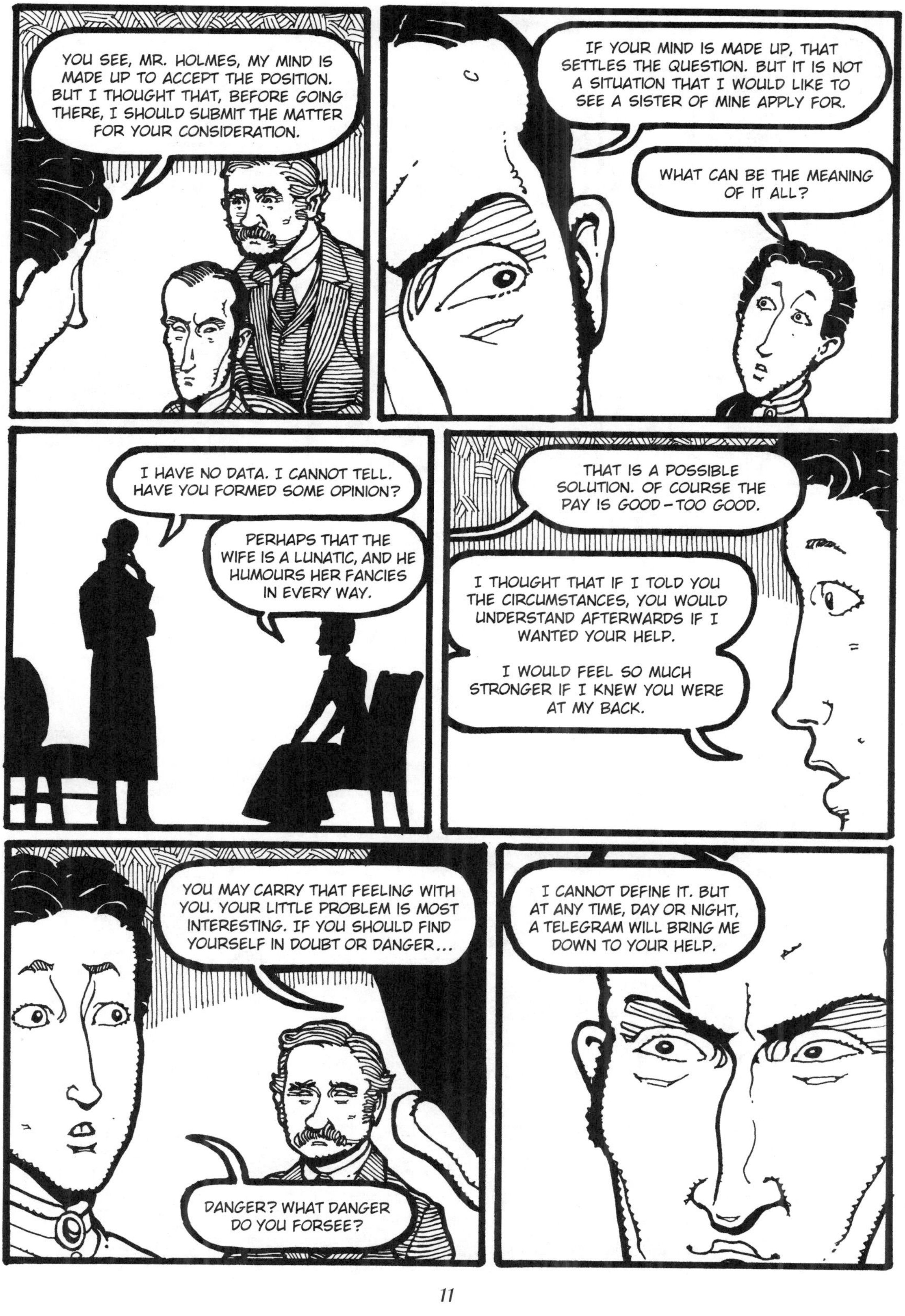
YOU SEE, MR. HOLMES, MY MIND IS MADE UP TO ACCEPT THE POSITION. BUT I THOUGHT THAT, BEFORE GOING THERE, I SHOULD SUBMIT THE MATTER FOR YOUR CONSIDERATION.
IF YOUR MIND IS MADE UP, THAT SETTLES THE QUESTION. BUT IT IS NOT A SITUATION THAT I WOULD LIKE TO SEE A SISTER OF MINE APPLY FOR.
WHAT CAN BE THE MEANING OF IT ALL?
I HAVE NO DATA. I CANNOT TELL. HAVE YOU FORMED SOME OPINION?
PERHAPS THAT THE WIFE IS A LUNATIC, AND HE HUMOURS HER FANCIES IN EVERY WAY.
THAT IS A POSSIBLE SOLUTION. OF COURSE THE PAY IS GOOD–TOO GOOD.
I THOUGHT THAT IF I TOLD YOU THE CIRCUMSTANCES, YOU WOULD UNDERSTAND AFTERWARDS IF I WANTED YOUR HELP.
I WOULD FEEL SO MUCH STRONGER IF I KNEW YOU WERE AT MY BACK.
YOU MAY CARRY THAT FEELING WITH YOU. YOUR LITTLE PROBLEM IS MOST INTERESTING. IF YOU SHOULD FIND YOURSELF IN DOUBT OR DANGER...
DANGER? WHAT DANGER DO YOU FORSEE?
I CANNOT DEFINE IT. BUT AT ANY TIME, DAY OR NIGHT, A TELEGRAM WILL BRING ME DOWN TO YOUR HELP.

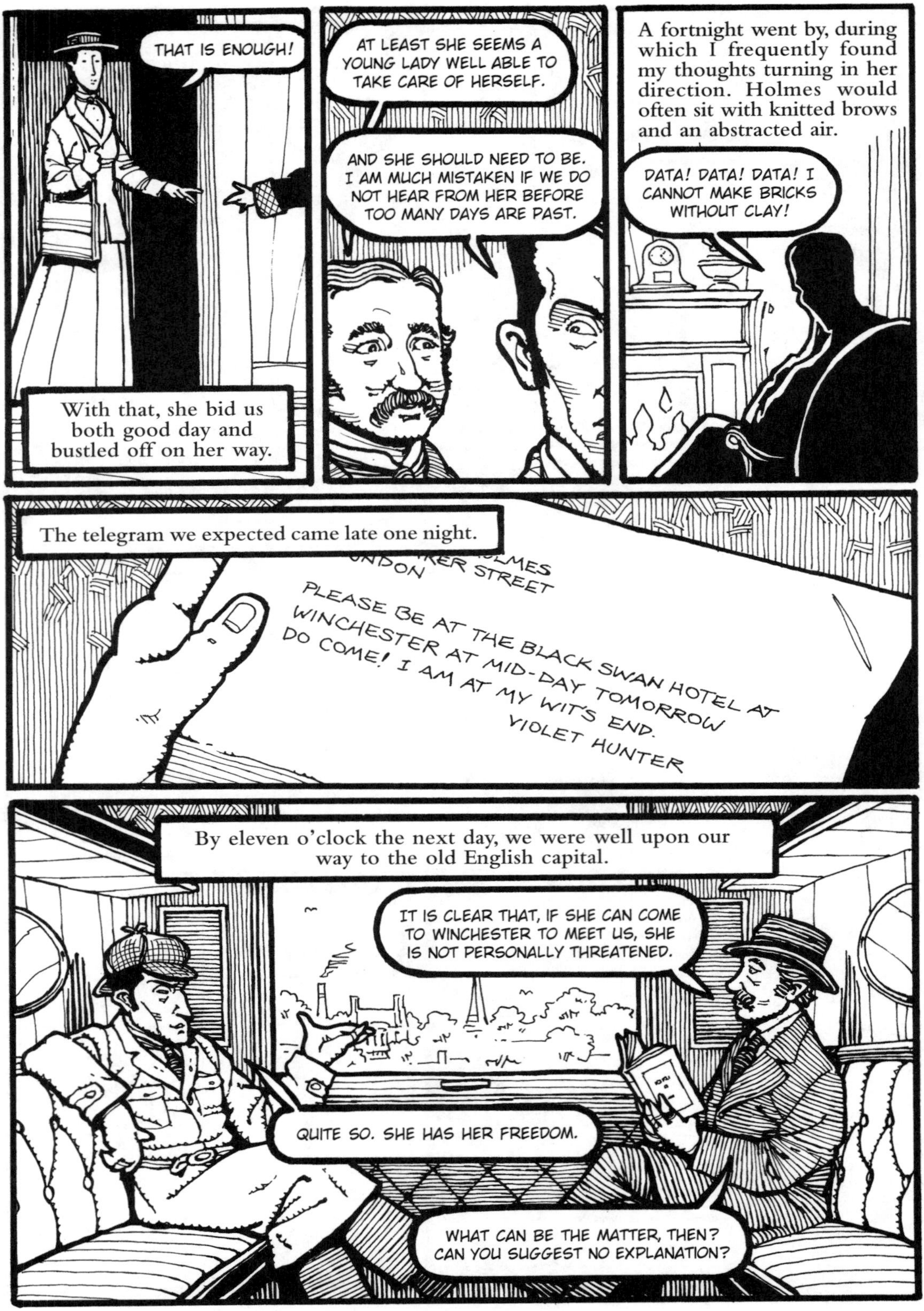
THAT IS ENOUGH!
With that, she bid us both good day and bustled off on her way.
AT LEAST SHE SEEMS A YOUNG LADY WELL ABLE TO TAKE CARE OF HERSELF.
AND SHE SHOULD NEED TO BE. I AM MUCH MISTAKEN IF WE DO NOT HEAR FROM HER BEFORE TOO MANY DAYS ARE PAST.
A fortnight went by, during which I frequently found my thoughts turning in her direction. Holmes would often sit with knitted brows and an abstracted air.
DATA! DATA! DATA! I CANNOT MAKE BRICKS WITHOUT CLAY!
The telegram we expected came late one night.
PLEASE BE AT THE BLACK SWAN HOTEL AT WINCHESTER AT MID-DAY TOMORROW
DO COME! I AM AT MY WIT'S END.
VIOLET HUNTER
By eleven o'clock the next day, we were well upon our way to the old English capital.
IT IS CLEAR THAT, IF SHE CAN COME TO WINCHESTER TO MEET US, SHE IS NOT PERSONALLY THREATENED.
QUITE SO. SHE HAS HER FREEDOM.
WHAT CAN BE THE MATTER, THEN? CAN YOU SUGGEST NO EXPLANATION?

I HAVE DEVISED SEVEN SEPARATE EXPLANATIONS, EACH OF WHICH WOULD COVER THE FACTS AS WE KNOW THEM. BUT WHICH OF THEM IS CORRECT CAN ONLY BE DETERMINED BY THE FRESH INFORMATION WE SHALL NO DOUBT FIND WAITING FOR US.

THE BLACK SWAN
est. 1603

The Black Swan is an inn of repute on High Street. There we found the young lady awaiting us.

She had engaged a sitting room, with our lunch laid out.

I AM SO DELIGHTED THAT YOU HAVE COME. YOUR ADVICE WILL BE INVALUABLE TO ME.

PRAY TELL US WHAT HAS HAPPENED TO YOU.

I WILL DO SO, AND I MUST BE QUICK, FOR I HAVE PROMISED MR. RUCASTLE TO BE BACK BEFORE THREE. HE AND HIS WIFE ARE GOING OUT FOR THE EVENING.

LET US HAVE EVERYTHING IN ITS DUE ORDER.

13

WELL, IN THE FIRST PLACE, I MUST SAY THAT I HAVE MET WITH NO ACTUAL ILL-TREATMENT FROM MR. AND MRS. RUCASTLE. BUT I CANNOT UNDERSTAND THEM, AND I AM NOT EASY IN MY MIND ABOUT THEM.

WHAT CAN YOU NOT UNDERSTAND?

THE REASONS FOR THEIR CONDUCT. BUT YOU SHALL HAVE IT ALL JUST AS IT OCCURRED.

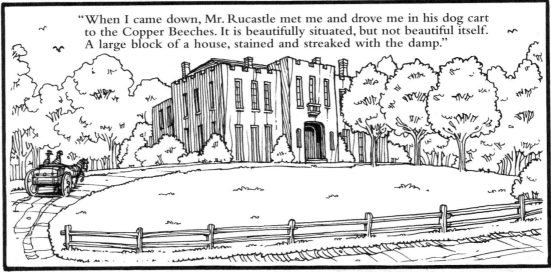

"When I came down, Mr. Rucastle met me and drove me in his dog cart to the Copper Beeches. It is beautifully situated, but not beautiful itself. A large block of a house, stained and streaked with the damp."

"My employer was as amiable as ever. He introduced me that evening to his wife and child."

"Mrs. Rucastle is not mad, but I found her to be a silent, pale-faced woman, much younger than her husband."

"She seemed to me colorless in mind as well as in feature. She impressed me neither favourably nor the reverse."

"He is kind to her in his bluff, boisterous fashion, and yet she has some secret sorrow, this woman. She would often be lost in deep, sad thought, and I have more than once surprised her in tears."

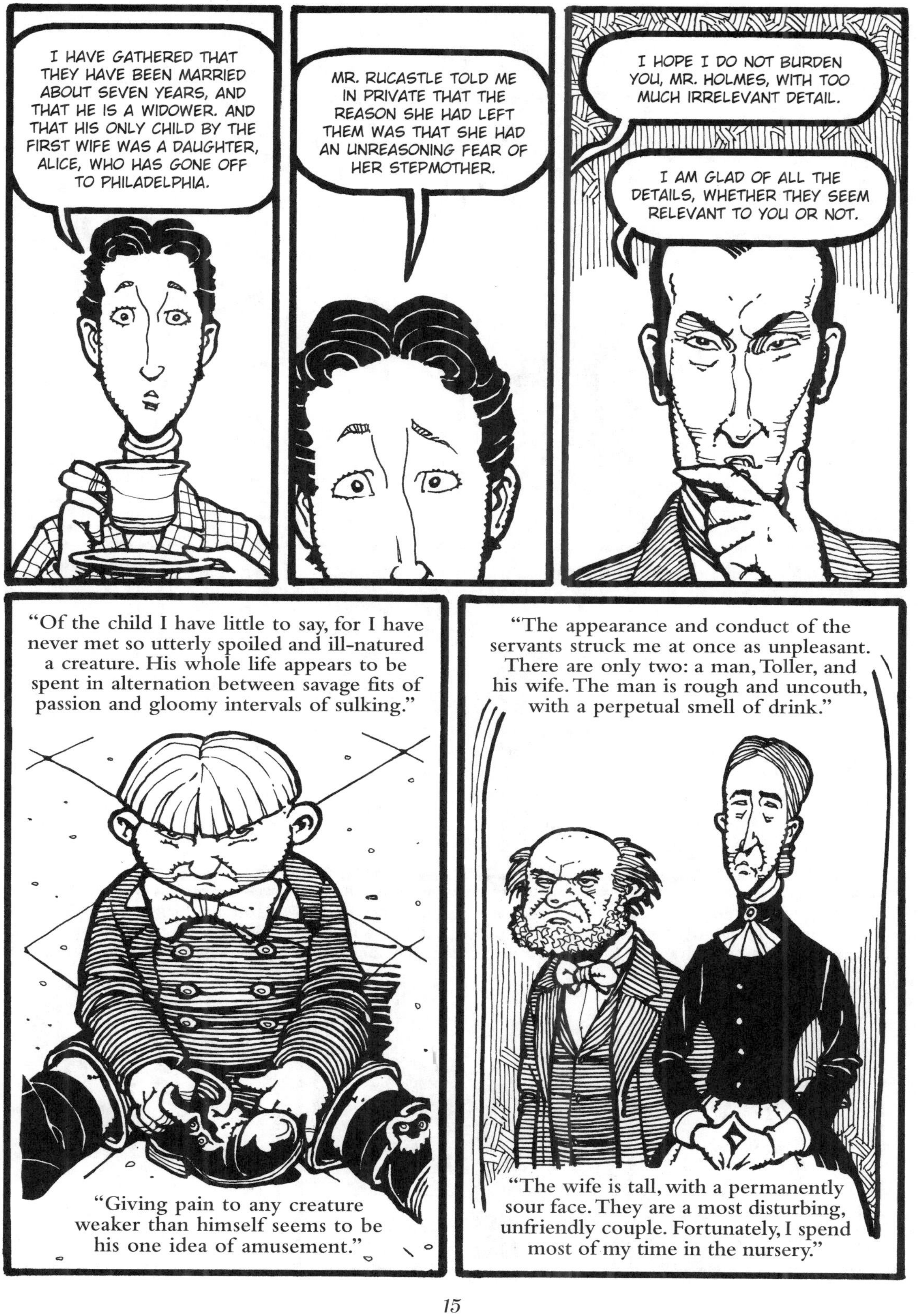
I HAVE GATHERED THAT THEY HAVE BEEN MARRIED ABOUT SEVEN YEARS, AND THAT HE IS A WIDOWER. AND THAT HIS ONLY CHILD BY THE FIRST WIFE WAS A DAUGHTER, ALICE, WHO HAS GONE OFF TO PHILADELPHIA.
MR. RUCASTLE TOLD ME IN PRIVATE THAT THE REASON SHE HAD LEFT THEM WAS THAT SHE HAD AN UNREASONING FEAR OF HER STEPMOTHER.
I HOPE I DO NOT BURDEN YOU, MR. HOLMES, WITH TOO MUCH IRRELEVANT DETAIL.
I AM GLAD OF ALL THE DETAILS, WHETHER THEY SEEM RELEVANT TO YOU OR NOT.
"Of the child I have little to say, for I have never met so utterly spoiled and ill-natured a creature. His whole life appears to be spent in alternation between savage fits of passion and gloomy intervals of sulking."
"Giving pain to any creature weaker than himself seems to be his one idea of amusement."
"The appearance and conduct of the servants struck me at once as unpleasant. There are only two: a man, Toller, and his wife. The man is rough and uncouth, with a perpetual smell of drink."
"The wife is tall, with a permanently sour face. They are a most disturbing, unfriendly couple. Fortunately, I spend most of my time in the nursery."

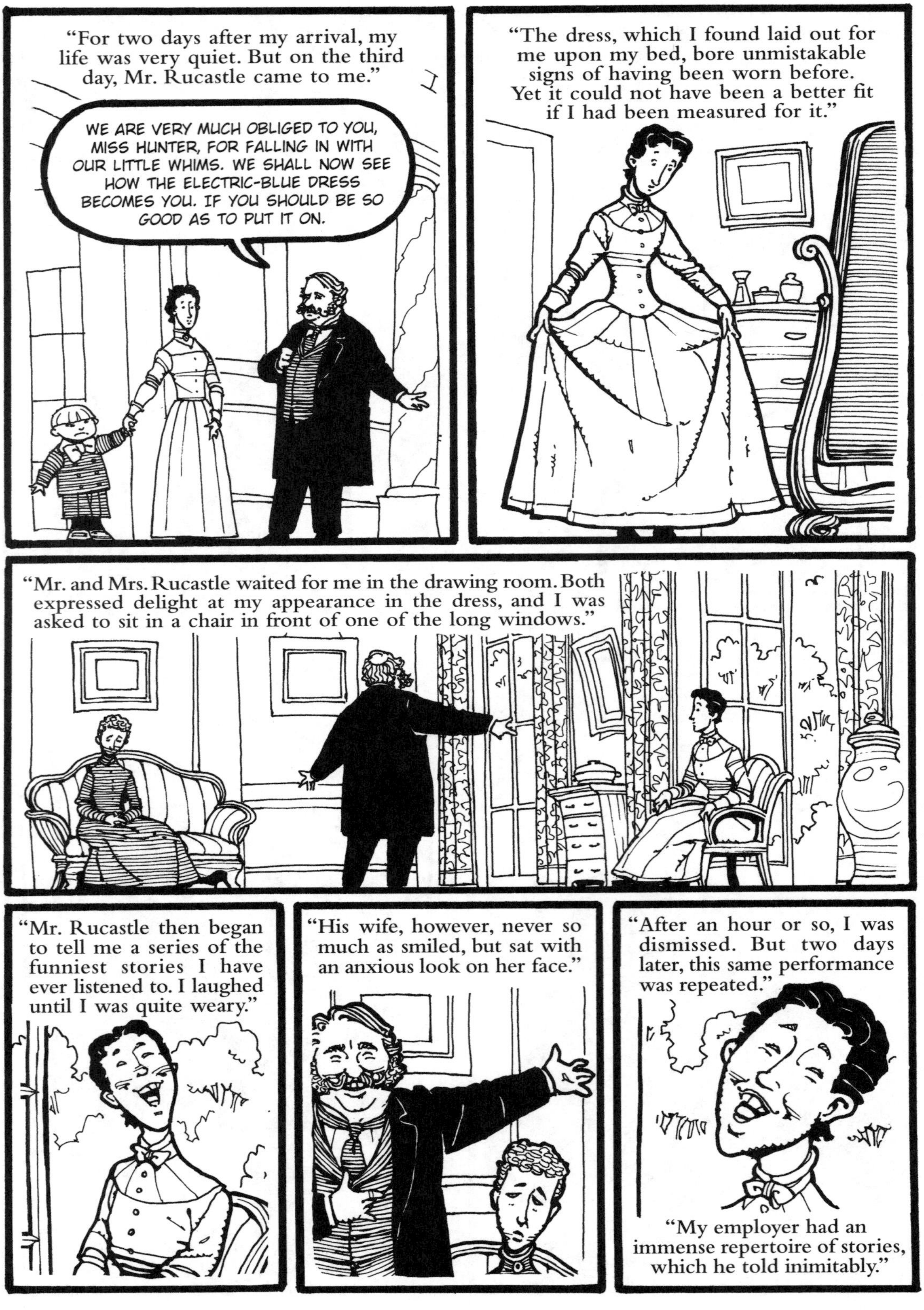
"For two days after my arrival, my life was very quiet. But on the third day, Mr. Rucastle came to me."
WE ARE VERY MUCH OBLIGED TO YOU, MISS HUNTER, FOR FALLING IN WITH OUR LITTLE WHIMS. WE SHALL NOW SEE HOW THE ELECTRIC-BLUE DRESS BECOMES YOU. IF YOU SHOULD BE SO GOOD AS TO PUT IT ON.
"The dress, which I found laid out for me upon my bed, bore unmistakable signs of having been worn before. Yet it could not have been a better fit if I had been measured for it."
"Mr. and Mrs. Rucastle waited for me in the drawing room. Both expressed delight at my appearance in the dress, and I was asked to sit in a chair in front of one of the long windows."
"Mr. Rucastle then began to tell me a series of the funniest stories I have ever listened to. I laughed until I was quite weary."
"His wife, however, never so much as smiled, but sat with an anxious look on her face."
"After an hour or so, I was dismissed. But two days later, this same performance was repeated."
"My employer had an immense repertoire of stories, which he told inimitably."

YOU CAN EASILY IMAGINE, MR. HOLMES, HOW CURIOUS I BECAME AS TO WHAT THE MEANING OF THIS COULD POSSIBLY BE.

"Mr. Rucastle was always very careful, I observed, to keep my face turned from the window – so I became consumed with the desire to see what was going on behind my back."

"I soon devised a means. My hand mirror had recently been broken, so I concealed a piece of the glass in my handkerchief."

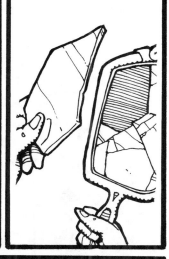

"On the next occasion, in the midst of my laughter, I put my handkerchief up to my eyes."

"In the reflection, I perceived a man standing in the Southhampton Road, leaning against the railings and looking in my direction."

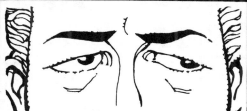

"I glanced at Mrs. Rucastle to find her eyes fixed upon me with a searching gaze."

"I am convinced she had divined that I had a mirror, for she rose and drew down the blind."

THERE IS AN IMPERTINENT FELLOW LOITERING OUT ON THE ROAD AND STARING UP AT MISS HUNTER.

"Since then, I have not sat at the window, nor have I worn the blue dress."

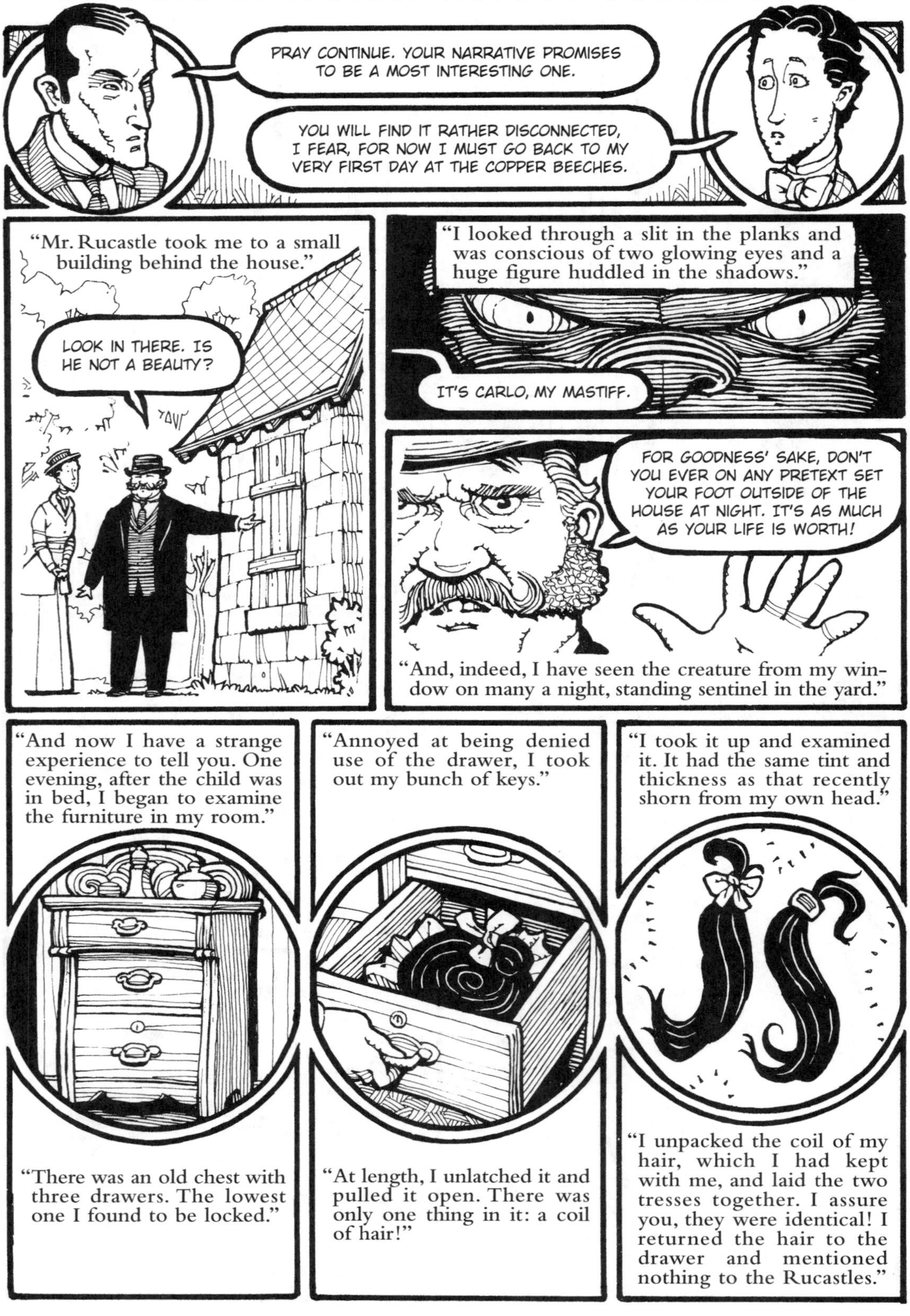
PRAY CONTINUE. YOUR NARRATIVE PROMISES TO BE A MOST INTERESTING ONE.
YOU WILL FIND IT RATHER DISCONNECTED, I FEAR, FOR NOW I MUST GO BACK TO MY VERY FIRST DAY AT THE COPPER BEECHES.
"Mr. Rucastle took me to a small building behind the house."
LOOK IN THERE. IS HE NOT A BEAUTY?
"I looked through a slit in the planks and was conscious of two glowing eyes and a huge figure huddled in the shadows."
IT'S CARLO, MY MASTIFF.
FOR GOODNESS' SAKE, DON'T YOU EVER ON ANY PRETEXT SET YOUR FOOT OUTSIDE OF THE HOUSE AT NIGHT. IT'S AS MUCH AS YOUR LIFE IS WORTH!
"And, indeed, I have seen the creature from my window on many a night, standing sentinel in the yard."
"And now I have a strange experience to tell you. One evening, after the child was in bed, I began to examine the furniture in my room."
"There was an old chest with three drawers. The lowest one I found to be locked."
"Annoyed at being denied use of the drawer, I took out my bunch of keys."
"At length, I unlatched it and pulled it open. There was only one thing in it: a coil of hair!"
"I took it up and examined it. It had the same tint and thickness as that recently shorn from my own head."
"I unpacked the coil of my hair, which I had kept with me, and laid the two tresses together. I assure you, they were identical! I returned the hair to the drawer and mentioned nothing to the Rucastles."

"And now for another strange incident. After a while, I had a pretty good plan of the whole house in my head. There was one wing, however, which appeared not to be inhabited at all."

"A door near the rear stairway led to this wing – but it was invariably locked."

"One day, I met Mr. Rucastle coming out through this door. His face was distorted with anger, a very different person to the jovial man to whom I was accustomed."

"He locked the door and hurried past me without a word or a look."

"This aroused my curiosity, so I went outside for a walk and found the windows of the deserted wing."

"There were four in a row, three of them merely dirty – the fourth shuttered up."

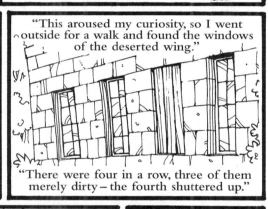

"Mr. Rucastle came out to me, as merry and jovial as ever."

YOU SEEM TO HAVE A SUITE OF SPARE ROOMS IN THIS PART OF THE HOUSE.

YES, PHOTOGRAPHY IS ONE OF MY HOBBIES. I HAVE MADE A DARKROOM IN THIS WING.

BUT DEAR ME! WHAT AN OBSERVANT YOUNG LADY WE HAVE COME UPON! WHO WOULD HAVE BELIEVED IT?

WELL, MR. HOLMES, AS YOU MIGHT IMAGINE, FROM THAT MOMENT, I WAS ALL ON FIRE TO SEE THOSE ROOMS!

IT WAS NOT MERE CURIOSITY, BUT MORE A FEELING OF DUTY – A FEELING THAT SOME GOOD MIGHT COME OF IT.

"It was only yesterday that the chance came. As I came up the stairs, I spied a key in the door—left there, no doubt, by Toller in his drunken state."

"I turned the key and slipped through the door."

"In the little passage in front of me, there were three doors in a line."

"The first and third were unlocked, and each led to an empty room."

"But the centre door was tightly locked. Across it was fastened an iron bar, as if to keep someone inside."

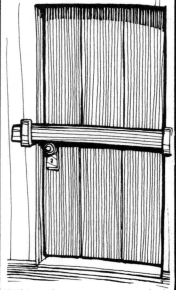

"This door corresponded clearly with the shuttered window outside, yet I could see by a glimmer of light beneath it that the room was not in total darkness."

"Suddenly, I heard the sound of footsteps within the room and saw a shadow pass against the dim light."

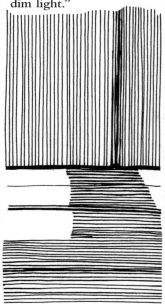

"A mad, unreasoning terror rose up in me at the sight, Mr. Holmes."

"My overstrung nerves failed me, and I turned and ran. Ran as though some dreadful hand were behind me, clutching at my dress."

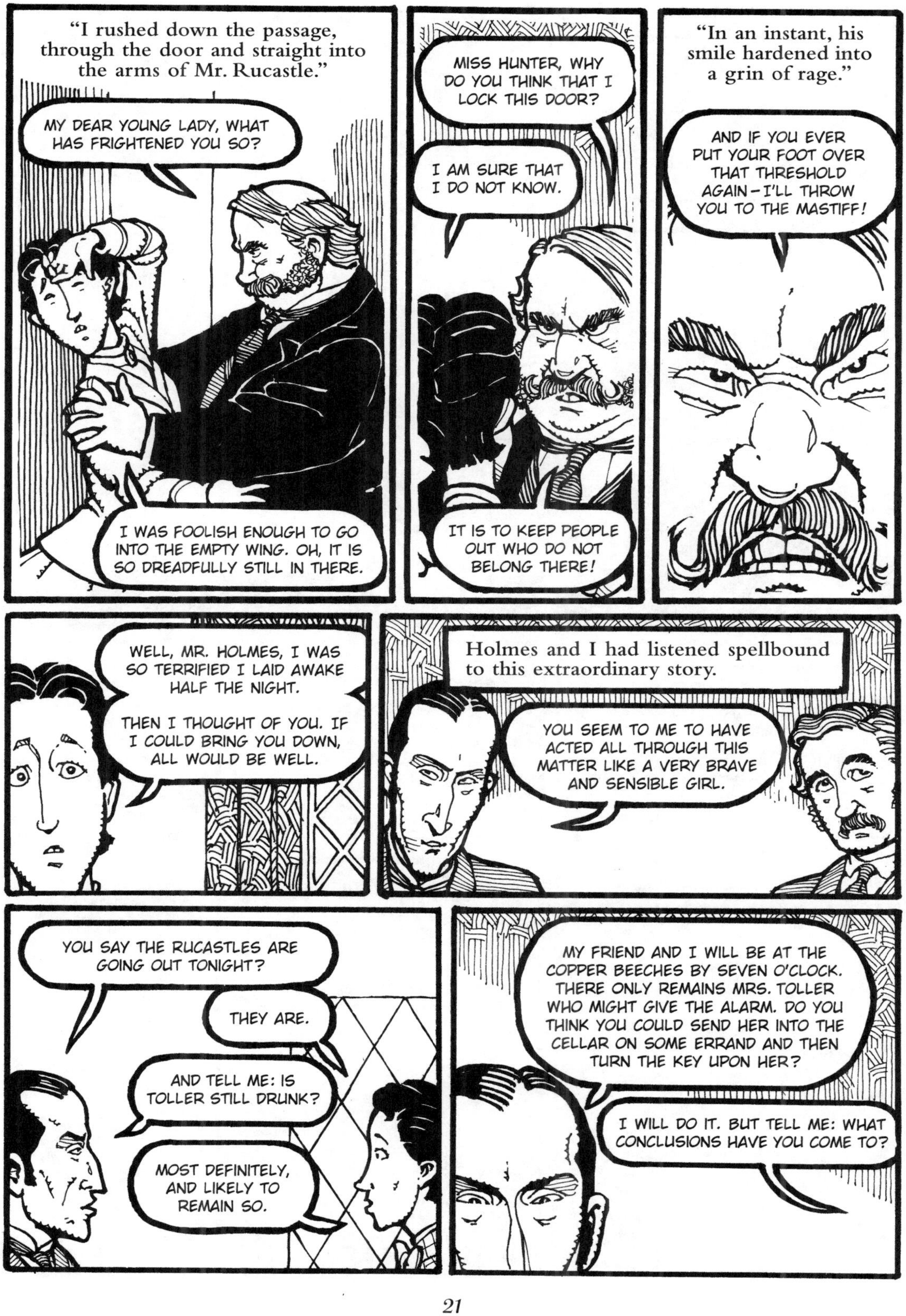
"I rushed down the passage, through the door and straight into the arms of Mr. Rucastle."
MY DEAR YOUNG LADY, WHAT HAS FRIGHTENED YOU SO?
I WAS FOOLISH ENOUGH TO GO INTO THE EMPTY WING. OH, IT IS SO DREADFULLY STILL IN THERE.
MISS HUNTER, WHY DO YOU THINK THAT I LOCK THIS DOOR?
I AM SURE THAT I DO NOT KNOW.
IT IS TO KEEP PEOPLE OUT WHO DO NOT BELONG THERE!
"In an instant, his smile hardened into a grin of rage."
AND IF YOU EVER PUT YOUR FOOT OVER THAT THRESHOLD AGAIN – I'LL THROW YOU TO THE MASTIFF!
WELL, MR. HOLMES, I WAS SO TERRIFIED I LAID AWAKE HALF THE NIGHT.
THEN I THOUGHT OF YOU. IF I COULD BRING YOU DOWN, ALL WOULD BE WELL.
Holmes and I had listened spellbound to this extraordinary story.
YOU SEEM TO ME TO HAVE ACTED ALL THROUGH THIS MATTER LIKE A VERY BRAVE AND SENSIBLE GIRL.
YOU SAY THE RUCASTLES ARE GOING OUT TONIGHT?
THEY ARE.
AND TELL ME: IS TOLLER STILL DRUNK?
MOST DEFINITELY, AND LIKELY TO REMAIN SO.
MY FRIEND AND I WILL BE AT THE COPPER BEECHES BY SEVEN O'CLOCK. THERE ONLY REMAINS MRS. TOLLER WHO MIGHT GIVE THE ALARM. DO YOU THINK YOU COULD SEND HER INTO THE CELLAR ON SOME ERRAND AND THEN TURN THE KEY UPON HER?
I WILL DO IT. BUT TELL ME: WHAT CONCLUSIONS HAVE YOU COME TO?

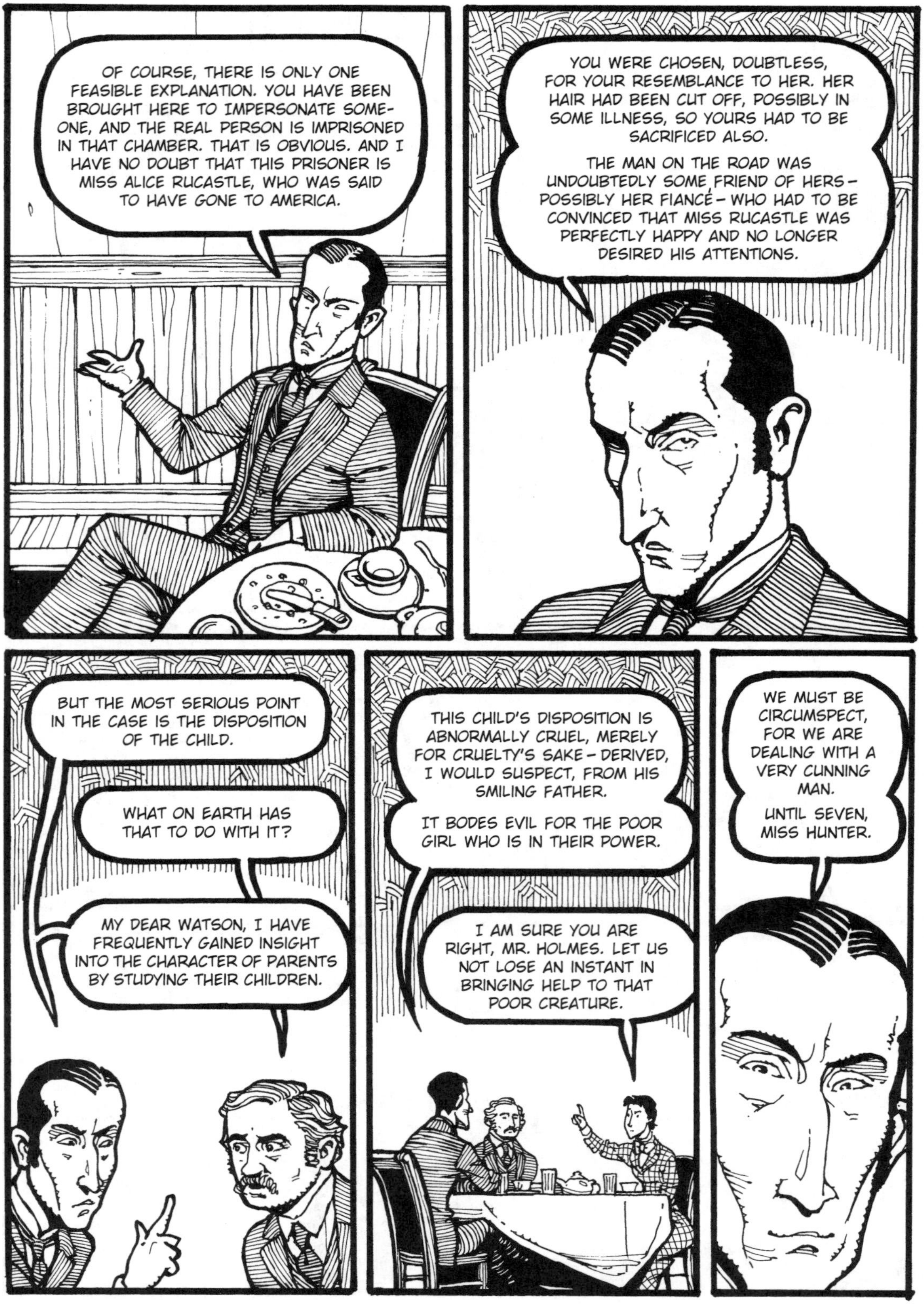
OF COURSE, THERE IS ONLY ONE FEASIBLE EXPLANATION. YOU HAVE BEEN BROUGHT HERE TO IMPERSONATE SOMEONE, AND THE REAL PERSON IS IMPRISONED IN THAT CHAMBER. THAT IS OBVIOUS. AND I HAVE NO DOUBT THAT THIS PRISONER IS MISS ALICE RUCASTLE, WHO WAS SAID TO HAVE GONE TO AMERICA.
YOU WERE CHOSEN, DOUBTLESS, FOR YOUR RESEMBLANCE TO HER. HER HAIR HAD BEEN CUT OFF, POSSIBLY IN SOME ILLNESS, SO YOURS HAD TO BE SACRIFICED ALSO.
THE MAN ON THE ROAD WAS UNDOUBTEDLY SOME FRIEND OF HERS – POSSIBLY HER FIANCÉ – WHO HAD TO BE CONVINCED THAT MISS RUCASTLE WAS PERFECTLY HAPPY AND NO LONGER DESIRED HIS ATTENTIONS.
BUT THE MOST SERIOUS POINT IN THE CASE IS THE DISPOSITION OF THE CHILD.
WHAT ON EARTH HAS THAT TO DO WITH IT?
MY DEAR WATSON, I HAVE FREQUENTLY GAINED INSIGHT INTO THE CHARACTER OF PARENTS BY STUDYING THEIR CHILDREN.
THIS CHILD'S DISPOSITION IS ABNORMALLY CRUEL, MERELY FOR CRUELTY'S SAKE – DERIVED, I WOULD SUSPECT, FROM HIS SMILING FATHER.
IT BODES EVIL FOR THE POOR GIRL WHO IS IN THEIR POWER.
I AM SURE YOU ARE RIGHT, MR. HOLMES. LET US NOT LOSE AN INSTANT IN BRINGING HELP TO THAT POOR CREATURE.
WE MUST BE CIRCUMSPECT, FOR WE ARE DEALING WITH A VERY CUNNING MAN.
UNTIL SEVEN, MISS HUNTER.

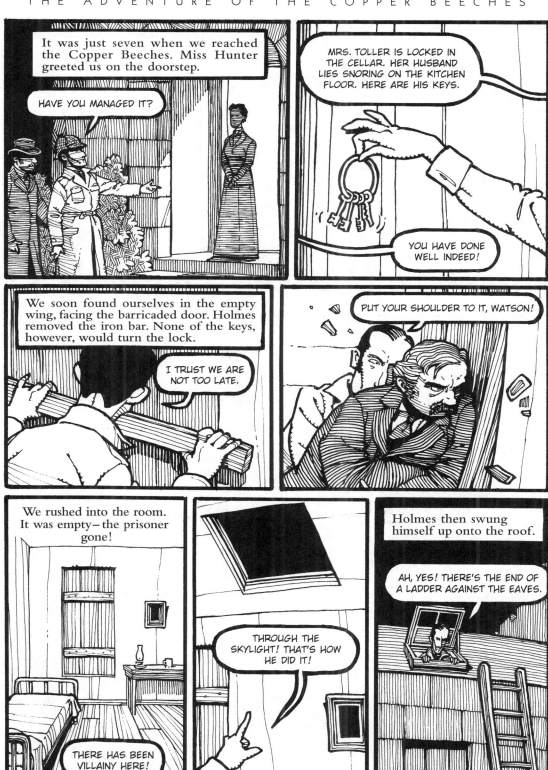

It was just seven when we reached the Copper Beeches. Miss Hunter greeted us on the doorstep.

HAVE YOU MANAGED IT?

MRS. TOLLER IS LOCKED IN THE CELLAR. HER HUSBAND LIES SNORING ON THE KITCHEN FLOOR. HERE ARE HIS KEYS.

YOU HAVE DONE WELL INDEED!

We soon found ourselves in the empty wing, facing the barricaded door. Holmes removed the iron bar. None of the keys, however, would turn the lock.

I TRUST WE ARE NOT TOO LATE.

PUT YOUR SHOULDER TO IT, WATSON!

We rushed into the room. It was empty—the prisoner gone!

THERE HAS BEEN VILLAINY HERE!

THROUGH THE SKYLIGHT! THAT'S HOW HE DID IT!

Holmes then swung himself up onto the roof.

AH, YES! THERE'S THE END OF A LADDER AGAINST THE EAVES.

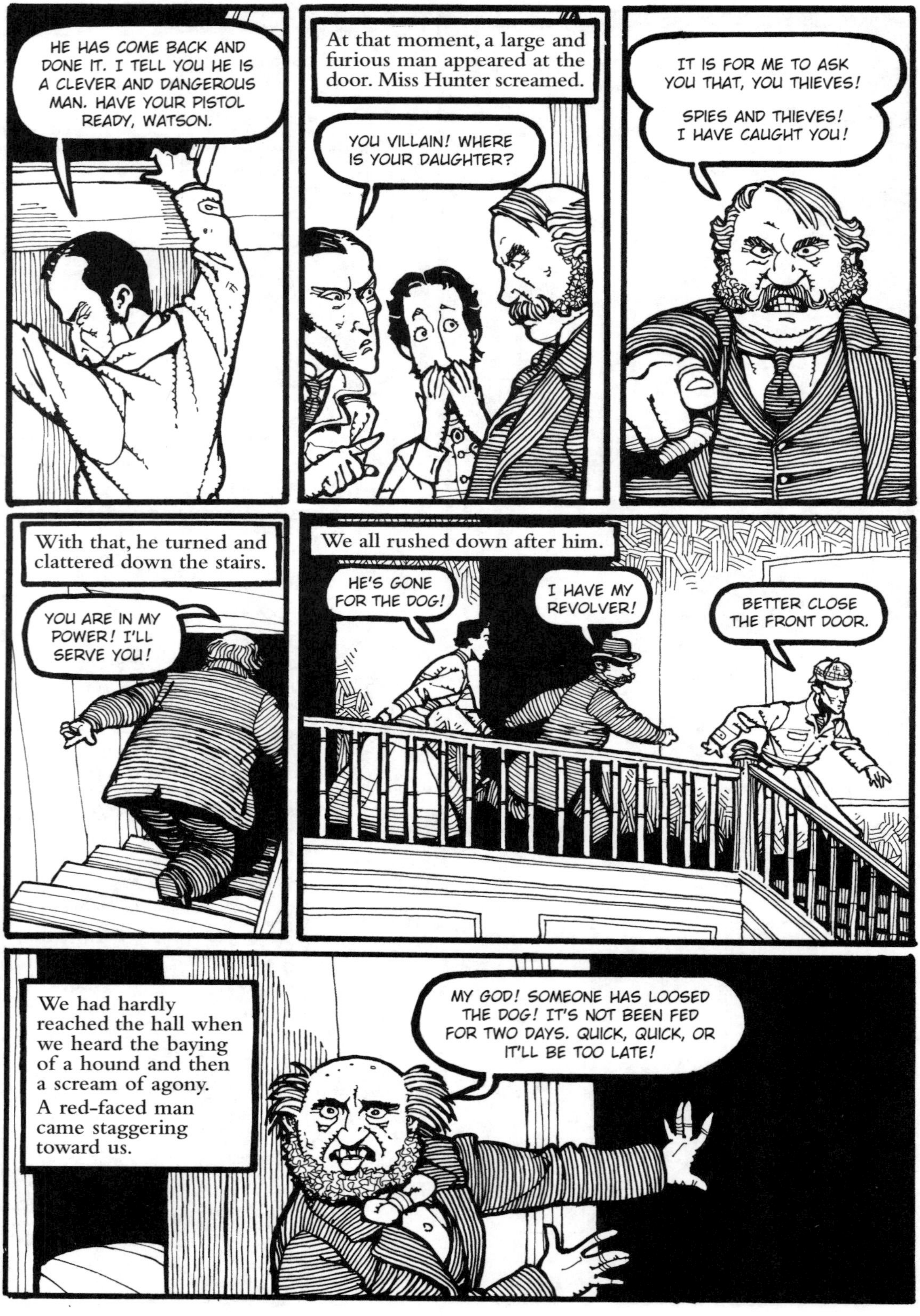
HE HAS COME BACK AND DONE IT. I TELL YOU HE IS A CLEVER AND DANGEROUS MAN. HAVE YOUR PISTOL READY, WATSON.
At that moment, a large and furious man appeared at the door. Miss Hunter screamed.
YOU VILLAIN! WHERE IS YOUR DAUGHTER?
IT IS FOR ME TO ASK YOU THAT, YOU THIEVES!
SPIES AND THIEVES! I HAVE CAUGHT YOU!
With that, he turned and clattered down the stairs.
YOU ARE IN MY POWER! I'LL SERVE YOU!
We all rushed down after him.
HE'S GONE FOR THE DOG!
I HAVE MY REVOLVER!
BETTER CLOSE THE FRONT DOOR.
We had hardly reached the hall when we heard the baying of a hound and then a scream of agony.
A red-faced man came staggering toward us.
MY GOD! SOMEONE HAS LOOSED THE DOG! IT'S NOT BEEN FED FOR TWO DAYS. QUICK, QUICK, OR IT'LL BE TOO LATE!

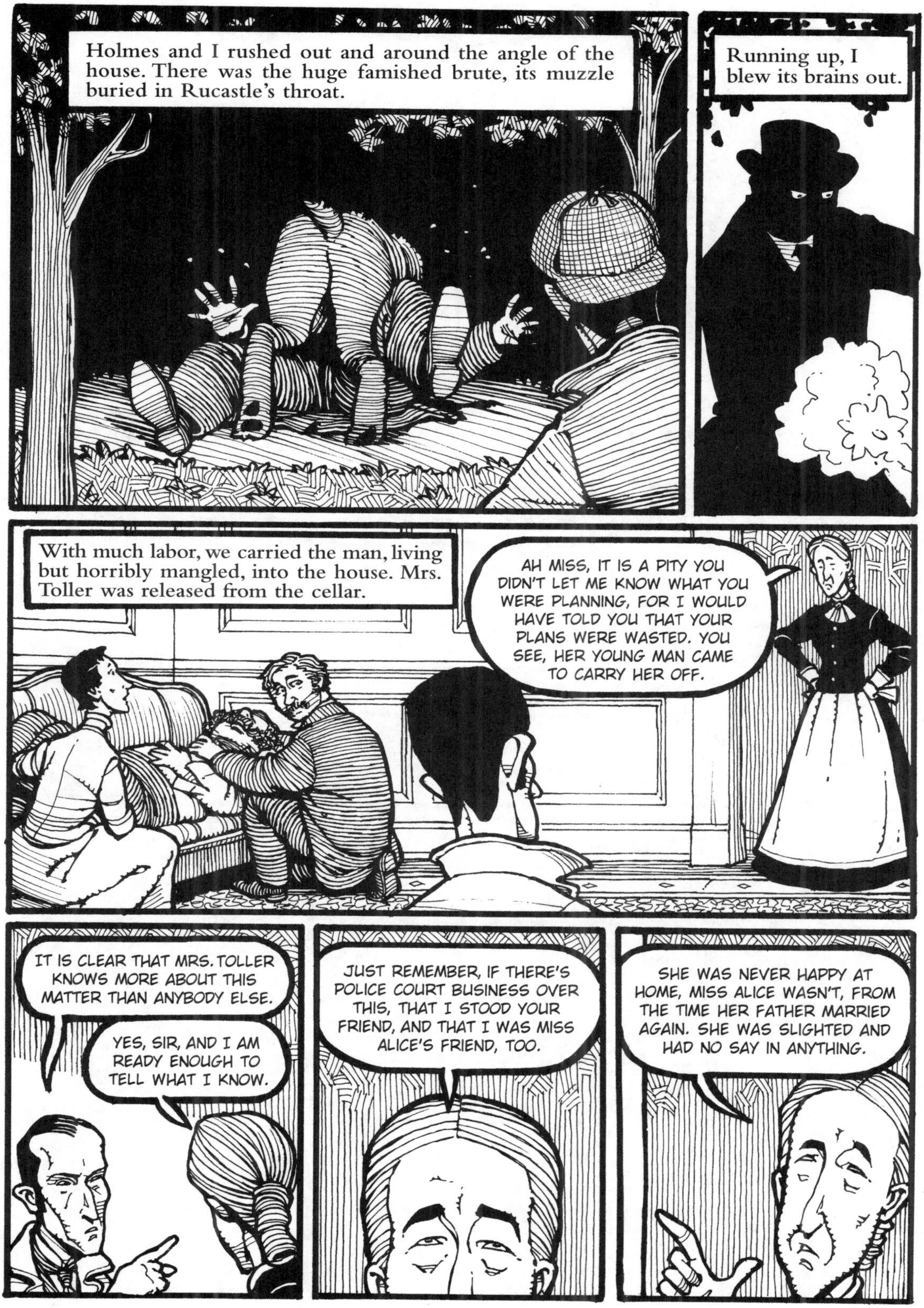
Holmes and I rushed out and around the angle of the house. There was the huge famished brute, its muzzle buried in Rucastle's throat.
Running up, I blew its brains out.
With much labor, we carried the man, living but horribly mangled, into the house. Mrs. Toller was released from the cellar.
AH MISS, IT IS A PITY YOU DIDN'T LET ME KNOW WHAT YOU WERE PLANNING, FOR I WOULD HAVE TOLD YOU THAT YOUR PLANS WERE WASTED. YOU SEE, HER YOUNG MAN CAME TO CARRY HER OFF.
IT IS CLEAR THAT MRS. TOLLER KNOWS MORE ABOUT THIS MATTER THAN ANYBODY ELSE.
YES, SIR, AND I AM READY ENOUGH TO TELL WHAT I KNOW.
JUST REMEMBER, IF THERE'S POLICE COURT BUSINESS OVER THIS, THAT I STOOD YOUR FRIEND, AND THAT I WAS MISS ALICE'S FRIEND, TOO.
SHE WAS NEVER HAPPY AT HOME, MISS ALICE WASN'T, FROM THE TIME HER FATHER MARRIED AGAIN. SHE WAS SLIGHTED AND HAD NO SAY IN ANYTHING.

YOU SEE, MISS ALICE HAD MONEY OF HER OWN, BY TERMS OF HER MOTHER'S WILL, BUT SHE WAS SO QUIET AND PATIENT, SHE JUST LEFT EVERYTHING IN HER FATHER'S HANDS.

THEN SHE MET MR. FOWLER, WHO WANTED TO MARRY HER.

BUT MR. RUCASTLE WANTED HER TO SIGN A PAPER SO THAT, IF SHE MARRIED OR NOT, HE WOULD RETAIN MANAGEMENT OF HER MONEY.

WHEN SHE REFUSED, HE KEPT ON WORRYING HER UNTIL SHE GOT BRAIN FEVER — AND FOR SIX WEEKS SHE WAS AT DEATH'S DOOR.

SHE RECOVERED, ALL WORN TO A SHADOW AND WITH HER BEAUTIFUL HAIR CUT OFF. BUT HER YOUNG MAN STUCK TO HER AS TRUE AS A MAN COULD BE.

MR. RUCASTLE THEN TOOK TO THIS SYSTEM OF IMPRISONMENT, I PRESUME, AND HIRED MISS HUNTER IN ORDER TO GET RID OF MR. FOWLER.

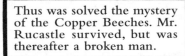

YOU HAVE IT SIR, JUST AS IT HAPPENED.

WE OWE YOU AN APOLOGY, MRS. TOLLER. YOU HAVE CERTAINLY CLEARED UP EVERYTHING WHICH PUZZLED US.

Thus was solved the mystery of the Copper Beeches. Mr. Rucastle survived, but was thereafter a broken man.

Miss Rucastle and Mr. Fowler were married the day after their flight. He now holds a government appointment on the Island of Mauritius.

As to Miss Violet Hunter, Holmes manifested no further interest in her once she had ceased to be the centre of a problem.

She is now the head of a private school at Walsall, where I believe that she has met with considerable success.

When the great wars of the Spanish Succession had finally been brought to an end, the vast number of privateers which had been fitted out by the contending parties found their occupation gone. Some took to the more peaceful but less lucrative ways of ordinary commerce, others were absorbed into the fishing fleets, and a few of the more reckless hoisted the Jolly Roger, declaring a private war against the human race.

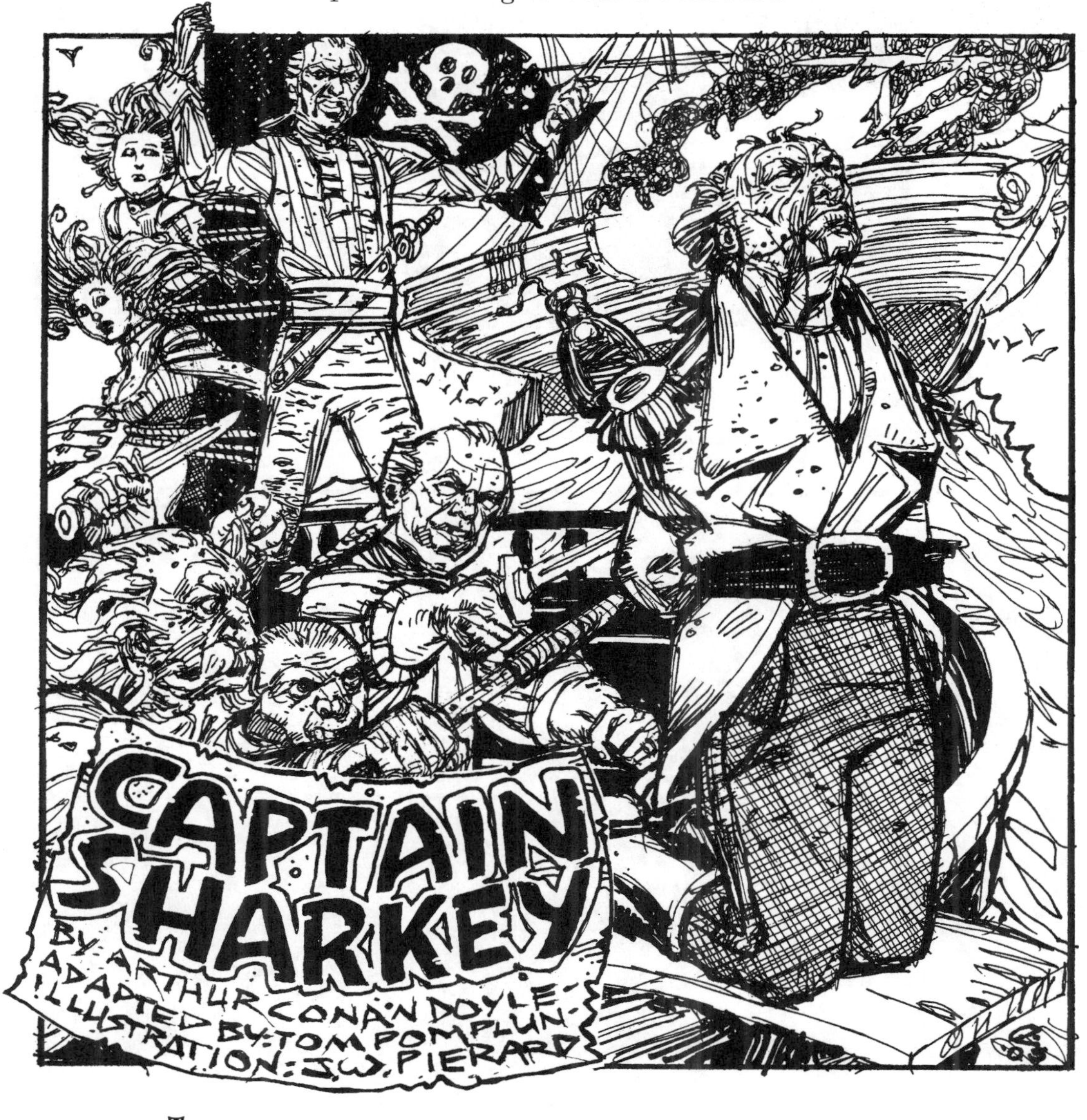
CAPTAIN SHARKEY
BY: ARTHUR CONAN DOYLE-
ADAPTED BY: TOM POMPLUN-
ILLUSTRATION: J.W. PIERARD

They were the more to be dreaded because they had none of the discipline and restraint of their predecessors, the Buccaneers. This new breed rendered an account to no man, and treated their prisoners according to the drunken whim of the moment. It took a stout seaman in those days to ply his calling in the Caribbean Gulf.

Such a man was Captain John Scarrow, of the *Morning Star,* and yet he breathed a long sigh of relief when he sunk anchor beneath the guns of the citadel of Basseterre. St. Kitts was his final port of call, and early next morning his bowsprit would be pointed for England.

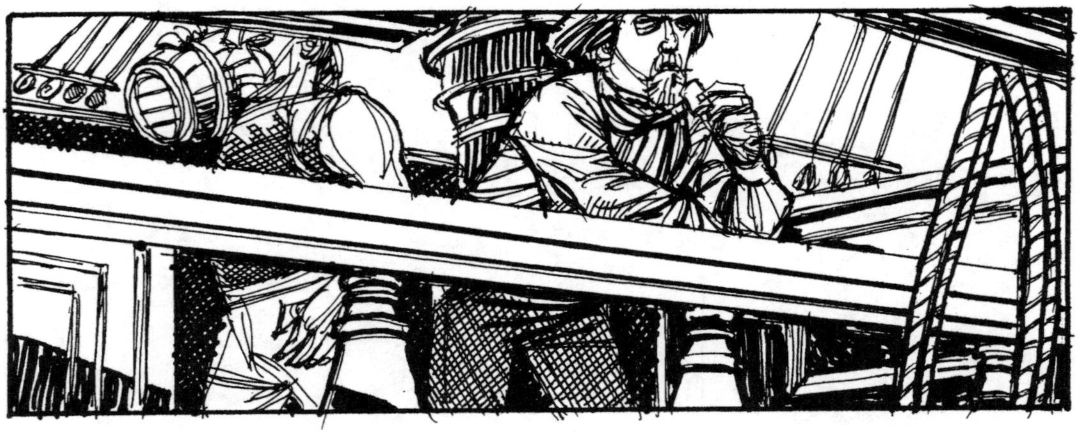

He had had enough of these robber-haunted seas. Ever since he had left Maracaibo with his full lading, he had winced at every topsail which glimmered over the edge of the tropical sea, and had been assailed continually by stories of villainy and outrage.

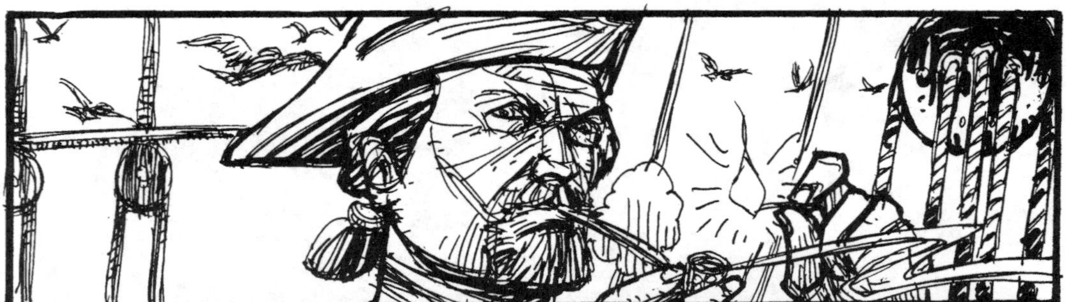

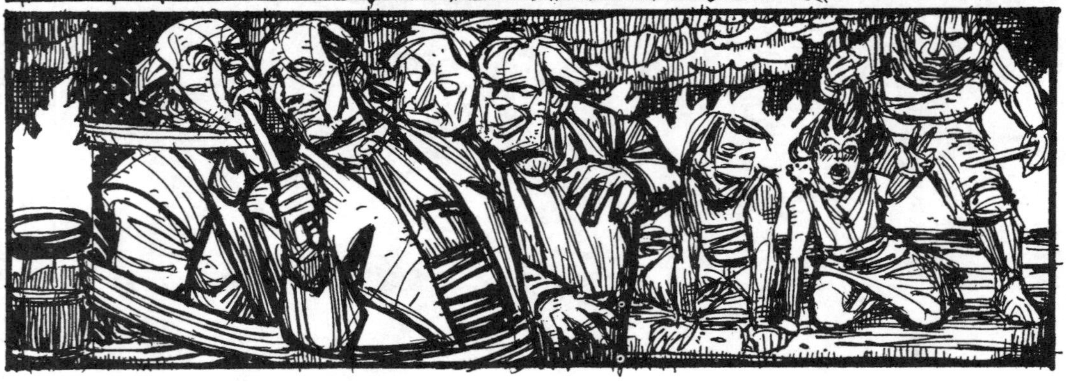

The worst of the bad lot was Captain Sharkey, whose twenty-gun barque, *Happy Delivery,* had recently passed down the coast, littering it with gutted vessels and murdered men. Dreadful anecdotes were told of his grim pleasantries and inflexible ferocity.

So nervous was Captain Scarrow, with his new ship and her valuable lading, that he struck out to the west, far from the usual track of commerce. And yet even in those solitary waters he had been unable to shake off all traces of Captain Sharkey.

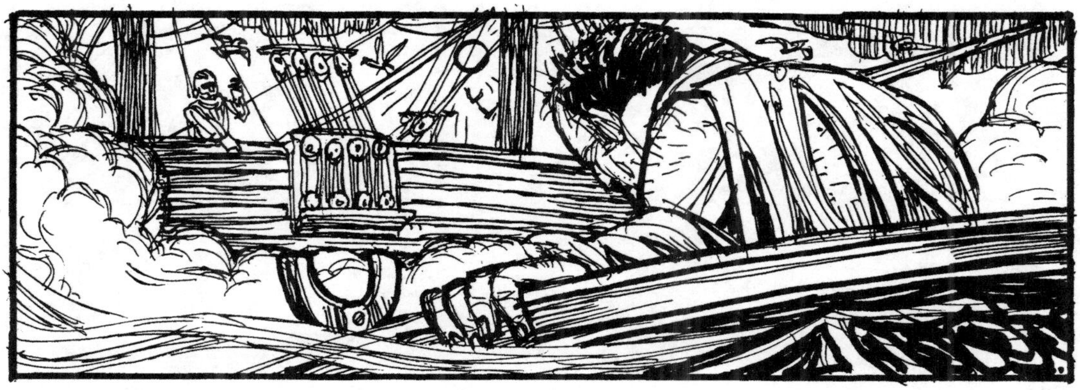

One morning they had spied a skiff adrift upon the face of the ocean. Its only occupant was a delirious seaman, the sole survivor of a schooner which had been scuttled by the dreadful Sharkey. For a week he had been adrift beneath a tropical sun, near to death.

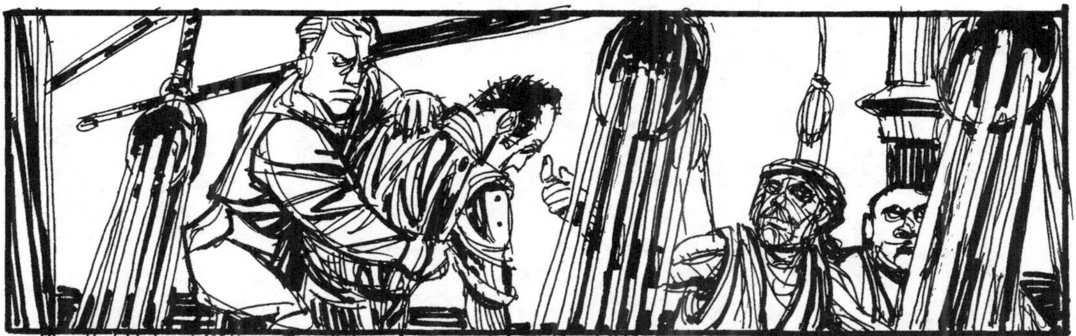

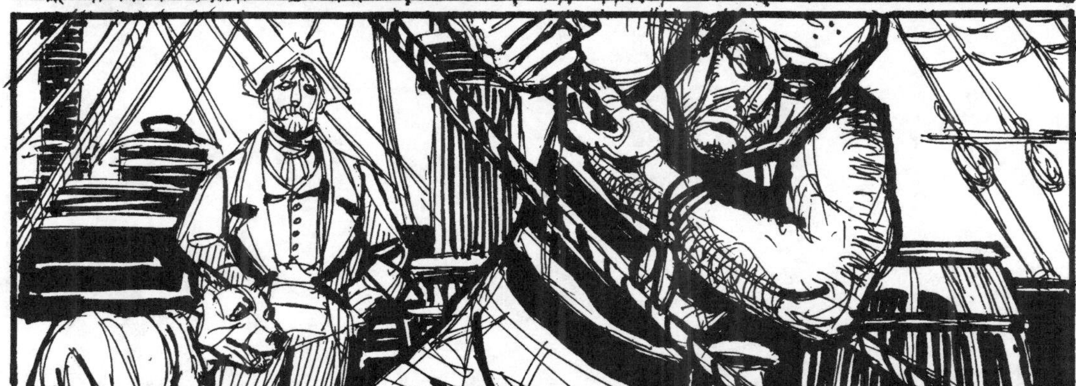

But water and nursing soon transformed Hiram Evanson, the name he gave, into the strongest and smartest sailor on the ship. It was no bad find for Captain Scarrow, for such a seaman as this big New Englander was a prize worth having.

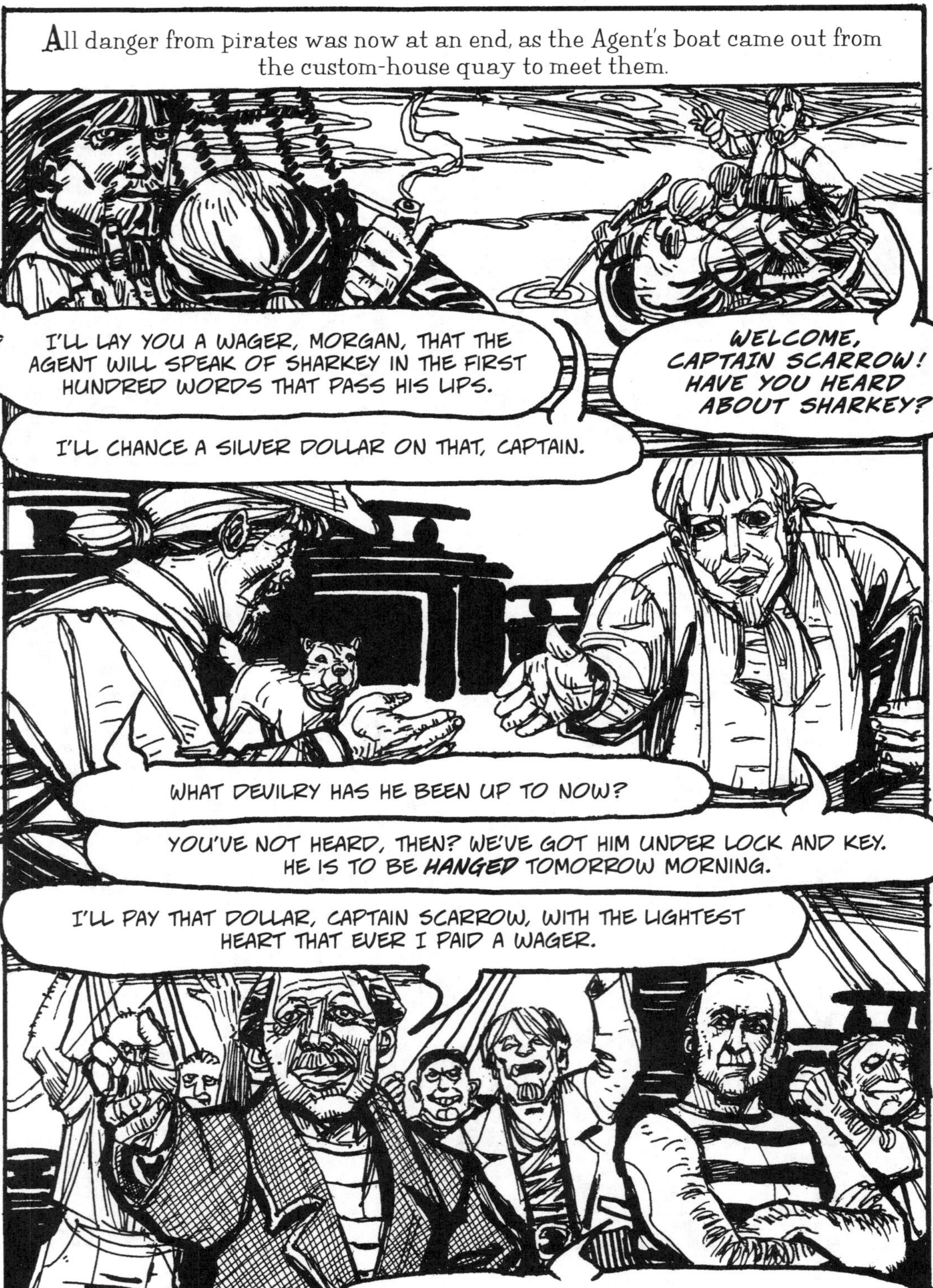
All danger from pirates was now at an end, as the Agent's boat came out from the custom-house quay to meet them.
I'LL LAY YOU A WAGER, MORGAN, THAT THE AGENT WILL SPEAK OF SHARKEY IN THE FIRST HUNDRED WORDS THAT PASS HIS LIPS.
I'LL CHANCE A SILVER DOLLAR ON THAT, CAPTAIN.
WELCOME, CAPTAIN SCARROW! HAVE YOU HEARD ABOUT SHARKEY?
WHAT DEVILRY HAS HE BEEN UP TO NOW?
YOU'VE NOT HEARD, THEN? WE'VE GOT HIM UNDER LOCK AND KEY. HE IS TO BE HANGED TOMORROW MORNING.
I'LL PAY THAT DOLLAR, CAPTAIN SCARROW, WITH THE LIGHTEST HEART THAT EVER I PAID A WAGER.
YOU'RE SURE IT IS SHARKEY?... HOW CAME THE VILLAIN TO BE TAKEN?

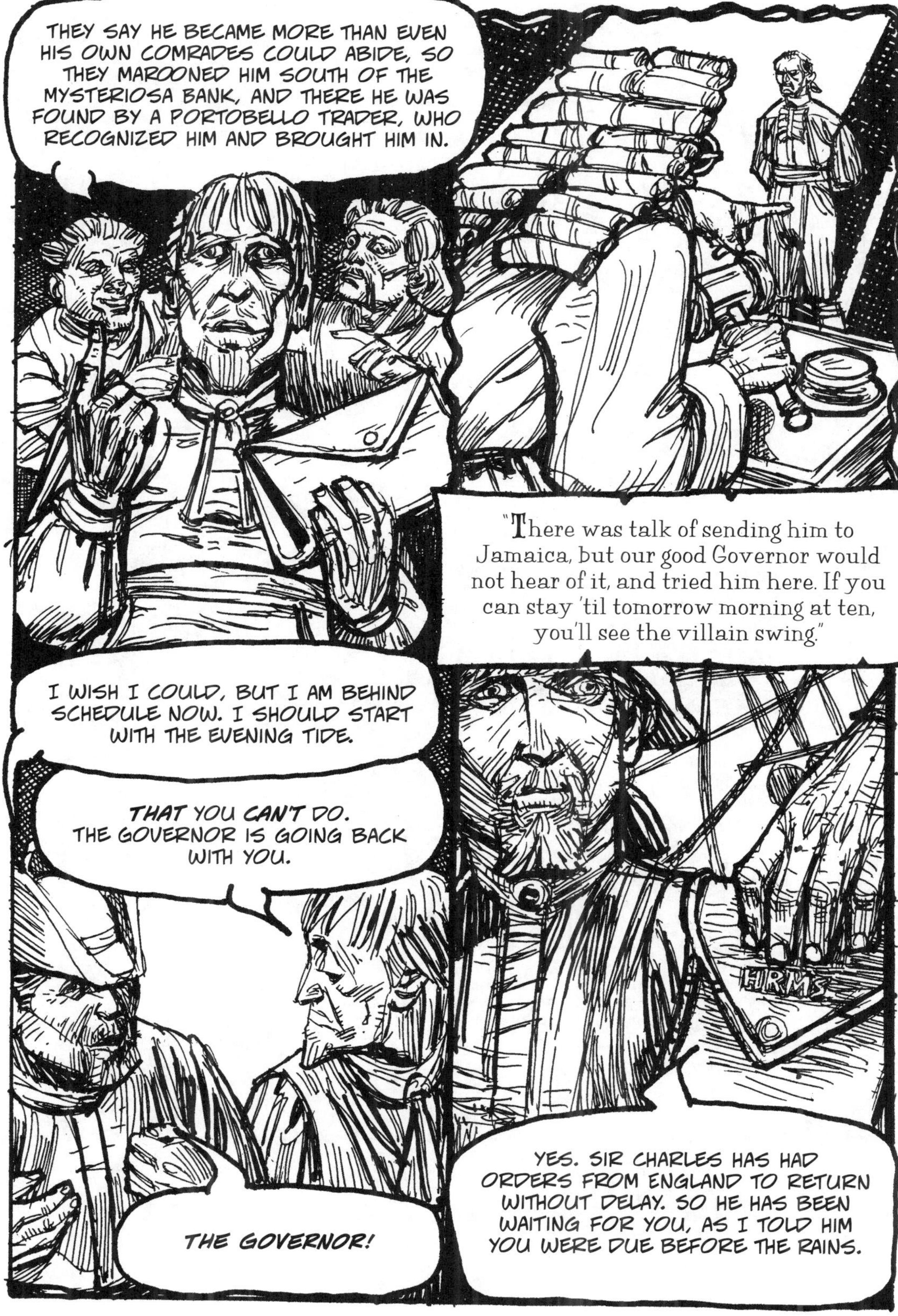
THEY SAY HE BECAME MORE THAN EVEN HIS OWN COMRADES COULD ABIDE, SO THEY MAROONED HIM SOUTH OF THE MYSTERIOSA BANK, AND THERE HE WAS FOUND BY A PORTOBELLO TRADER, WHO RECOGNIZED HIM AND BROUGHT HIM IN.
"There was talk of sending him to Jamaica, but our good Governor would not hear of it, and tried him here. If you can stay 'til tomorrow morning at ten, you'll see the villain swing."
I WISH I COULD, BUT I AM BEHIND SCHEDULE NOW. I SHOULD START WITH THE EVENING TIDE.
THAT YOU CAN'T DO. THE GOVERNOR IS GOING BACK WITH YOU.
THE GOVERNOR!
YES. SIR CHARLES HAS HAD ORDERS FROM ENGLAND TO RETURN WITHOUT DELAY. SO HE HAS BEEN WAITING FOR YOU, AS I TOLD HIM YOU WERE DUE BEFORE THE RAINS.
HRMS

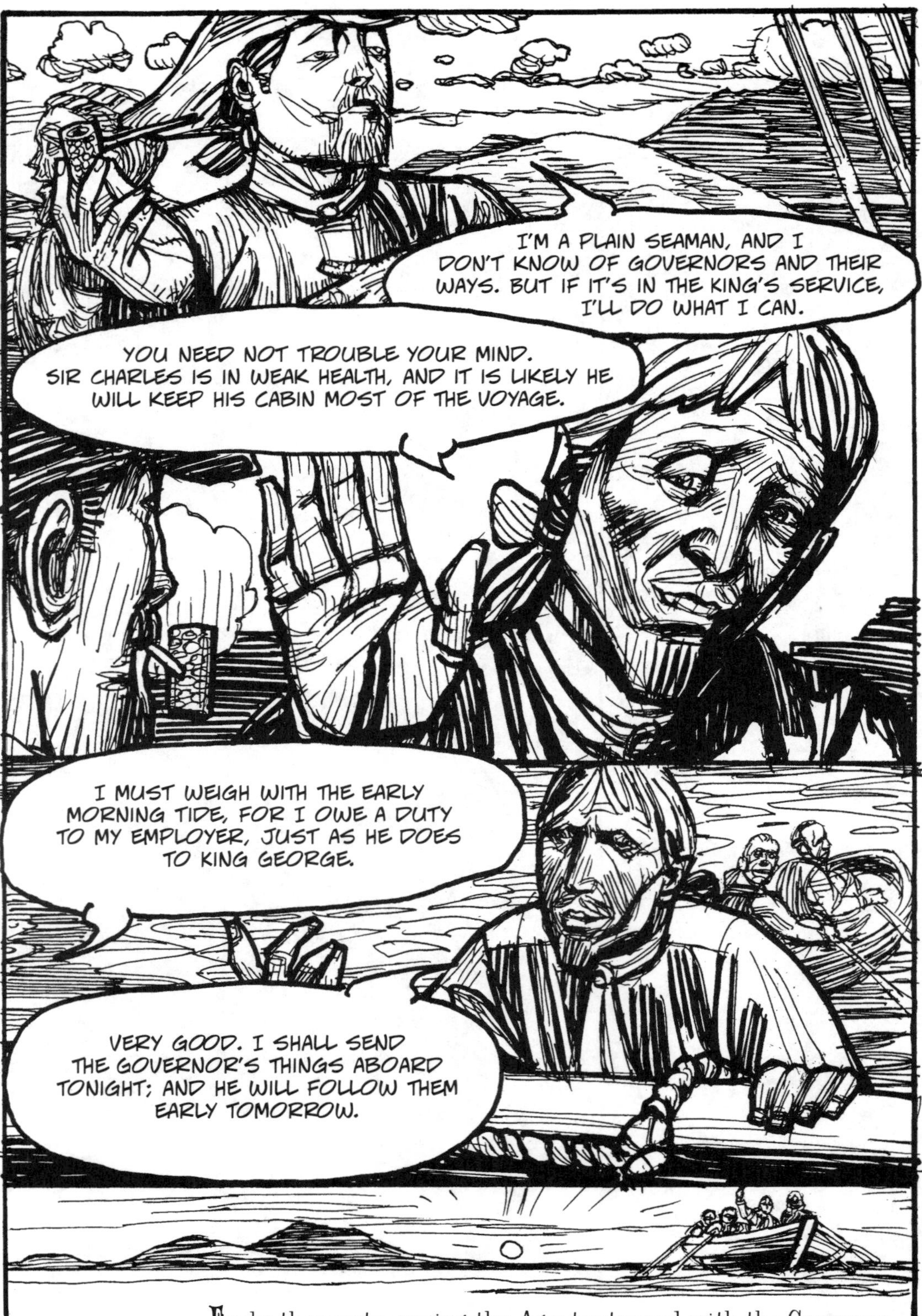
I'M A PLAIN SEAMAN, AND I DON'T KNOW OF GOVERNORS AND THEIR WAYS. BUT IF IT'S IN THE KING'S SERVICE, I'LL DO WHAT I CAN.
YOU NEED NOT TROUBLE YOUR MIND. SIR CHARLES IS IN WEAK HEALTH, AND IT IS LIKELY HE WILL KEEP HIS CABIN MOST OF THE VOYAGE.
I MUST WEIGH WITH THE EARLY MORNING TIDE, FOR I OWE A DUTY TO MY EMPLOYER, JUST AS HE DOES TO KING GEORGE.
VERY GOOD. I SHALL SEND THE GOVERNOR'S THINGS ABOARD TONIGHT; AND HE WILL FOLLOW THEM EARLY TOMORROW.

Early the next morning, the Agent returned with the Governor.

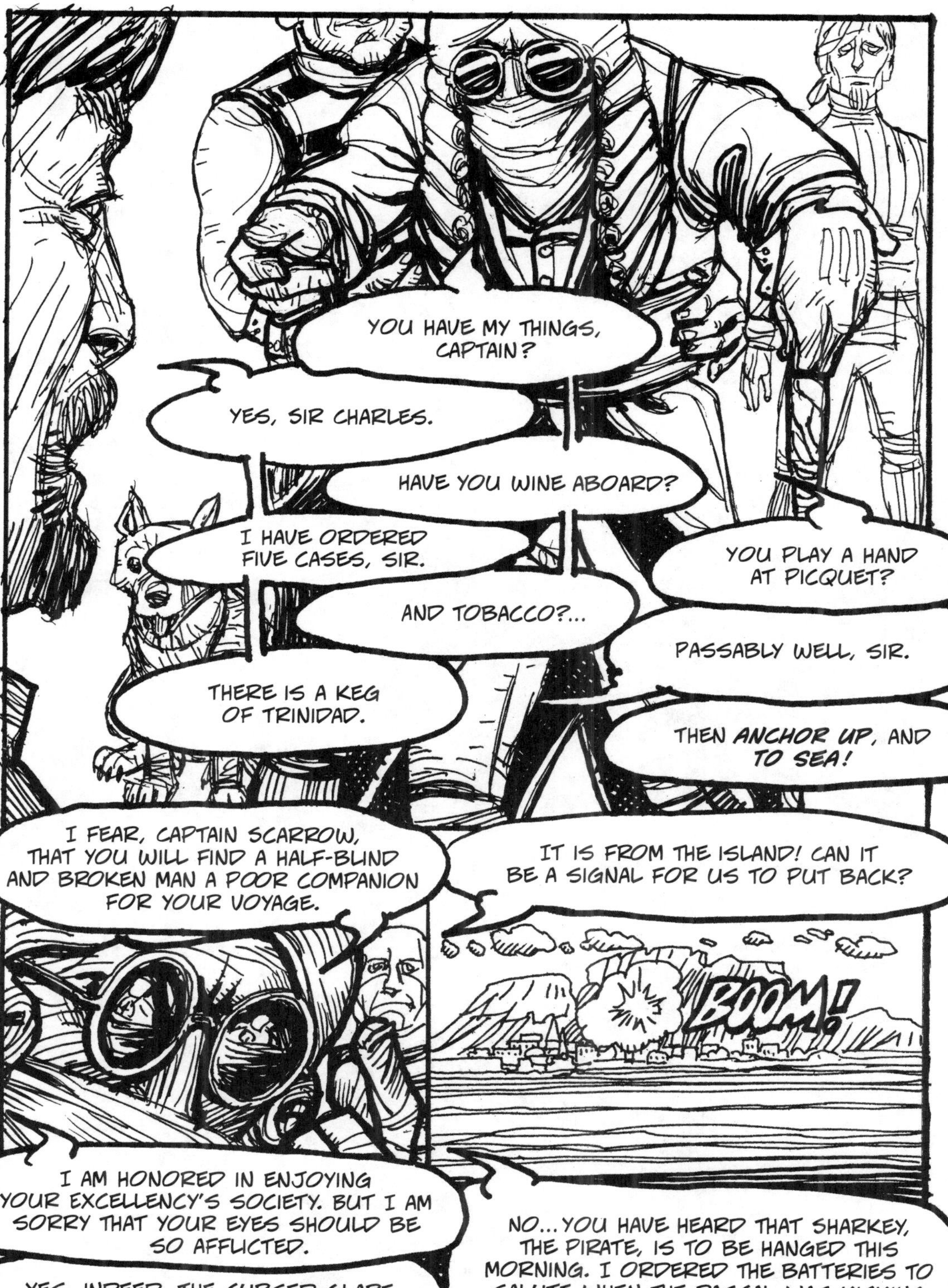
YOU HAVE MY THINGS, CAPTAIN?
YES, SIR CHARLES.
HAVE YOU WINE ABOARD?
I HAVE ORDERED FIVE CASES, SIR.
AND TOBACCO?...
THERE IS A KEG OF TRINIDAD.
YOU PLAY A HAND AT PICQUET?
PASSABLY WELL, SIR.
THEN ANCHOR UP, AND TO SEA!
I FEAR, CAPTAIN SCARROW, THAT YOU WILL FIND A HALF-BLIND AND BROKEN MAN A POOR COMPANION FOR YOUR VOYAGE.
I AM HONORED IN ENJOYING YOUR EXCELLENCY'S SOCIETY. BUT I AM SORRY THAT YOUR EYES SHOULD BE SO AFFLICTED.
YES, INDEED. THE CURSED GLARE OF THE SUN HAS GONE FAR TO BURN THEM OUT. BUT HARK!
BOOM!
IT IS FROM THE ISLAND! CAN IT BE A SIGNAL FOR US TO PUT BACK?
NO... YOU HAVE HEARD THAT SHARKEY, THE PIRATE, IS TO BE HANGED THIS MORNING. I ORDERED THE BATTERIES TO SALUTE WHEN THE RASCAL WAS KICKING HIS LAST, SO THAT I MIGHT KNOW OF IT. THERE'S AN END OF SHARKEY!

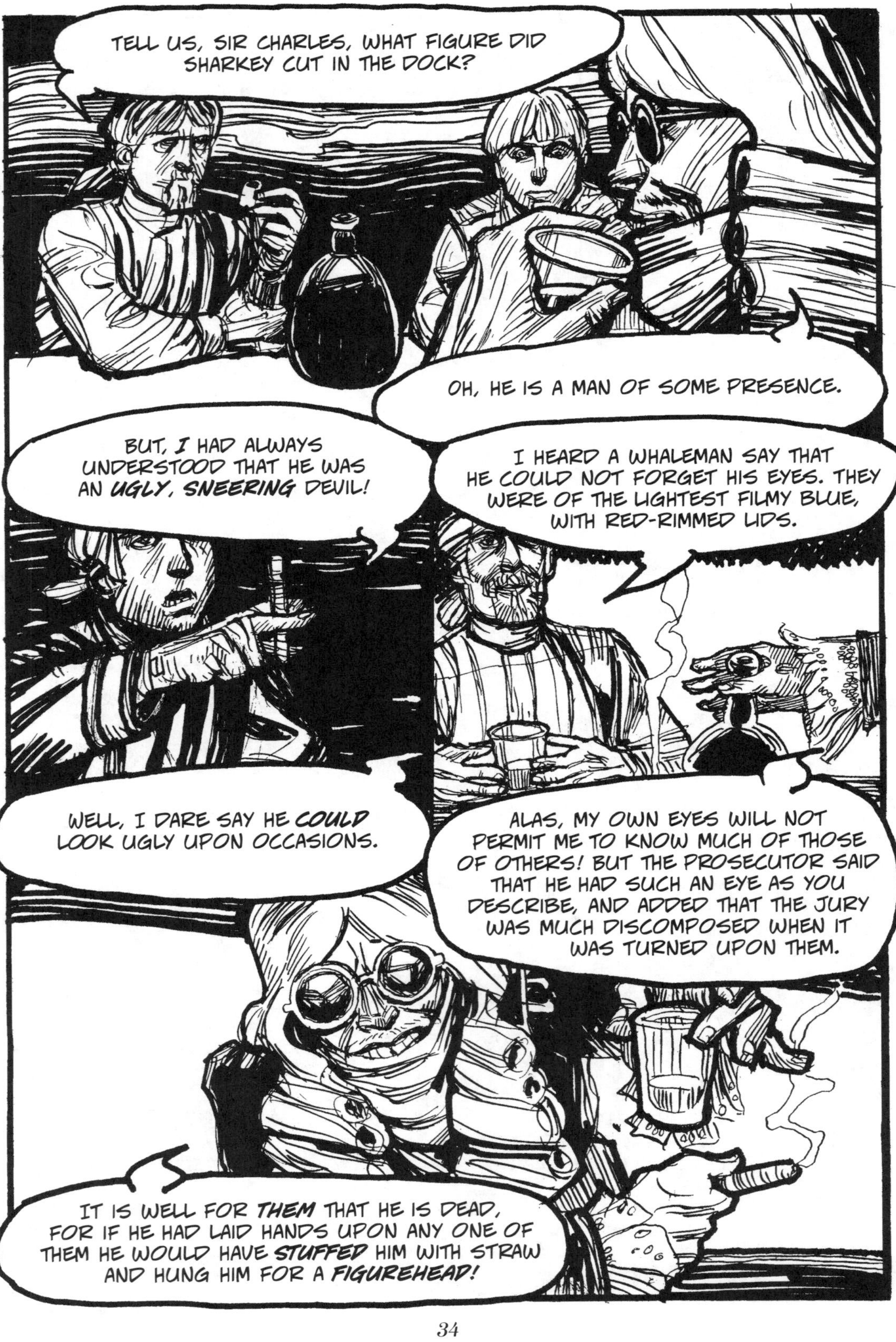
TELL US, SIR CHARLES, WHAT FIGURE DID SHARKEY CUT IN THE DOCK?
OH, HE IS A MAN OF SOME PRESENCE.
BUT, I HAD ALWAYS UNDERSTOOD THAT HE WAS AN UGLY, SNEERING DEVIL!
I HEARD A WHALEMAN SAY THAT HE COULD NOT FORGET HIS EYES. THEY WERE OF THE LIGHTEST FILMY BLUE, WITH RED-RIMMED LIDS.
WELL, I DARE SAY HE COULD LOOK UGLY UPON OCCASIONS.
ALAS, MY OWN EYES WILL NOT PERMIT ME TO KNOW MUCH OF THOSE OF OTHERS! BUT THE PROSECUTOR SAID THAT HE HAD SUCH AN EYE AS YOU DESCRIBE, AND ADDED THAT THE JURY WAS MUCH DISCOMPOSED WHEN IT WAS TURNED UPON THEM.
IT IS WELL FOR THEM THAT HE IS DEAD, FOR IF HE HAD LAID HANDS UPON ANY ONE OF THEM HE WOULD HAVE STUFFED HIM WITH STRAW AND HUNG HIM FOR A FIGUREHEAD!

The Governor insisted on broaching another bottle, after which the seamen were glad at last to stagger off – the Mate to his watch, and the Captain to his bunk.

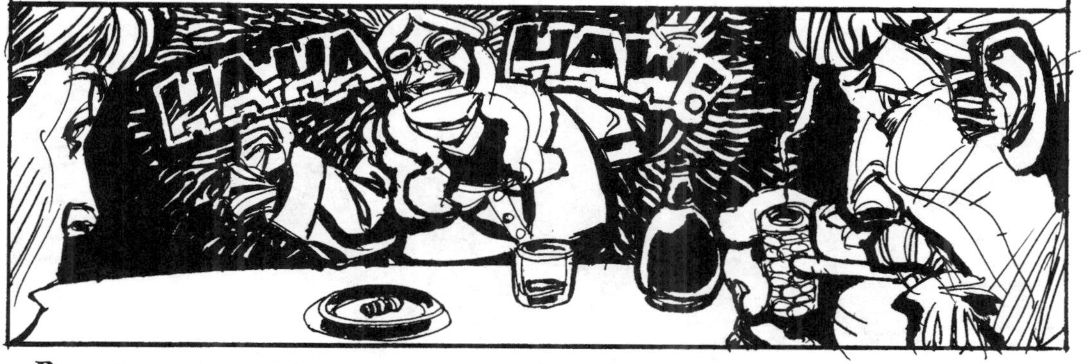
HAHA HAW!

But when, after his four hours' spell, the Mate came down again, he was amazed to see the Governor still seated sedately at his lonely table.

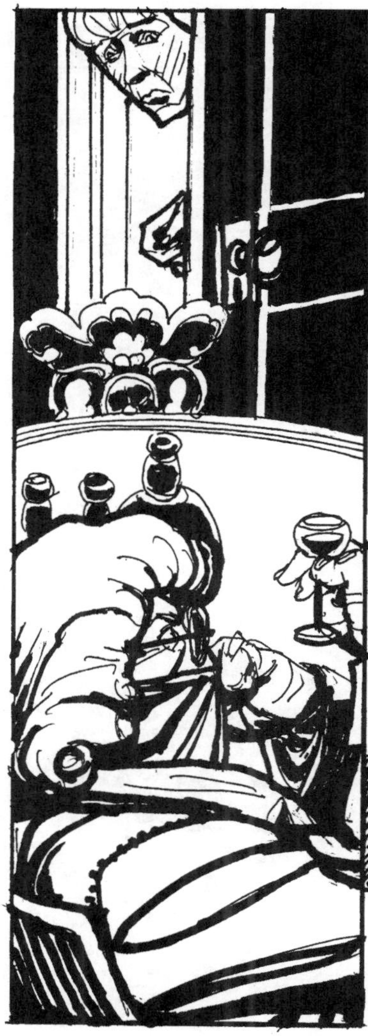

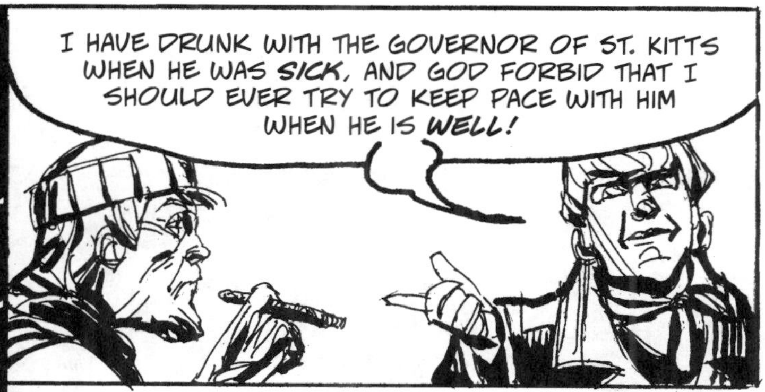
I HAVE DRUNK WITH THE GOVERNOR OF ST. KITTS WHEN HE WAS *SICK*, AND GOD FORBID THAT I SHOULD EVER TRY TO KEEP PACE WITH HIM WHEN HE IS ***WELL!***

From the first day of the voyage, the infirm Governor had begun to recover his strength, and before they were halfway across the Atlantic, he was, save only for his eyes, as well as any man upon the ship

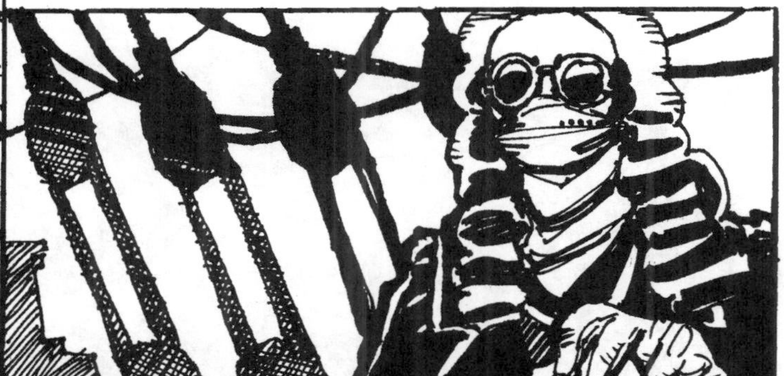

And never a night passed that he did not repeat the performance of his first one. Yet he would be out upon deck in the early morning as fresh as the best of them.

And he made up for the deficiency of his eyes by obtaining leave from the Captain that the New England castaway should lead him about, and, above all, that he should stand behind him when he played cards, for unaided he could not tell the king from the knave.

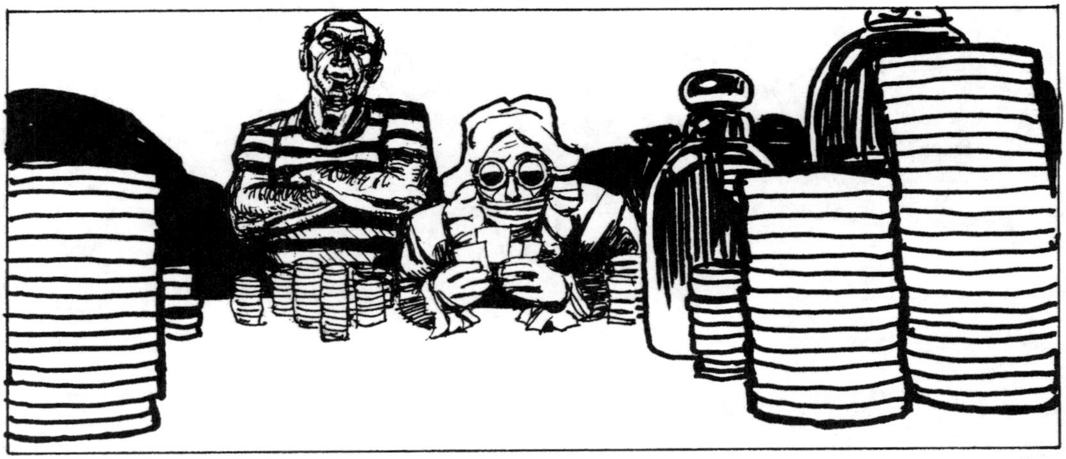

It was natural that Evanson should do the Governor willing service, since the one was the victim of the vile Sharkey and the other was his avenger.

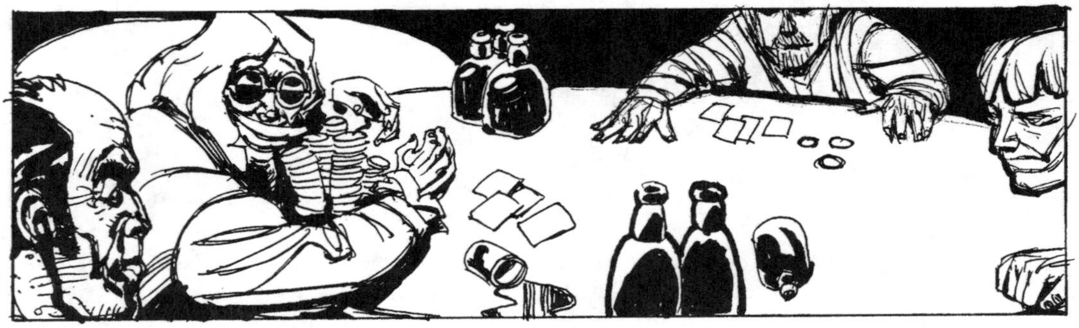

Between them there was little in the pockets either of Captain Scarrow or of Morgan by the time they sighted England.

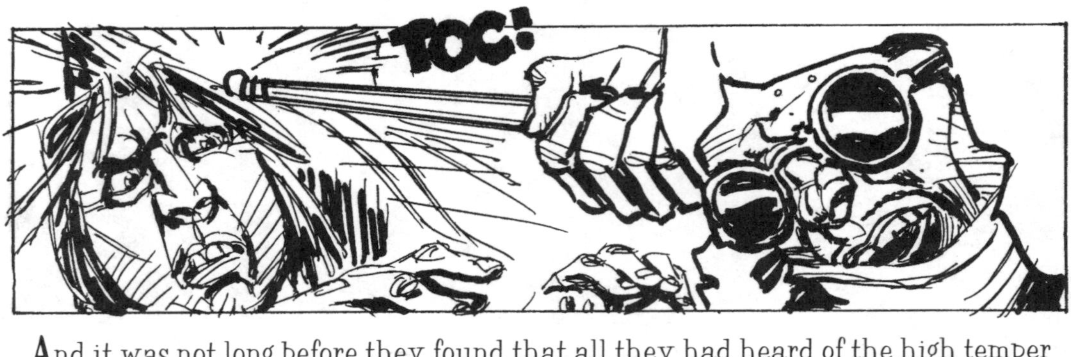
TOC!

And it was not long before they found that all they had heard of the high temper of Sir Charles Ewan fell short of the mark. He bristled at the slightest opposition, and he once cracked his cane over the head of the Carpenter when the man had accidentally jostled him upon the deck.

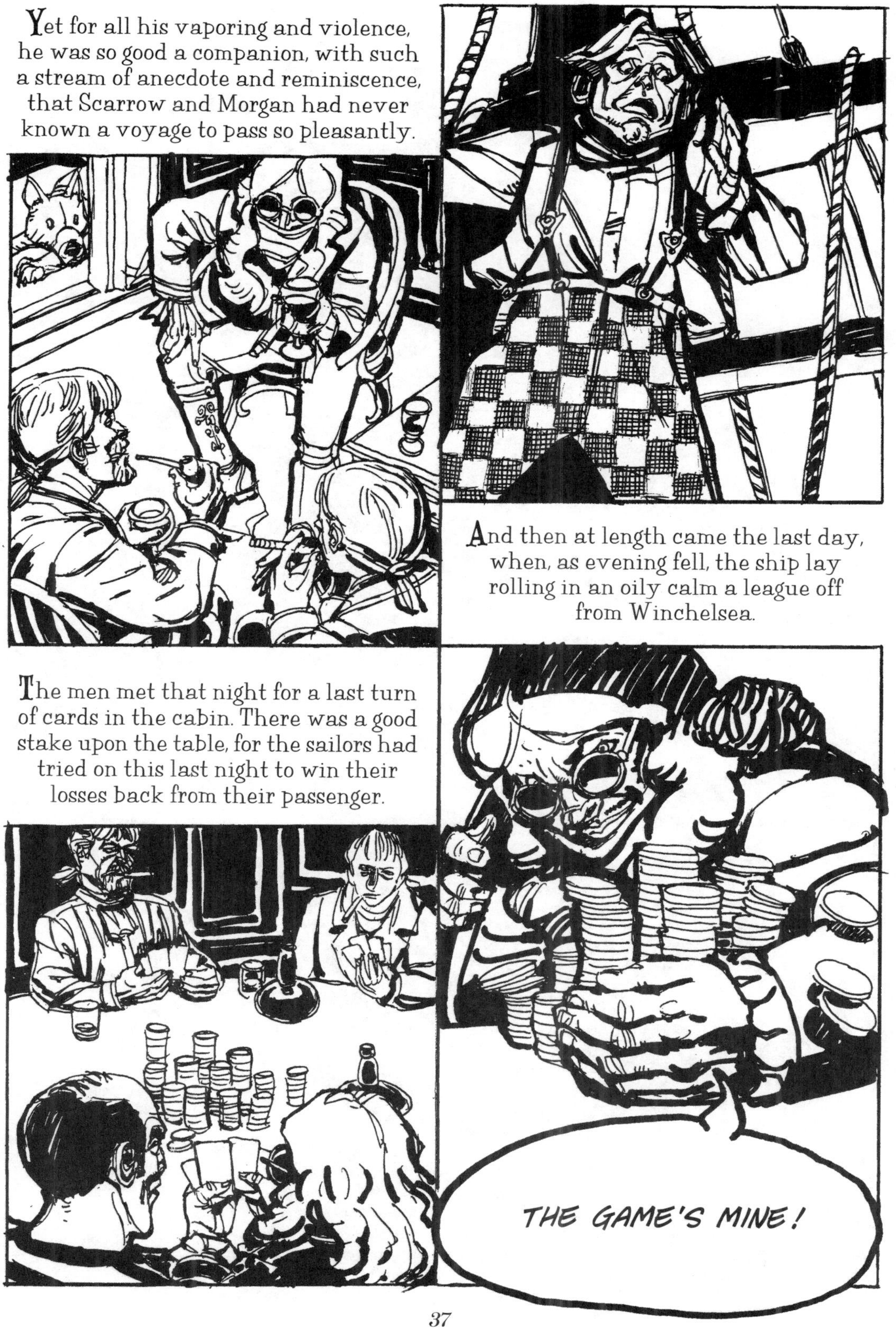
Yet for all his vaporing and violence, he was so good a companion, with such a stream of anecdote and reminiscence, that Scarrow and Morgan had never known a voyage to pass so pleasantly.
And then at length came the last day, when, as evening fell, the ship lay rolling in an oily calm a league off from Winchelsea.
The men met that night for a last turn of cards in the cabin. There was a good stake upon the table, for the sailors had tried on this last night to win their losses back from their passenger.
THE GAME'S MINE!

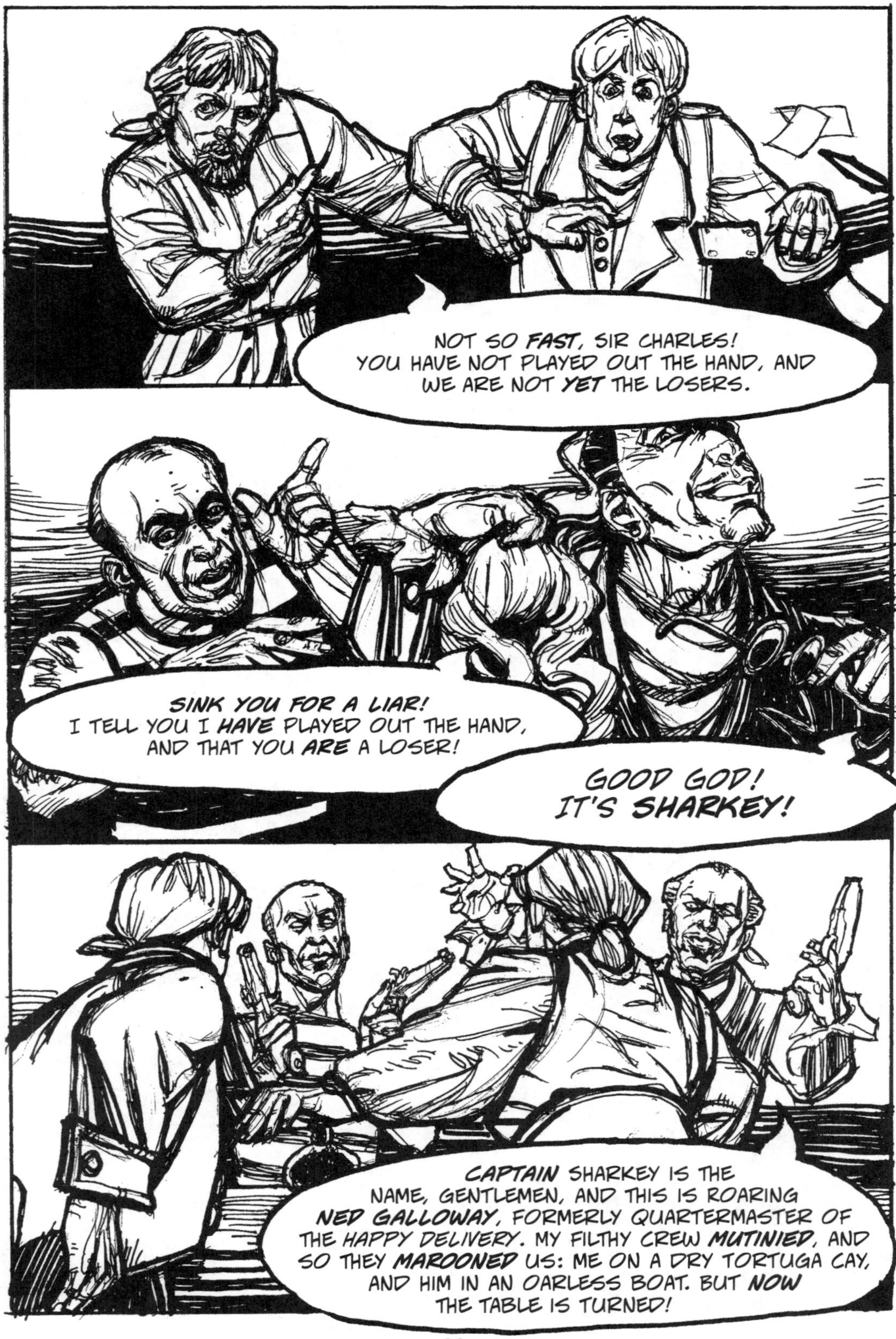
NOT SO **FAST**, SIR CHARLES! YOU HAVE NOT PLAYED OUT THE HAND, AND WE ARE NOT **YET** THE LOSERS.
SINK YOU FOR A LIAR! I TELL YOU I **HAVE** PLAYED OUT THE HAND, AND THAT YOU **ARE** A LOSER!
GOOD GOD! IT'S **SHARKEY!**
CAPTAIN SHARKEY IS THE NAME, GENTLEMEN, AND THIS IS ROARING **NED GALLOWAY**, FORMERLY QUARTERMASTER OF THE *HAPPY DELIVERY*. MY FILTHY CREW **MUTINIED**, AND SO THEY **MAROONED** US: ME ON A DRY TORTUGA CAY, AND HIM IN AN OARLESS BOAT. BUT **NOW** THE TABLE IS TURNED!

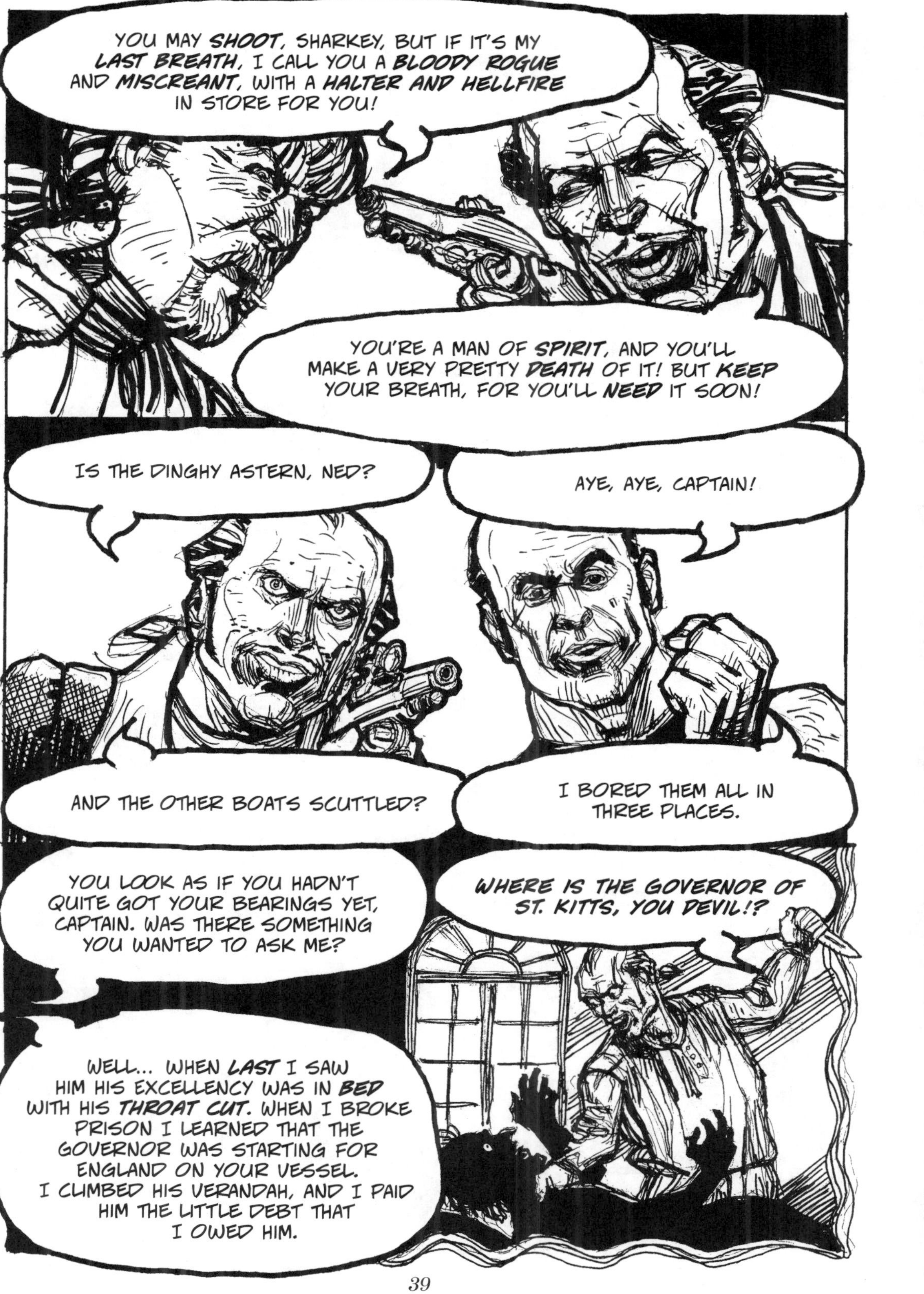
YOU MAY SHOOT, SHARKEY, BUT IF IT'S MY LAST BREATH, I CALL YOU A BLOODY ROGUE AND MISCREANT, WITH A HALTER AND HELLFIRE IN STORE FOR YOU!
YOU'RE A MAN OF SPIRIT, AND YOU'LL MAKE A VERY PRETTY DEATH OF IT! BUT KEEP YOUR BREATH, FOR YOU'LL NEED IT SOON!
IS THE DINGHY ASTERN, NED?
AYE, AYE, CAPTAIN!
AND THE OTHER BOATS SCUTTLED?
I BORED THEM ALL IN THREE PLACES.
YOU LOOK AS IF YOU HADN'T QUITE GOT YOUR BEARINGS YET, CAPTAIN. WAS THERE SOMETHING YOU WANTED TO ASK ME?
WHERE IS THE GOVERNOR OF ST. KITTS, YOU DEVIL!?
WELL... WHEN LAST I SAW HIM HIS EXCELLENCY WAS IN BED WITH HIS THROAT CUT. WHEN I BROKE PRISON I LEARNED THAT THE GOVERNOR WAS STARTING FOR ENGLAND ON YOUR VESSEL. I CLIMBED HIS VERANDAH, AND I PAID HIM THE LITTLE DEBT THAT I OWED HIM.

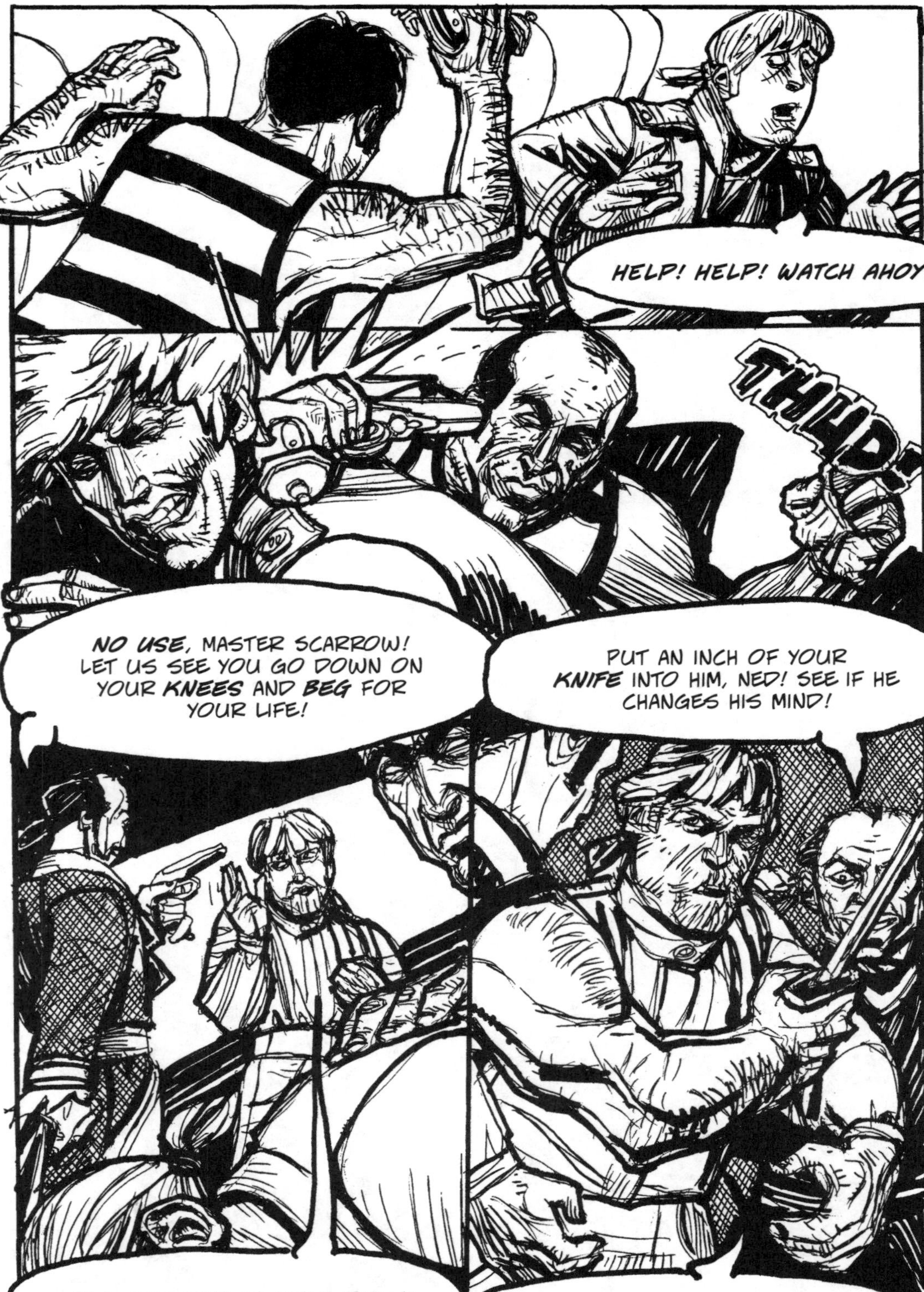
HELP! HELP! WATCH AHOY!
THUD!
NO USE, MASTER SCARROW! LET US SEE YOU GO DOWN ON YOUR KNEES AND BEG FOR YOUR LIFE!
PUT AN INCH OF YOUR KNIFE INTO HIM, NED! SEE IF HE CHANGES HIS MIND!
I'LL SEE YOU IN HELL FIRST!
YOU MAY PUT IN SIX INCHES, AND STILL I WON'T!

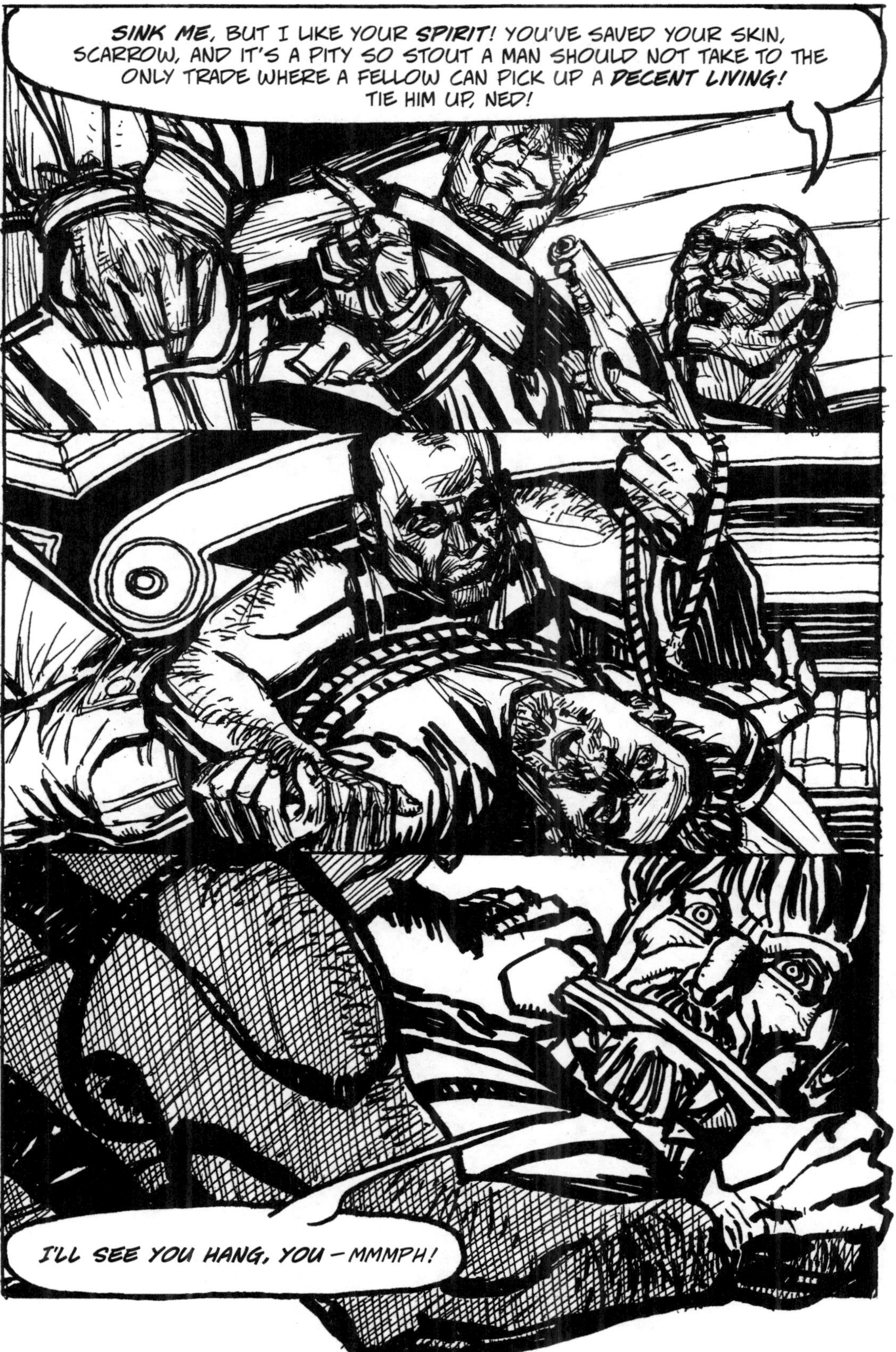
SINK ME, BUT I LIKE YOUR SPIRIT! YOU'VE SAVED YOUR SKIN, SCARROW, AND IT'S A PITY SO STOUT A MAN SHOULD NOT TAKE TO THE ONLY TRADE WHERE A FELLOW CAN PICK UP A DECENT LIVING! TIE HIM UP, NED!
I'LL SEE YOU HANG, YOU—MMMPH!

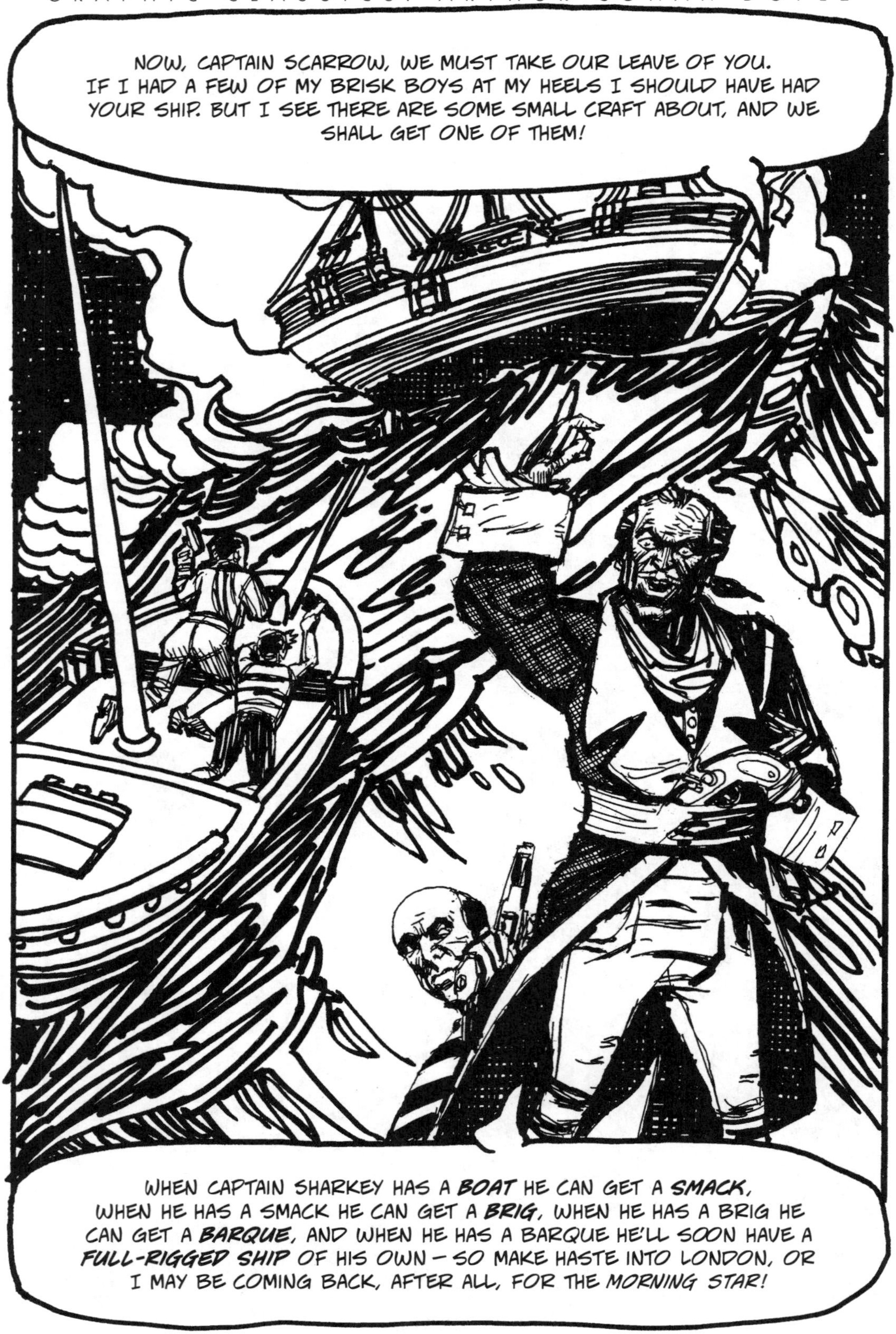
NOW, CAPTAIN SCARROW, WE MUST TAKE OUR LEAVE OF YOU. IF I HAD A FEW OF MY BRISK BOYS AT MY HEELS I SHOULD HAVE HAD YOUR SHIP. BUT I SEE THERE ARE SOME SMALL CRAFT ABOUT, AND WE SHALL GET ONE OF THEM!
WHEN CAPTAIN SHARKEY HAS A ***BOAT*** HE CAN GET A ***SMACK***, WHEN HE HAS A SMACK HE CAN GET A ***BRIG***, WHEN HE HAS A BRIG HE CAN GET A ***BARQUE***, AND WHEN HE HAS A BARQUE HE'LL SOON HAVE A ***FULL-RIGGED SHIP*** OF HIS OWN – SO MAKE HASTE INTO LONDON, OR I MAY BE COMING BACK, AFTER ALL, FOR THE *MORNING STAR*!

As Captain Scarrow strained at his bonds, he heard footsteps pass up the companion and along the quarter-deck to where the dinghy hung in the stern, and then the splash of the boat in the water.

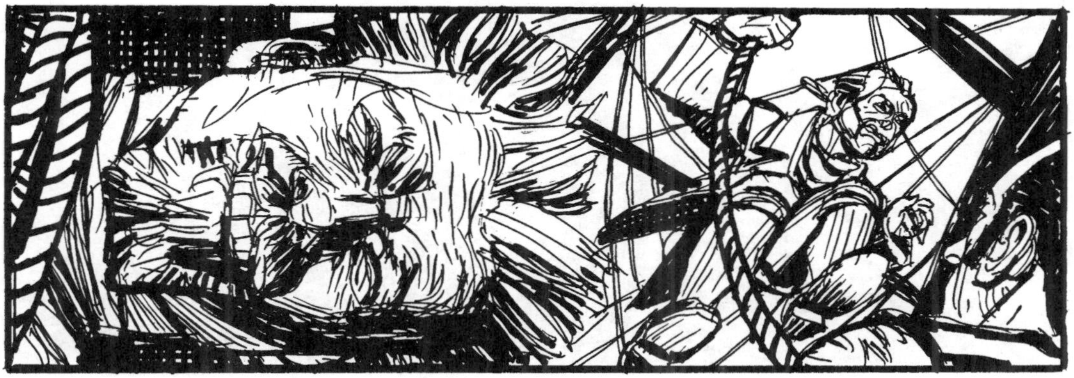

In a mad fury he tore at his ropes, until at last he rolled from the table, kicked open the cabin door, and rushed on to the deck.

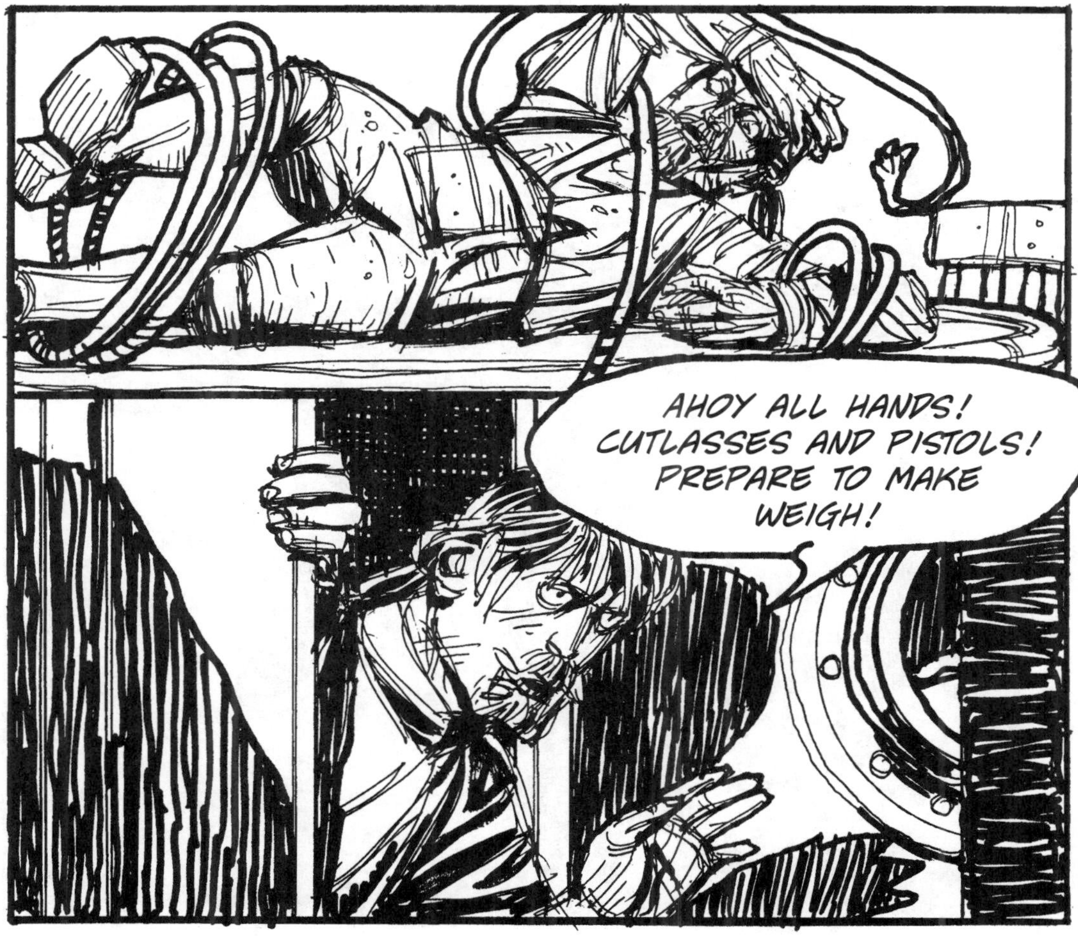
AHOY ALL HANDS! CUTLASSES AND PISTOLS! PREPARE TO MAKE WEIGH!

The captain gave a bitter curse as he realized it was too late. He had been beaten and outwitted at every point. The boats had all been damaged. Above was a cloudless, starlit sky, with neither wind nor the promise of it.

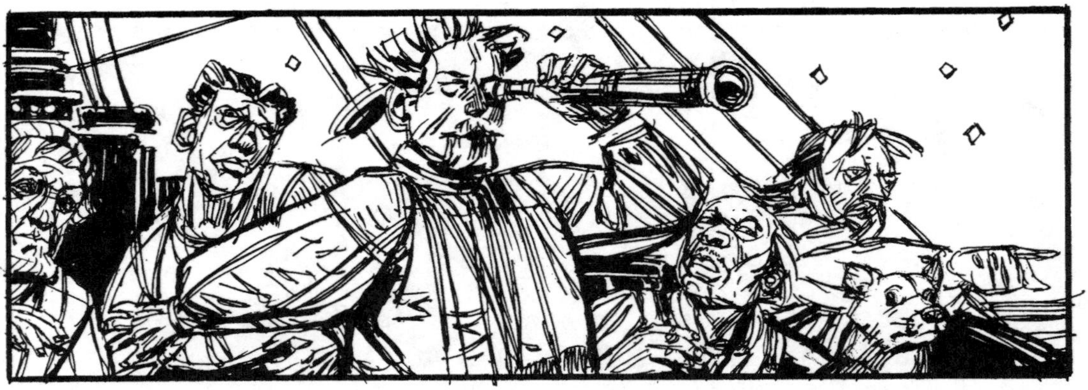

Far away lay a fishing-smack, and approaching them was the little dinghy, steadily drawing nearer.

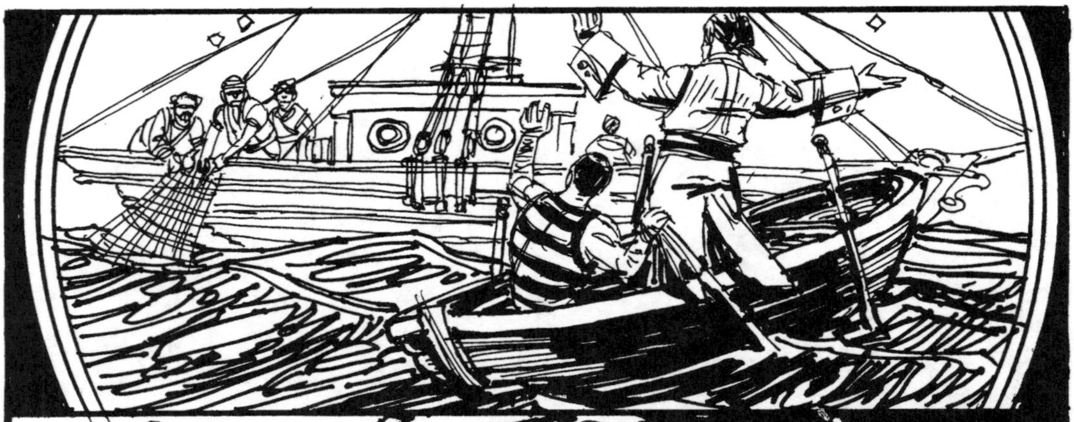

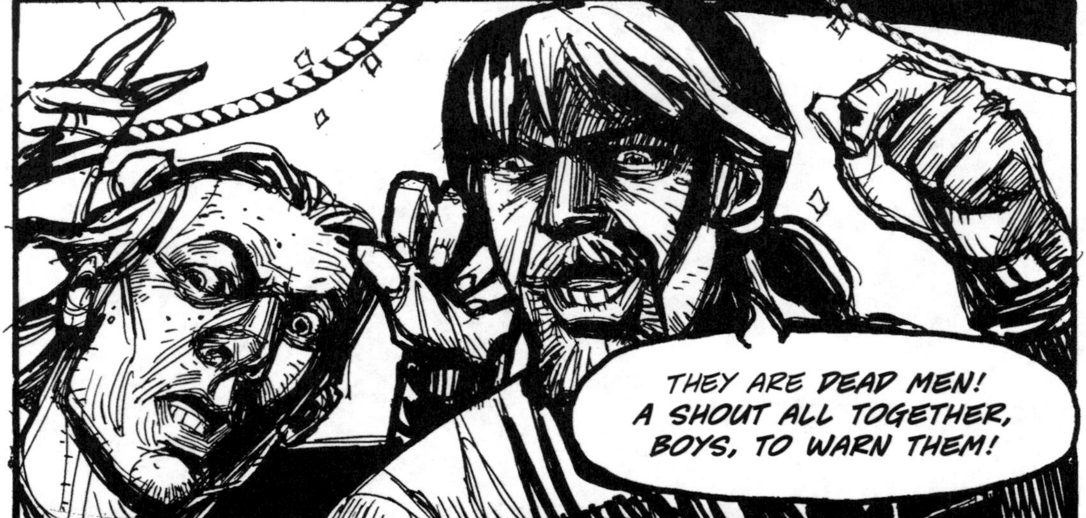
THEY ARE DEAD MEN! A SHOUT ALL TOGETHER, BOYS, TO WARN THEM!

But it was too late. There were two rapid pistol shots, a scream, and then another shot, followed by silence. The fishermen had disappeared.

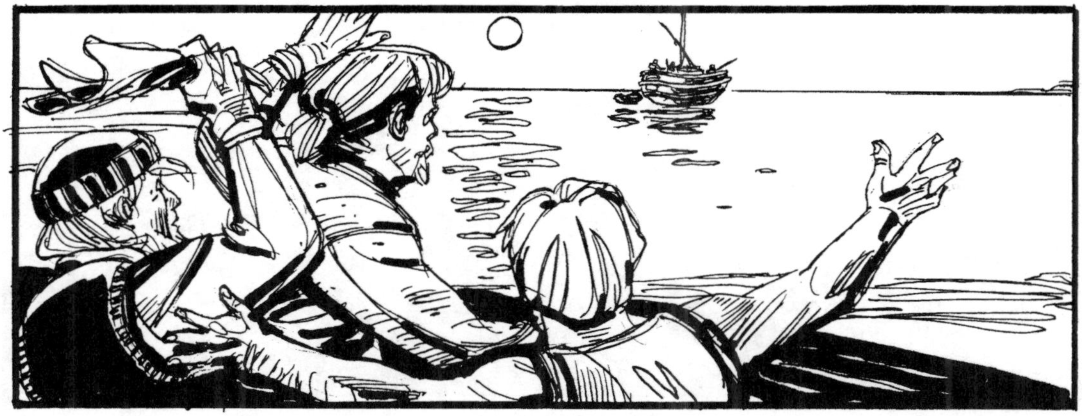

And then, as the first puffs of a land-breeze suddenly came out from the Sussex shore, the boom swung out, the mainsail filled, and the little craft crept out with her nose to the Atlantic.

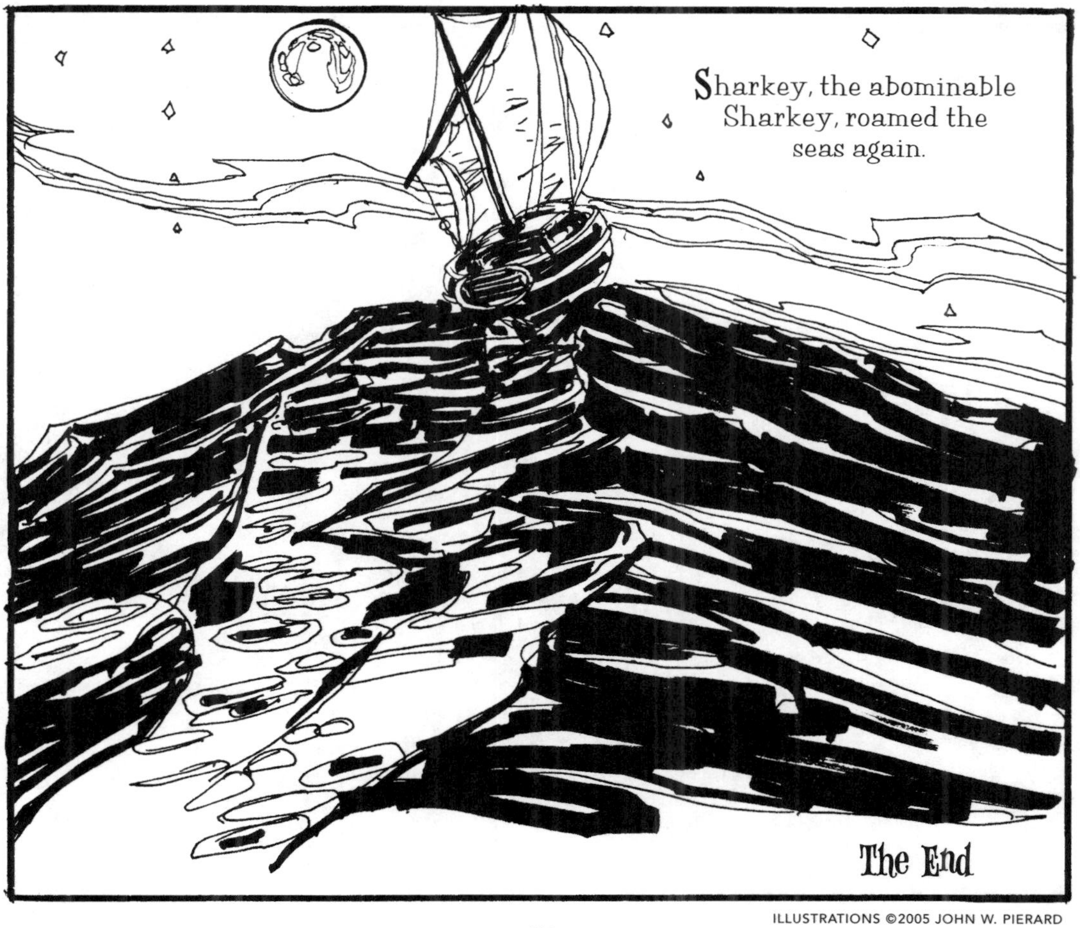
Sharkey, the abominable Sharkey, roamed the seas again.
The End

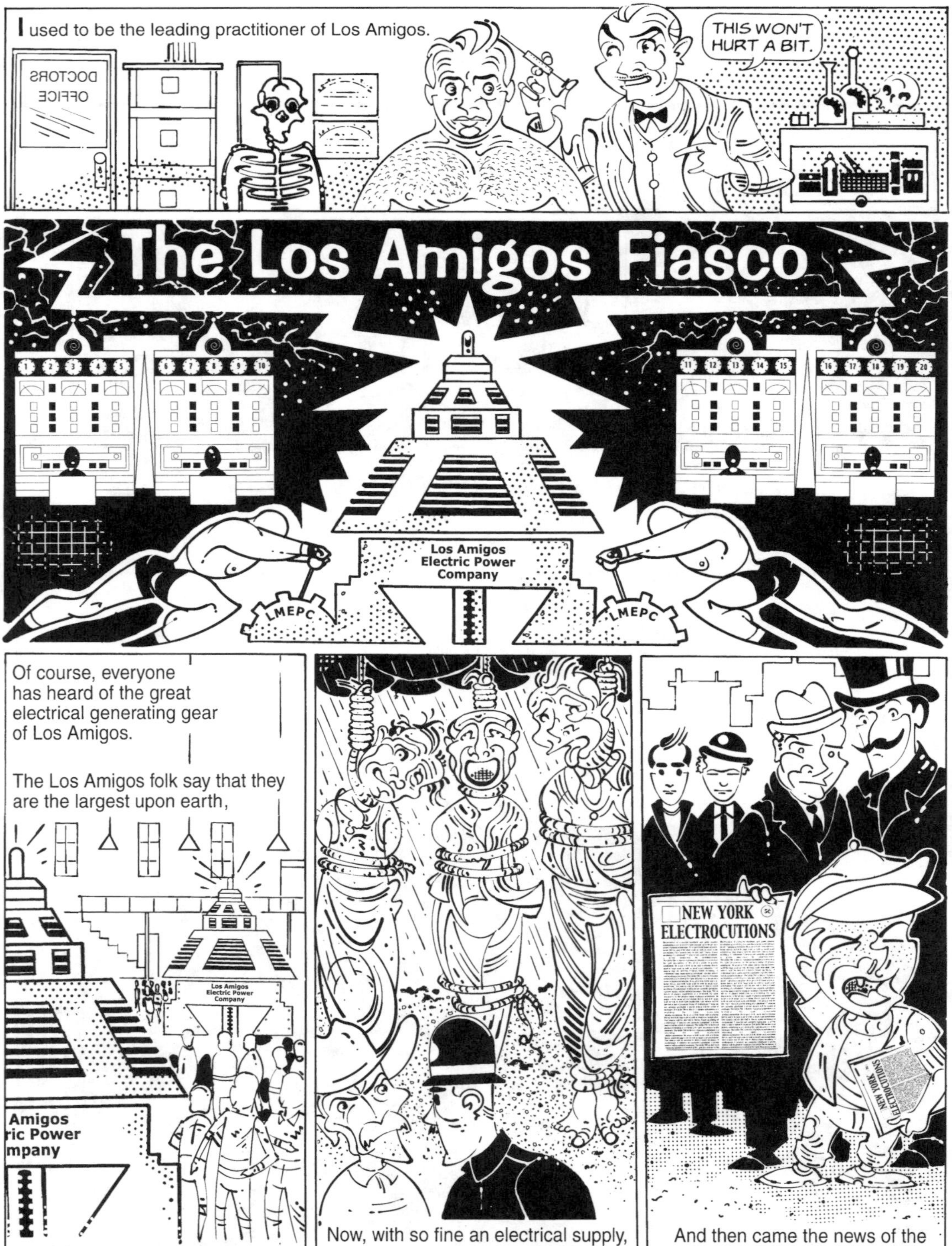
I used to be the leading practitioner of Los Amigos.
THIS WON'T HURT A BIT.
The Los Amigos Fiasco
Los Amigos Electric Power Company
LMEPC
LMEPC
Of course, everyone has heard of the great electrical generating gear of Los Amigos.
The Los Amigos folk say that they are the largest upon earth,
Los Amigos Electric Power Company
Amigos ric Power mpany
supplying power to our town, as well as dozens of little townlets and villages all round, which receive their supply from the same centre.
Now, with so fine an electrical supply, it seemed to be a sinful waste of hemp that the Los Amigos criminals should perish in the old-fashioned manner.
NEW YORK ELECTROCUTIONS
NEW YORK ELECTROCUTIONS
And then came the news of the electrocutions in the East, and how the results had not after all been so instantaneous as had been hoped.

The Western engineers raised their eyebrows when they read of the puny shocks by which these men had perished, and they vowed in Los Amigos that when an irreclaimable came their way he should have the run of all the big dynamos. And what the result of that would be none could predict, save that it must be absolutely blasting and deadly.

Some prophesied combustion.

And some disintegration and disappearance.

They were waiting eagerly to settle the question by actual demonstration, and it was just at that moment that Duncan Warner came that way.

Warner had been wanted by the law, and by nobody else, for many years.

HALT!

HA HA HA HA HA HA HA HA

Desperado, murderer, robber,

he was a man beyond the pale of human pity.

His advocate did all he knew, but the cards lay against him,

GUILTY!

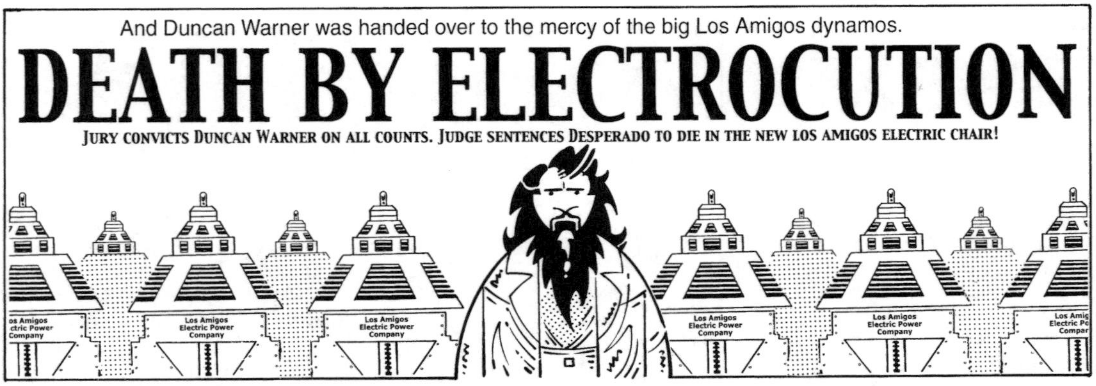
And Duncan Warner was handed over to the mercy of the big Los Amigos dynamos.
DEATH BY ELECTROCUTION
JURY CONVICTS DUNCAN WARNER ON ALL COUNTS. JUDGE SENTENCES DESPERADO TO DIE IN THE NEW LOS AMIGOS ELECTRIC CHAIR!
Los Amigos Electric Power Company
Los Amigos Electric Power Company
Los Amigos Electric Power Company
Los Amigos Electric Power Company
Los Amigos Electric Power Company

The town council had chosen four experts to look after the arrangements. Three of them were admirable.

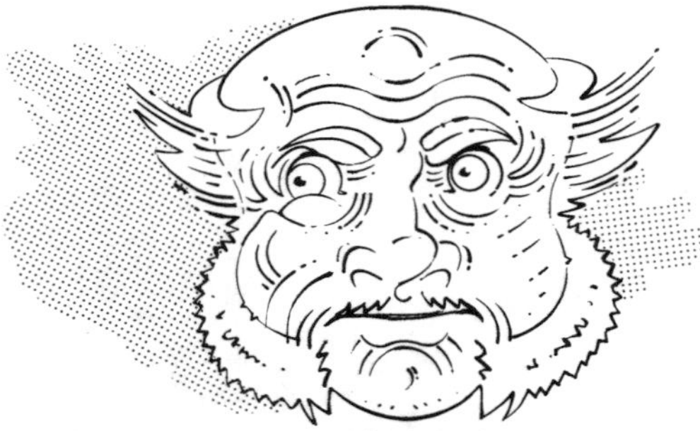

There was Joseph M'Conner, the very man who had designed the dynamos,

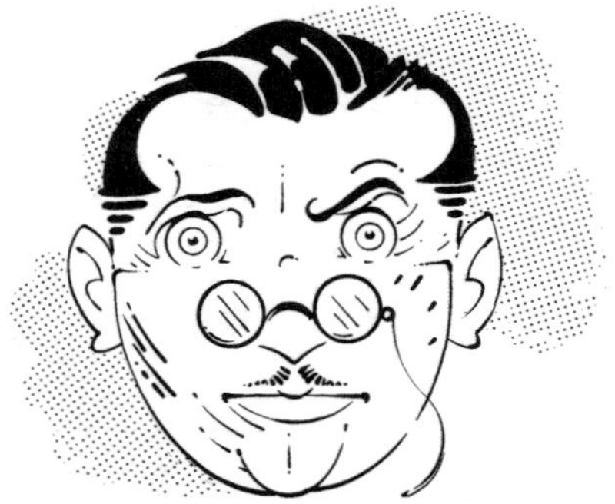

and there was Joshua Westmacott, the chairman of the Los Amigos Electrical Supply Company, Limited.

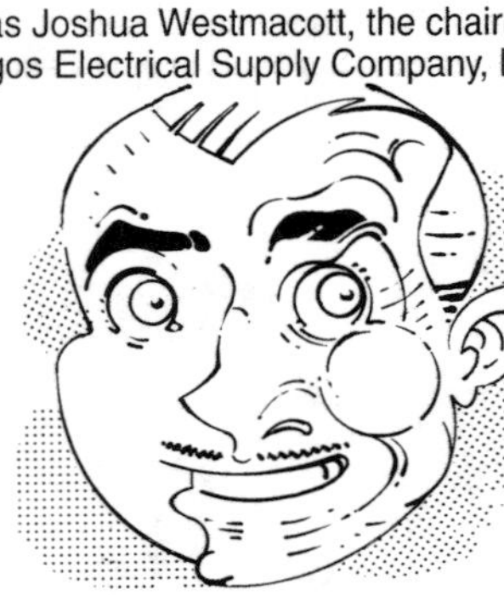

Then there was myself as the chief medical man,

and lastly an old German of the name of Peter Stulpnagel.

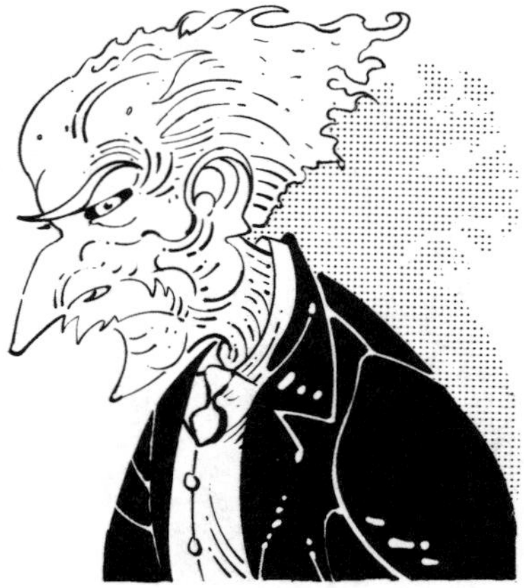

It was said that he had been a wonderful electrician at home, and he was eternally working with wires and insulators and Leyden jars; but, as he never seemed to get any further, or to have any results worth publishing, he came at last to be regarded as a harmless crank, who had made science his hobby. We three practical men smiled when we heard that he had been elected as our colleague, and at the meeting we fixed it all up very nicely among ourselves without much thought of the old fellow who sat with his ears scooped forward in his hands, for he was a trifle hard of hearing, taking no more part in the proceedings than the gentlemen of the press who scribbled their notes on the back benches.

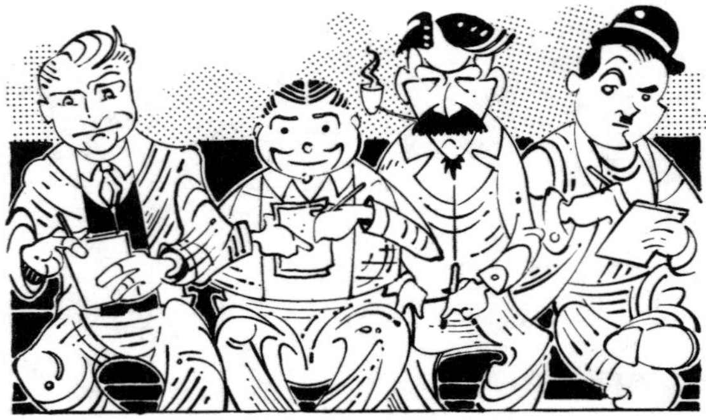

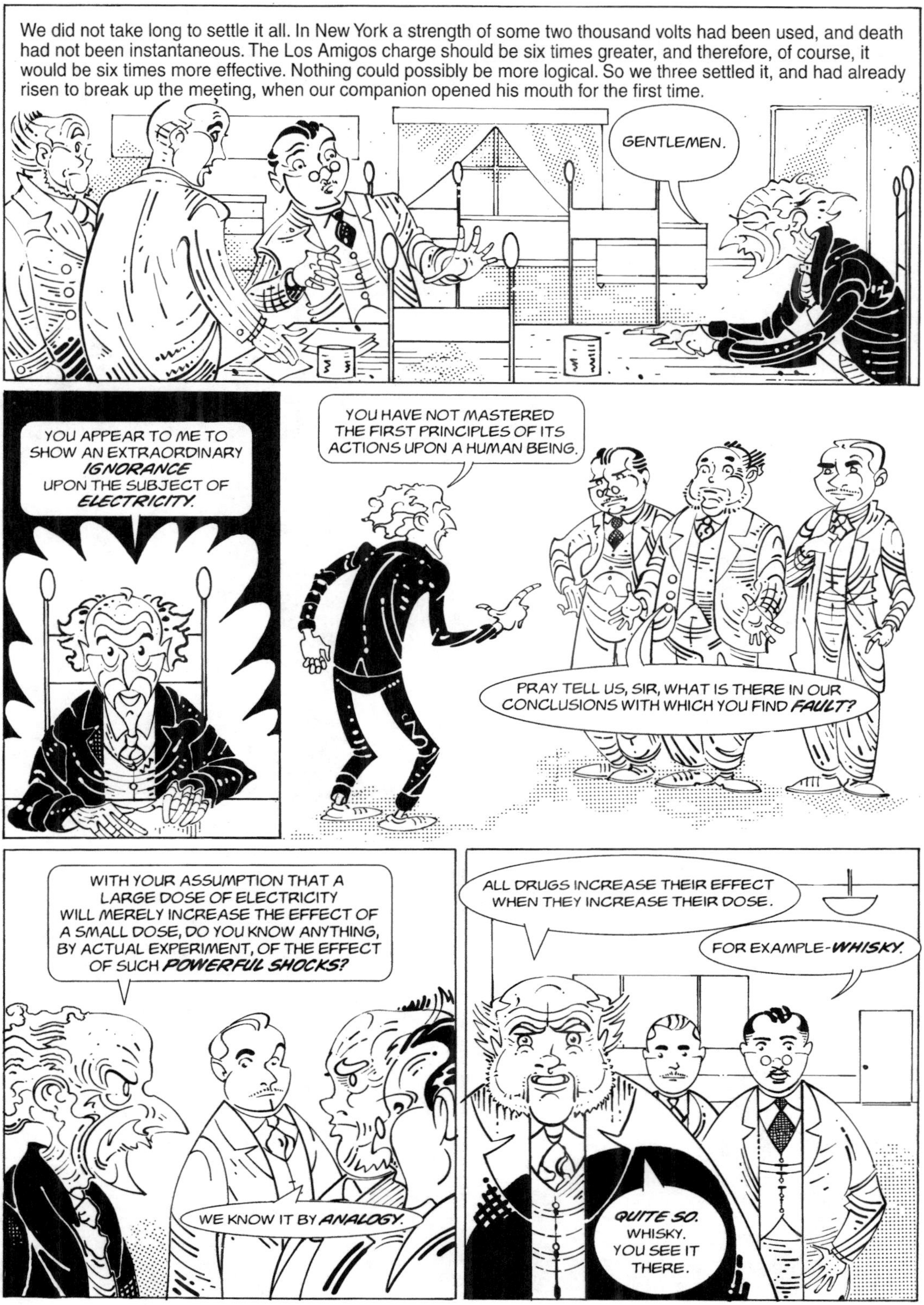
We did not take long to settle it all. In New York a strength of some two thousand volts had been used, and death had not been instantaneous. The Los Amigos charge should be six times greater, and therefore, of course, it would be six times more effective. Nothing could possibly be more logical. So we three settled it, and had already risen to break up the meeting, when our companion opened his mouth for the first time.
GENTLEMEN.
YOU APPEAR TO ME TO SHOW AN EXTRAORDINARY IGNORANCE UPON THE SUBJECT OF ELECTRICITY.
YOU HAVE NOT MASTERED THE FIRST PRINCIPLES OF ITS ACTIONS UPON A HUMAN BEING.
PRAY TELL US, SIR, WHAT IS THERE IN OUR CONCLUSIONS WITH WHICH YOU FIND FAULT?
WITH YOUR ASSUMPTION THAT A LARGE DOSE OF ELECTRICITY WILL MERELY INCREASE THE EFFECT OF A SMALL DOSE, DO YOU KNOW ANYTHING, BY ACTUAL EXPERIMENT, OF THE EFFECT OF SUCH POWERFUL SHOCKS?
WE KNOW IT BY ANALOGY.
ALL DRUGS INCREASE THEIR EFFECT WHEN THEY INCREASE THEIR DOSE.
FOR EXAMPLE-WHISKY.
QUITE SO. WHISKY. YOU SEE IT THERE.

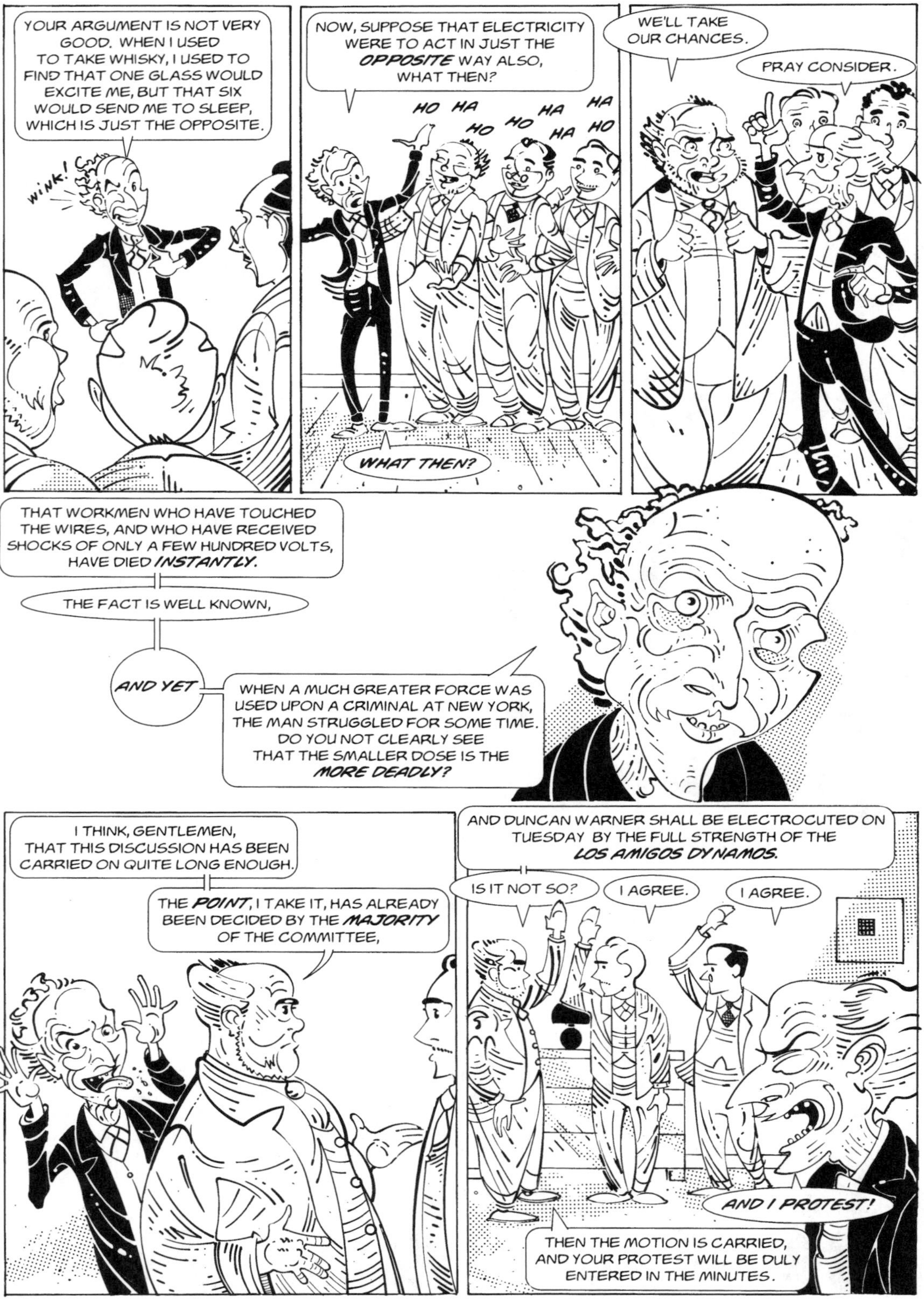
YOUR ARGUMENT IS NOT VERY GOOD. WHEN I USED TO TAKE WHISKY, I USED TO FIND THAT ONE GLASS WOULD EXCITE ME, BUT THAT SIX WOULD SEND ME TO SLEEP, WHICH IS JUST THE OPPOSITE.
WINK!
NOW, SUPPOSE THAT ELECTRICITY WERE TO ACT IN JUST THE OPPOSITE WAY ALSO, WHAT THEN?
HO HA HO HO HA HA HA HO
WHAT THEN?
WE'LL TAKE OUR CHANCES.
PRAY CONSIDER.
THAT WORKMEN WHO HAVE TOUCHED THE WIRES, AND WHO HAVE RECEIVED SHOCKS OF ONLY A FEW HUNDRED VOLTS, HAVE DIED INSTANTLY.
THE FACT IS WELL KNOWN,
AND YET
WHEN A MUCH GREATER FORCE WAS USED UPON A CRIMINAL AT NEW YORK, THE MAN STRUGGLED FOR SOME TIME. DO YOU NOT CLEARLY SEE THAT THE SMALLER DOSE IS THE MORE DEADLY?
I THINK, GENTLEMEN, THAT THIS DISCUSSION HAS BEEN CARRIED ON QUITE LONG ENOUGH.
THE POINT, I TAKE IT, HAS ALREADY BEEN DECIDED BY THE MAJORITY OF THE COMMITTEE,
AND DUNCAN WARNER SHALL BE ELECTROCUTED ON TUESDAY BY THE FULL STRENGTH OF THE LOS AMIGOS DYNAMOS.
IS IT NOT SO?
I AGREE.
I AGREE.
AND I PROTEST!
THEN THE MOTION IS CARRIED, AND YOUR PROTEST WILL BE DULY ENTERED IN THE MINUTES.

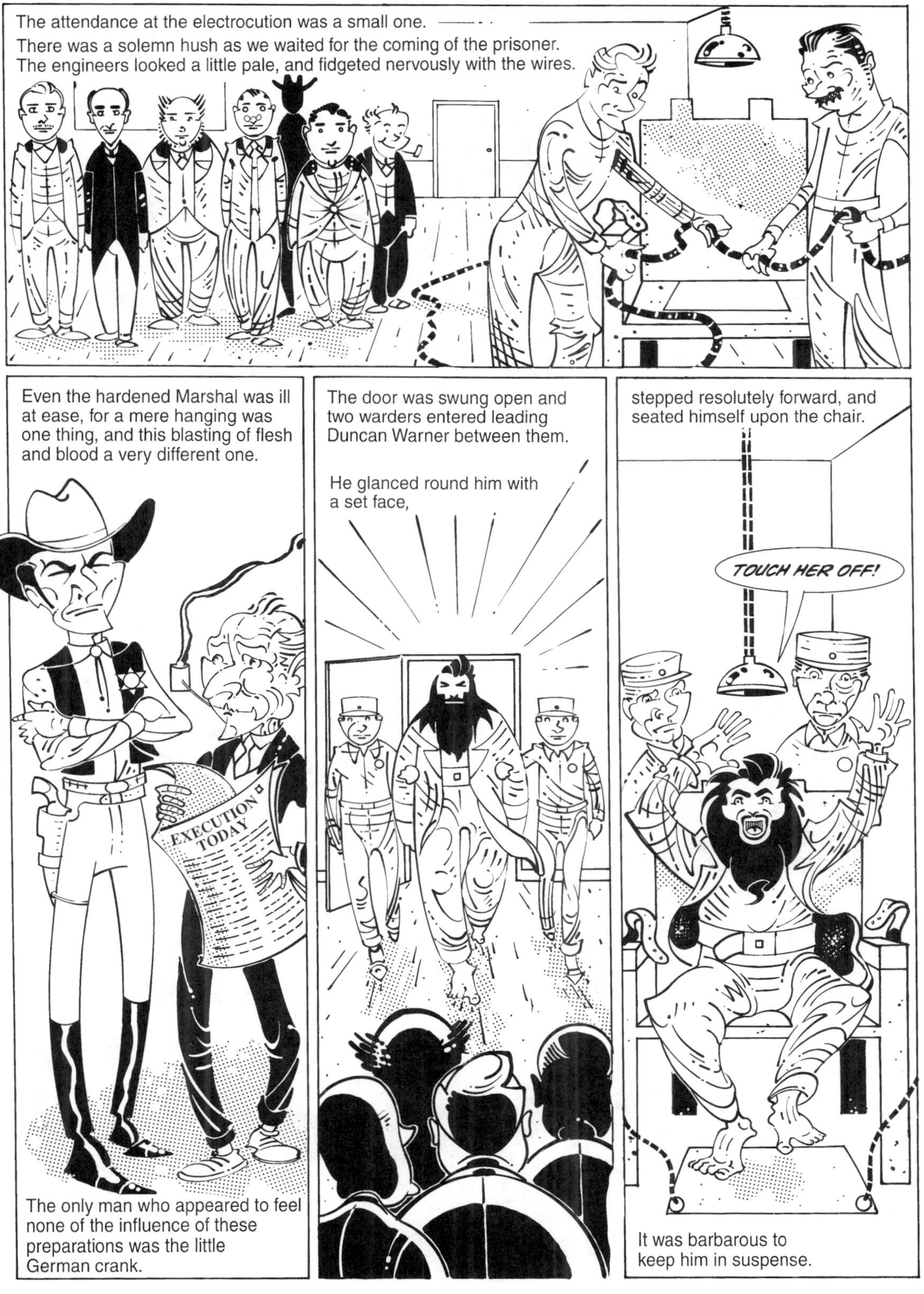
The attendance at the electrocution was a small one.
There was a solemn hush as we waited for the coming of the prisoner.
The engineers looked a little pale, and fidgeted nervously with the wires.
Even the hardened Marshal was ill at ease, for a mere hanging was one thing, and this blasting of flesh and blood a very different one.
EXECUTION TODAY
The only man who appeared to feel none of the influence of these preparations was the little German crank.
The door was swung open and two warders entered leading Duncan Warner between them.
He glanced round him with a set face,
stepped resolutely forward, and seated himself upon the chair.
TOUCH HER OFF!
It was barbarous to keep him in suspense.

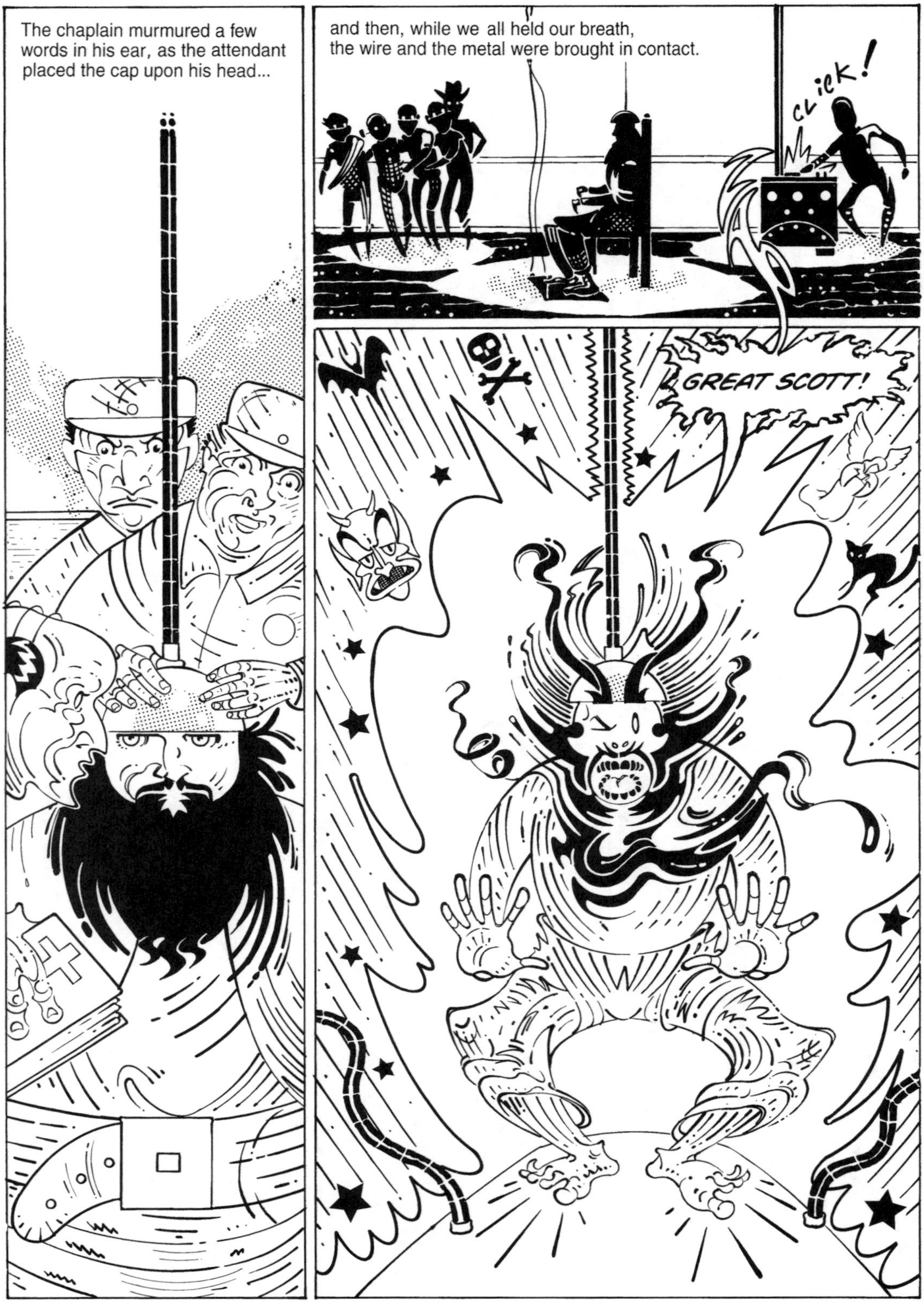
The chaplain murmured a few words in his ear, as the attendant placed the cap upon his head...
and then, while we all held our breath, the wire and the metal were brought in contact.
CLICK!
GREAT SCOTT!

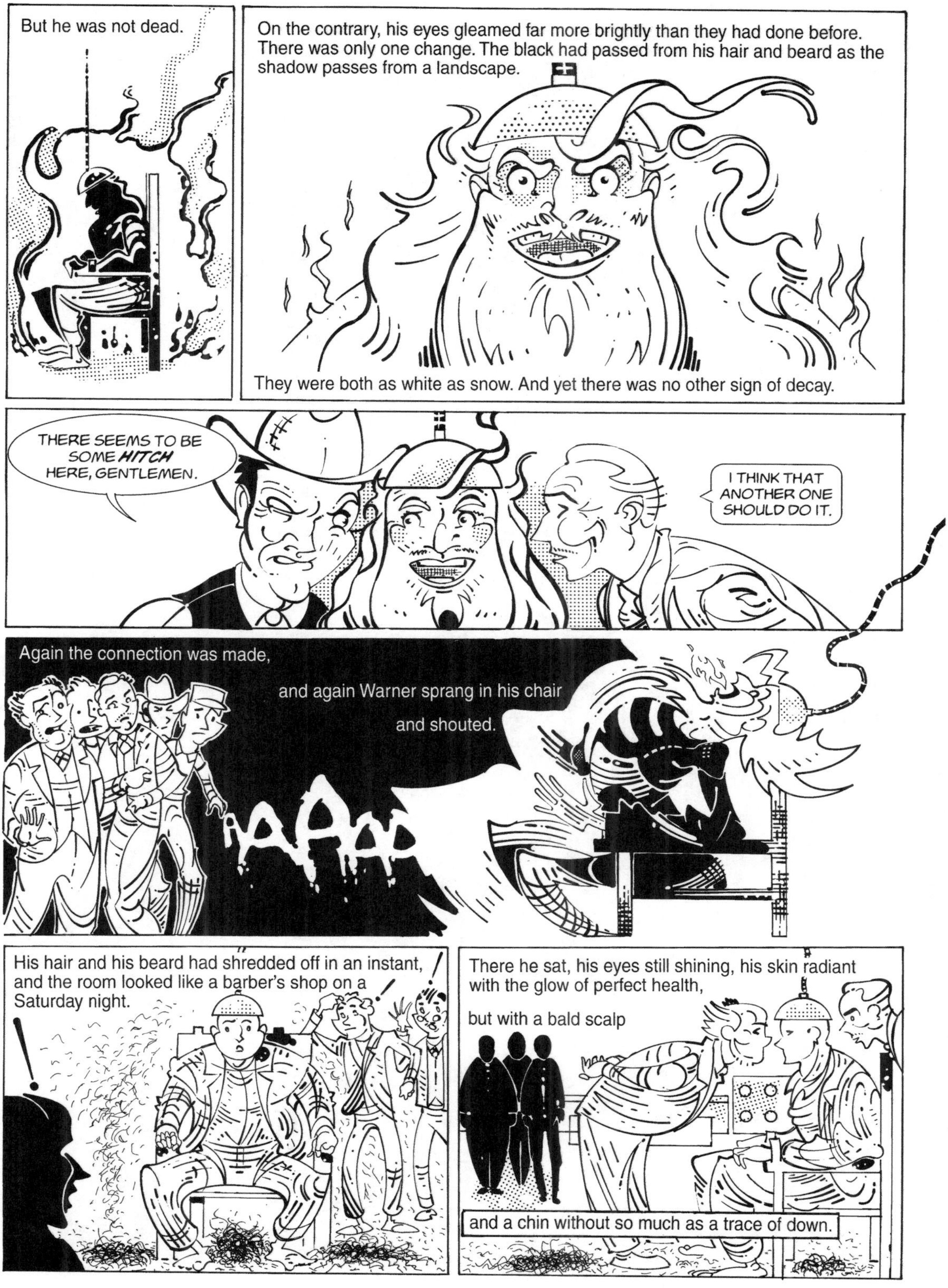
But he was not dead.
On the contrary, his eyes gleamed far more brightly than they had done before. There was only one change. The black had passed from his hair and beard as the shadow passes from a landscape.
They were both as white as snow. And yet there was no other sign of decay.
THERE SEEMS TO BE SOME HITCH HERE, GENTLEMEN.
I THINK THAT ANOTHER ONE SHOULD DO IT.
Again the connection was made,
and again Warner sprang in his chair
and shouted.
iAAAA
His hair and his beard had shredded off in an instant, and the room looked like a barber's shop on a Saturday night.
There he sat, his eyes still shining, his skin radiant with the glow of perfect health,
but with a bald scalp
and a chin without so much as a trace of down.

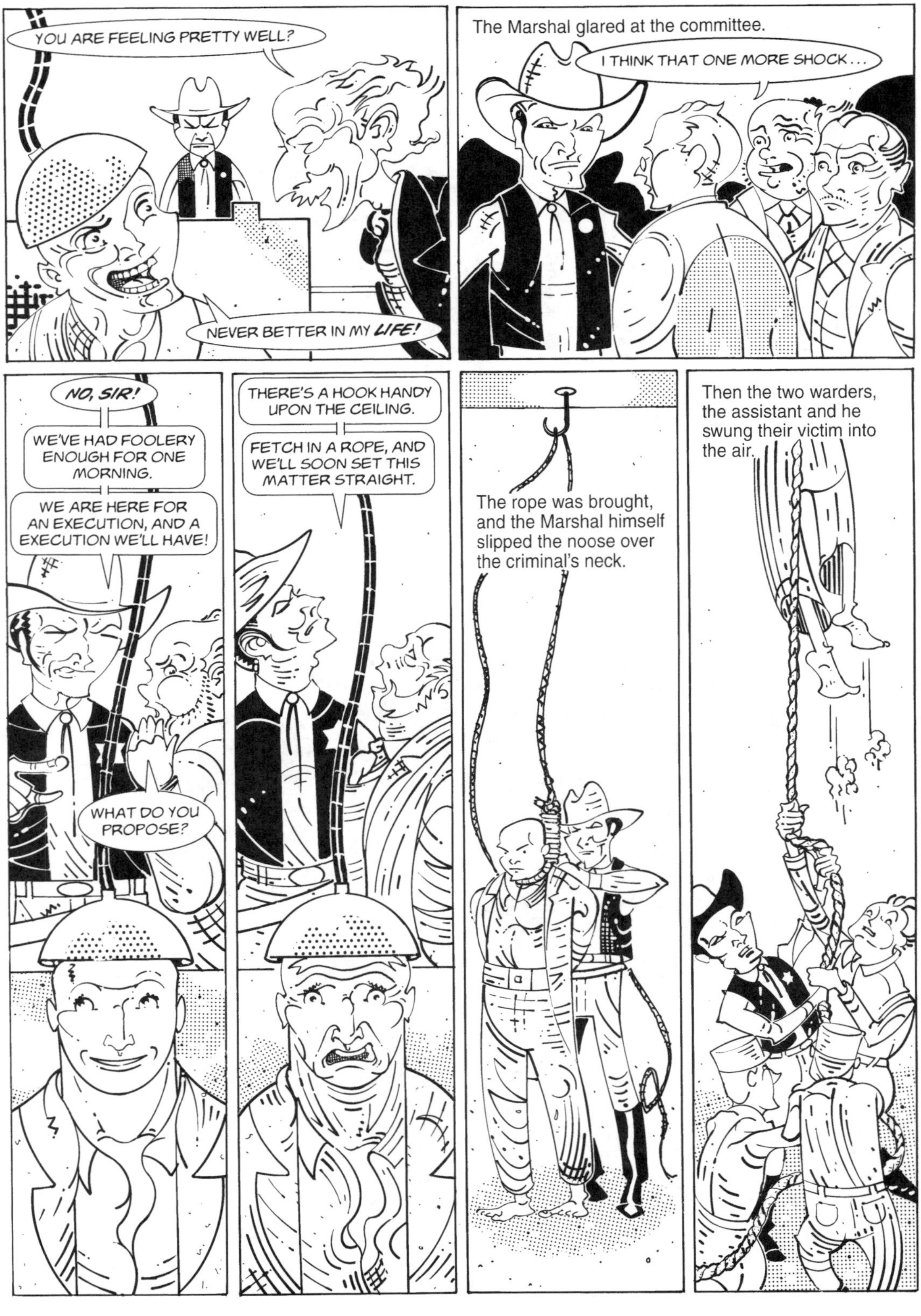
YOU ARE FEELING PRETTY WELL?
NEVER BETTER IN MY LIFE!
The Marshal glared at the committee.
I THINK THAT ONE MORE SHOCK...
NO, SIR!
WE'VE HAD FOOLERY ENOUGH FOR ONE MORNING.
WE ARE HERE FOR AN EXECUTION, AND A EXECUTION WE'LL HAVE!
WHAT DO YOU PROPOSE?
THERE'S A HOOK HANDY UPON THE CEILING.
FETCH IN A ROPE, AND WE'LL SOON SET THIS MATTER STRAIGHT.
The rope was brought, and the Marshal himself slipped the noose over the criminal's neck.
Then the two warders, the assistant and he swung their victim into the air.

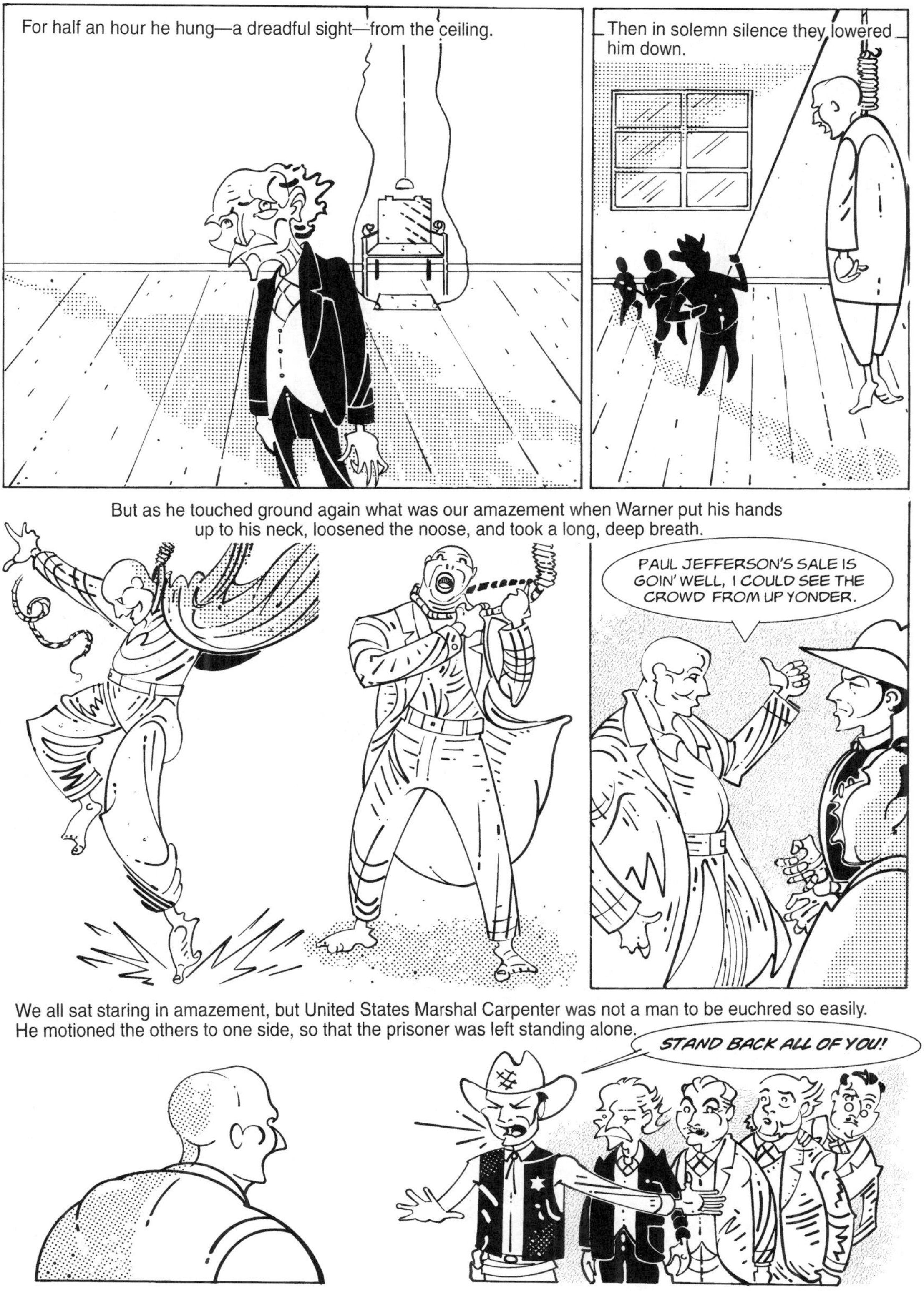
For half an hour he hung—a dreadful sight—from the ceiling.
Then in solemn silence they lowered him down.
But as he touched ground again what was our amazement when Warner put his hands up to his neck, loosened the noose, and took a long, deep breath.
PAUL JEFFERSON'S SALE IS GOIN' WELL, I COULD SEE THE CROWD FROM UP YONDER.
We all sat staring in amazement, but United States Marshal Carpenter was not a man to be euchred so easily. He motioned the others to one side, so that the prisoner was left standing alone.
STAND BACK ALL OF YOU!

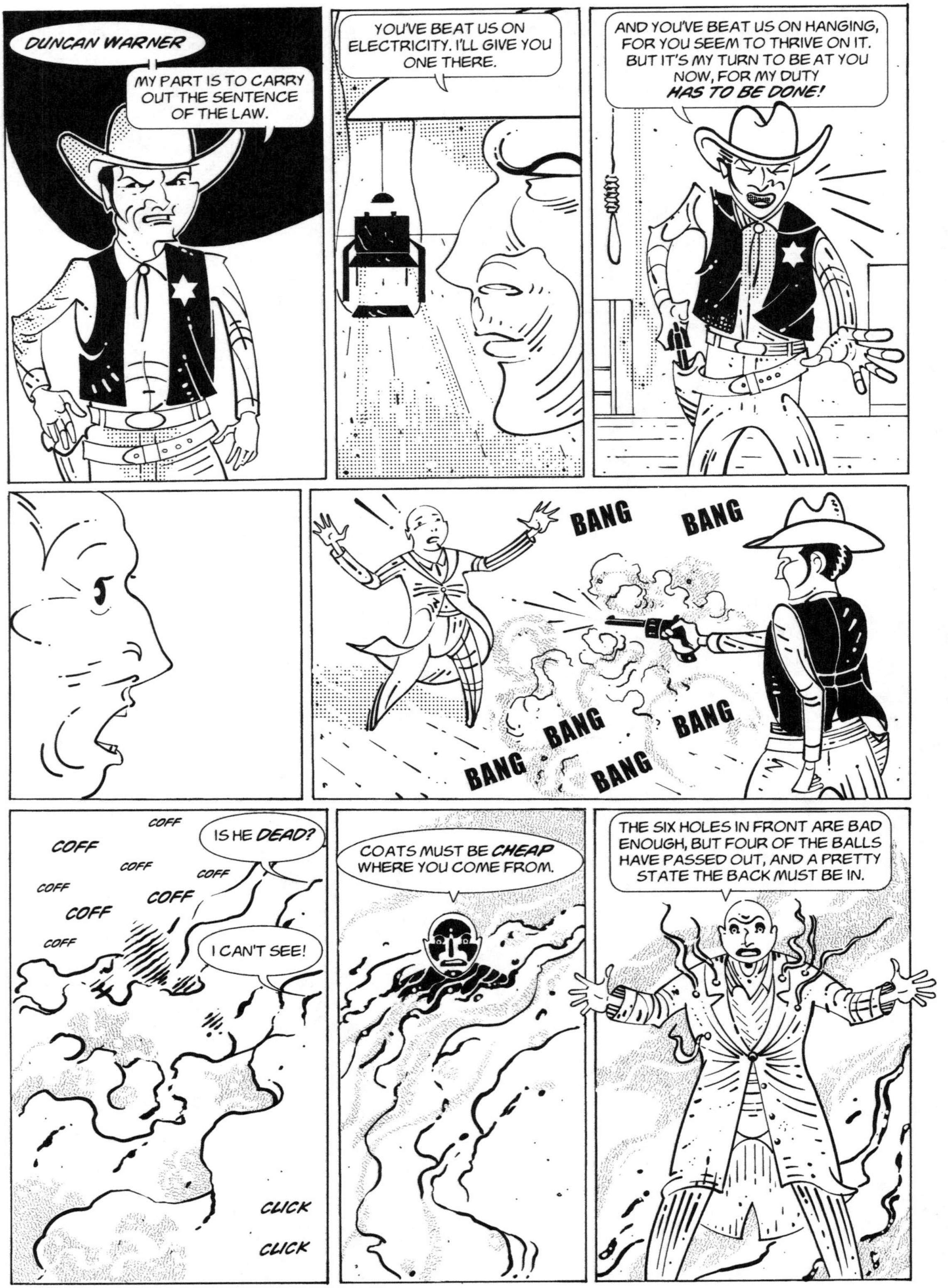
DUNCAN WARNER
MY PART IS TO CARRY OUT THE SENTENCE OF THE LAW.
YOU'VE BEAT US ON ELECTRICITY. I'LL GIVE YOU ONE THERE.
AND YOU'VE BEAT US ON HANGING, FOR YOU SEEM TO THRIVE ON IT. BUT IT'S MY TURN TO BE AT YOU NOW, FOR MY DUTY HAS TO BE DONE!
BANG BANG
BANG BANG BANG BANG
COFF COFF COFF COFF COFF COFF COFF
IS HE DEAD?
I CAN'T SEE!
CLICK
CLICK
COATS MUST BE CHEAP WHERE YOU COME FROM.
THE SIX HOLES IN FRONT ARE BAD ENOUGH, BUT FOUR OF THE BALLS HAVE PASSED OUT, AND A PRETTY STATE THE BACK MUST BE IN.

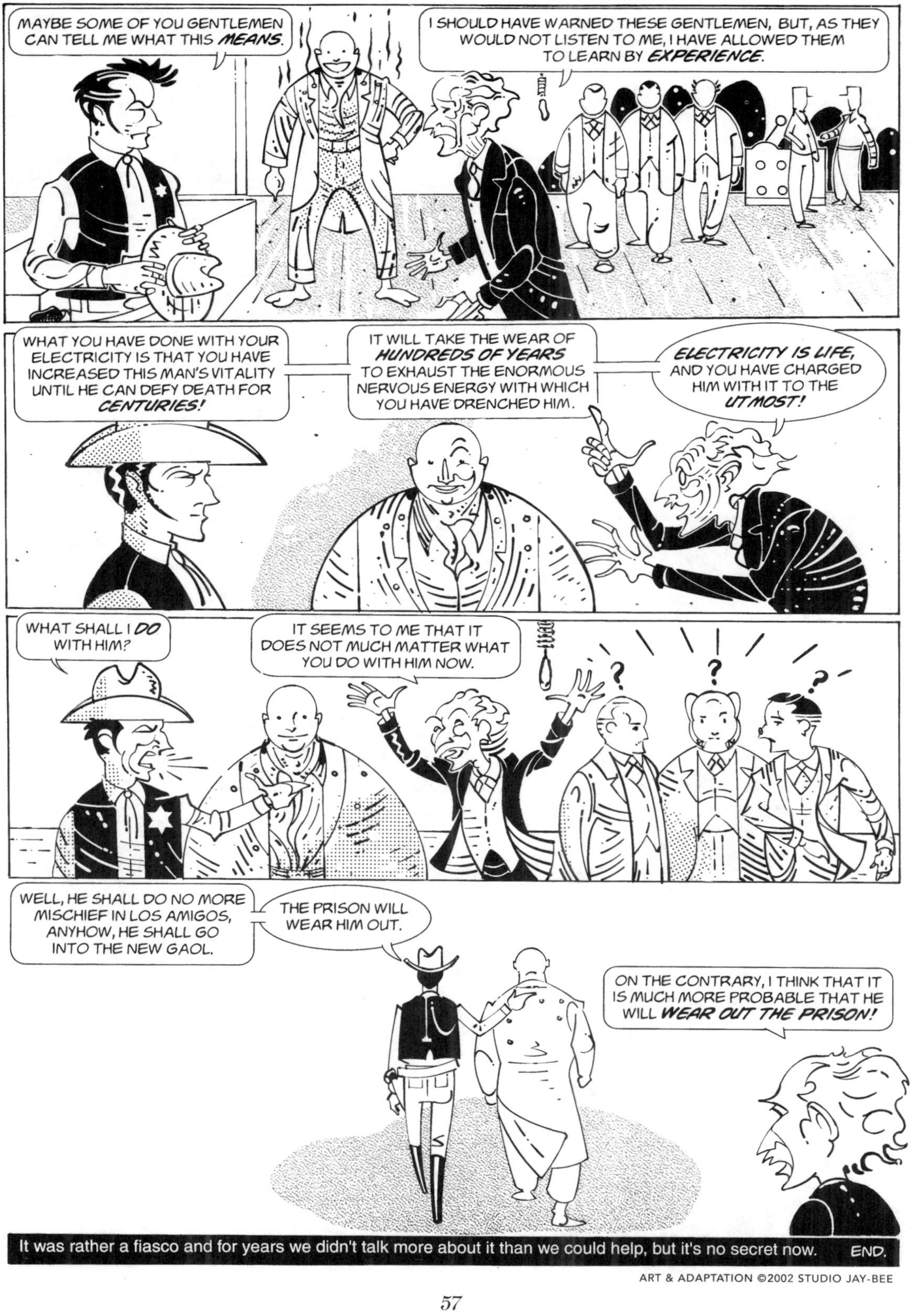
MAYBE SOME OF YOU GENTLEMEN CAN TELL ME WHAT THIS MEANS.
I SHOULD HAVE WARNED THESE GENTLEMEN, BUT, AS THEY WOULD NOT LISTEN TO ME, I HAVE ALLOWED THEM TO LEARN BY EXPERIENCE.
WHAT YOU HAVE DONE WITH YOUR ELECTRICITY IS THAT YOU HAVE INCREASED THIS MAN'S VITALITY UNTIL HE CAN DEFY DEATH FOR CENTURIES!
IT WILL TAKE THE WEAR OF HUNDREDS OF YEARS TO EXHAUST THE ENORMOUS NERVOUS ENERGY WITH WHICH YOU HAVE DRENCHED HIM.
ELECTRICITY IS LIFE, AND YOU HAVE CHARGED HIM WITH IT TO THE UTMOST!
WHAT SHALL I DO WITH HIM?
IT SEEMS TO ME THAT IT DOES NOT MUCH MATTER WHAT YOU DO WITH HIM NOW.
?
?
?
WELL, HE SHALL DO NO MORE MISCHIEF IN LOS AMIGOS, ANYHOW, HE SHALL GO INTO THE NEW GAOL.
THE PRISON WILL WEAR HIM OUT.
ON THE CONTRARY, I THINK THAT IT IS MUCH MORE PROBABLE THAT HE WILL WEAR OUT THE PRISON!
It was rather a fiasco and for years we didn't talk more about it than we could help, but it's no secret now.
END.

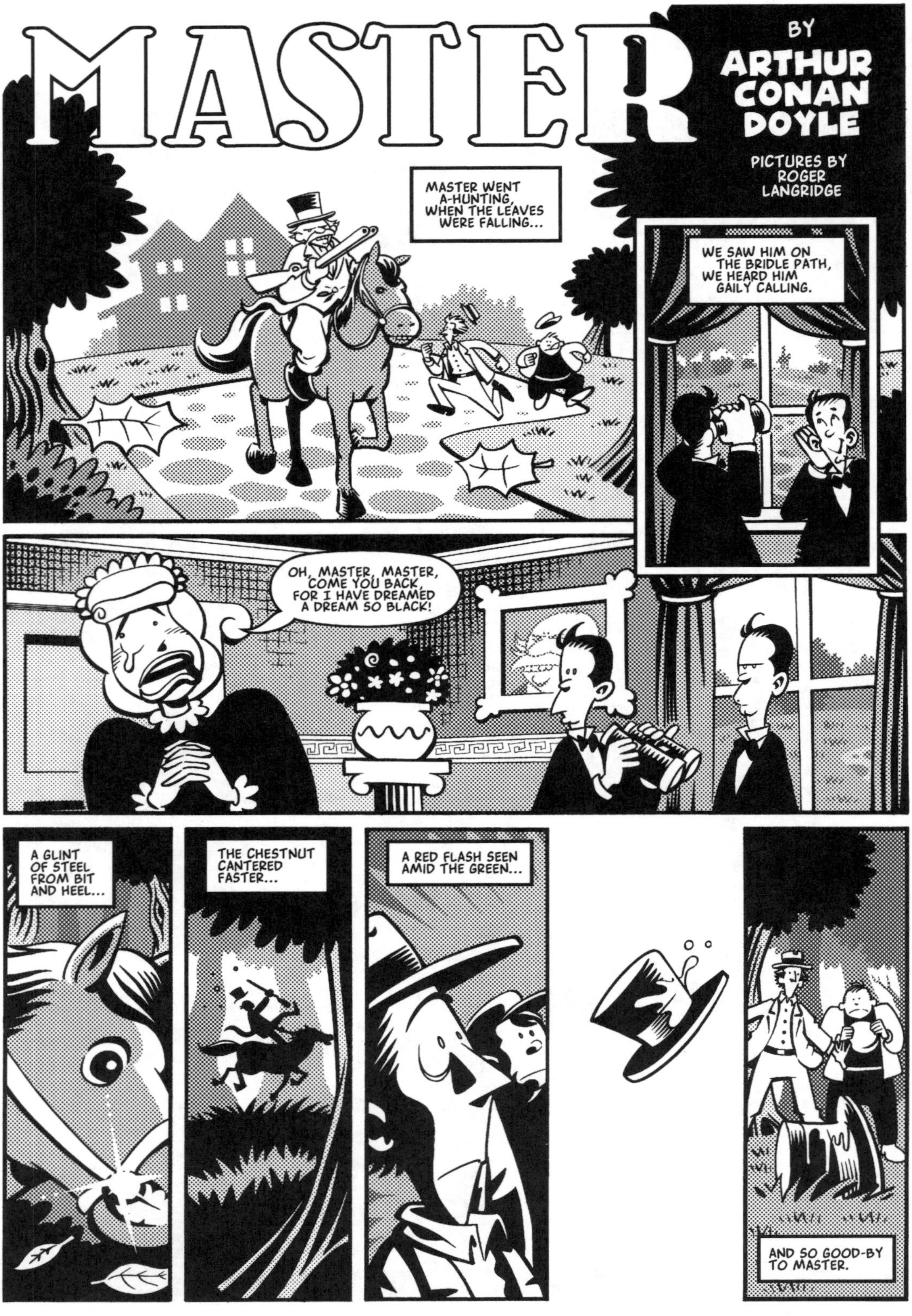
MASTER
BY
ARTHUR CONAN DOYLE
PICTURES BY ROGER LANGRIDGE
MASTER WENT A-HUNTING, WHEN THE LEAVES WERE FALLING...
WE SAW HIM ON THE BRIDLE PATH, WE HEARD HIM GAILY CALLING.
OH, MASTER, MASTER, COME YOU BACK, FOR I HAVE DREAMED A DREAM SO BLACK!
A GLINT OF STEEL FROM BIT AND HEEL...
THE CHESTNUT CANTERED FASTER...
A RED FLASH SEEN AMID THE GREEN...
AND SO GOOD-BY TO MASTER.

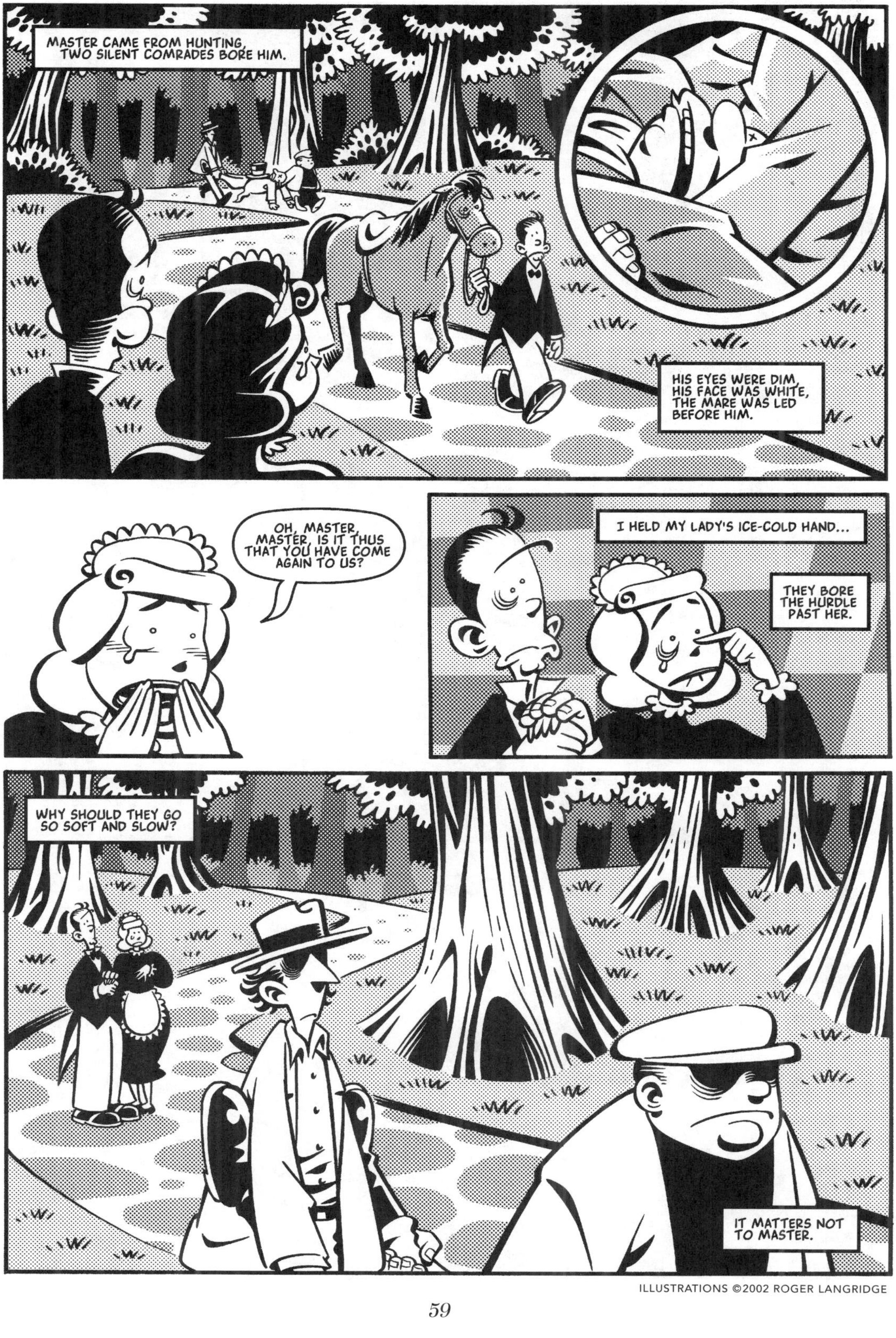
MASTER CAME FROM HUNTING, TWO SILENT COMRADES BORE HIM.
HIS EYES WERE DIM, HIS FACE WAS WHITE, THE MARE WAS LED BEFORE HIM.
OH, MASTER, MASTER, IS IT THUS THAT YOU HAVE COME AGAIN TO US?
I HELD MY LADY'S ICE-COLD HAND...
THEY BORE THE HURDLE PAST HER.
WHY SHOULD THEY GO SO SOFT AND SLOW?
IT MATTERS NOT TO MASTER.

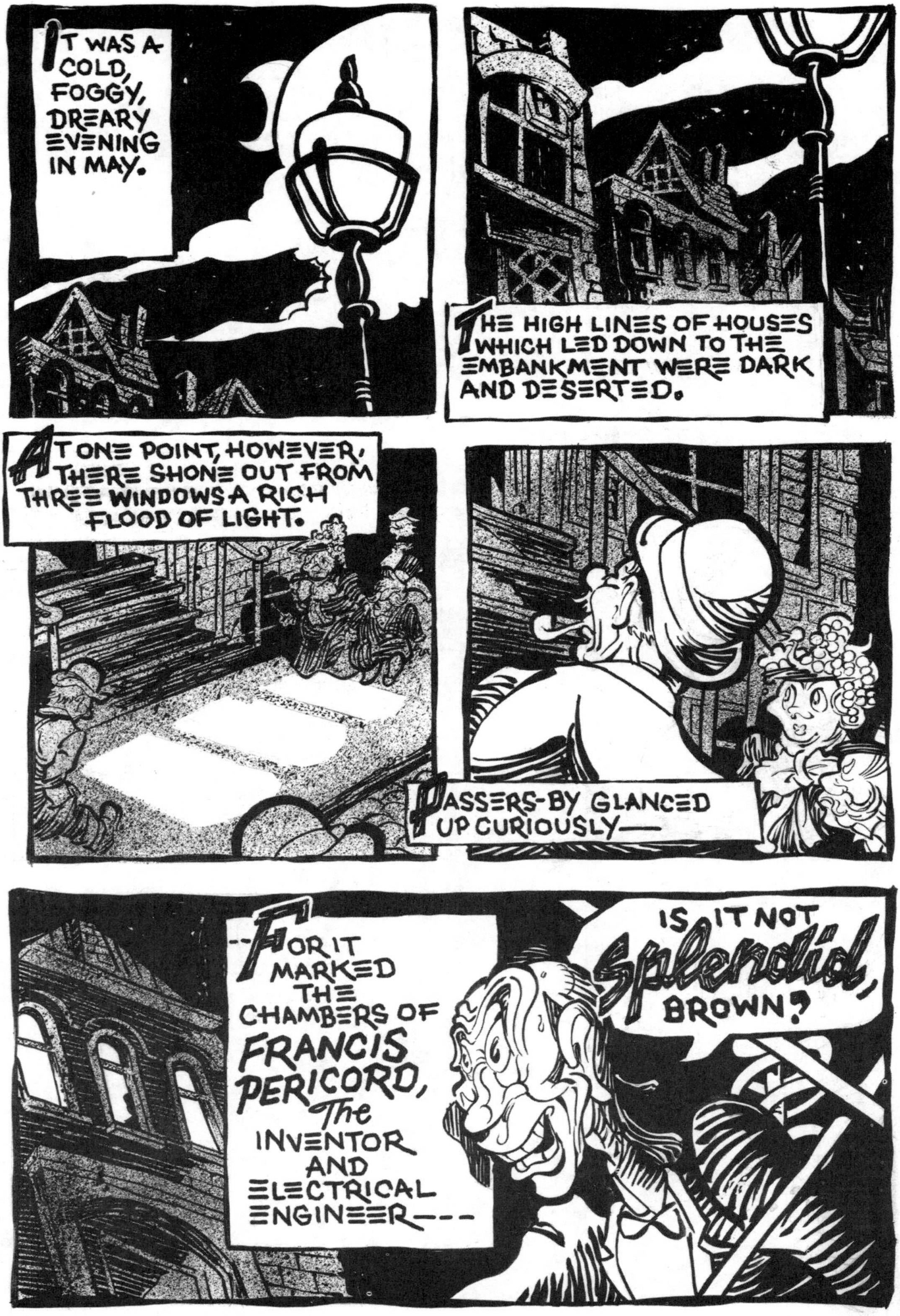
IT WAS A COLD, FOGGY, DREARY EVENING IN MAY.
THE HIGH LINES OF HOUSES WHICH LED DOWN TO THE EMBANKMENT WERE DARK AND DESERTED.
AT ONE POINT, HOWEVER, THERE SHONE OUT FROM THREE WINDOWS A RICH FLOOD OF LIGHT.
PASSERS-BY GLANCED UP CURIOUSLY—
--FOR IT MARKED THE CHAMBERS OF FRANCIS PERICORD, The INVENTOR AND ELECTRICAL ENGINEER---
IS IT NOT splendid, BROWN?

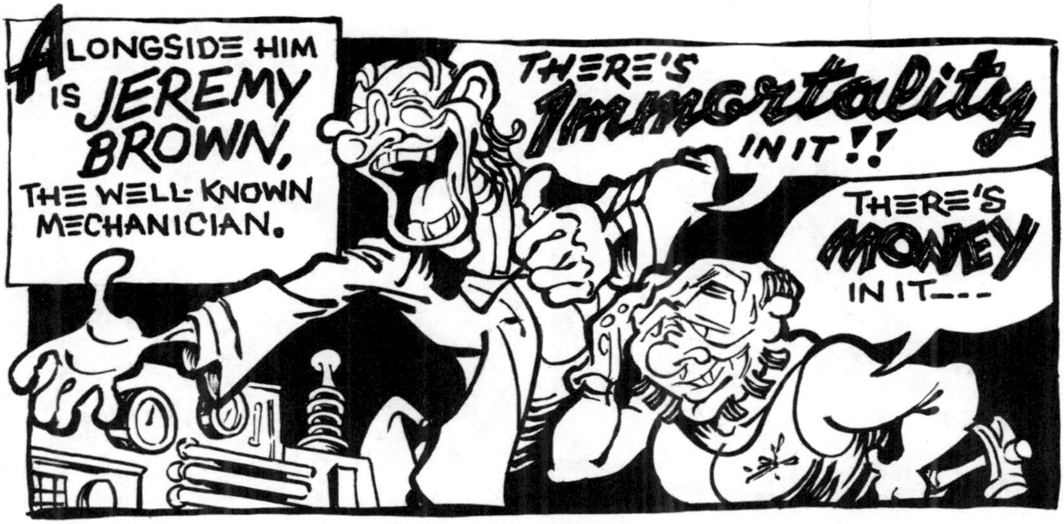
ALONGSIDE HIM IS JEREMY BROWN, THE WELL-KNOWN MECHANICIAN.
THERE'S Immortality IN IT!!
THERE'S MONEY IN IT---

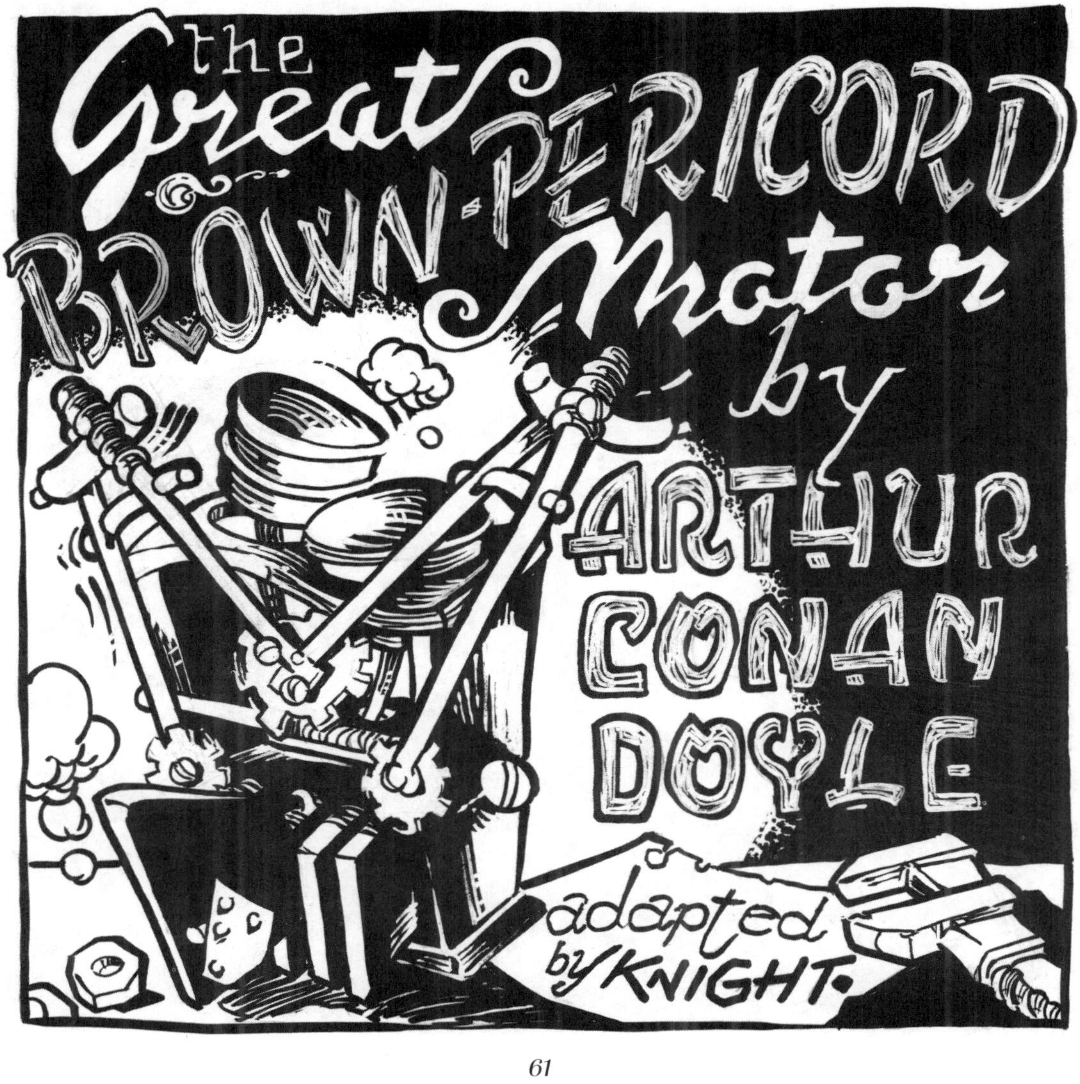
the Great BROWN-PERICORD Motor
by ARTHUR CONAN DOYLE
adapted by KNIGHT.

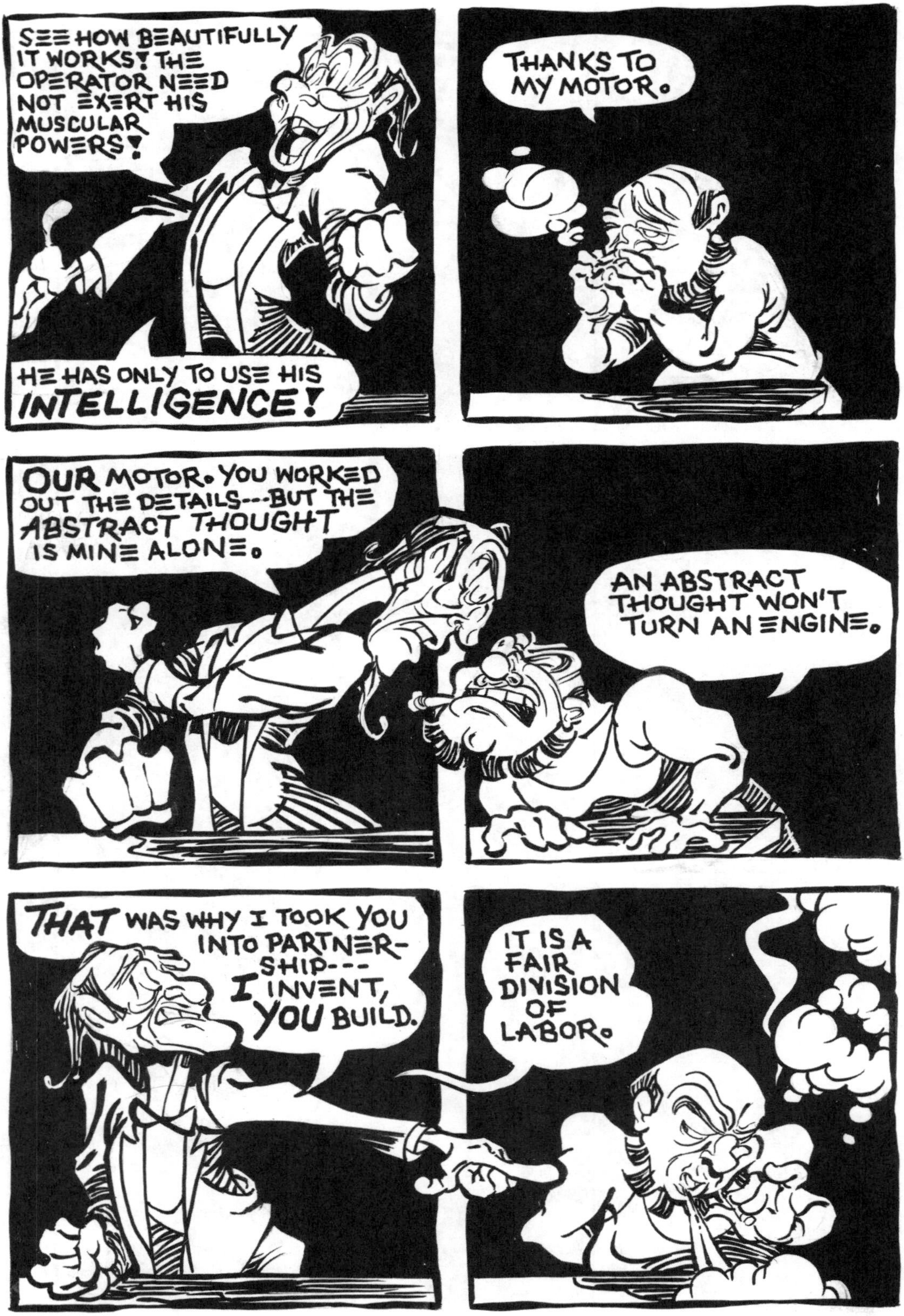
SEE HOW BEAUTIFULLY IT WORKS! THE OPERATOR NEED NOT EXERT HIS MUSCULAR POWERS!
HE HAS ONLY TO USE HIS INTELLIGENCE!
THANKS TO MY MOTOR.
OUR MOTOR. YOU WORKED OUT THE DETAILS---BUT THE ABSTRACT THOUGHT IS MINE ALONE.
AN ABSTRACT THOUGHT WON'T TURN AN ENGINE.
THAT WAS WHY I TOOK YOU INTO PARTNER-SHIP--- I INVENT, YOU BUILD.
IT IS A FAIR DIVISION OF LABOR.

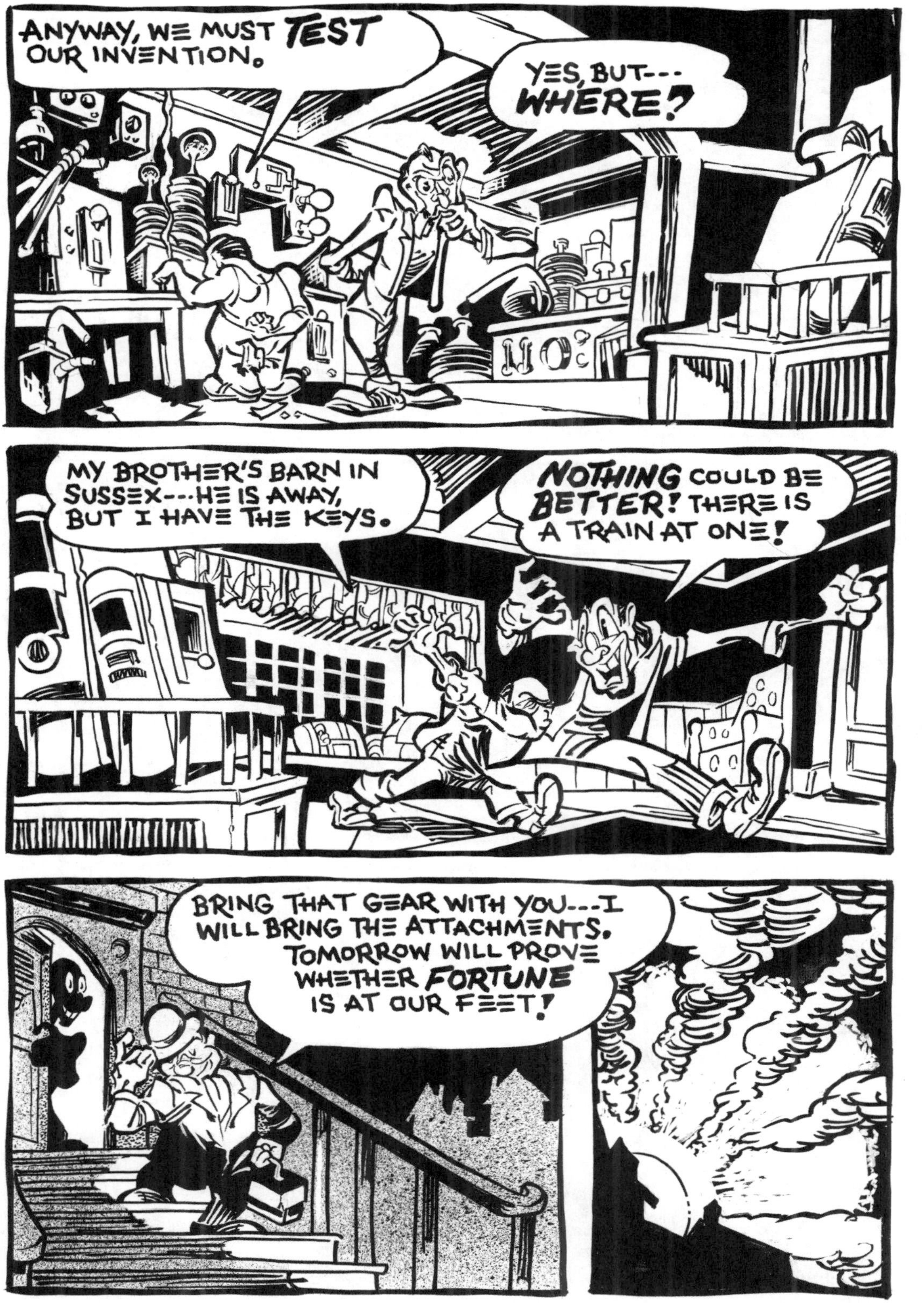
ANYWAY, WE MUST TEST OUR INVENTION.
YES, BUT--- WHERE?
MY BROTHER'S BARN IN SUSSEX---HE IS AWAY, BUT I HAVE THE KEYS.
NOTHING COULD BE BETTER! THERE IS A TRAIN AT ONE!
BRING THAT GEAR WITH YOU---I WILL BRING THE ATTACHMENTS. TOMORROW WILL PROVE WHETHER FORTUNE IS AT OUR FEET!

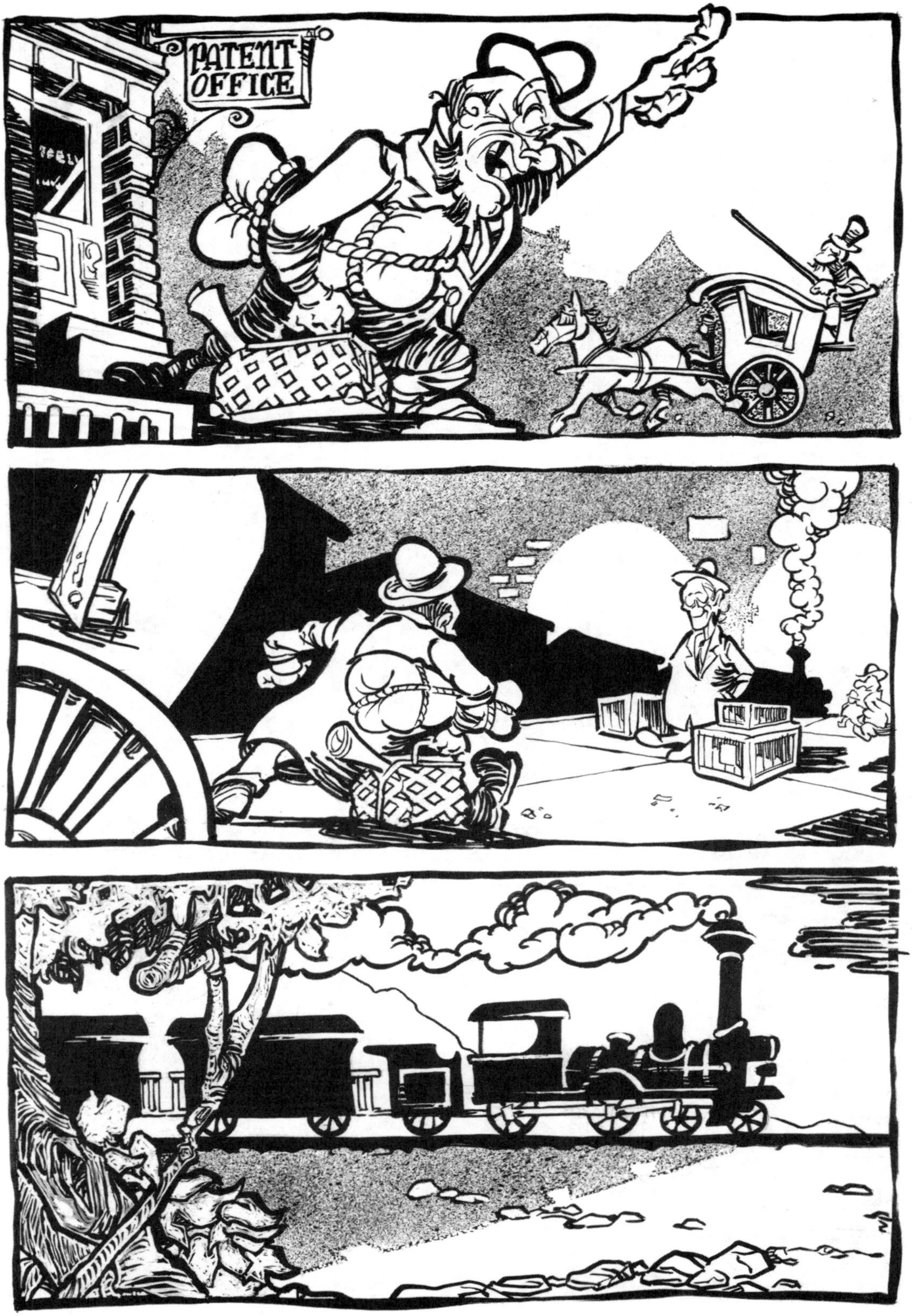
PATENT OFFICE

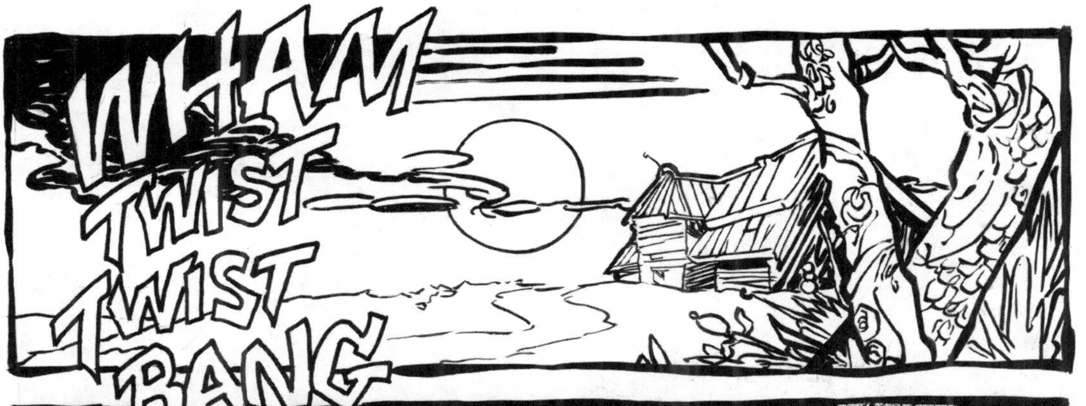
WHAM
TWIST
TWIST
BANG

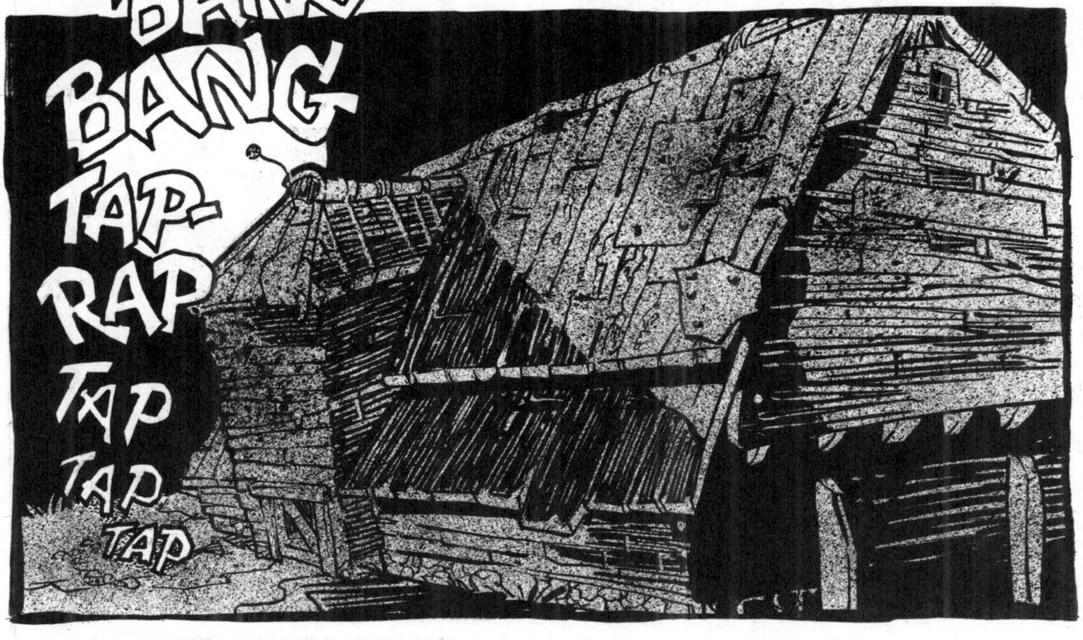
BANG
TAP-
RAP
TAP
TAP
TAP

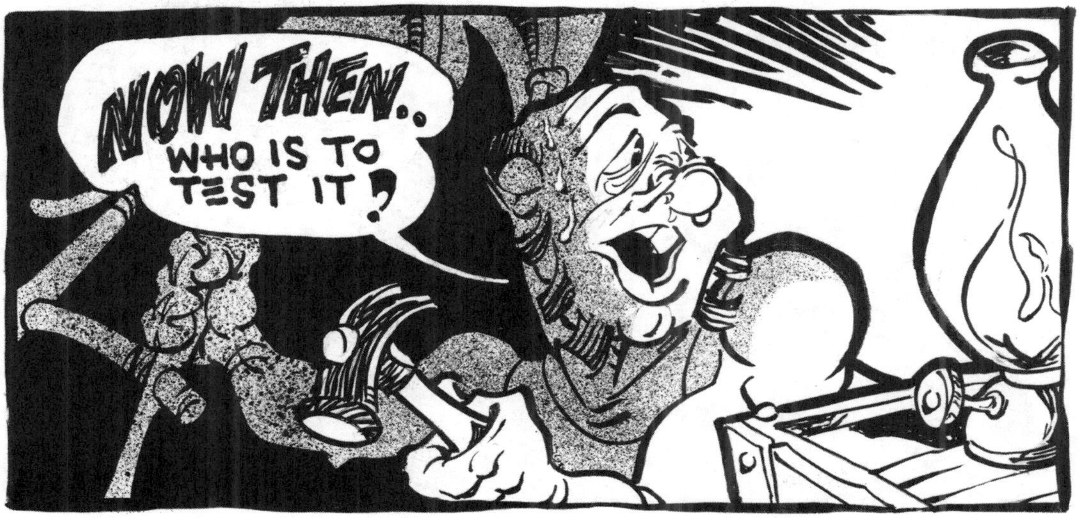
NOW THEN.. WHO IS TO TEST IT?

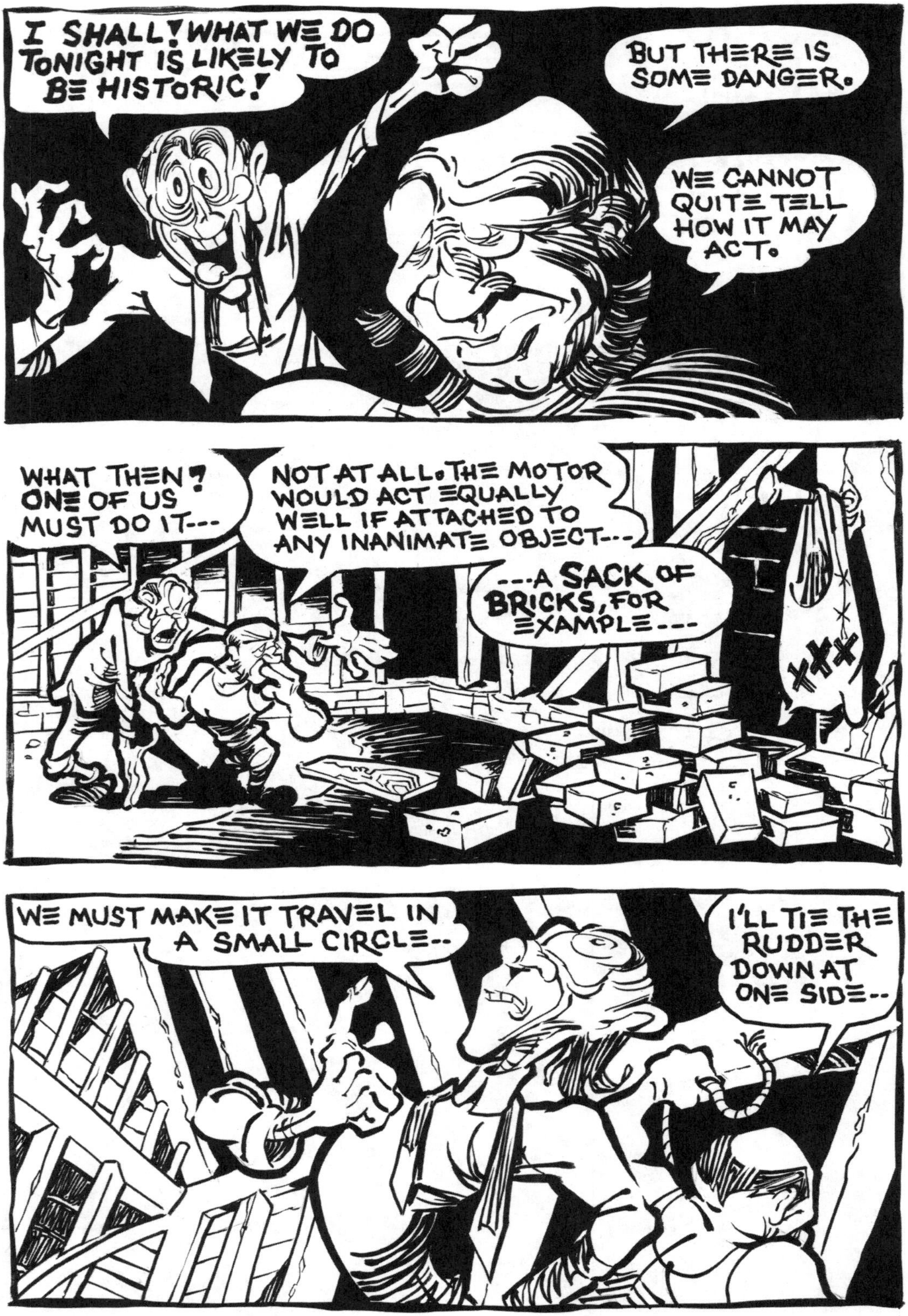
I SHALL! WHAT WE DO TONIGHT IS LIKELY TO BE HISTORIC!
BUT THERE IS SOME DANGER.
WE CANNOT QUITE TELL HOW IT MAY ACT.
WHAT THEN? ONE OF US MUST DO IT---
NOT AT ALL. THE MOTOR WOULD ACT EQUALLY WELL IF ATTACHED TO ANY INANIMATE OBJECT---
---A SACK OF BRICKS, FOR EXAMPLE---
WE MUST MAKE IT TRAVEL IN A SMALL CIRCLE--
I'LL TIE THE RUDDER DOWN AT ONE SIDE--

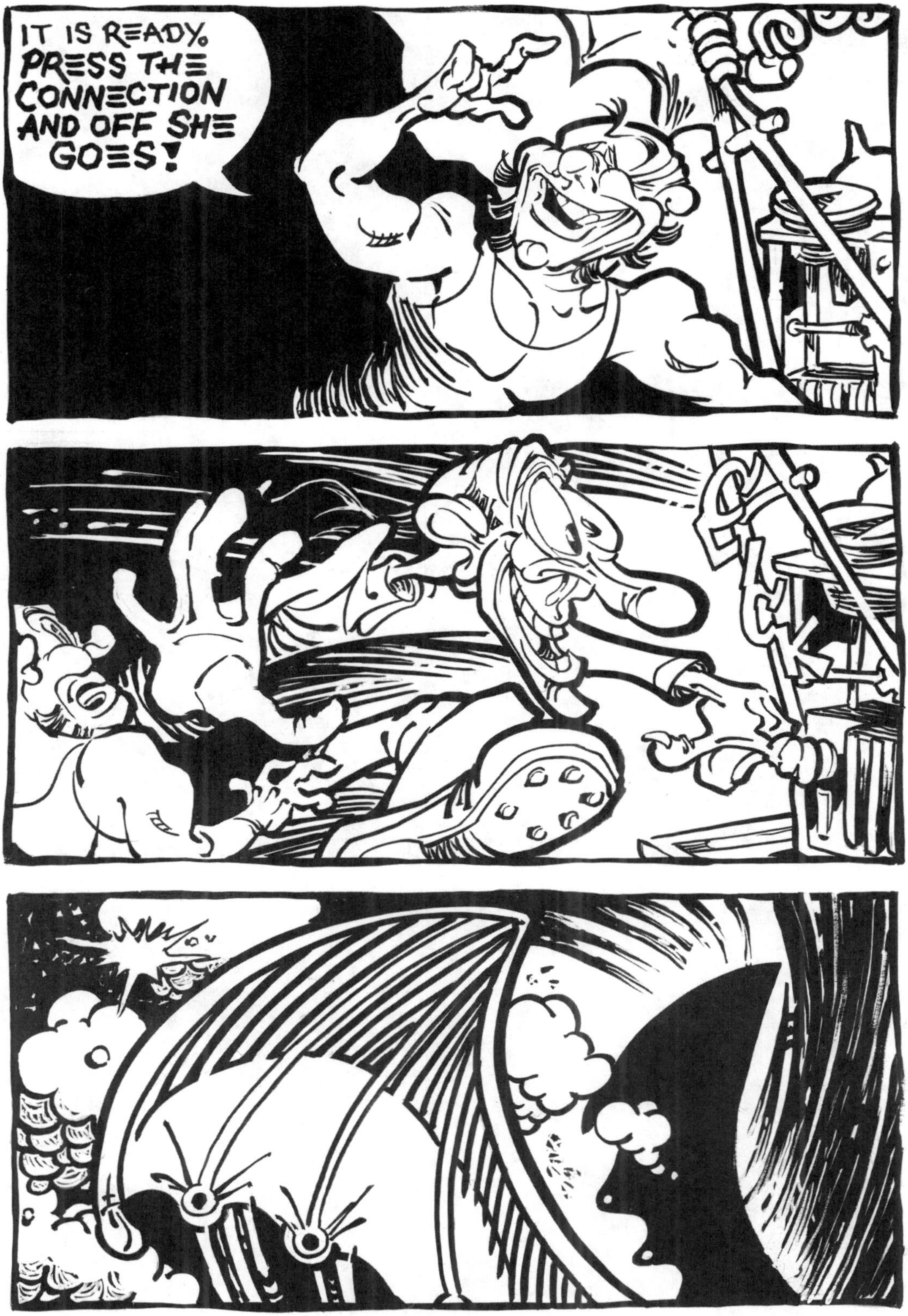
IT IS READY. PRESS THE CONNECTION AND OFF SHE GOES!

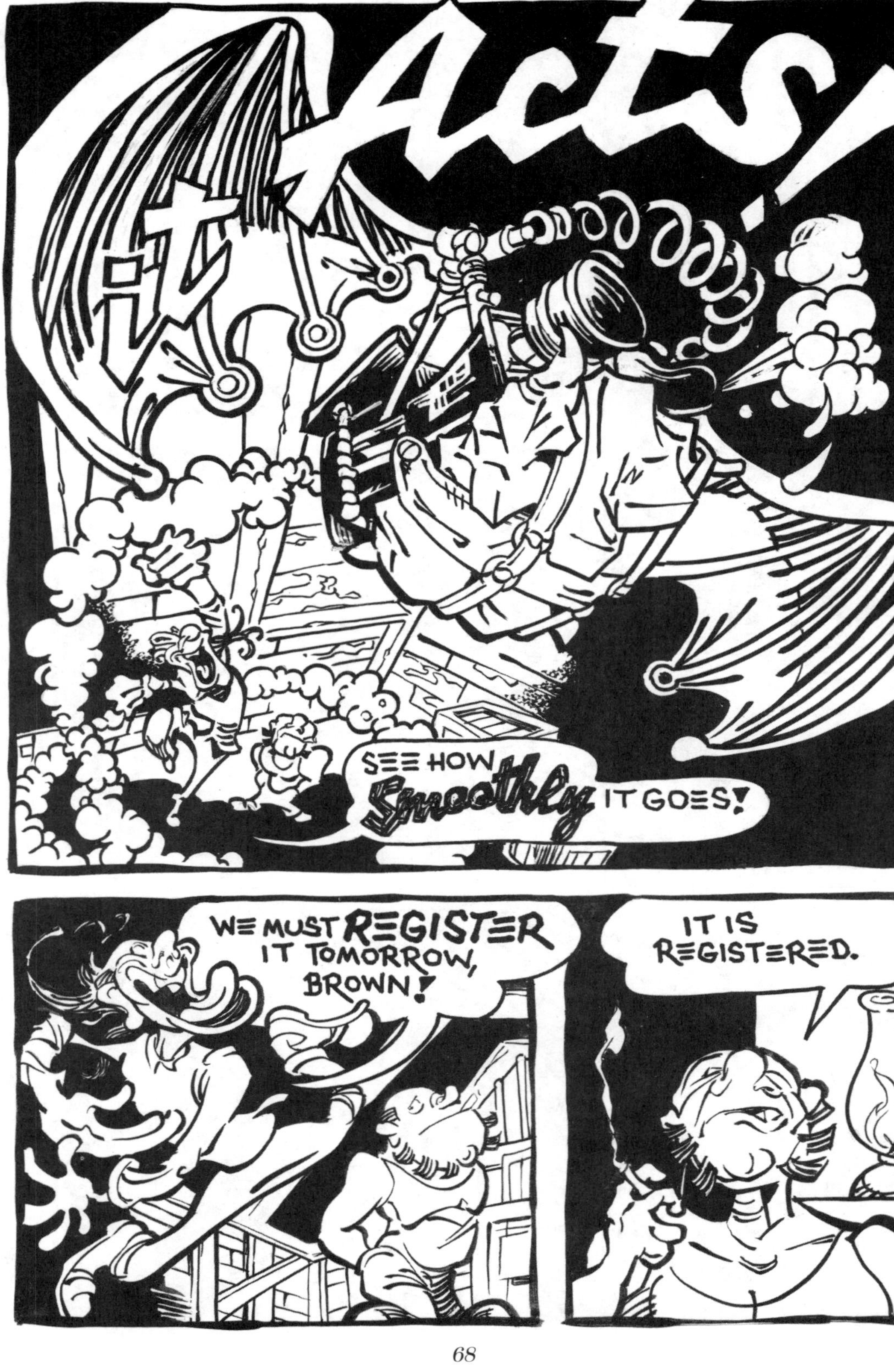
it Acts!
SEE HOW Smoothly IT GOES!
WE MUST REGISTER IT TOMORROW, BROWN!
IT IS REGISTERED.

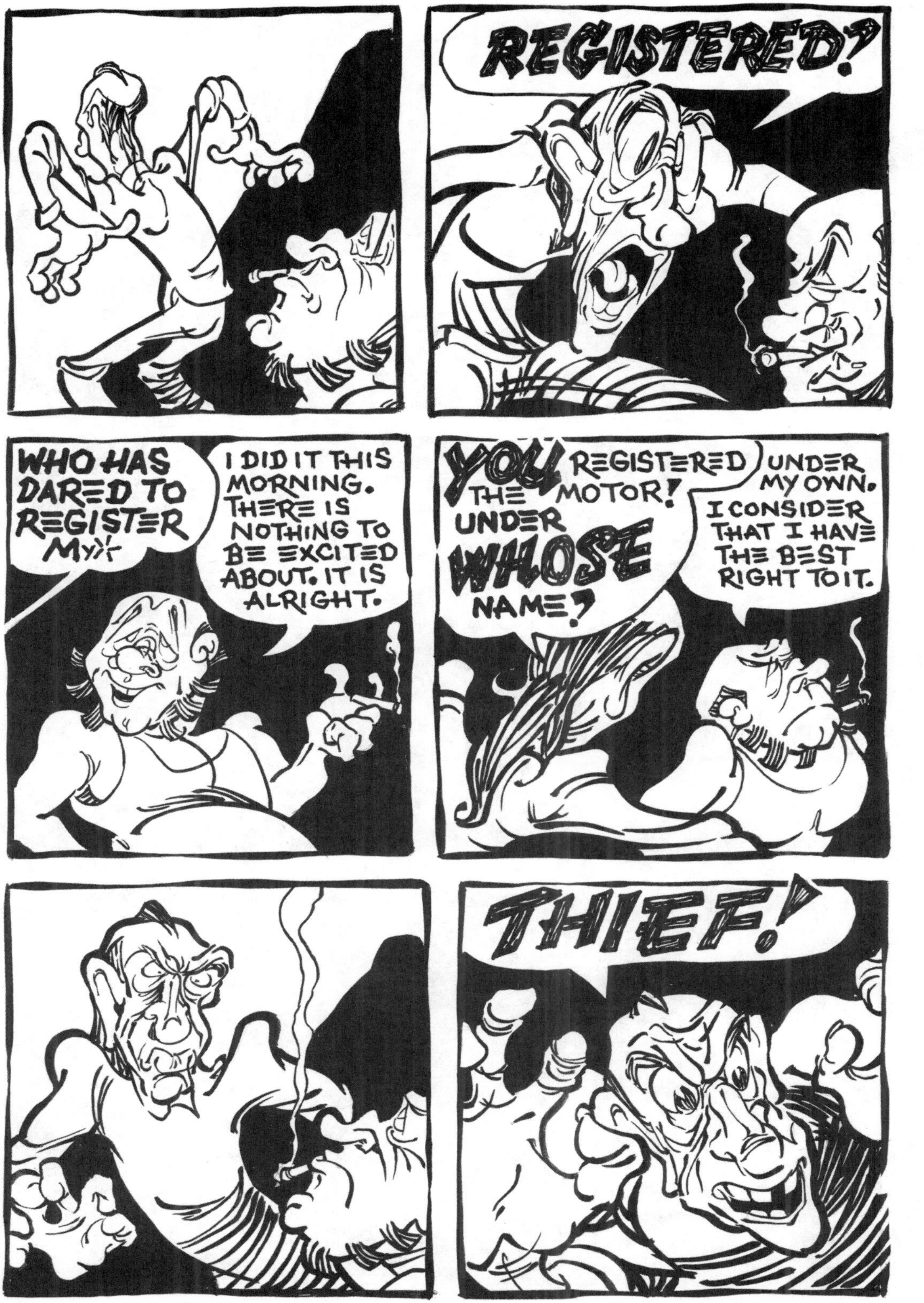
REGISTERED?
WHO HAS DARED TO REGISTER MY*
I DID IT THIS MORNING. THERE IS NOTHING TO BE EXCITED ABOUT. IT IS ALRIGHT.
YOU REGISTERED THE MOTOR! UNDER WHOSE NAME?
UNDER MY OWN. I CONSIDER THAT I HAVE THE BEST RIGHT TO IT.
THIEF!

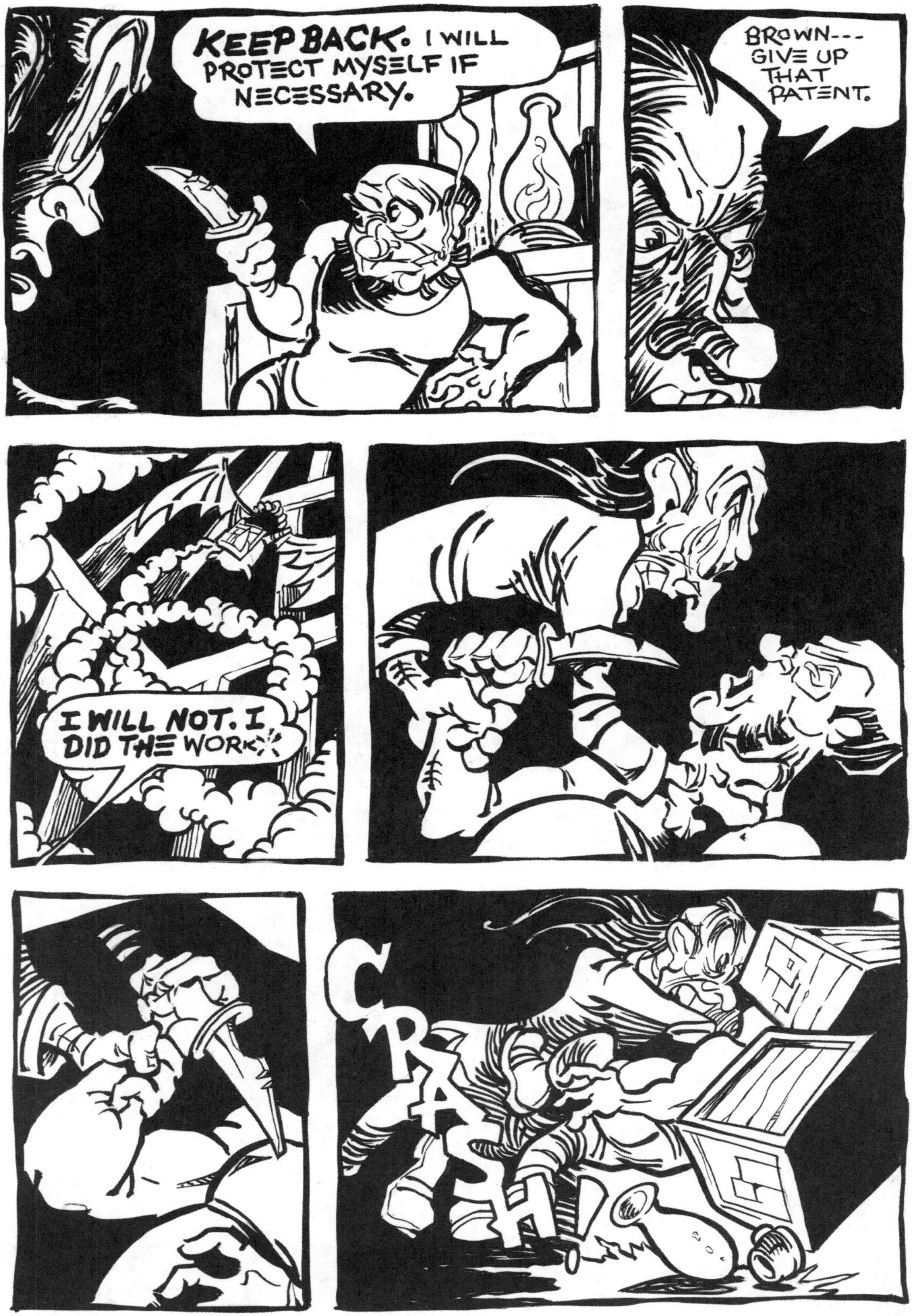
KEEP BACK. I WILL PROTECT MYSELF IF NECESSARY.
BROWN--- GIVE UP THAT PATENT.
I WILL NOT. I DID THE WORK!
CRASH!

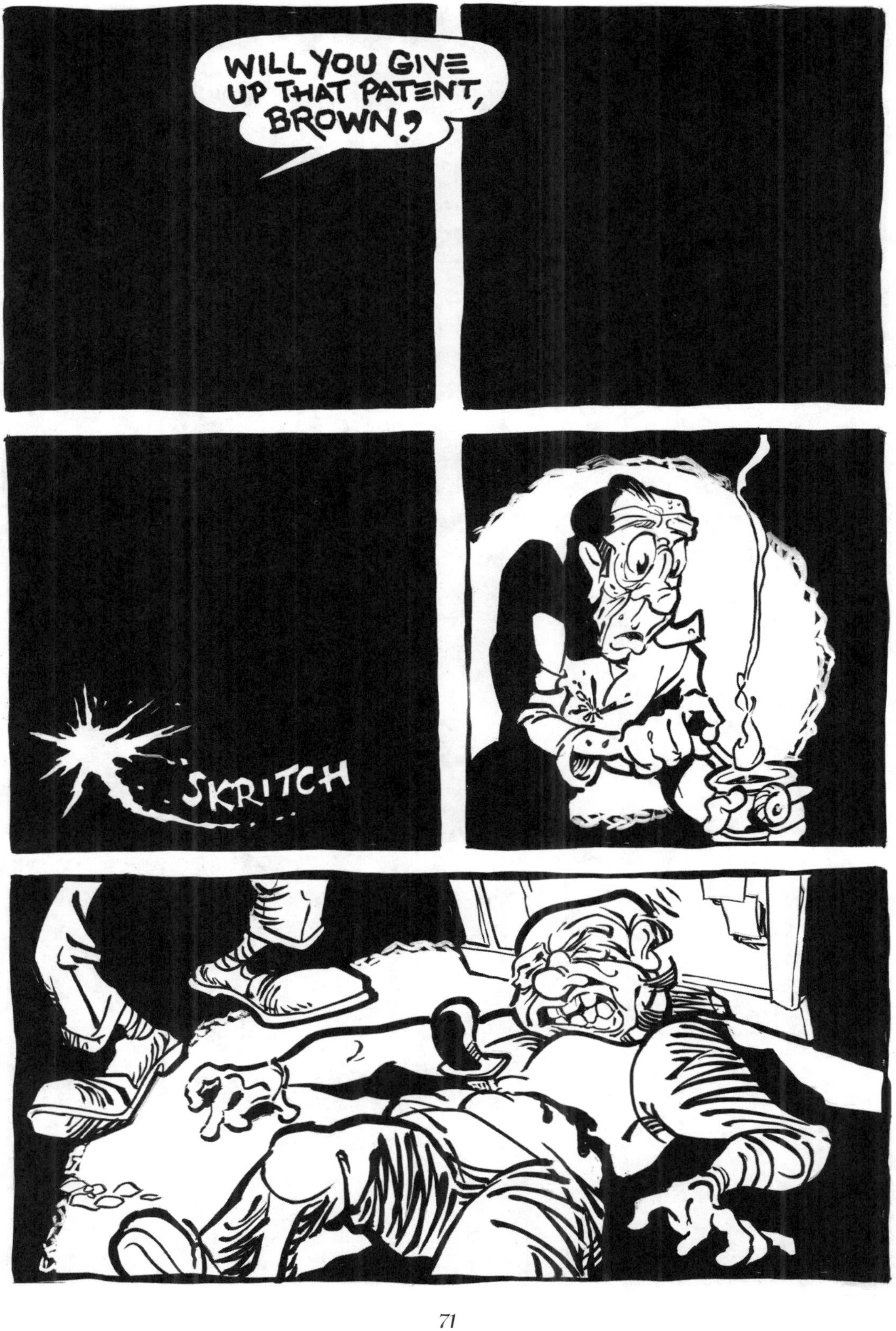
WILL YOU GIVE UP THAT PATENT, BROWN?
SKRITCH

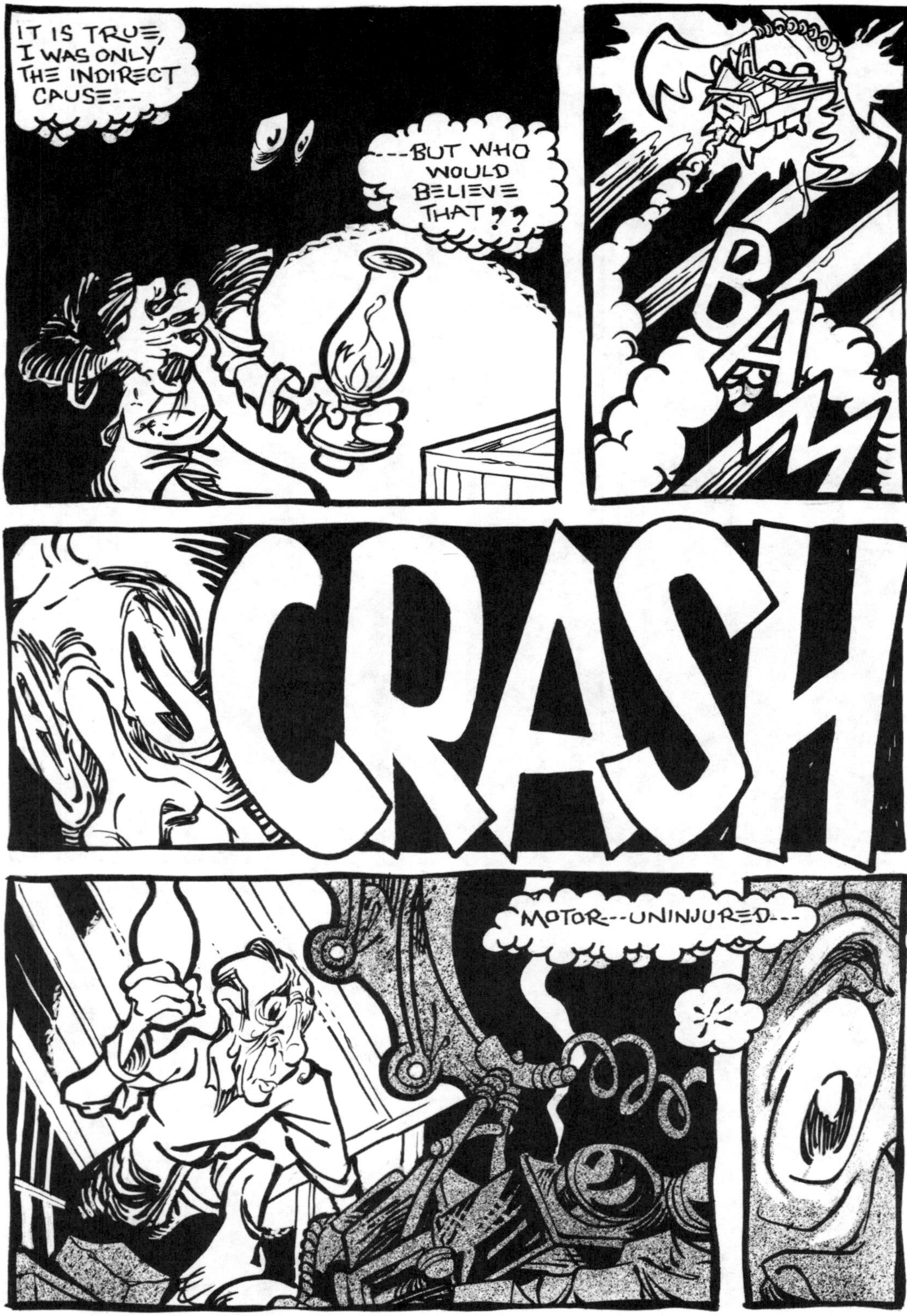
IT IS TRUE, I WAS ONLY THE INDIRECT CAUSE---
---BUT WHO WOULD BELIEVE THAT??
BAM
CRASH
MOTOR---UNINJURED---

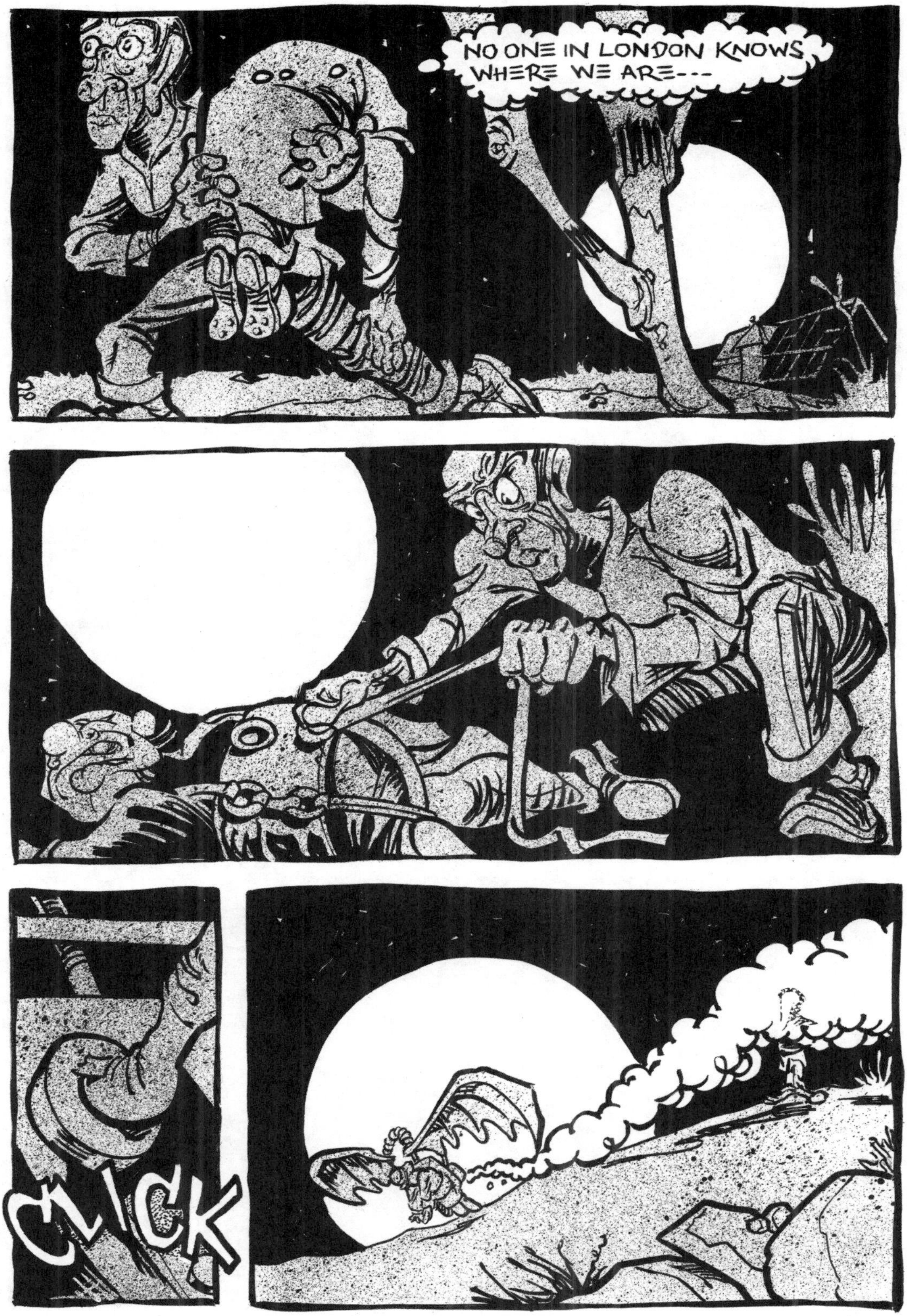
NO ONE IN LONDON KNOWS WHERE WE ARE---
CLICK

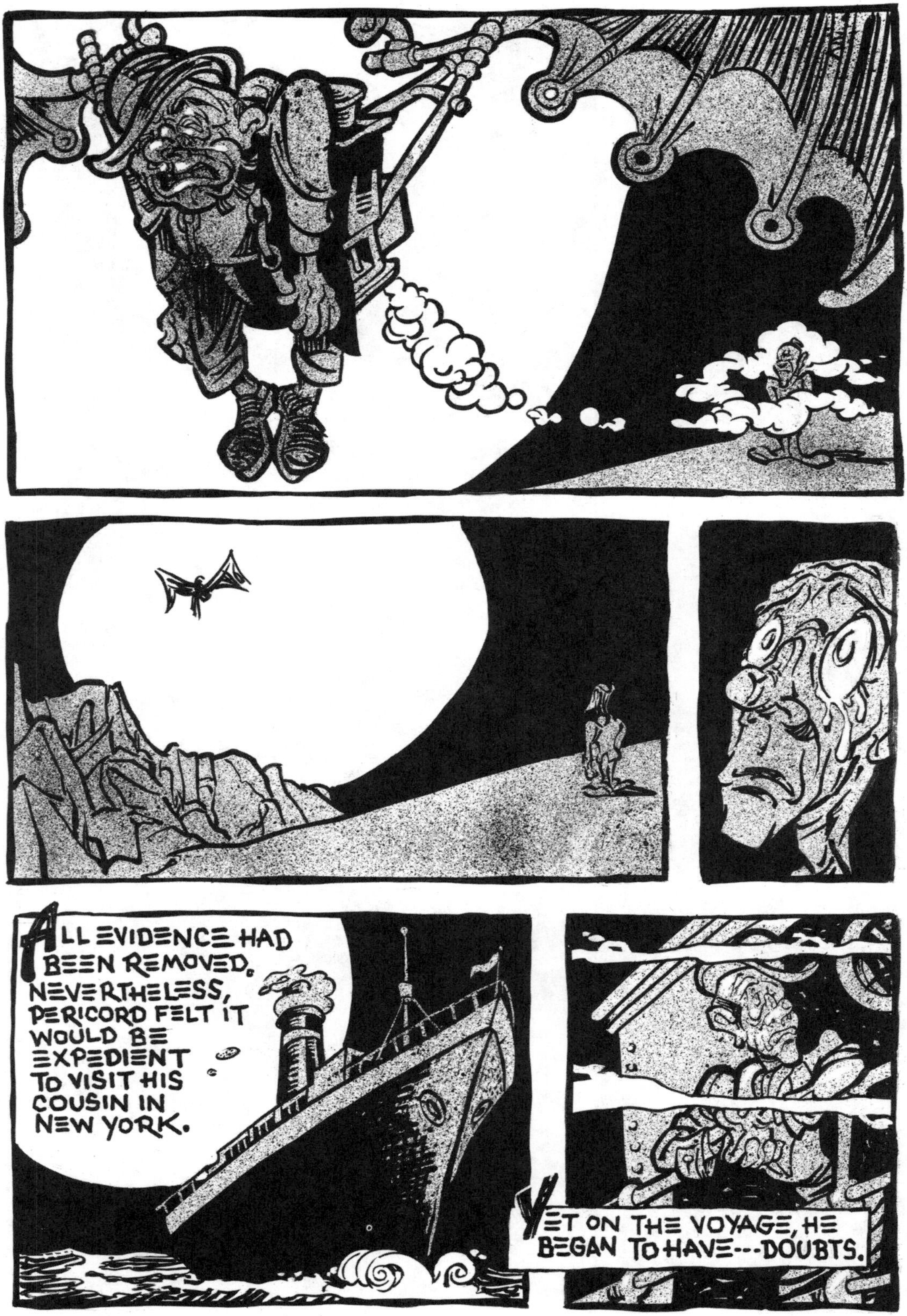
ALL EVIDENCE HAD BEEN REMOVED.
NEVERTHELESS, PERICORD FELT IT WOULD BE EXPEDIENT TO VISIT HIS COUSIN IN NEW YORK.
YET ON THE VOYAGE, HE BEGAN TO HAVE---DOUBTS.

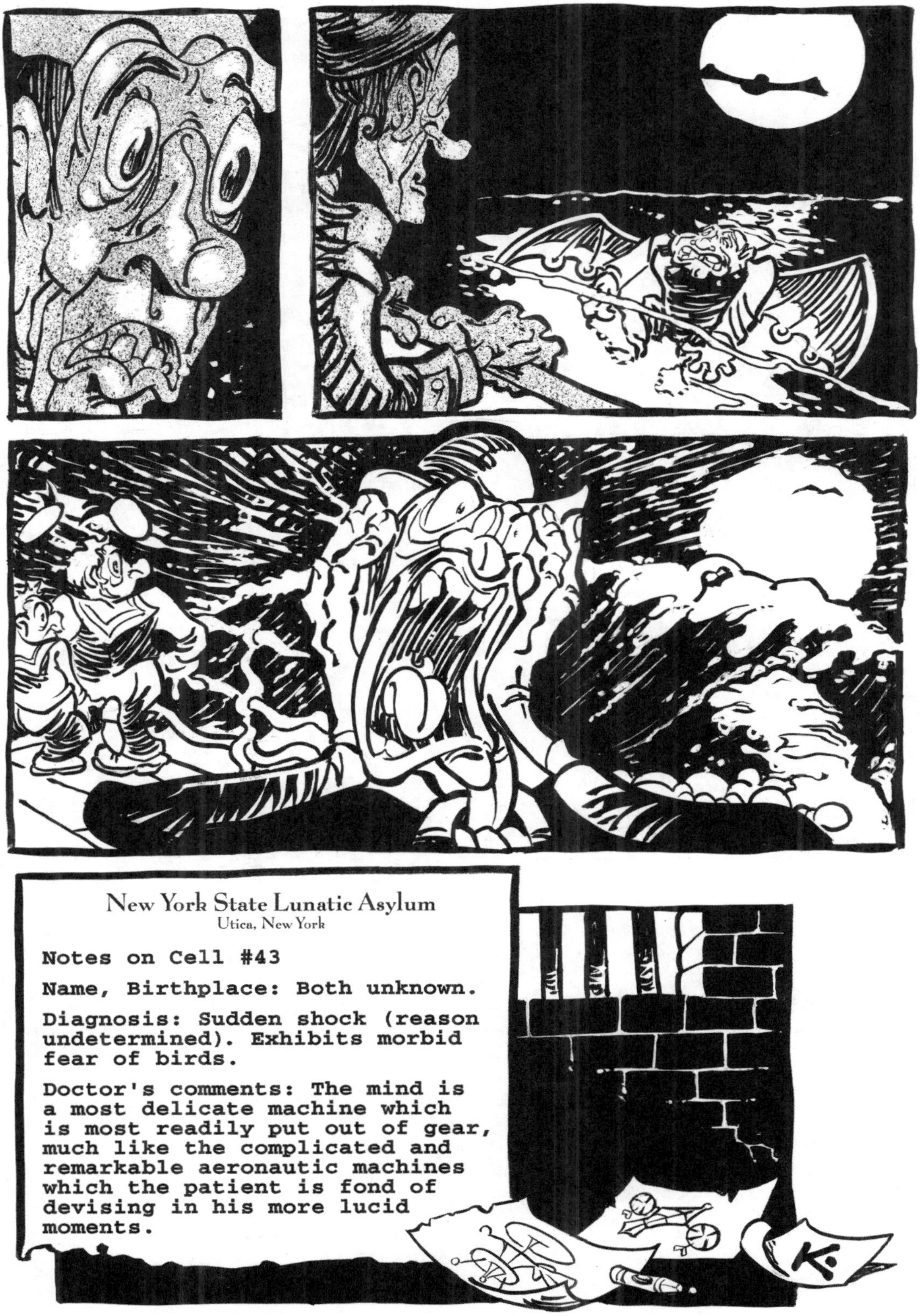
New York State Lunatic Asylum
Utica, New York
Notes on Cell #43
Name, Birthplace: Both unknown.
Diagnosis: Sudden shock (reason undetermined). Exhibits morbid fear of birds.
Doctor's comments: The mind is a most delicate machine which is most readily put out of gear, much like the complicated and remarkable aeronautic machines which the patient is fond of devising in his more lucid moments.

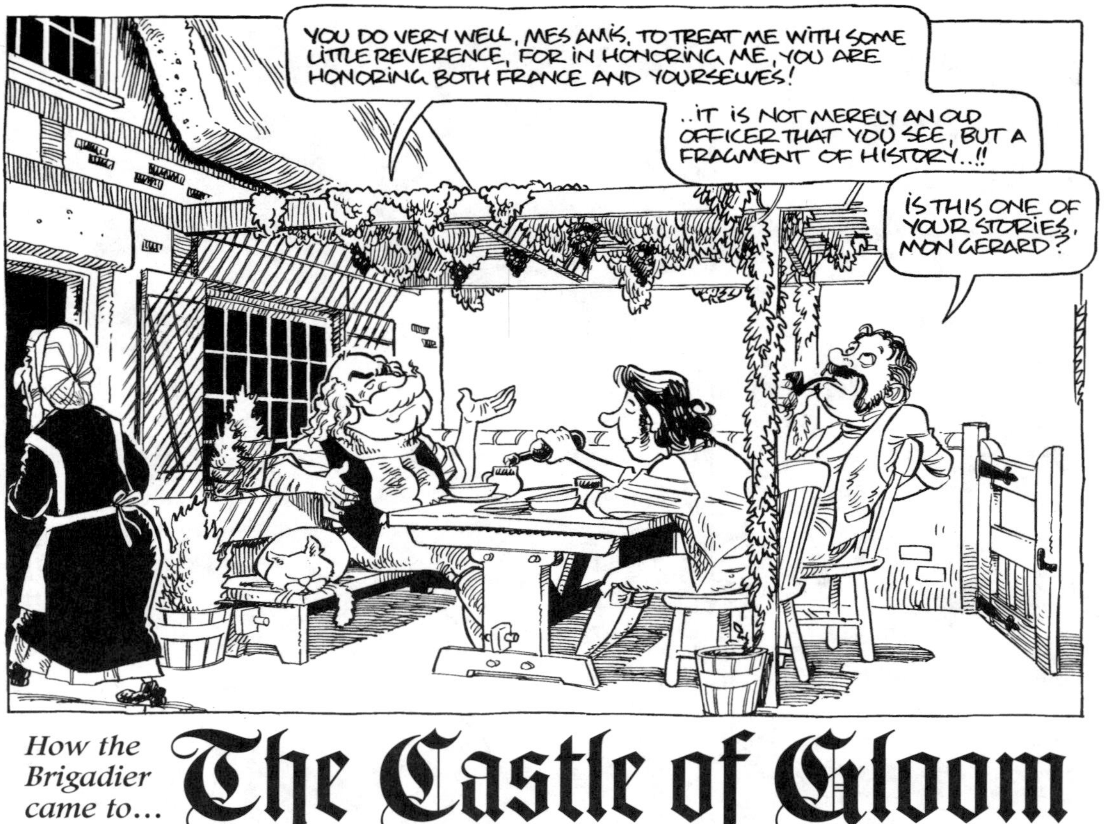
YOU DO VERY WELL, MES AMIS, TO TREAT ME WITH SOME LITTLE REVERENCE, FOR IN HONORING ME, YOU ARE HONORING BOTH FRANCE AND YOURSELVES!
..IT IS NOT MERELY AN OLD OFFICER THAT YOU SEE, BUT A FRAGMENT OF HISTORY..!!
IS THIS ONE OF YOUR STORIES, MON GERARD?

How the Brigadier came to…

The Castle of Gloom

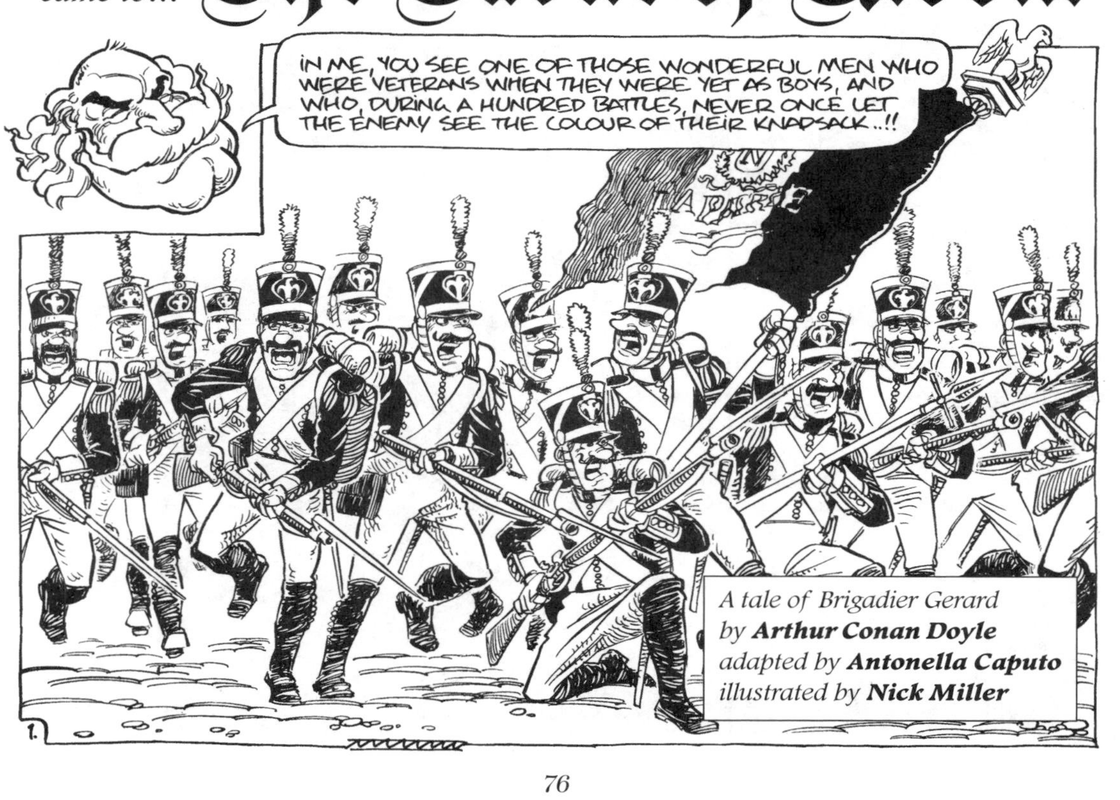
IN ME, YOU SEE ONE OF THOSE WONDERFUL MEN WHO WERE VETERANS WHEN THEY WERE YET AS BOYS, AND WHO, DURING A HUNDRED BATTLES, NEVER ONCE LET THE ENEMY SEE THE COLOUR OF THEIR KNAPSACK..!!
1.

A tale of Brigadier Gerard
by ***Arthur Conan Doyle***
adapted by ***Antonella Caputo***
illustrated by ***Nick Miller***

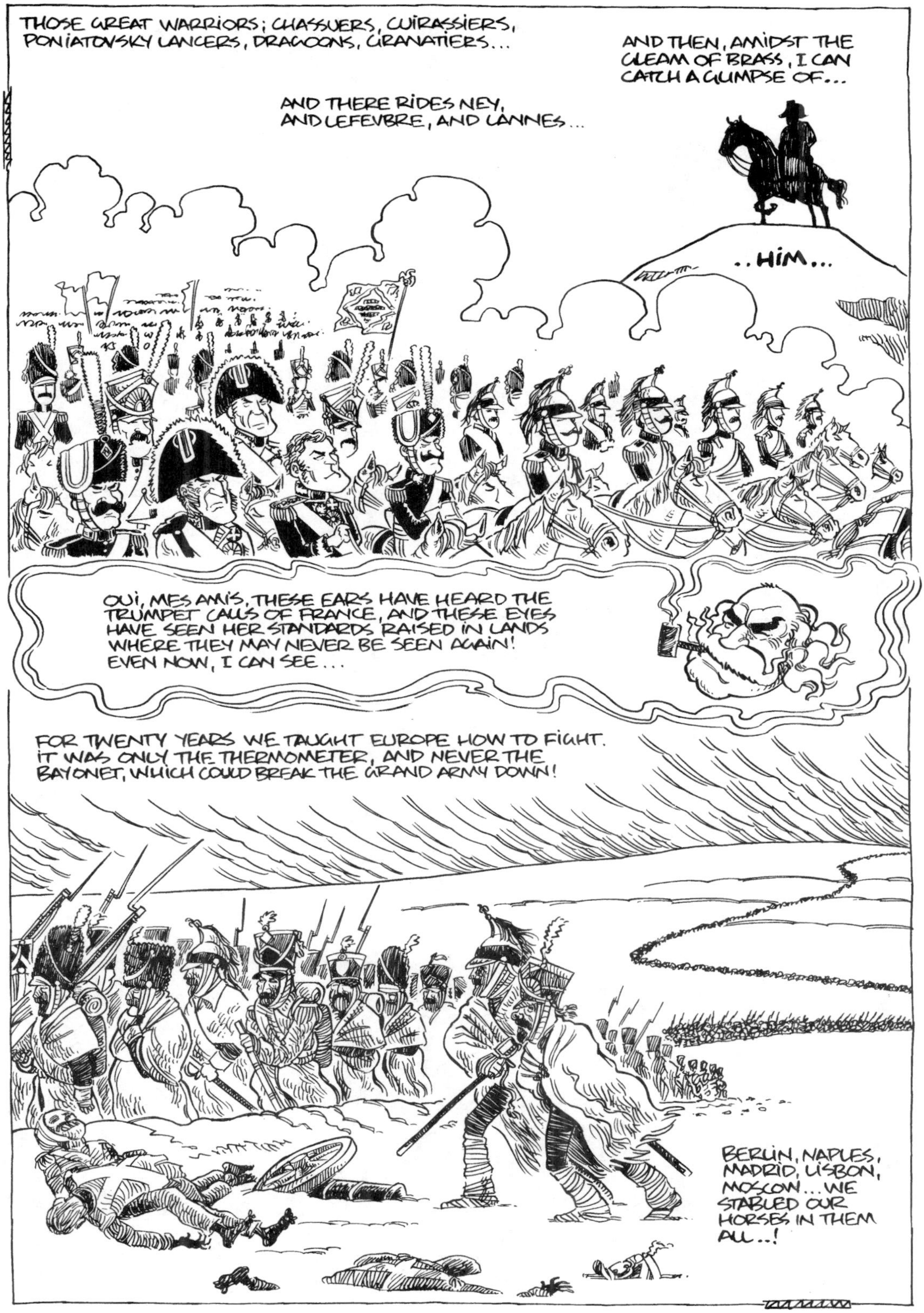
THOSE GREAT WARRIORS; CHASSUERS, CUIRASSIERS, PONIATOVSKY LANCERS, DRAGOONS, GRANATIERS...
AND THERE RIDES NEY, AND LEFEVBRE, AND LANNES...
AND THEN, AMIDST THE GLEAM OF BRASS, I CAN CATCH A GLIMPSE OF...
..HIM...
OUI, MES AMIS, THESE EARS HAVE HEARD THE TRUMPET CALLS OF FRANCE, AND THESE EYES HAVE SEEN HER STANDARDS RAISED IN LANDS WHERE THEY MAY NEVER BE SEEN AGAIN! EVEN NOW, I CAN SEE...
FOR TWENTY YEARS WE TAUGHT EUROPE HOW TO FIGHT. IT WAS ONLY THE THERMOMETER, AND NEVER THE BAYONET, WHICH COULD BREAK THE GRAND ARMY DOWN!
BERLIN, NAPLES, MADRID, LISBON, MOSCOW... WE STABLED OUR HORSES IN THEM ALL...!

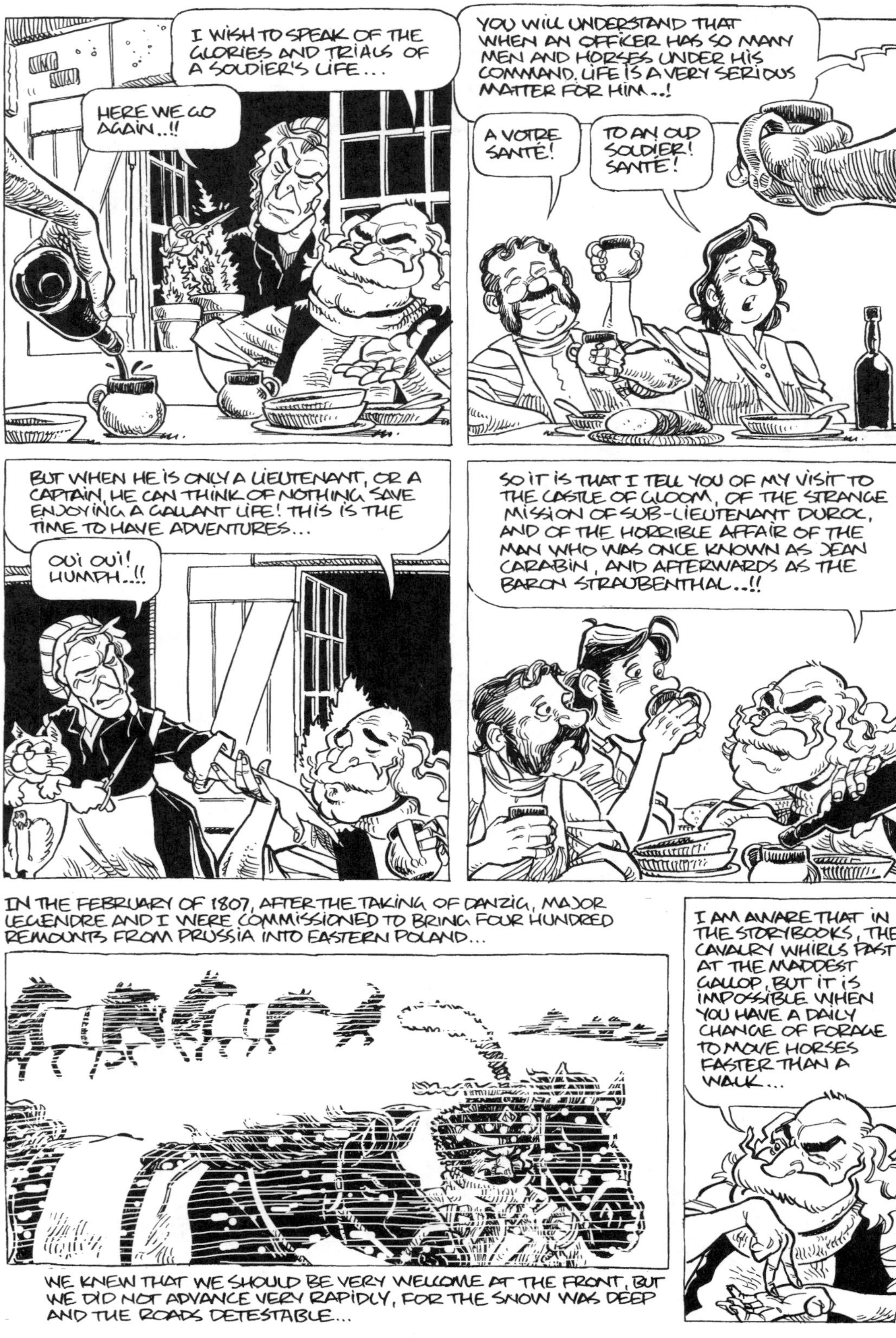
I WISH TO SPEAK OF THE GLORIES AND TRIALS OF A SOLDIER'S LIFE...
HERE WE GO AGAIN..!!
YOU WILL UNDERSTAND THAT WHEN AN OFFICER HAS SO MANY MEN AND HORSES UNDER HIS COMMAND, LIFE IS A VERY SERIOUS MATTER FOR HIM..!
A VOTRE SANTÉ!
TO AN OLD SOLDIER! SANTÉ!
BUT WHEN HE IS ONLY A LIEUTENANT, OR A CAPTAIN, HE CAN THINK OF NOTHING SAVE ENJOYING A GALLANT LIFE! THIS IS THE TIME TO HAVE ADVENTURES...
OUI OUI! HUMPH..!!
SO IT IS THAT I TELL YOU OF MY VISIT TO THE CASTLE OF GLOOM, OF THE STRANGE MISSION OF SUB-LIEUTENANT DUROC, AND OF THE HORRIBLE AFFAIR OF THE MAN WHO WAS ONCE KNOWN AS JEAN CARABIN, AND AFTERWARDS AS THE BARON STRAUBENTHAL..!!
IN THE FEBRUARY OF 1807, AFTER THE TAKING OF DANZIG, MAJOR LEGENDRE AND I WERE COMMISSIONED TO BRING FOUR HUNDRED REMOUNTS FROM PRUSSIA INTO EASTERN POLAND...
WE KNEW THAT WE SHOULD BE VERY WELCOME AT THE FRONT, BUT WE DID NOT ADVANCE VERY RAPIDLY, FOR THE SNOW WAS DEEP AND THE ROADS DETESTABLE...
I AM AWARE THAT IN THE STORYBOOKS, THE CAVALRY WHIRLS PAST AT THE MADDEST GALLOP, BUT IT IS IMPOSSIBLE WHEN YOU HAVE A DAILY CHANGE OF FORAGE TO MOVE HORSES FASTER THAN A WALK...
3.

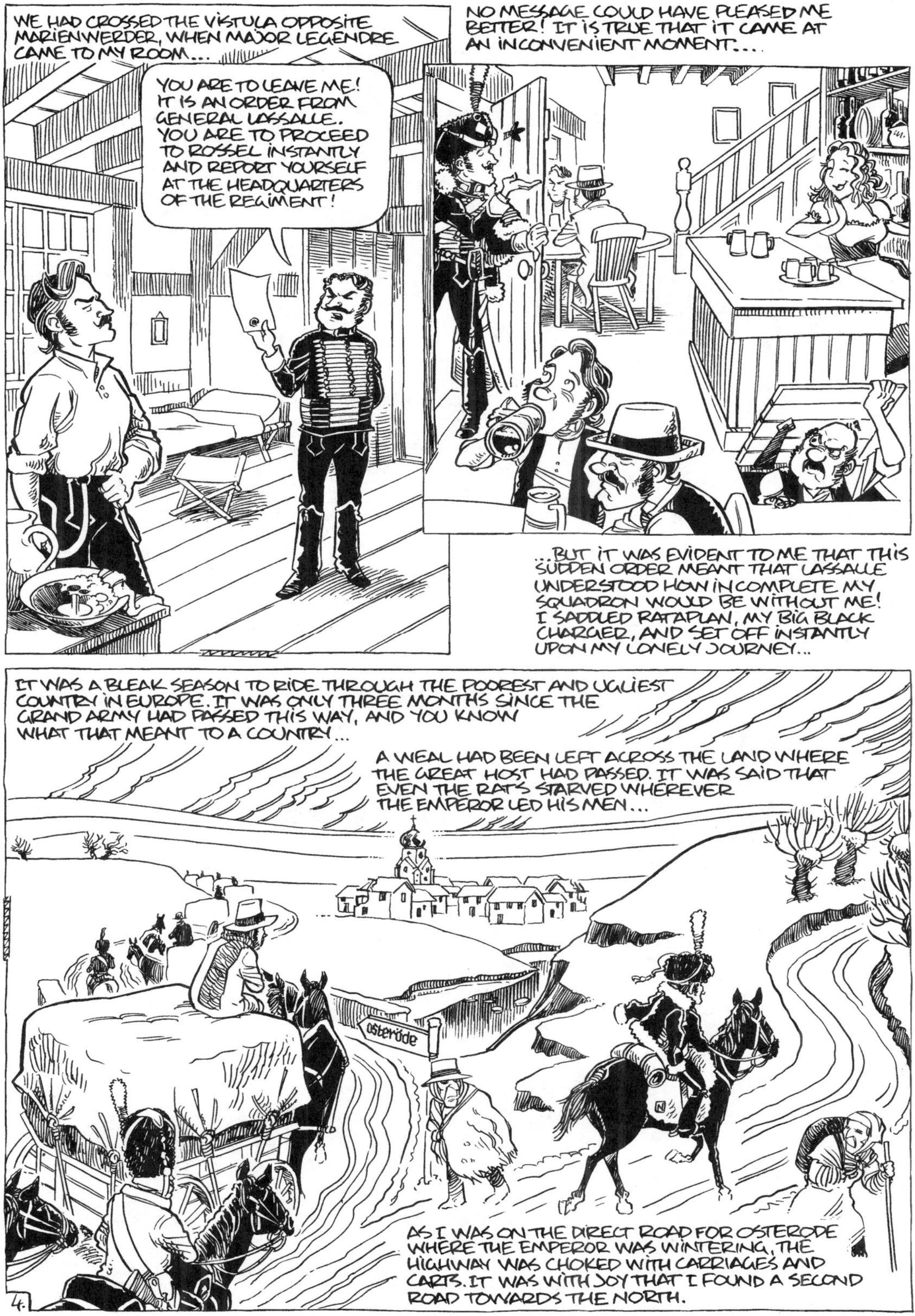
WE HAD CROSSED THE VISTULA OPPOSITE MARIENWERDER, WHEN MAJOR LEGENDRE CAME TO MY ROOM...
YOU ARE TO LEAVE ME! IT IS AN ORDER FROM GENERAL LASSALLE. YOU ARE TO PROCEED TO ROSSEL INSTANTLY AND REPORT YOURSELF AT THE HEADQUARTERS OF THE REGIMENT!
NO MESSAGE COULD HAVE PLEASED ME BETTER! IT IS TRUE THAT IT CAME AT AN INCONVENIENT MOMENT...
...BUT IT WAS EVIDENT TO ME THAT THIS SUDDEN ORDER MEANT THAT LASSALLE UNDERSTOOD HOW INCOMPLETE MY SQUADRON WOULD BE WITHOUT ME! I SADDLED RATAPLAN, MY BIG BLACK CHARGER, AND SET OFF INSTANTLY UPON MY LONELY JOURNEY...
IT WAS A BLEAK SEASON TO RIDE THROUGH THE POOREST AND UGLIEST COUNTRY IN EUROPE. IT WAS ONLY THREE MONTHS SINCE THE GRAND ARMY HAD PASSED THIS WAY, AND YOU KNOW WHAT THAT MEANT TO A COUNTRY...
A WEAL HAD BEEN LEFT ACROSS THE LAND WHERE THE GREAT HOST HAD PASSED. IT WAS SAID THAT EVEN THE RATS STARVED WHEREVER THE EMPEROR LED HIS MEN...
osteröde
AS I WAS ON THE DIRECT ROAD FOR OSTERODE WHERE THE EMPEROR WAS WINTERING, THE HIGHWAY WAS CHOKED WITH CARRIAGES AND CARTS. IT WAS WITH JOY THAT I FOUND A SECOND ROAD TOWARDS THE NORTH.

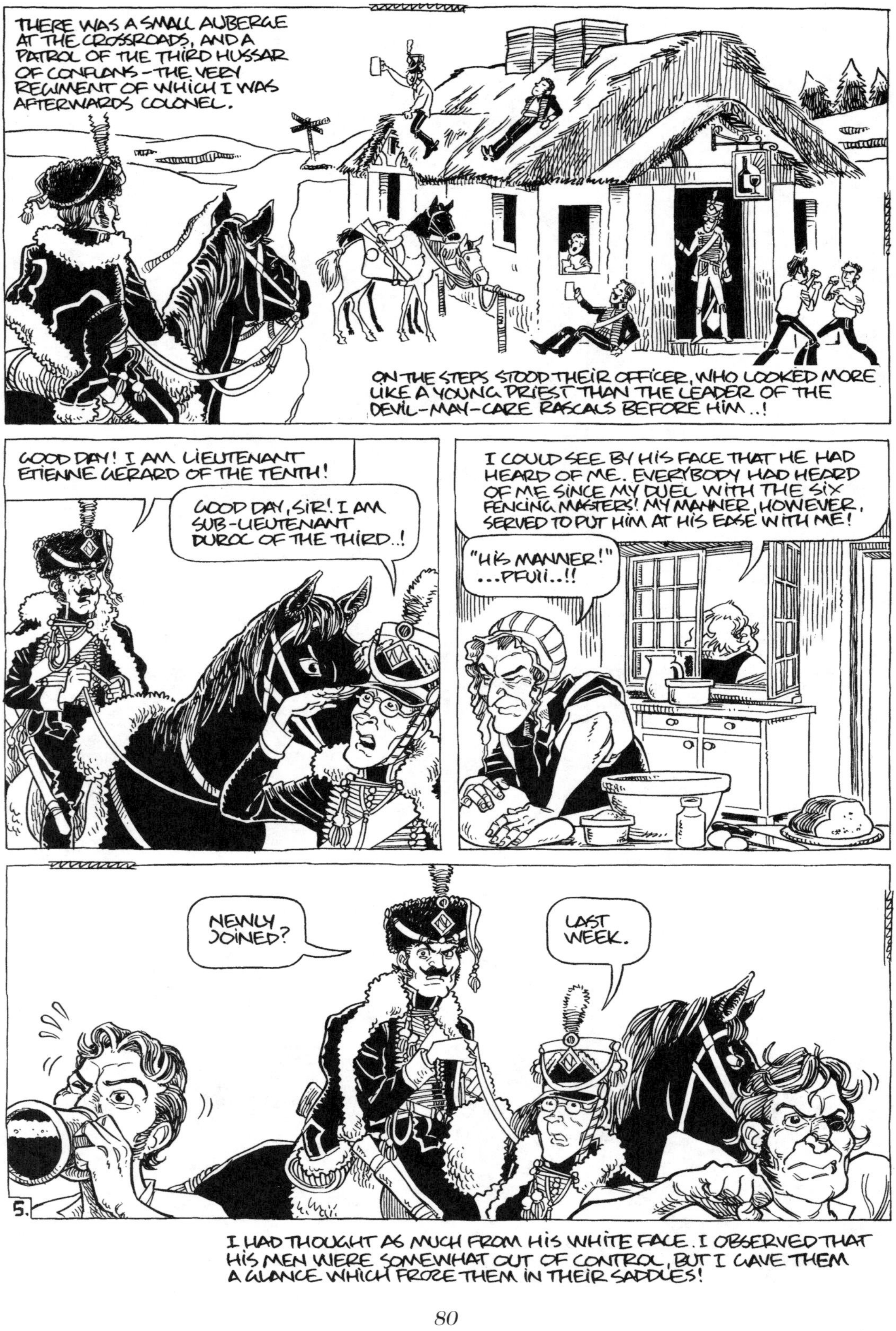
THERE WAS A SMALL AUBERGE AT THE CROSSROADS, AND A PATROL OF THE THIRD HUSSAR OF CONFLANS – THE VERY REGIMENT OF WHICH I WAS AFTERWARDS COLONEL.
ON THE STEPS STOOD THEIR OFFICER, WHO LOOKED MORE LIKE A YOUNG PRIEST THAN THE LEADER OF THE DEVIL-MAY-CARE RASCALS BEFORE HIM..!
GOOD DAY! I AM LIEUTENANT ETIENNE GERARD OF THE TENTH!
GOOD DAY, SIR! I AM SUB-LIEUTENANT DUROC OF THE THIRD..!
I COULD SEE BY HIS FACE THAT HE HAD HEARD OF ME. EVERYBODY HAD HEARD OF ME SINCE MY DUEL WITH THE SIX FENCING MASTERS! MY MANNER, HOWEVER, SERVED TO PUT HIM AT HIS EASE WITH ME!
"HIS MANNER!" ...PFUII..!!
NEWLY JOINED?
LAST WEEK.
5.

I HAD THOUGHT AS MUCH FROM HIS WHITE FACE. I OBSERVED THAT HIS MEN WERE SOMEWHAT OUT OF CONTROL, BUT I GAVE THEM A GLANCE WHICH FROZE THEM IN THEIR SADDLES!

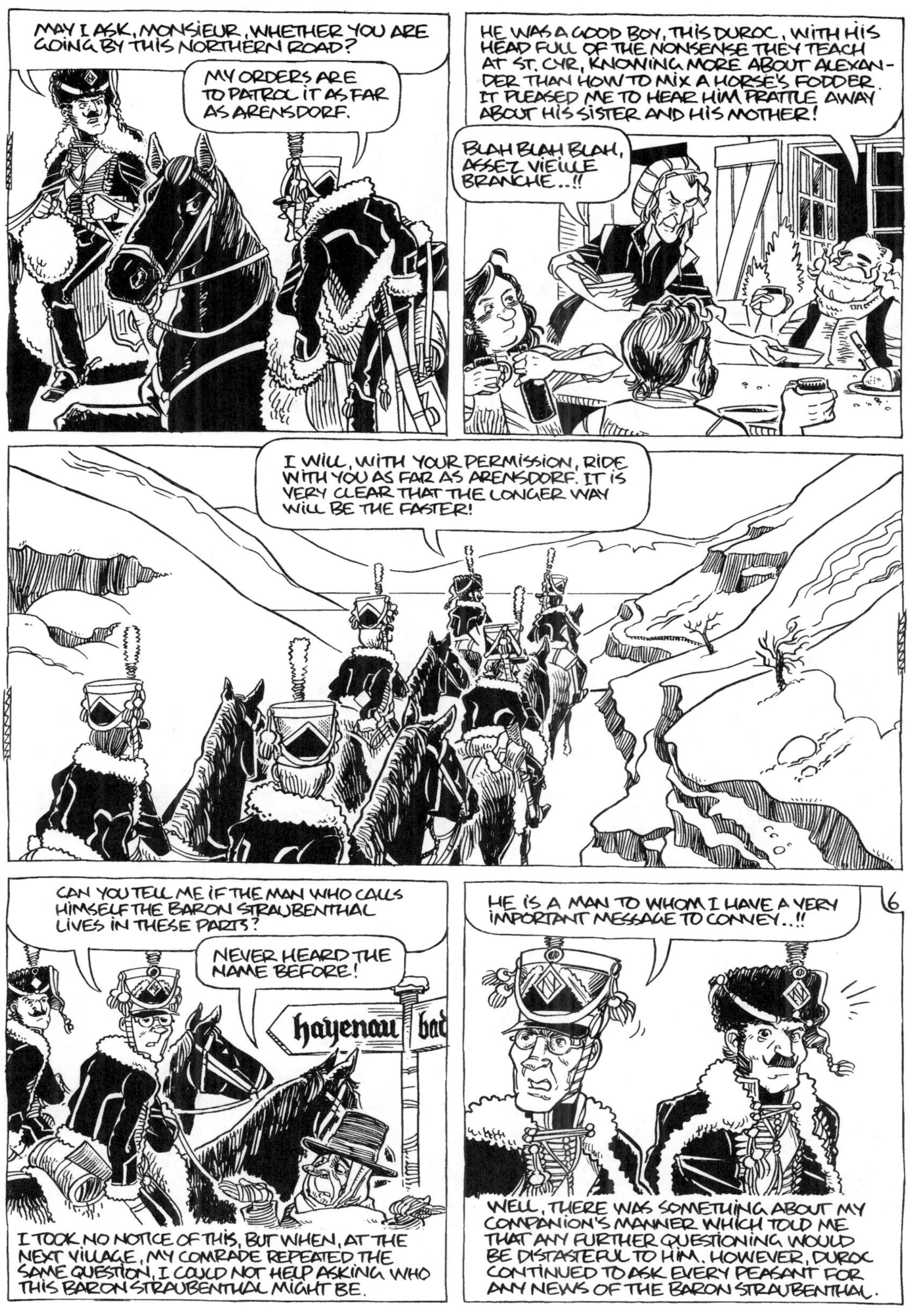
MAY I ASK, MONSIEUR, WHETHER YOU ARE GOING BY THIS NORTHERN ROAD?
MY ORDERS ARE TO PATROL IT AS FAR AS ARENSDORF.
HE WAS A GOOD BOY, THIS DUROC, WITH HIS HEAD FULL OF THE NONSENSE THEY TEACH AT ST. CYR, KNOWING MORE ABOUT ALEXANDER THAN HOW TO MIX A HORSE'S FODDER. IT PLEASED ME TO HEAR HIM PRATTLE AWAY ABOUT HIS SISTER AND HIS MOTHER!
BLAH BLAH BLAH, ASSEZ VIEILLE BRANCHE..!!
I WILL, WITH YOUR PERMISSION, RIDE WITH YOU AS FAR AS ARENSDORF. IT IS VERY CLEAR THAT THE LONGER WAY WILL BE THE FASTER!
CAN YOU TELL ME IF THE MAN WHO CALLS HIMSELF THE BARON STRAUBENTHAL LIVES IN THESE PARTS?
NEVER HEARD THE NAME BEFORE!
hayenau
I TOOK NO NOTICE OF THIS, BUT WHEN, AT THE NEXT VILLAGE, MY COMRADE REPEATED THE SAME QUESTION, I COULD NOT HELP ASKING WHO THIS BARON STRAUBENTHAL MIGHT BE.
6
HE IS A MAN TO WHOM I HAVE A VERY IMPORTANT MESSAGE TO CONVEY..!!
WELL, THERE WAS SOMETHING ABOUT MY COMPANION'S MANNER WHICH TOLD ME THAT ANY FURTHER QUESTIONING WOULD BE DISTASTEFUL TO HIM. HOWEVER, DUROC CONTINUED TO ASK EVERY PEASANT FOR ANY NEWS OF THE BARON STRAUBENTHAL.

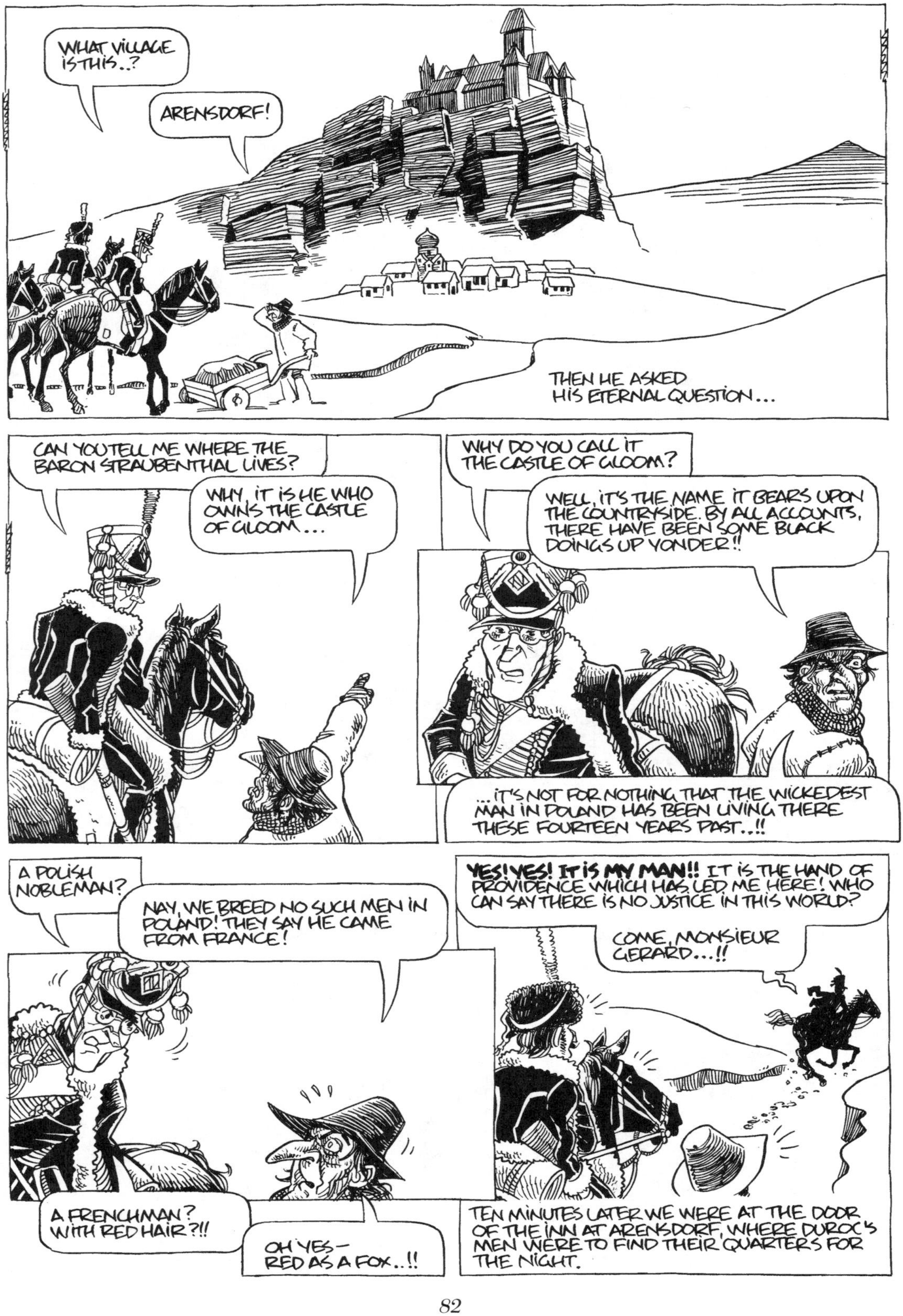
WHAT VILLAGE IS THIS..?
ARENSDORF!
THEN HE ASKED HIS ETERNAL QUESTION...
CAN YOU TELL ME WHERE THE BARON STRAUBENTHAL LIVES?
WHY, IT IS HE WHO OWNS THE CASTLE OF GLOOM...
WHY DO YOU CALL IT THE CASTLE OF GLOOM?
WELL, IT'S THE NAME IT BEARS UPON THE COUNTRYSIDE. BY ALL ACCOUNTS, THERE HAVE BEEN SOME BLACK DOINGS UP YONDER!!
...IT'S NOT FOR NOTHING THAT THE WICKEDEST MAN IN POLAND HAS BEEN LIVING THERE THESE FOURTEEN YEARS PAST..!!
A POLISH NOBLEMAN?
NAY, WE BREED NO SUCH MEN IN POLAND! THEY SAY HE CAME FROM FRANCE!
A FRENCHMAN? WITH RED HAIR?!!
OH YES— RED AS A FOX..!!
YES! YES! IT IS MY MAN!! IT IS THE HAND OF PROVIDENCE WHICH HAS LED ME HERE! WHO CAN SAY THERE IS NO JUSTICE IN THIS WORLD?
COME, MONSIEUR GERARD...!!
TEN MINUTES LATER WE WERE AT THE DOOR OF THE INN AT ARENSDORF, WHERE DUROC'S MEN WERE TO FIND THEIR QUARTERS FOR THE NIGHT.

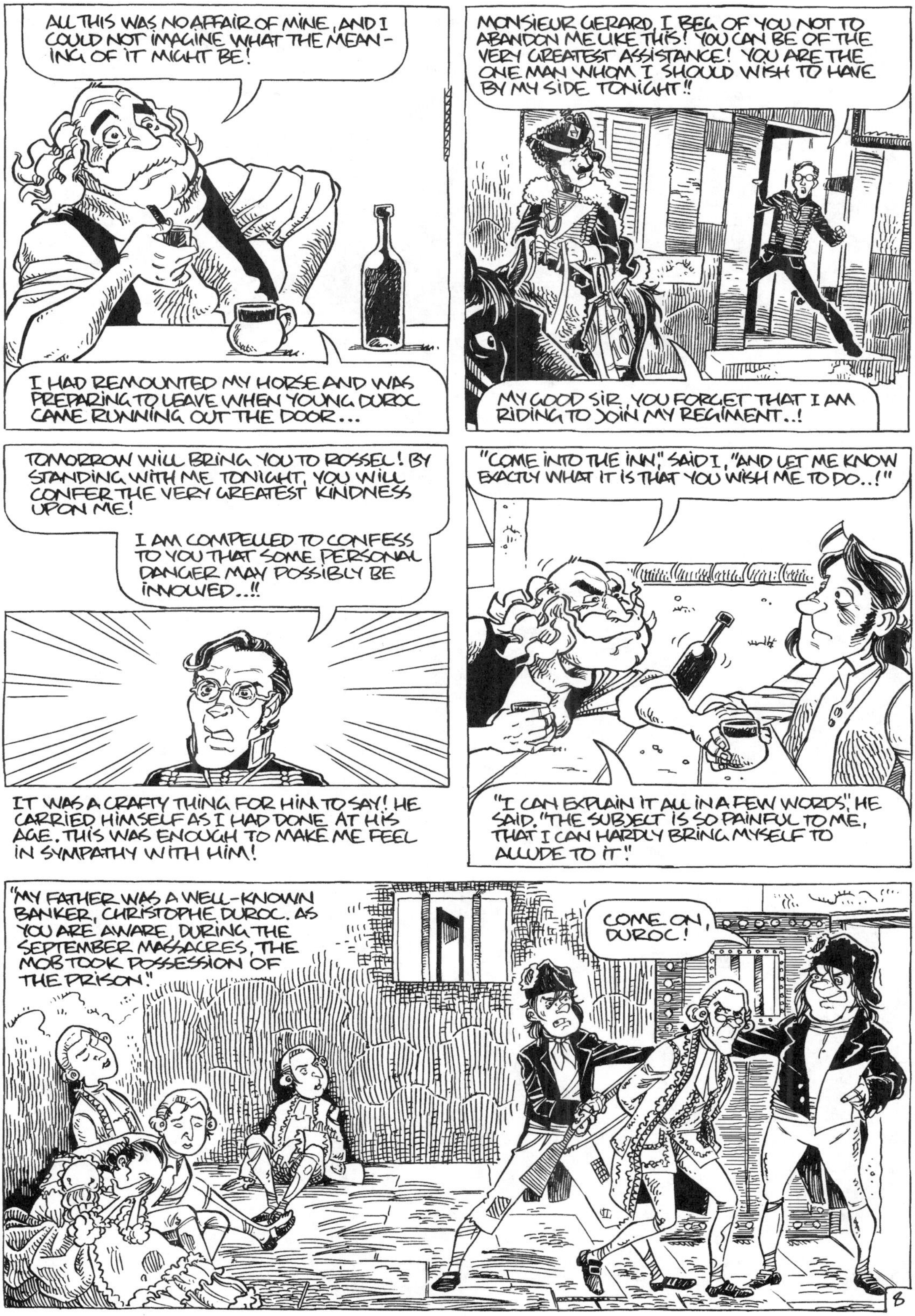
ALL THIS WAS NO AFFAIR OF MINE, AND I COULD NOT IMAGINE WHAT THE MEANING OF IT MIGHT BE!
I HAD REMOUNTED MY HORSE AND WAS PREPARING TO LEAVE WHEN YOUNG DUROC CAME RUNNING OUT THE DOOR...
MONSIEUR GERARD, I BEG OF YOU NOT TO ABANDON ME LIKE THIS! YOU CAN BE OF THE VERY GREATEST ASSISTANCE! YOU ARE THE ONE MAN WHOM I SHOULD WISH TO HAVE BY MY SIDE TONIGHT!!
MY GOOD SIR, YOU FORGET THAT I AM RIDING TO JOIN MY REGIMENT..!
TOMORROW WILL BRING YOU TO ROSSEL! BY STANDING WITH ME TONIGHT, YOU WILL CONFER THE VERY GREATEST KINDNESS UPON ME!
I AM COMPELLED TO CONFESS TO YOU THAT SOME PERSONAL DANGER MAY POSSIBLY BE INVOLVED..!!
IT WAS A CRAFTY THING FOR HIM TO SAY! HE CARRIED HIMSELF AS I HAD DONE AT HIS AGE. THIS WAS ENOUGH TO MAKE ME FEEL IN SYMPATHY WITH HIM!
"COME INTO THE INN," SAID I, "AND LET ME KNOW EXACTLY WHAT IT IS THAT YOU WISH ME TO DO..!"
"I CAN EXPLAIN IT ALL IN A FEW WORDS," HE SAID, "THE SUBJECT IS SO PAINFUL TO ME, THAT I CAN HARDLY BRING MYSELF TO ALLUDE TO IT."
"MY FATHER WAS A WELL-KNOWN BANKER, CHRISTOPHE DUROC. AS YOU ARE AWARE, DURING THE SEPTEMBER MASSACRES, THE MOB TOOK POSSESSION OF THE PRISON."
COME ON, DUROC!
8

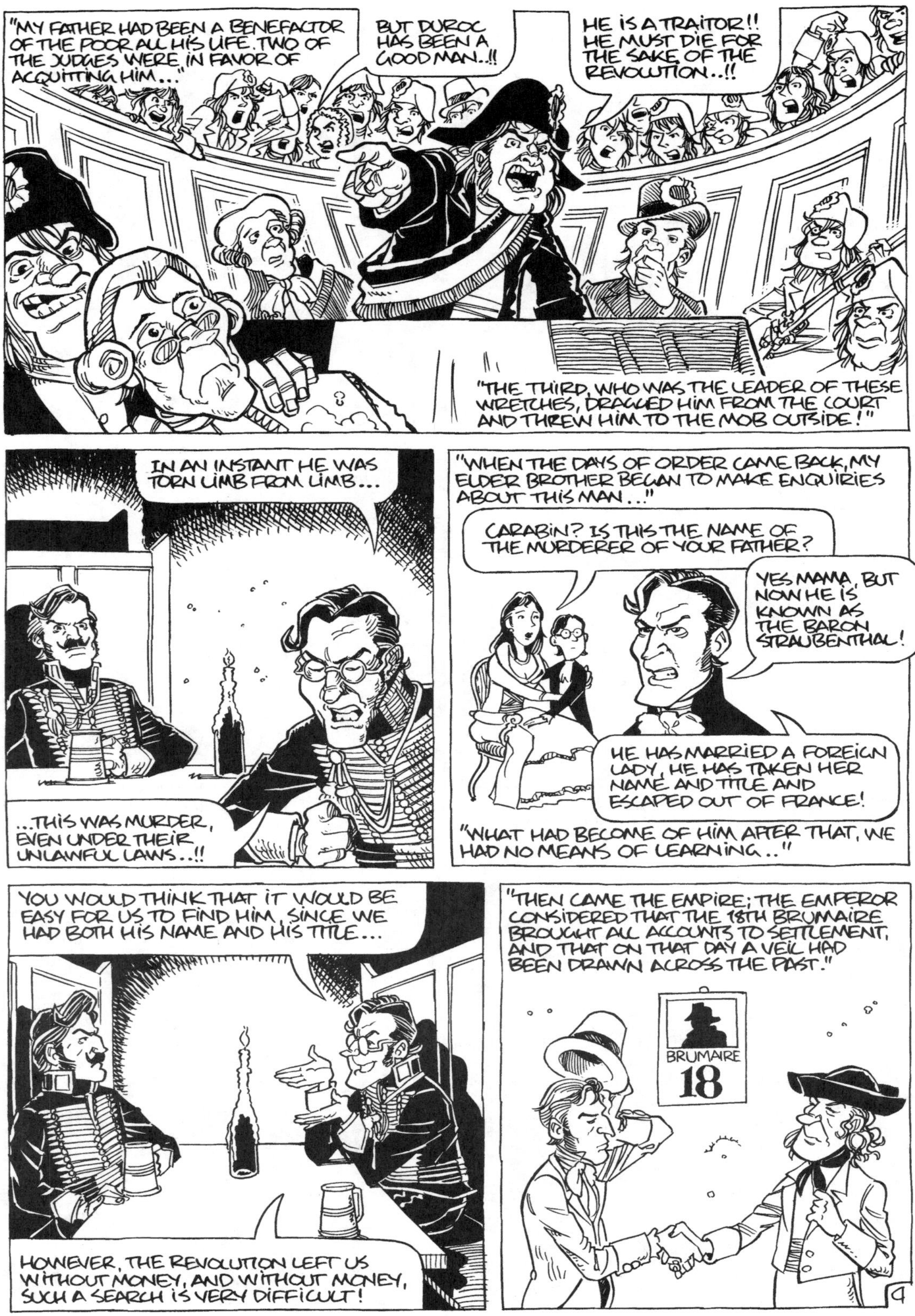
"MY FATHER HAD BEEN A BENEFACTOR OF THE POOR ALL HIS LIFE. TWO OF THE JUDGES WERE IN FAVOR OF ACQUITTING HIM..."
BUT DUROC HAS BEEN A GOOD MAN..!!
HE IS A TRAITOR!! HE MUST DIE FOR THE SAKE OF THE REVOLUTION..!!
"THE THIRD, WHO WAS THE LEADER OF THESE WRETCHES, DRAGGED HIM FROM THE COURT AND THREW HIM TO THE MOB OUTSIDE!"
IN AN INSTANT HE WAS TORN LIMB FROM LIMB...
...THIS WAS MURDER, EVEN UNDER THEIR UNLAWFUL LAWS..!!
"WHEN THE DAYS OF ORDER CAME BACK, MY ELDER BROTHER BEGAN TO MAKE ENQUIRIES ABOUT THIS MAN..."
CARABIN? IS THIS THE NAME OF THE MURDERER OF YOUR FATHER?
YES MAMA, BUT NOW HE IS KNOWN AS THE BARON STRAUBENTHAL!
HE HAS MARRIED A FOREIGN LADY, HE HAS TAKEN HER NAME AND TITLE AND ESCAPED OUT OF FRANCE!
"WHAT HAD BECOME OF HIM AFTER THAT, WE HAD NO MEANS OF LEARNING.."
YOU WOULD THINK THAT IT WOULD BE EASY FOR US TO FIND HIM, SINCE WE HAD BOTH HIS NAME AND HIS TITLE...
HOWEVER, THE REVOLUTION LEFT US WITHOUT MONEY, AND WITHOUT MONEY, SUCH A SEARCH IS VERY DIFFICULT!
"THEN CAME THE EMPIRE; THE EMPEROR CONSIDERED THAT THE 18TH BRUMAIRE BROUGHT ALL ACCOUNTS TO SETTLEMENT, AND THAT ON THAT DAY A VEIL HAD BEEN DRAWN ACROSS THE PAST."
BRUMAIRE
18

"MY BROTHER JOINED THE ARMY. HE ASKED EVERYWHERE FOR THE BARON STRAUBENTHAL. LAST OCTOBER, HE WAS KILLED AT JENA.

"THEN IT BECAME MY TURN, AND I HAD THE GOOD FORTUNE TO HEAR OF THE MAN WITHIN A FORTNIGHT OF JOINING MY REGIMENT!"

NOW, I FIND MYSELF IN THE COMPANY OF ONE WHOSE NAME IS NEVER MENTIONED THROUGH-OUT THE ARMY, SAVE IN CONNECTION WITH SOME DARING AND GENEROUS DEED!

HOW CAN I BE OF SERVICE TO YOU?

BY COMING WITH ME TO THE CASTLE AT ONCE! I WISH YOU TO BE WITH ME!

BUT WHAT DO YOU INTEND TO DO?

I SHALL KNOW WHAT TO DO WHEN I FIND THE VILLAIN..!!

IT WAS NEVER IN MY NATURE TO REFUSE AN ADVENTURE! AND BESIDES, I HAD EVERY SYMPATHY WITH THE LAD'S FEELINGS. I HELD OUT MY HAND TO HIM THEREFORE.

"I MUST BE ON MY WAY FOR ROSSEL TOMORROW MORNING", SAID I, "BUT TONIGHT, I AM YOURS!"

TO TELL THE TRUTH, I HATE TO SEE A CAVALRYMAN WALK, AS HE IS THE MOST GALLANT THING UPON THE EARTH WHEN HE HAS HIS SADDLE BETWEEN HIS KNEES, SO HE IS THE MOST CLUMSY WHEN HE HAS HIS SABRE IN ONE HAND AND TURNS HIS TOES FOR FEAR OF CATCHING THE ROWEL OF HIS SPURS.

HOWEVER, IT WAS BUT A MILE TO THE CASTLE, SO WE DID NOT DISTURB OUR HORSES.

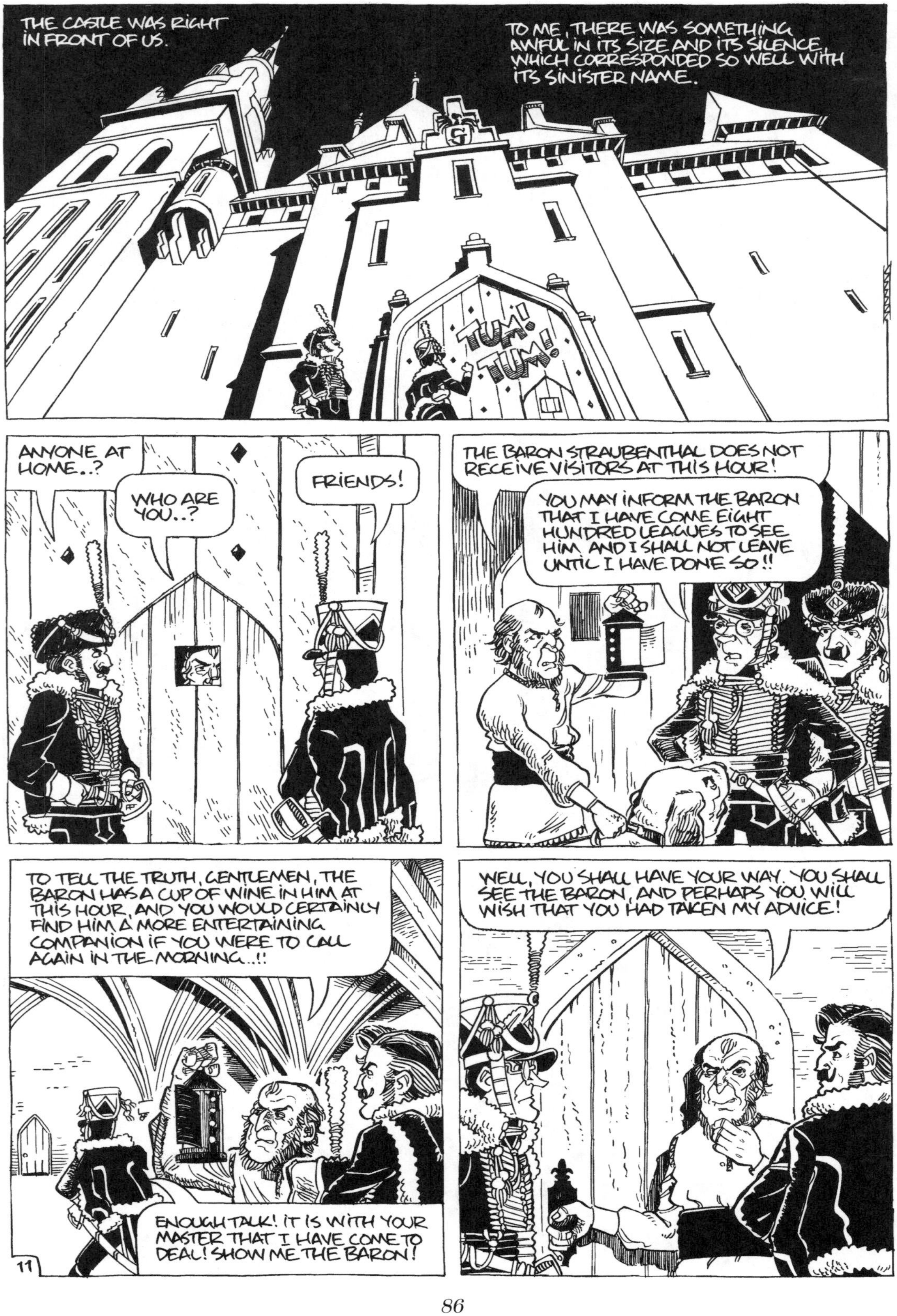
THE CASTLE WAS RIGHT IN FRONT OF US.
TO ME, THERE WAS SOMETHING AWFUL IN ITS SIZE AND ITS SILENCE, WHICH CORRESPONDED SO WELL WITH ITS SINISTER NAME.
TUM! TUM!
ANYONE AT HOME..?
WHO ARE YOU..?
FRIENDS!
THE BARON STRAUBENTHAL DOES NOT RECEIVE VISITORS AT THIS HOUR!
YOU MAY INFORM THE BARON THAT I HAVE COME EIGHT HUNDRED LEAGUES TO SEE HIM, AND I SHALL NOT LEAVE UNTIL I HAVE DONE SO!!
TO TELL THE TRUTH, GENTLEMEN, THE BARON HAS A CUP OF WINE IN HIM AT THIS HOUR, AND YOU WOULD CERTAINLY FIND HIM A MORE ENTERTAINING COMPANION IF YOU WERE TO CALL AGAIN IN THE MORNING..!!
ENOUGH TALK! IT IS WITH YOUR MASTER THAT I HAVE COME TO DEAL! SHOW ME THE BARON!
11
WELL, YOU SHALL HAVE YOUR WAY. YOU SHALL SEE THE BARON, AND PERHAPS YOU WILL WISH THAT YOU HAD TAKEN MY ADVICE!

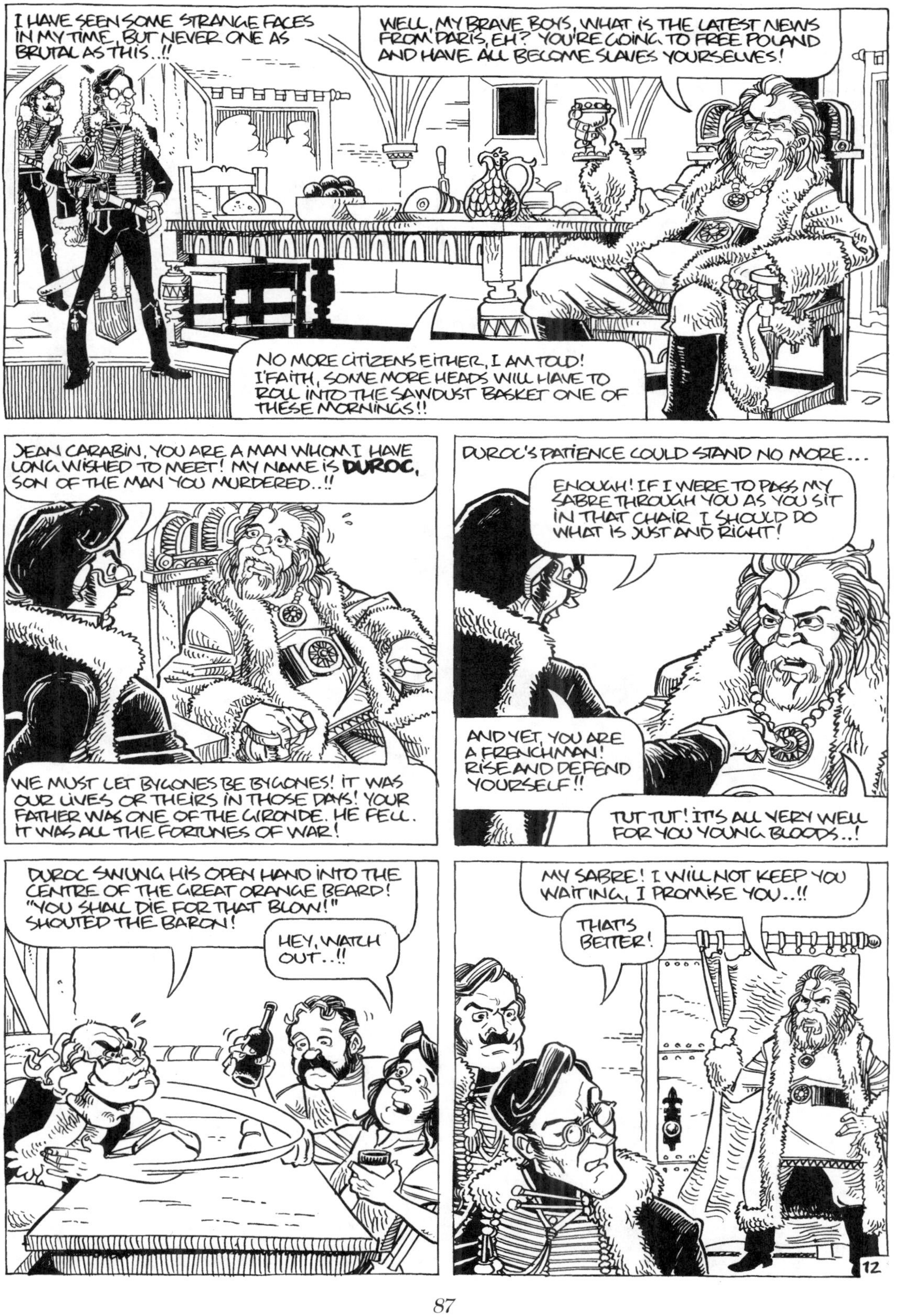
I HAVE SEEN SOME STRANGE FACES IN MY TIME, BUT NEVER ONE AS BRUTAL AS THIS..!!
WELL, MY BRAVE BOYS, WHAT IS THE LATEST NEWS FROM PARIS, EH? YOU'RE GOING TO FREE POLAND AND HAVE ALL BECOME SLAVES YOURSELVES!
NO MORE CITIZENS EITHER, I AM TOLD! I'FAITH, SOME MORE HEADS WILL HAVE TO ROLL INTO THE SAWDUST BASKET ONE OF THESE MORNINGS!!
JEAN CARABIN, YOU ARE A MAN WHOM I HAVE LONG WISHED TO MEET! MY NAME IS **DUROC**, SON OF THE MAN YOU MURDERED..!!
WE MUST LET BYGONES BE BYGONES! IT WAS OUR LIVES OR THEIRS IN THOSE DAYS! YOUR FATHER WAS ONE OF THE GIRONDE. HE FELL. IT WAS ALL THE FORTUNES OF WAR!
DUROC'S PATIENCE COULD STAND NO MORE...
ENOUGH! IF I WERE TO PASS MY SABRE THROUGH YOU AS YOU SIT IN THAT CHAIR I SHOULD DO WHAT IS JUST AND RIGHT!
AND YET, YOU ARE A FRENCHMAN! RISE AND DEFEND YOURSELF!!
TUT TUT! IT'S ALL VERY WELL FOR YOU YOUNG BLOODS..!
DUROC SWUNG HIS OPEN HAND INTO THE CENTRE OF THE GREAT ORANGE BEARD! "YOU SHALL DIE FOR THAT BLOW!" SHOUTED THE BARON!
HEY, WATCH OUT..!!
MY SABRE! I WILL NOT KEEP YOU WAITING, I PROMISE YOU..!!
THAT'S BETTER!
12

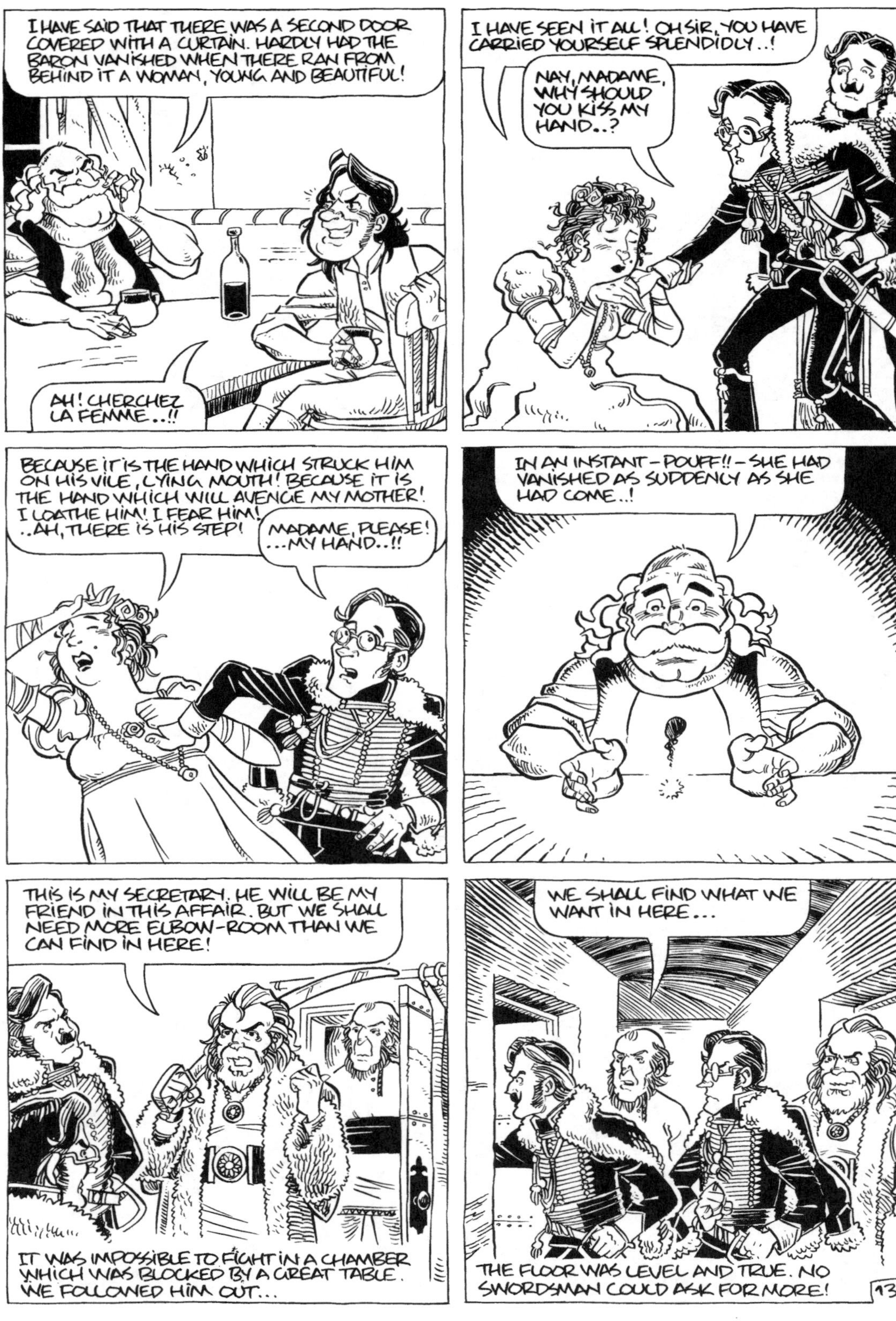
I HAVE SAID THAT THERE WAS A SECOND DOOR COVERED WITH A CURTAIN. HARDLY HAD THE BARON VANISHED WHEN THERE RAN FROM BEHIND IT A WOMAN, YOUNG AND BEAUTIFUL!
AH! CHERCHEZ LA FEMME..!!
I HAVE SEEN IT ALL! OH SIR, YOU HAVE CARRIED YOURSELF SPLENDIDLY..!
NAY, MADAME, WHY SHOULD YOU KISS MY HAND..?
BECAUSE IT IS THE HAND WHICH STRUCK HIM ON HIS VILE, LYING MOUTH! BECAUSE IT IS THE HAND WHICH WILL AVENGE MY MOTHER! I LOATHE HIM! I FEAR HIM! ..AH, THERE IS HIS STEP!
MADAME, PLEASE! ...MY HAND..!!
IN AN INSTANT - POUFF!! - SHE HAD VANISHED AS SUDDENLY AS SHE HAD COME..!
THIS IS MY SECRETARY. HE WILL BE MY FRIEND IN THIS AFFAIR. BUT WE SHALL NEED MORE ELBOW-ROOM THAN WE CAN FIND IN HERE!
IT WAS IMPOSSIBLE TO FIGHT IN A CHAMBER WHICH WAS BLOCKED BY A GREAT TABLE. WE FOLLOWED HIM OUT...
WE SHALL FIND WHAT WE WANT IN HERE...
THE FLOOR WAS LEVEL AND TRUE. NO SWORDSMAN COULD ASK FOR MORE!
13

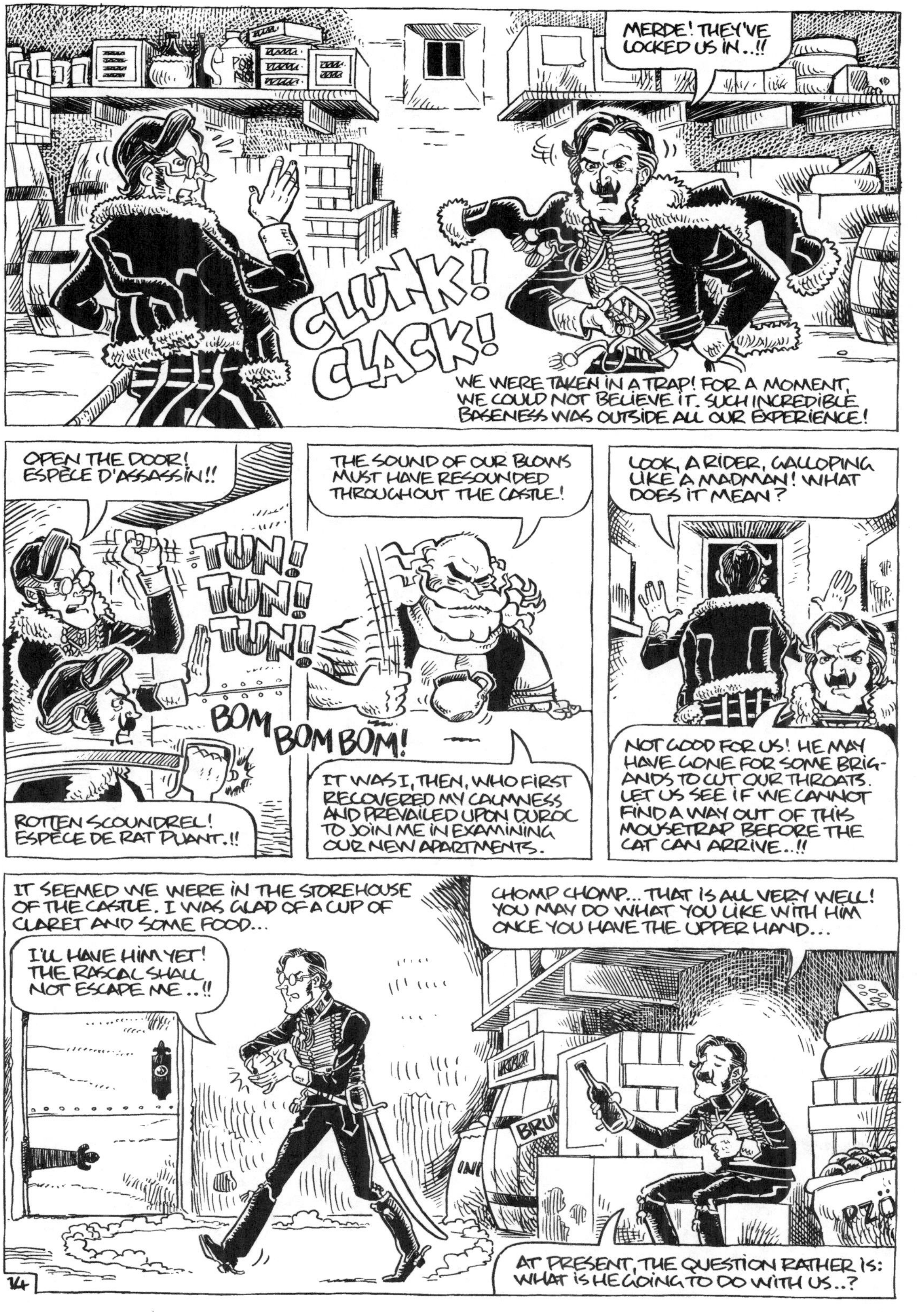
MERDE! THEY'VE LOCKED US IN..!!
CLUNK! CLACK!
WE WERE TAKEN IN A TRAP! FOR A MOMENT, WE COULD NOT BELIEVE IT. SUCH INCREDIBLE BASENESS WAS OUTSIDE ALL OUR EXPERIENCE!
OPEN THE DOOR! ESPÈCE D'ASSASSIN!!
TUN! TUN! TUN!
BOM BOM BOM!
ROTTEN SCOUNDREL! ESPÈCE DE RAT PUANT.!!
THE SOUND OF OUR BLOWS MUST HAVE RESOUNDED THROUGHOUT THE CASTLE!
IT WAS I, THEN, WHO FIRST RECOVERED MY CALMNESS AND PREVAILED UPON DUROC TO JOIN ME IN EXAMINING OUR NEW APARTMENTS.
LOOK, A RIDER, GALLOPING LIKE A MADMAN! WHAT DOES IT MEAN?
NOT GOOD FOR US! HE MAY HAVE GONE FOR SOME BRIGANDS TO CUT OUR THROATS. LET US SEE IF WE CANNOT FIND A WAY OUT OF THIS MOUSETRAP BEFORE THE CAT CAN ARRIVE..!!
IT SEEMED WE WERE IN THE STOREHOUSE OF THE CASTLE. I WAS GLAD OF A CUP OF CLARET AND SOME FOOD...
I'LL HAVE HIM YET! THE RASCAL SHALL NOT ESCAPE ME..!!
CHOMP CHOMP... THAT IS ALL VERY WELL! YOU MAY DO WHAT YOU LIKE WITH HIM ONCE YOU HAVE THE UPPER HAND...
AT PRESENT, THE QUESTION RATHER IS: WHAT IS HE GOING TO DO WITH US..?
14

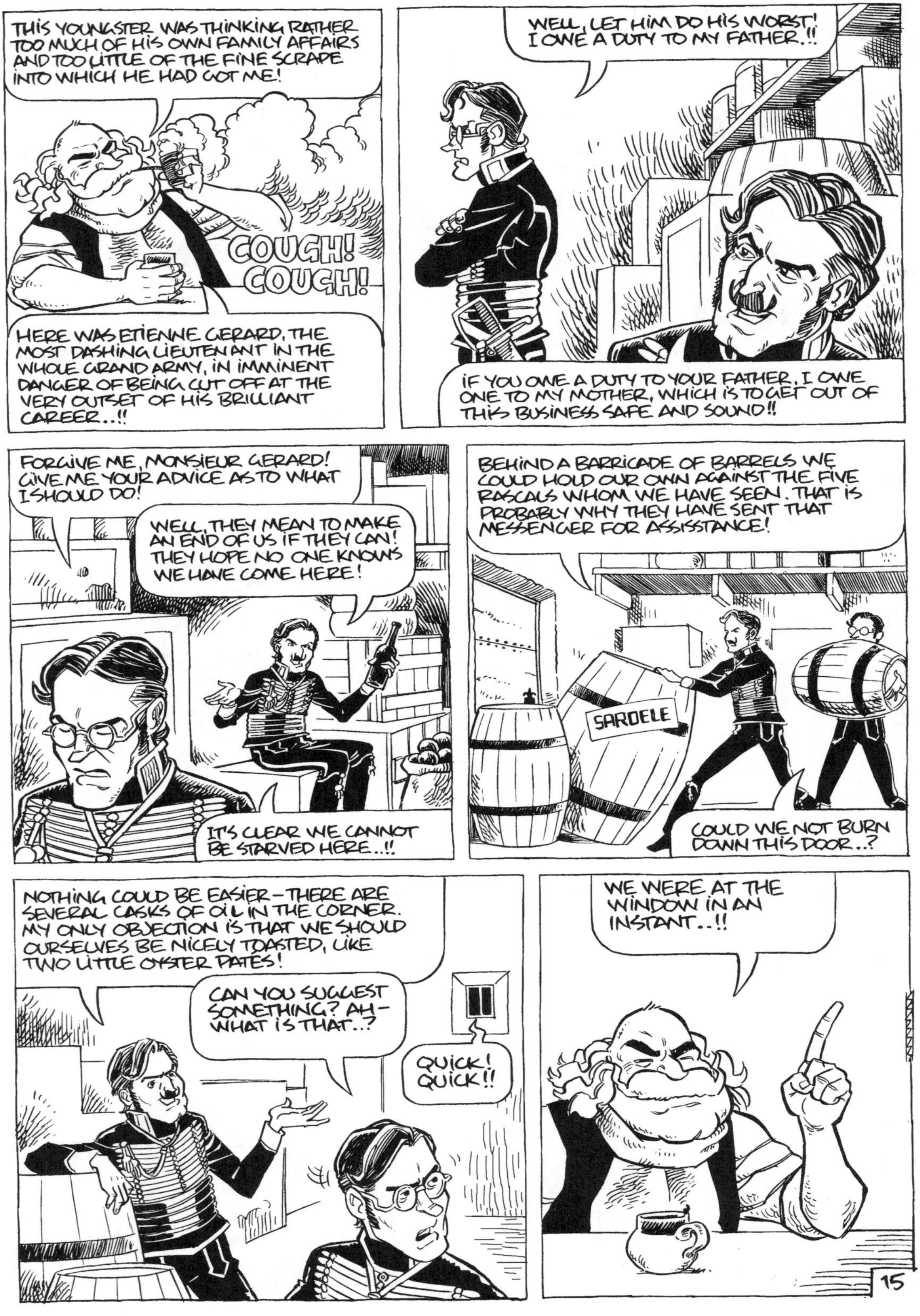
THIS YOUNGSTER WAS THINKING RATHER TOO MUCH OF HIS OWN FAMILY AFFAIRS AND TOO LITTLE OF THE FINE SCRAPE INTO WHICH HE HAD GOT ME!
COUGH! COUGH!
HERE WAS ETIENNE GERARD, THE MOST DASHING LIEUTENANT IN THE WHOLE GRAND ARMY, IN IMMINENT DANGER OF BEING CUT OFF AT THE VERY OUTSET OF HIS BRILLIANT CAREER..!!
WELL, LET HIM DO HIS WORST! I OWE A DUTY TO MY FATHER..!!
IF YOU OWE A DUTY TO YOUR FATHER, I OWE ONE TO MY MOTHER, WHICH IS TO GET OUT OF THIS BUSINESS SAFE AND SOUND!!
FORGIVE ME, MONSIEUR GERARD! GIVE ME YOUR ADVICE AS TO WHAT I SHOULD DO!
WELL, THEY MEAN TO MAKE AN END OF US IF THEY CAN! THEY HOPE NO ONE KNOWS WE HAVE COME HERE!
IT'S CLEAR WE CANNOT BE STARVED HERE..!!
BEHIND A BARRICADE OF BARRELS WE COULD HOLD OUR OWN AGAINST THE FIVE RASCALS WHOM WE HAVE SEEN. THAT IS PROBABLY WHY THEY HAVE SENT THAT MESSENGER FOR ASSISSTANCE!
SARDELE
COULD WE NOT BURN DOWN THIS DOOR..?
NOTHING COULD BE EASIER — THERE ARE SEVERAL CASKS OF OIL IN THE CORNER. MY ONLY OBJECTION IS THAT WE SHOULD OURSELVES BE NICELY TOASTED, LIKE TWO LITTLE OYSTER PATES!
CAN YOU SUGGEST SOMETHING? AH — WHAT IS THAT..?
QUICK! QUICK!!
WE WERE AT THE WINDOW IN AN INSTANT..!!
15

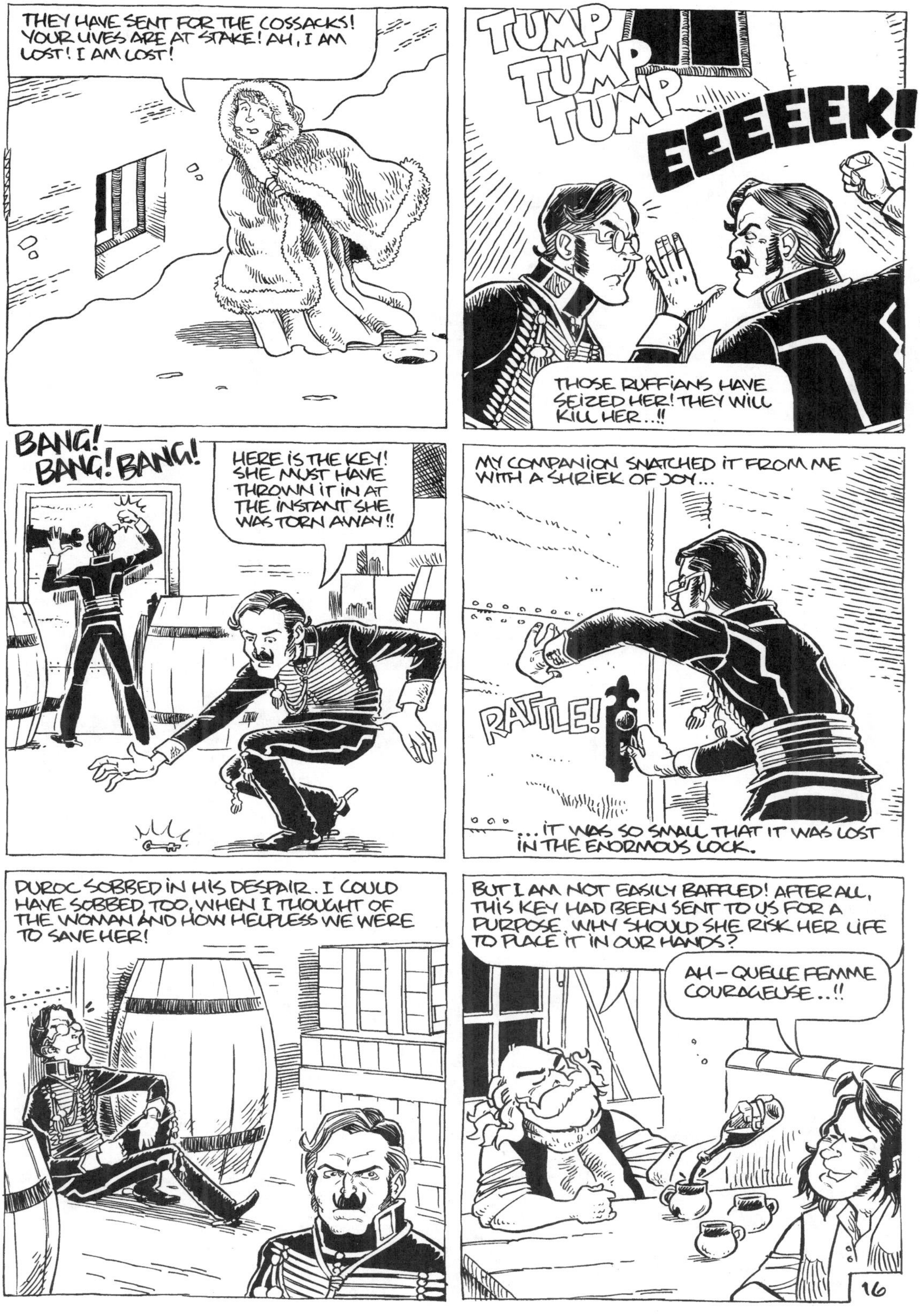
THEY HAVE SENT FOR THE COSSACKS! YOUR LIVES ARE AT STAKE! AH, I AM LOST! I AM LOST!
TUMP TUMP TUMP
EEEEEK!
THOSE RUFFIANS HAVE SEIZED HER! THEY WILL KILL HER..!!
BANG! BANG! BANG!
HERE IS THE KEY! SHE MUST HAVE THROWN IT IN AT THE INSTANT SHE WAS TORN AWAY!!
MY COMPANION SNATCHED IT FROM ME WITH A SHRIEK OF JOY...
RATTLE!
...IT WAS SO SMALL THAT IT WAS LOST IN THE ENORMOUS LOCK.
DUROC SOBBED IN HIS DESPAIR. I COULD HAVE SOBBED, TOO, WHEN I THOUGHT OF THE WOMAN AND HOW HELPLESS WE WERE TO SAVE HER!
BUT I AM NOT EASILY BAFFLED! AFTER ALL, THIS KEY HAD BEEN SENT TO US FOR A PURPOSE. WHY SHOULD SHE RISK HER LIFE TO PLACE IT IN OUR HANDS?
AH — QUELLE FEMME COURAGEUSE..!!
16

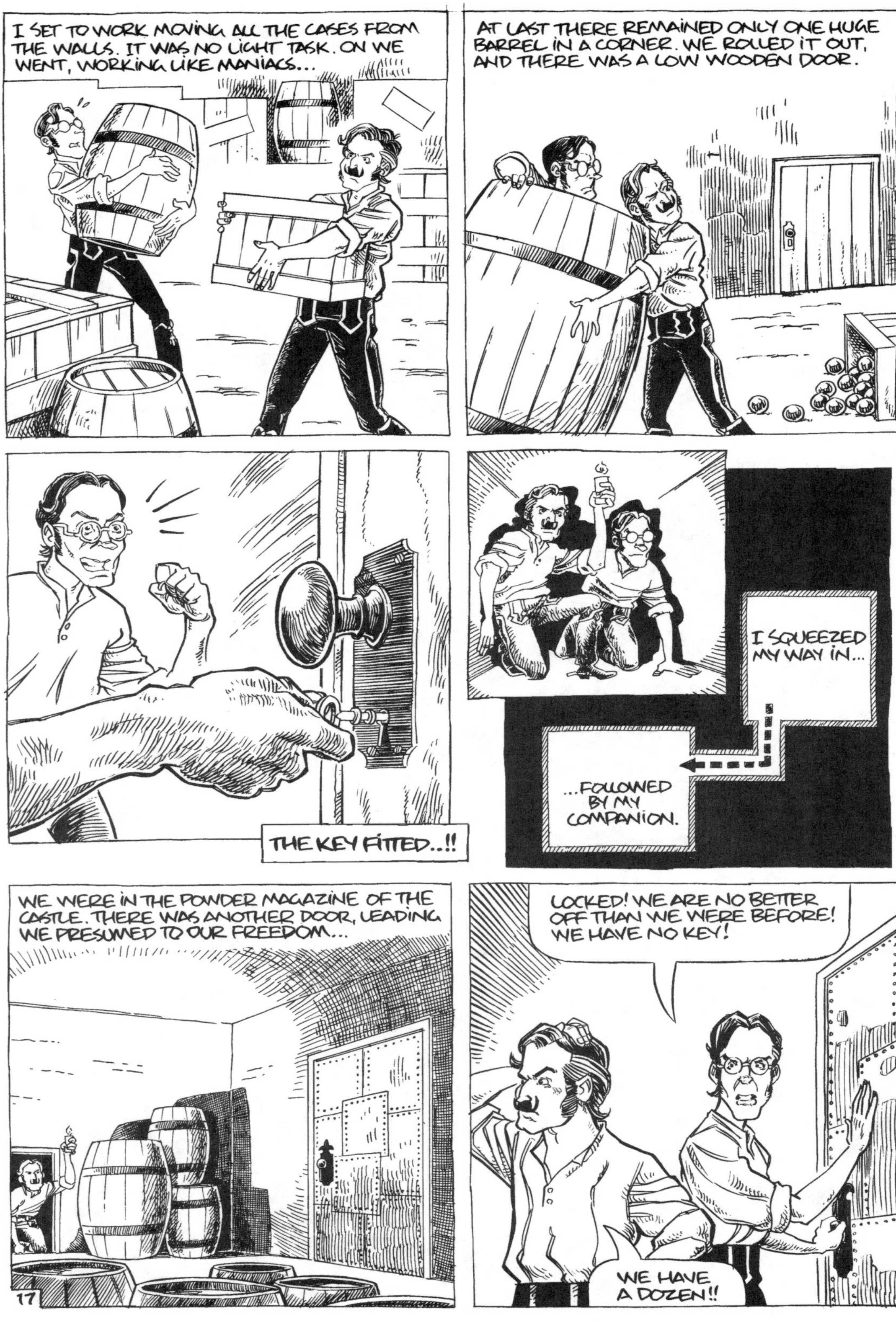
I SET TO WORK MOVING ALL THE CASES FROM THE WALLS. IT WAS NO LIGHT TASK. ON WE WENT, WORKING LIKE MANIACS...
AT LAST THERE REMAINED ONLY ONE HUGE BARREL IN A CORNER. WE ROLLED IT OUT, AND THERE WAS A LOW WOODEN DOOR.
THE KEY FITTED..!!
I SQUEEZED MY WAY IN...
...FOLLOWED BY MY COMPANION.
WE WERE IN THE POWDER MAGAZINE OF THE CASTLE. THERE WAS ANOTHER DOOR, LEADING WE PRESUMED TO OUR FREEDOM...
17
LOCKED! WE ARE NO BETTER OFF THAN WE WERE BEFORE! WE HAVE NO KEY!
WE HAVE A DOZEN!!

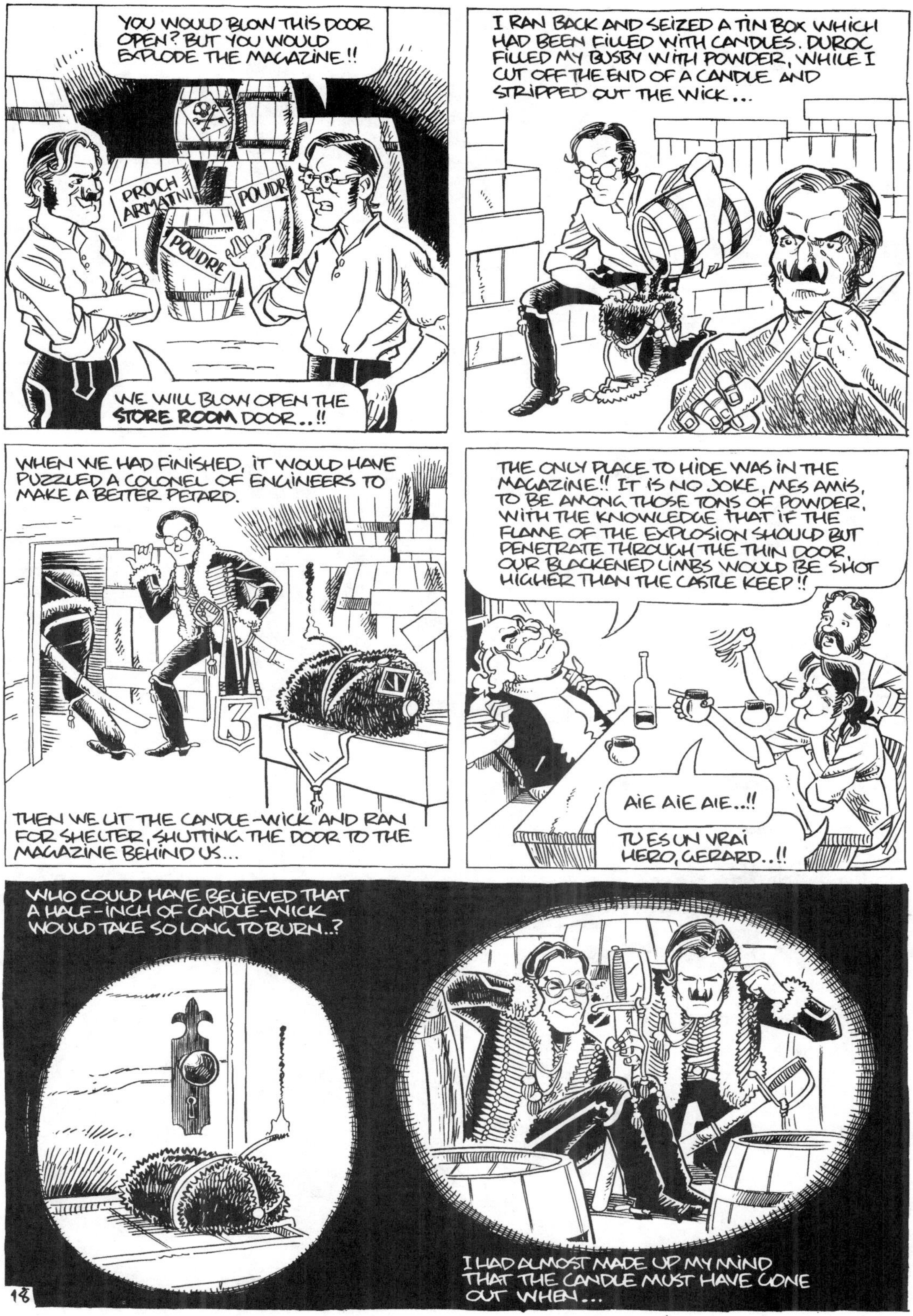
YOU WOULD BLOW THIS DOOR OPEN? BUT YOU WOULD EXPLODE THE MAGAZINE!!
PROCH ARMATNI
POUDR
POUDRE
WE WILL BLOW OPEN THE STORE ROOM DOOR..!!
I RAN BACK AND SEIZED A TIN BOX WHICH HAD BEEN FILLED WITH CANDLES. DUROC FILLED MY BUSBY WITH POWDER, WHILE I CUT OFF THE END OF A CANDLE AND STRIPPED OUT THE WICK...
WHEN WE HAD FINISHED, IT WOULD HAVE PUZZLED A COLONEL OF ENGINEERS TO MAKE A BETTER PETARD.
3
THEN WE LIT THE CANDLE-WICK AND RAN FOR SHELTER, SHUTTING THE DOOR TO THE MAGAZINE BEHIND US...
THE ONLY PLACE TO HIDE WAS IN THE MAGAZINE!! IT IS NO JOKE, MES AMIS, TO BE AMONG THOSE TONS OF POWDER, WITH THE KNOWLEDGE THAT IF THE FLAME OF THE EXPLOSION SHOULD BUT PENETRATE THROUGH THE THIN DOOR, OUR BLACKENED LIMBS WOULD BE SHOT HIGHER THAN THE CASTLE KEEP!!
AIE AIE AIE..!!
TU ES UN VRAI HERO, GERARD..!!
WHO COULD HAVE BELIEVED THAT A HALF-INCH OF CANDLE-WICK WOULD TAKE SO LONG TO BURN..?
I HAD ALMOST MADE UP MY MIND THAT THE CANDLE MUST HAVE GONE OUT WHEN...
18

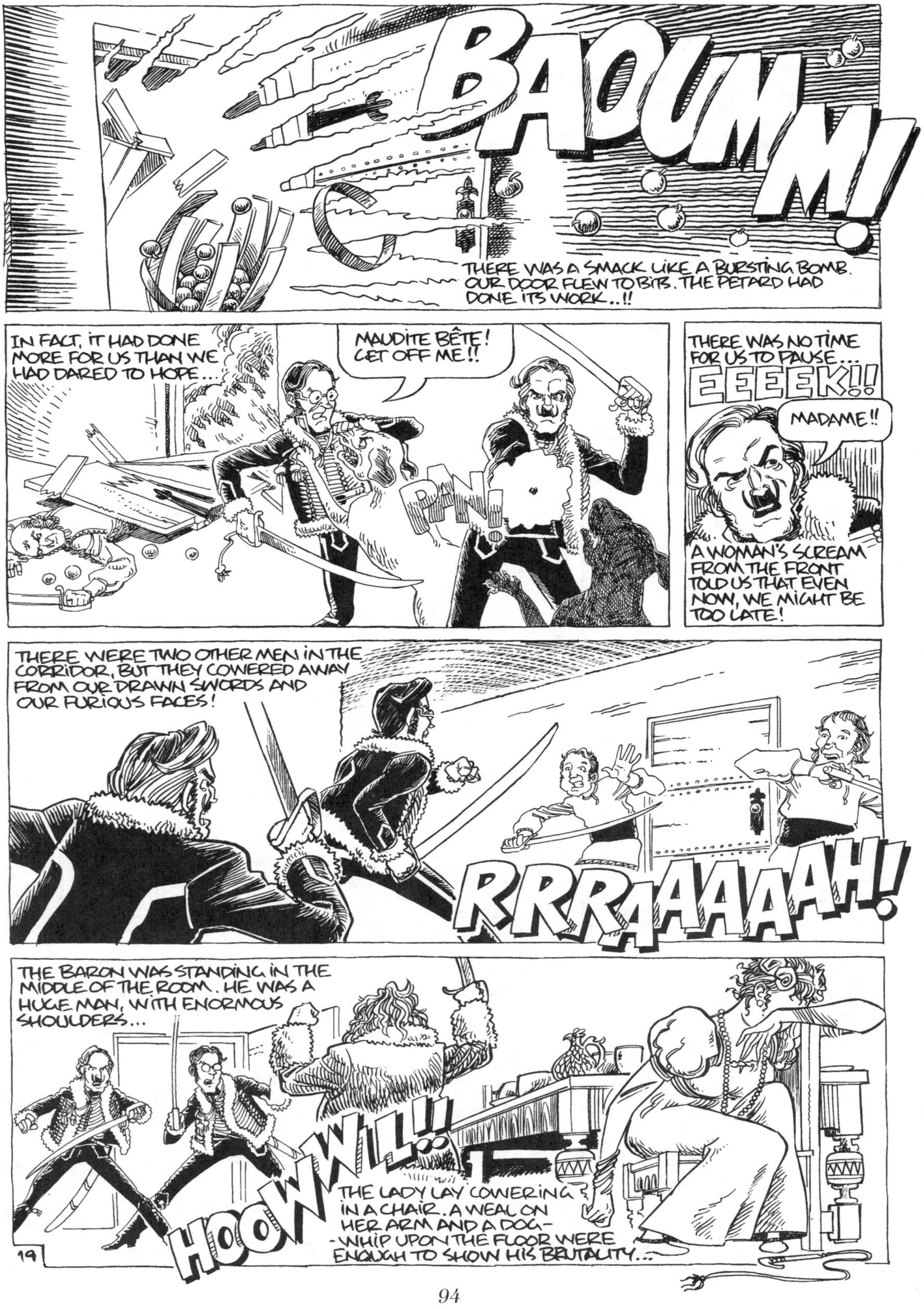
BAOUMM!
THERE WAS A SMACK LIKE A BURSTING BOMB. OUR DOOR FLEW TO BITS. THE PETARD HAD DONE ITS WORK..!!
IN FACT, IT HAD DONE MORE FOR US THAN WE HAD DARED TO HOPE...
MAUDITE BÊTE! GET OFF ME!!
PAN!
THERE WAS NO TIME FOR US TO PAUSE...
EEEEK!!
MADAME!!
A WOMAN'S SCREAM FROM THE FRONT TOLD US THAT EVEN NOW, WE MIGHT BE TOO LATE!
THERE WERE TWO OTHER MEN IN THE CORRIDOR, BUT THEY COWERED AWAY FROM OUR DRAWN SWORDS AND OUR FURIOUS FACES!
RRRAAAAAH!
THE BARON WAS STANDING IN THE MIDDLE OF THE ROOM. HE WAS A HUGE MAN, WITH ENORMOUS SHOULDERS...
HOOWWL!!..
THE LADY LAY COWERING IN A CHAIR. A WEAL ON HER ARM AND A DOG-WHIP UPON THE FLOOR WERE ENOUGH TO SHOW HIS BRUTALITY...
19

THE LAD KNEW SOMETHING OF HIS WEAPON, BUT IN SO NARROW A SPACE THE STRENGTH OF THE GIANT GAVE HIM THE ADVANTAGE...

HE WAS AN ADMIRABLE SWORDSMAN. TWICE HE TOUCHED DUROC, AND THEN...

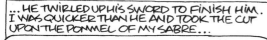

...HE TWIRLED UP HIS SWORD TO FINISH HIM. I WAS QUICKER THAN HE AND TOOK THE CUT UPON THE POMMEL OF MY SABRE...

EXCUSE ME, BUT YOU HAVE STILL TO DEAL WITH ETIENNE GERARD! TAKE YOUR BREATH SIR—I WILL AWAIT YOUR CONVENIENCE!

YOU HAVE NO CAUSE TO QUARREL WITH ME..!!

"I OWE YOU SOME LITTLE ATTENTION," SAID I, "FOR HAVING SHUT ME UP IN YOUR STORE ROOM! BESIDES, IF ALL OTHER WERE WANTING, I COULD SEE CAUSE ENOUGH ON THAT LADY'S ARM..!!

YOUR CHIVALRY DOES YOU PROUD, MON AMI..!!

"HAVE YOUR WAY, THEN!" HE SNARLED, AND LEAPT AT ME LIKE A MADMAN!!

HE KNEW THAT I WAS HIS MASTER. HE READ DEATH IN MY EYES, AND I COULD SEE THAT HE READ IT. HIS BREATH CAME SHORTER, AND IN THICKER GASPS...

20

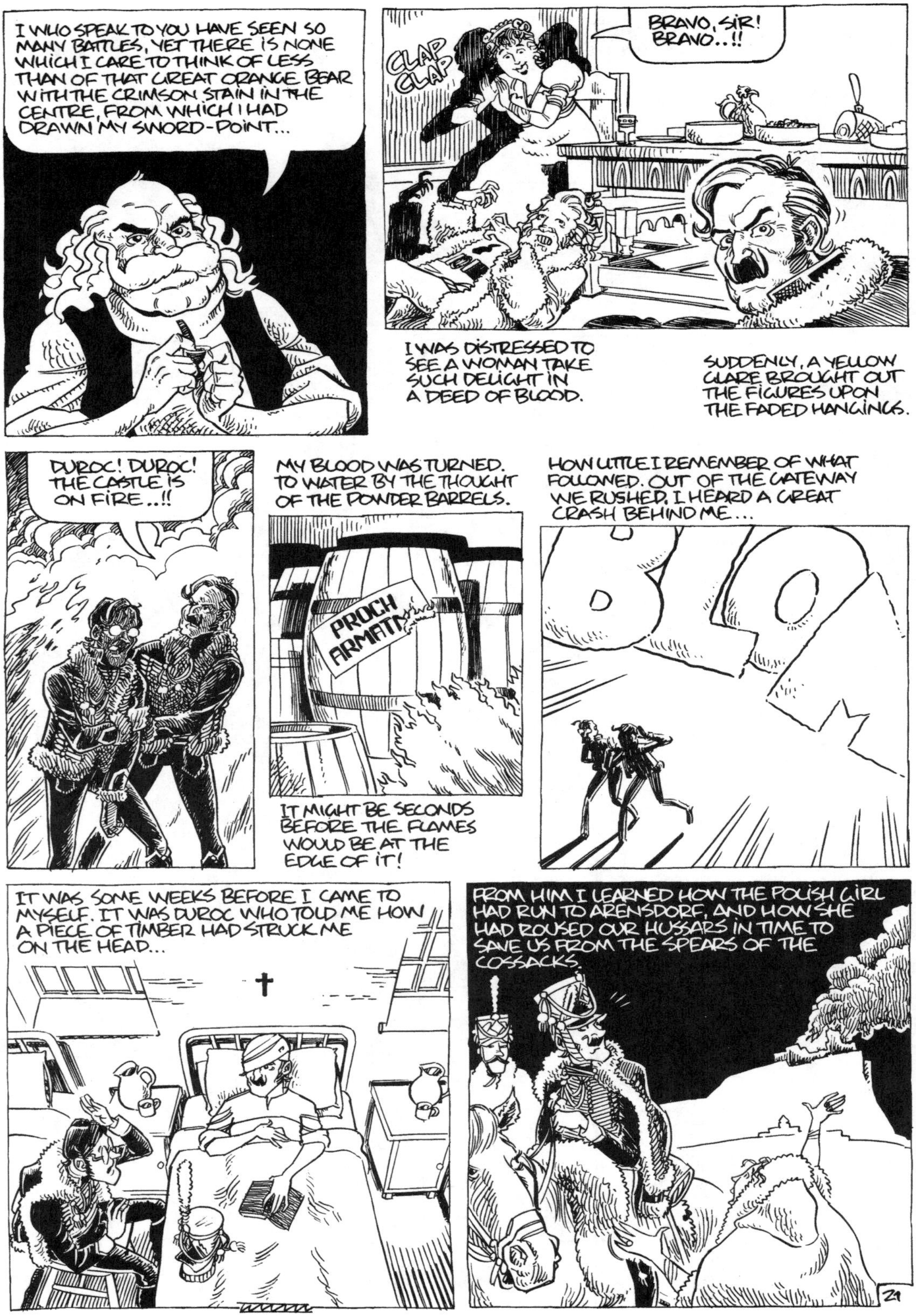
I WHO SPEAK TO YOU HAVE SEEN SO MANY BATTLES, YET THERE IS NONE WHICH I CARE TO THINK OF LESS THAN OF THAT GREAT ORANGE BEAR WITH THE CRIMSON STAIN IN THE CENTRE, FROM WHICH I HAD DRAWN MY SWORD-POINT...
CLAP CLAP
BRAVO, SIR! BRAVO..!!
I WAS DISTRESSED TO SEE A WOMAN TAKE SUCH DELIGHT IN A DEED OF BLOOD.
SUDDENLY, A YELLOW GLARE BROUGHT OUT THE FIGURES UPON THE FADED HANGINGS.
DUROC! DUROC! THE CASTLE IS ON FIRE..!!
MY BLOOD WAS TURNED. TO WATER BY THE THOUGHT OF THE POWDER BARRELS.
PROCH ARMATI
IT MIGHT BE SECONDS BEFORE THE FLAMES WOULD BE AT THE EDGE OF IT!
HOW LITTLE I REMEMBER OF WHAT FOLLOWED. OUT OF THE GATEWAY WE RUSHED. I HEARD A GREAT CRASH BEHIND ME...
BLO
IT WAS SOME WEEKS BEFORE I CAME TO MYSELF. IT WAS DUROC WHO TOLD ME HOW A PIECE OF TIMBER HAD STRUCK ME ON THE HEAD...
FROM HIM I LEARNED HOW THE POLISH GIRL HAD RUN TO ARENSDORF, AND HOW SHE HAD ROUSED OUR HUSSARS IN TIME TO SAVE US FROM THE SPEARS OF THE COSSACKS.

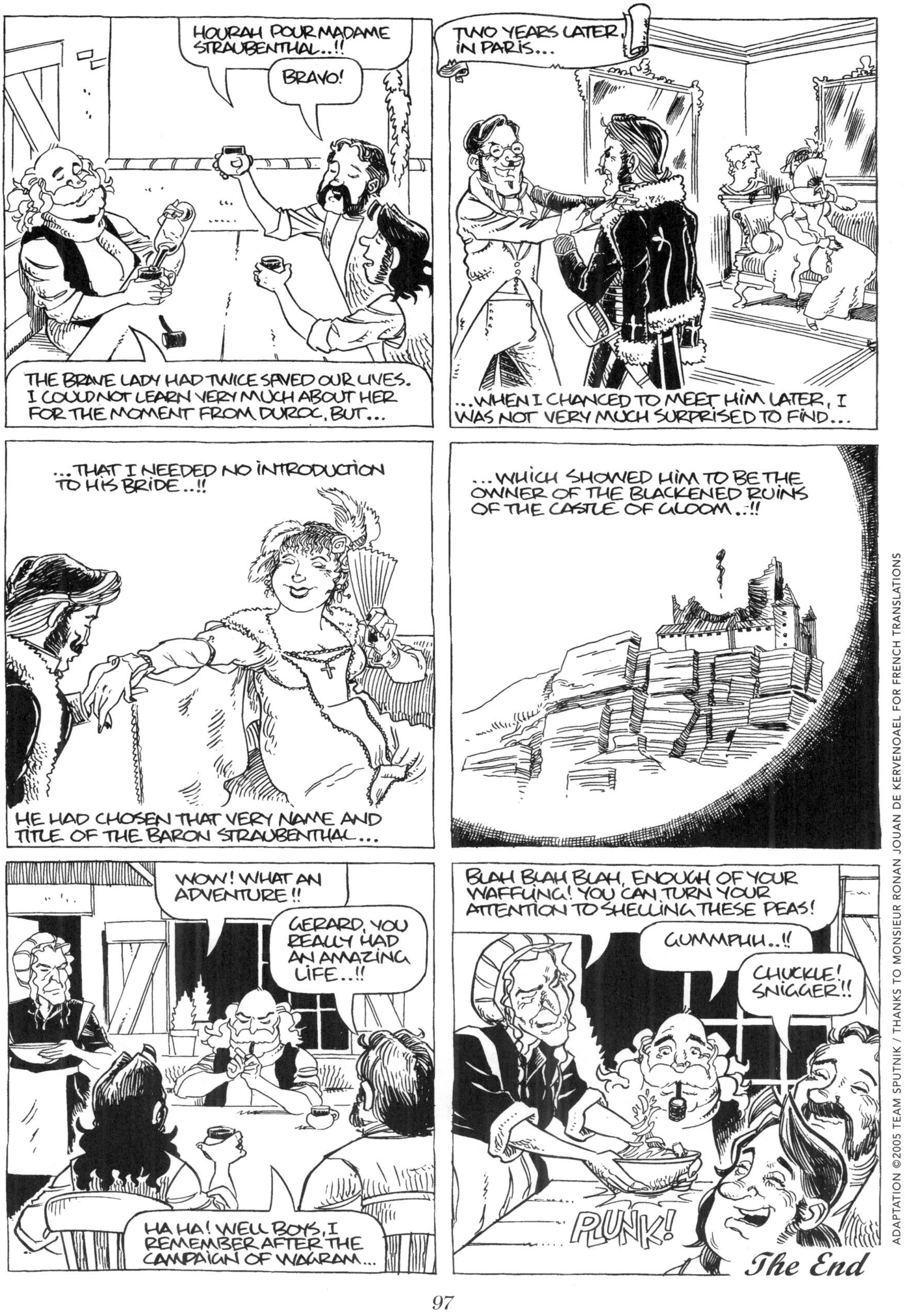
HOURAH POUR MADAME STRAUBENTHAL..!!
BRAVO!
THE BRAVE LADY HAD TWICE SAVED OUR LIVES. I COULD NOT LEARN VERY MUCH ABOUT HER FOR THE MOMENT FROM DUROC, BUT...
TWO YEARS LATER IN PARIS...
...WHEN I CHANCED TO MEET HIM LATER, I WAS NOT VERY MUCH SURPRISED TO FIND...
...THAT I NEEDED NO INTRODUCTION TO HIS BRIDE..!!
HE HAD CHOSEN THAT VERY NAME AND TITLE OF THE BARON STRAUBENTHAL...
...WHICH SHOWED HIM TO BE THE OWNER OF THE BLACKENED RUINS OF THE CASTLE OF GLOOM..!!
WOW! WHAT AN ADVENTURE!!
GERARD, YOU REALLY HAD AN AMAZING LIFE..!!
HA HA! WELL BOYS, I REMEMBER AFTER THE CAMPAIGN OF WAGRAM...
BLAH BLAH BLAH, ENOUGH OF YOUR WAFFLING! YOU CAN TURN YOUR ATTENTION TO SHELLING THESE PEAS!
GUMMPHH..!!
CHUCKLE! SNIGGER!!
PLUNK!

The End

Sherlock Holmes in

THE ADVENTURE OF THE ENGINEER'S THUMB

by **Arthur Conan Doyle**

adapted by **Rod Lott** • illustrated by **Simon Gane**

Of the only two problems which I myself submitted to my friend, Mr. Sherlock Holmes, the one of Mr. Hatherley's thumb is so strange in inception and so dramatic in details that it may be the more worthy of being placed upon record, even if it gave my friend fewer openings for those deductive methods of reasoning by which he achieved such remarkable results.

IN THE SUMMER OF 1889...

I had returned to civil practice, which had steadily increased. One morning, I was awakened by the maid tapping at the door.

TWO MEN FROM PADDINGTON ARE WAITING IN THE CONSULTING ROOM, DOCTOR!

Joe O'Brien was a guard at Paddington Station. I had cured him of a painful disease some years ago, and he never wearied of sending on every sufferer over whom he might have influence.

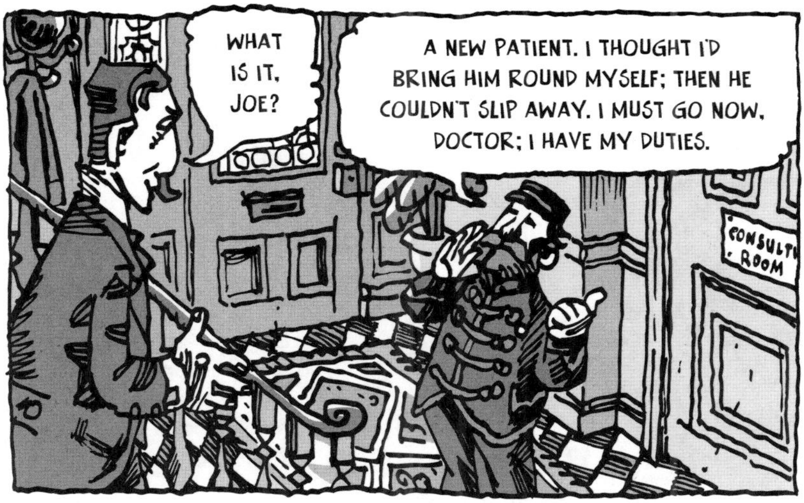
WHAT IS IT, JOE?
A NEW PATIENT. I THOUGHT I'D BRING HIM ROUND MYSELF; THEN HE COULDN'T SLIP AWAY. I MUST GO NOW, DOCTOR; I HAVE MY DUTIES.

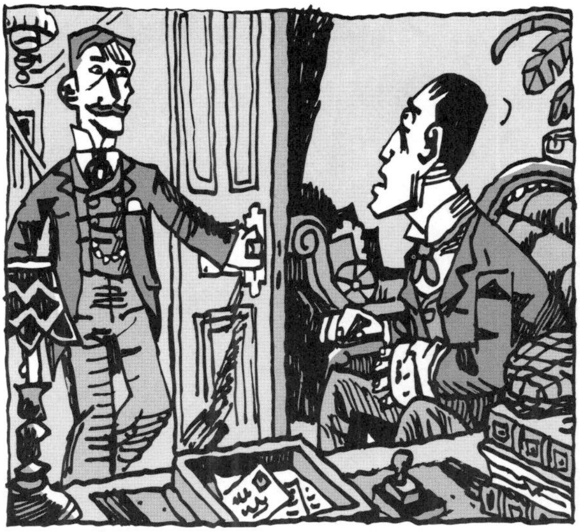

My patient gave me the impression of a man suffering from some strong agitation. Round one of his hands he had a handkerchief, mottled with bloodstains.

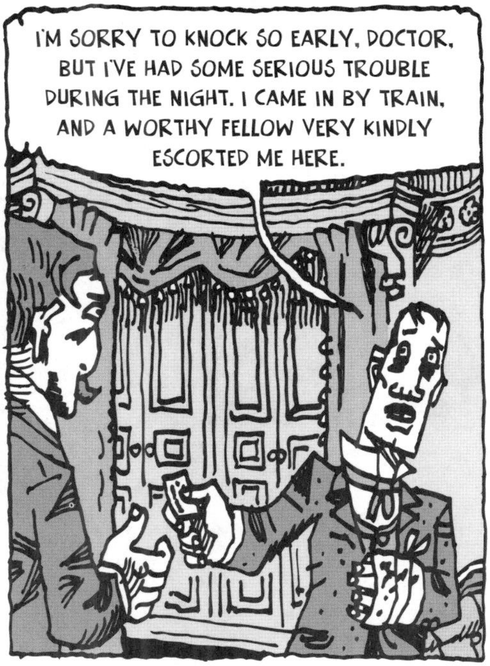
I'M SORRY TO KNOCK SO EARLY, DOCTOR, BUT I'VE HAD SOME SERIOUS TROUBLE DURING THE NIGHT. I CAME IN BY TRAIN, AND A WORTHY FELLOW VERY KINDLY ESCORTED ME HERE.

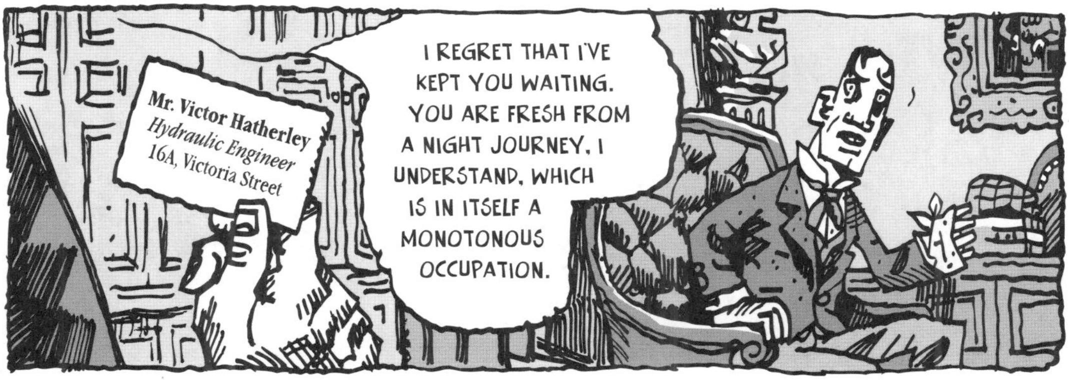
Mr. Victor Hatherley
Hydraulic Engineer
16A, Victoria Street
I REGRET THAT I'VE KEPT YOU WAITING. YOU ARE FRESH FROM A NIGHT JOURNEY, I UNDERSTAND, WHICH IS IN ITSELF A MONOTONOUS OCCUPATION.

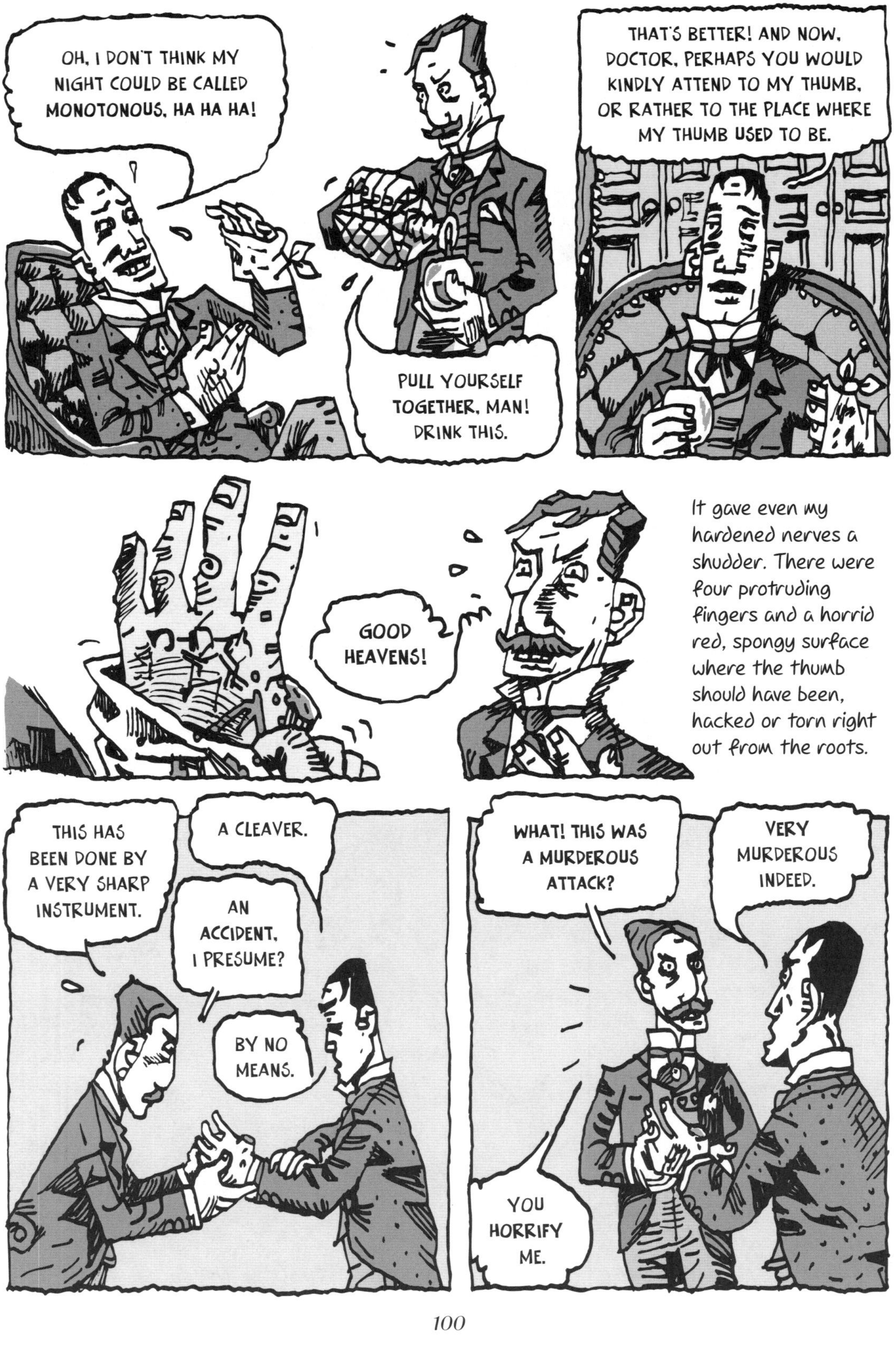
OH, I DON'T THINK MY NIGHT COULD BE CALLED MONOTONOUS, HA HA HA!
PULL YOURSELF TOGETHER, MAN! DRINK THIS.
THAT'S BETTER! AND NOW, DOCTOR, PERHAPS YOU WOULD KINDLY ATTEND TO MY THUMB, OR RATHER TO THE PLACE WHERE MY THUMB USED TO BE.
GOOD HEAVENS!
It gave even my hardened nerves a shudder. There were four protruding fingers and a horrid red, spongy surface where the thumb should have been, hacked or torn right out from the roots.
THIS HAS BEEN DONE BY A VERY SHARP INSTRUMENT.
A CLEAVER.
AN ACCIDENT, I PRESUME?
BY NO MEANS.
WHAT! THIS WAS A MURDEROUS ATTACK?
VERY MURDEROUS INDEED.
YOU HORRIFY ME.

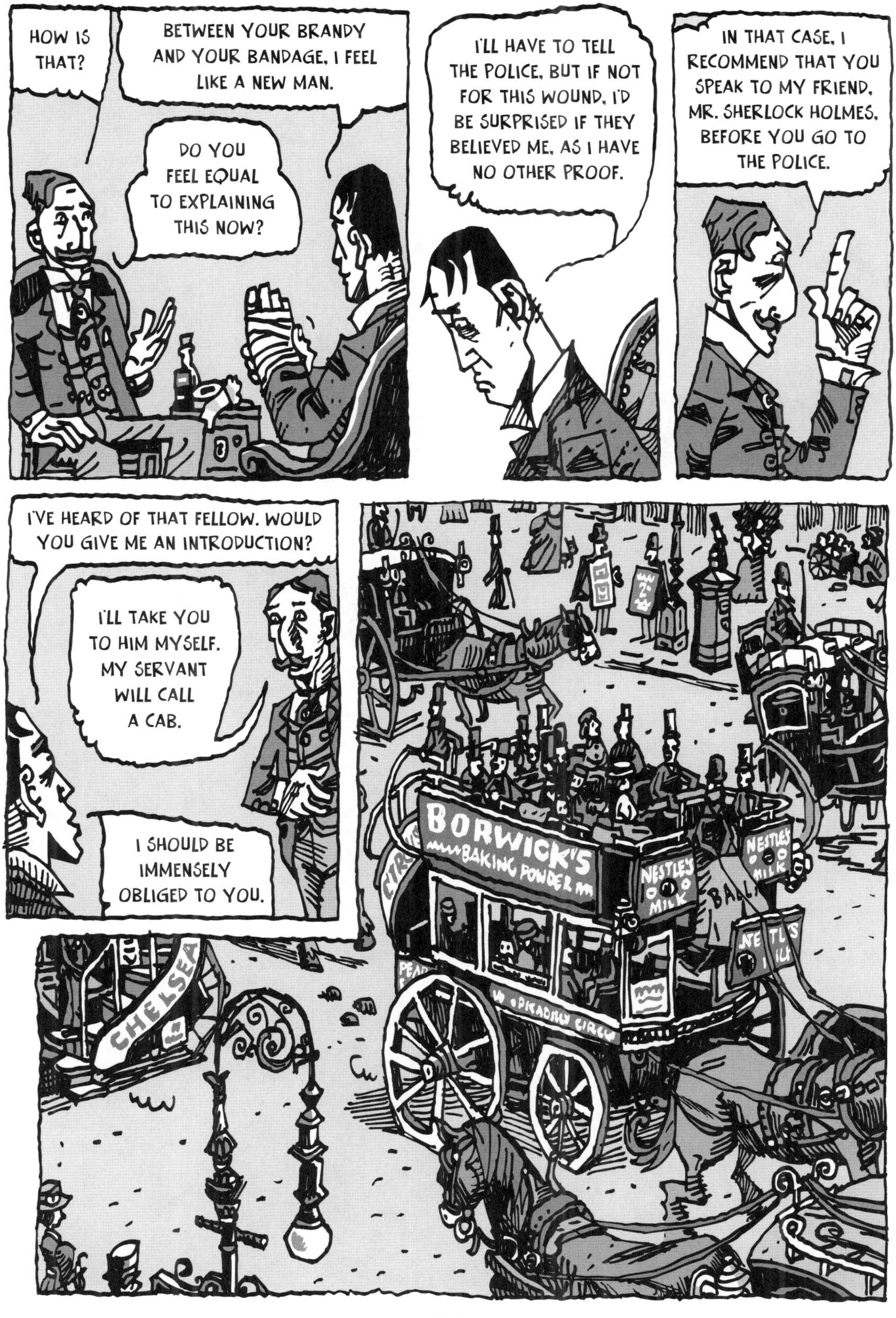
HOW IS THAT?
BETWEEN YOUR BRANDY AND YOUR BANDAGE, I FEEL LIKE A NEW MAN.
DO YOU FEEL EQUAL TO EXPLAINING THIS NOW?
I'LL HAVE TO TELL THE POLICE, BUT IF NOT FOR THIS WOUND, I'D BE SURPRISED IF THEY BELIEVED ME, AS I HAVE NO OTHER PROOF.
IN THAT CASE, I RECOMMEND THAT YOU SPEAK TO MY FRIEND, MR. SHERLOCK HOLMES, BEFORE YOU GO TO THE POLICE.
I'VE HEARD OF THAT FELLOW. WOULD YOU GIVE ME AN INTRODUCTION?
I'LL TAKE YOU TO HIM MYSELF. MY SERVANT WILL CALL A CAB.
I SHOULD BE IMMENSELY OBLIGED TO YOU.
BORWICK'S
BAKING POWDER
CHELSEA

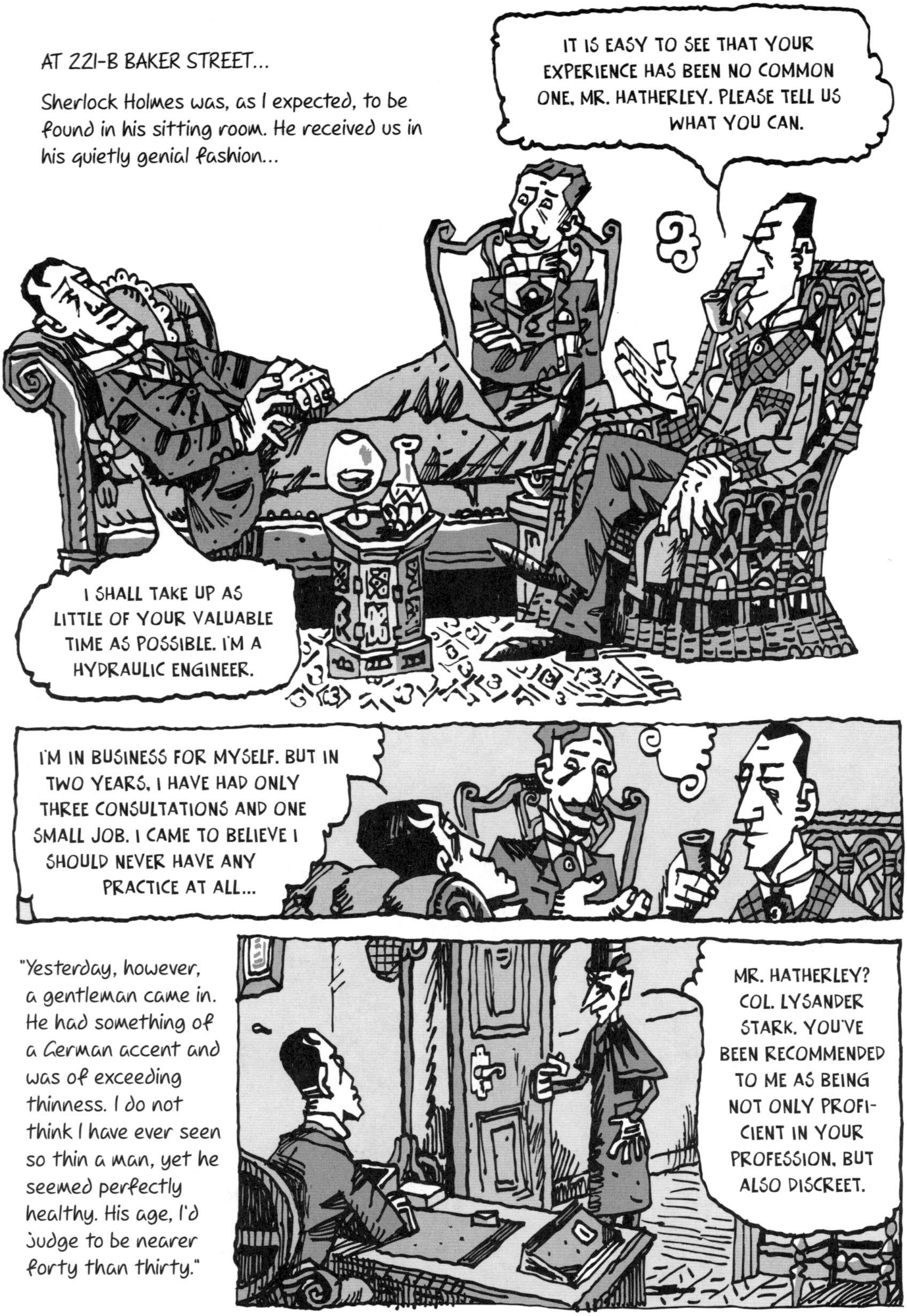
AT 221-B BAKER STREET...
Sherlock Holmes was, as I expected, to be found in his sitting room. He received us in his quietly genial fashion...
IT IS EASY TO SEE THAT YOUR EXPERIENCE HAS BEEN NO COMMON ONE, MR. HATHERLEY. PLEASE TELL US WHAT YOU CAN.
I SHALL TAKE UP AS LITTLE OF YOUR VALUABLE TIME AS POSSIBLE. I'M A HYDRAULIC ENGINEER.
I'M IN BUSINESS FOR MYSELF. BUT IN TWO YEARS, I HAVE HAD ONLY THREE CONSULTATIONS AND ONE SMALL JOB. I CAME TO BELIEVE I SHOULD NEVER HAVE ANY PRACTICE AT ALL...
"Yesterday, however, a gentleman came in. He had something of a German accent and was of exceeding thinness. I do not think I have ever seen so thin a man, yet he seemed perfectly healthy. His age, I'd judge to be nearer forty than thirty."
MR. HATHERLEY? COL. LYSANDER STARK. YOU'VE BEEN RECOMMENDED TO ME AS BEING NOT ONLY PROFI-CIENT IN YOUR PROFESSION, BUT ALSO DISCREET.

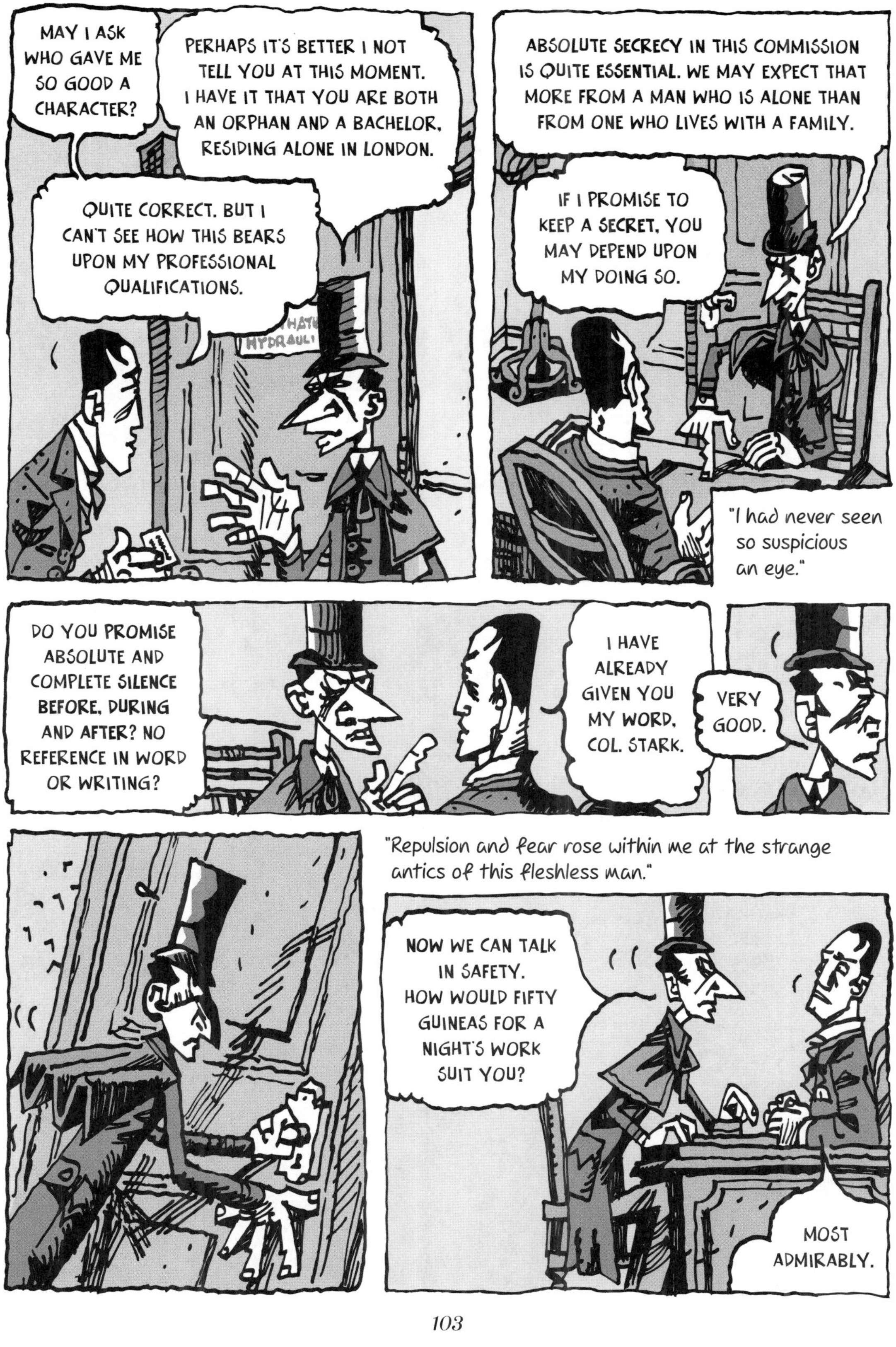
MAY I ASK WHO GAVE ME SO GOOD A CHARACTER?
PERHAPS IT'S BETTER I NOT TELL YOU AT THIS MOMENT. I HAVE IT THAT YOU ARE BOTH AN ORPHAN AND A BACHELOR, RESIDING ALONE IN LONDON.
QUITE CORRECT. BUT I CAN'T SEE HOW THIS BEARS UPON MY PROFESSIONAL QUALIFICATIONS.
ABSOLUTE SECRECY IN THIS COMMISSION IS QUITE ESSENTIAL. WE MAY EXPECT THAT MORE FROM A MAN WHO IS ALONE THAN FROM ONE WHO LIVES WITH A FAMILY.
IF I PROMISE TO KEEP A SECRET, YOU MAY DEPEND UPON MY DOING SO.
"I had never seen so suspicious an eye."
DO YOU PROMISE ABSOLUTE AND COMPLETE SILENCE BEFORE, DURING AND AFTER? NO REFERENCE IN WORD OR WRITING?
I HAVE ALREADY GIVEN YOU MY WORD, COL. STARK.
VERY GOOD.
"Repulsion and fear rose within me at the strange antics of this fleshless man."
NOW WE CAN TALK IN SAFETY. HOW WOULD FIFTY GUINEAS FOR A NIGHT'S WORK SUIT YOU?
MOST ADMIRABLY.

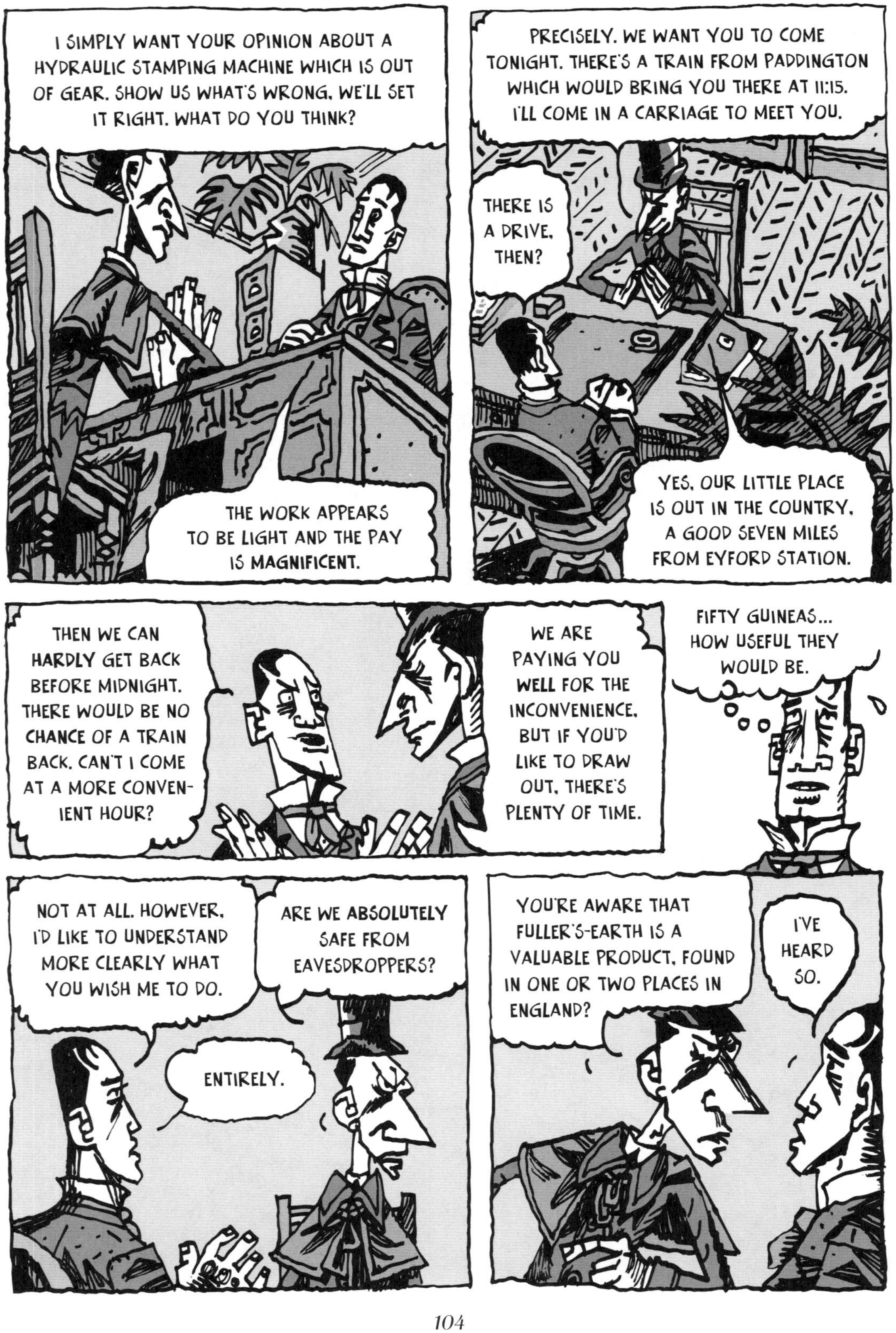
I SIMPLY WANT YOUR OPINION ABOUT A HYDRAULIC STAMPING MACHINE WHICH IS OUT OF GEAR. SHOW US WHAT'S WRONG, WE'LL SET IT RIGHT. WHAT DO YOU THINK?
THE WORK APPEARS TO BE LIGHT AND THE PAY IS **MAGNIFICENT.**
PRECISELY. WE WANT YOU TO COME TONIGHT. THERE'S A TRAIN FROM PADDINGTON WHICH WOULD BRING YOU THERE AT 11:15. I'LL COME IN A CARRIAGE TO MEET YOU.
THERE IS A DRIVE, THEN?
YES, OUR LITTLE PLACE IS OUT IN THE COUNTRY, A GOOD SEVEN MILES FROM EYFORD STATION.
THEN WE CAN **HARDLY** GET BACK BEFORE MIDNIGHT. THERE WOULD BE NO **CHANCE** OF A TRAIN BACK. CAN'T I COME AT A MORE CONVENIENT HOUR?
WE ARE PAYING YOU **WELL** FOR THE INCONVENIENCE, BUT IF YOU'D LIKE TO DRAW OUT, THERE'S PLENTY OF TIME.
FIFTY GUINEAS... HOW USEFUL THEY WOULD BE.
NOT AT ALL. HOWEVER, I'D LIKE TO UNDERSTAND MORE CLEARLY WHAT YOU WISH ME TO DO.
ARE WE **ABSOLUTELY** SAFE FROM EAVESDROPPERS?
ENTIRELY.
YOU'RE AWARE THAT FULLER'S-EARTH IS A VALUABLE PRODUCT, FOUND IN ONE OR TWO PLACES IN ENGLAND?
I'VE HEARD SO.

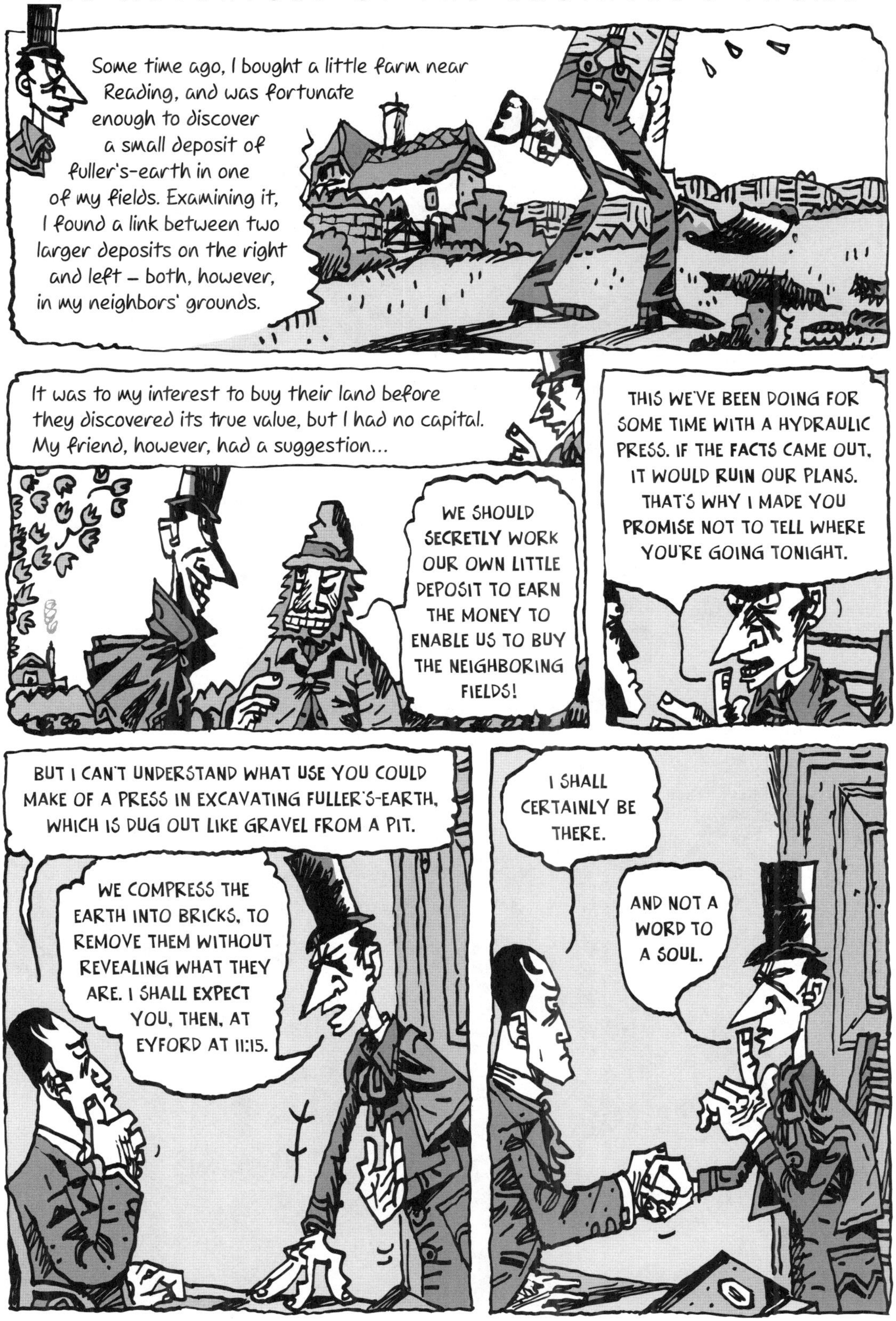
Some time ago, I bought a little farm near Reading, and was fortunate enough to discover a small deposit of fuller's-earth in one of my fields. Examining it, I found a link between two larger deposits on the right and left – both, however, in my neighbors' grounds.
It was to my interest to buy their land before they discovered its true value, but I had no capital. My friend, however, had a suggestion...
WE SHOULD SECRETLY WORK OUR OWN LITTLE DEPOSIT TO EARN THE MONEY TO ENABLE US TO BUY THE NEIGHBORING FIELDS!
THIS WE'VE BEEN DOING FOR SOME TIME WITH A HYDRAULIC PRESS. IF THE FACTS CAME OUT, IT WOULD RUIN OUR PLANS. THAT'S WHY I MADE YOU PROMISE NOT TO TELL WHERE YOU'RE GOING TONIGHT.
BUT I CAN'T UNDERSTAND WHAT USE YOU COULD MAKE OF A PRESS IN EXCAVATING FULLER'S-EARTH, WHICH IS DUG OUT LIKE GRAVEL FROM A PIT.
WE COMPRESS THE EARTH INTO BRICKS, TO REMOVE THEM WITHOUT REVEALING WHAT THEY ARE. I SHALL EXPECT YOU, THEN, AT EYFORD AT 11:15.
I SHALL CERTAINLY BE THERE.
AND NOT A WORD TO A SOUL.

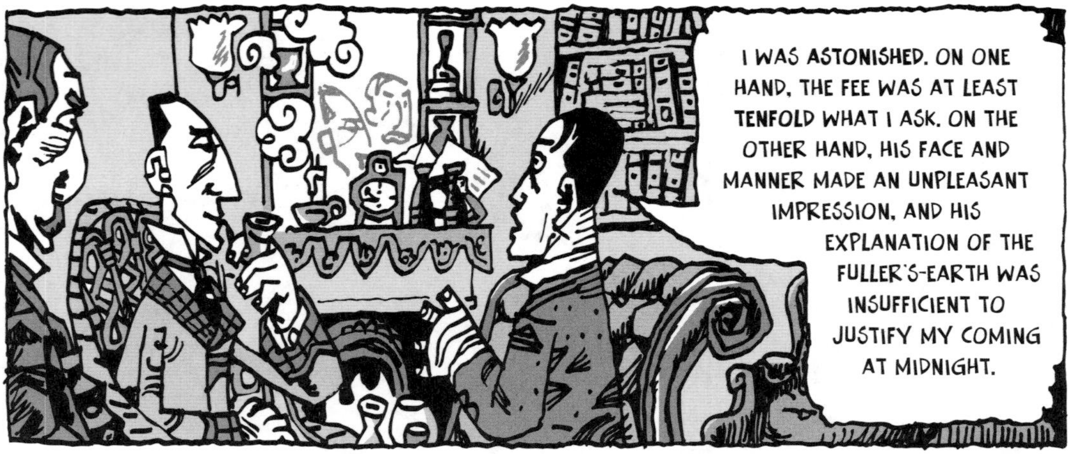
I WAS ASTONISHED. ON ONE HAND, THE FEE WAS AT LEAST TENFOLD WHAT I ASK. ON THE OTHER HAND, HIS FACE AND MANNER MADE AN UNPLEASANT IMPRESSION, AND HIS EXPLANATION OF THE FULLER'S-EARTH WAS INSUFFICIENT TO JUSTIFY MY COMING AT MIDNIGHT.
305

"However, I threw all fears to the winds. I was in time for the last train to Eyford. I was the only passenger there at 11 o'clock."

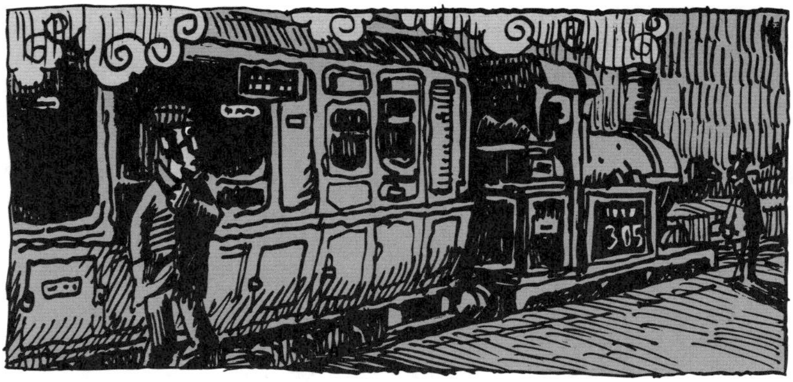

"As I passed through the gate, however, I found my acquaintance of the morning waiting in the shadow on the other side."

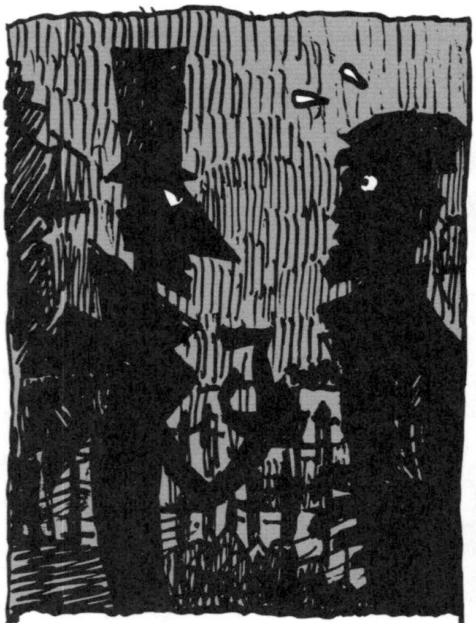
"Without a word, he grasped my arm and hurried me into a carriage. He drew up the windows on either side, and away we went quickly."

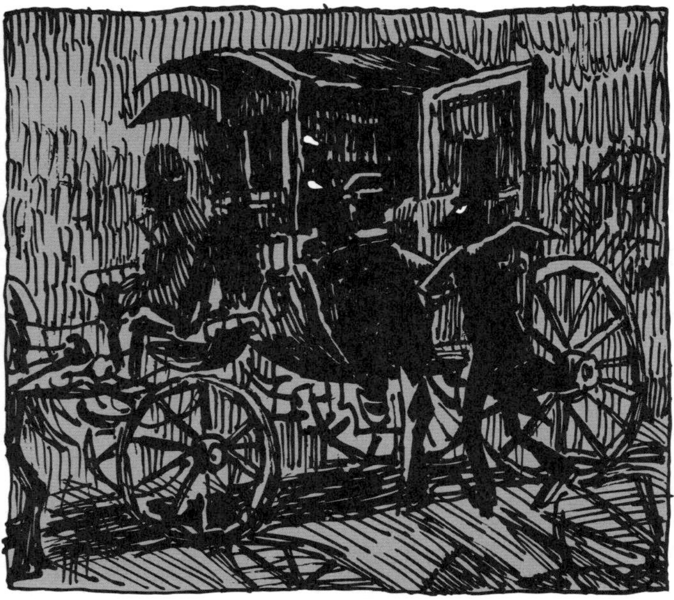

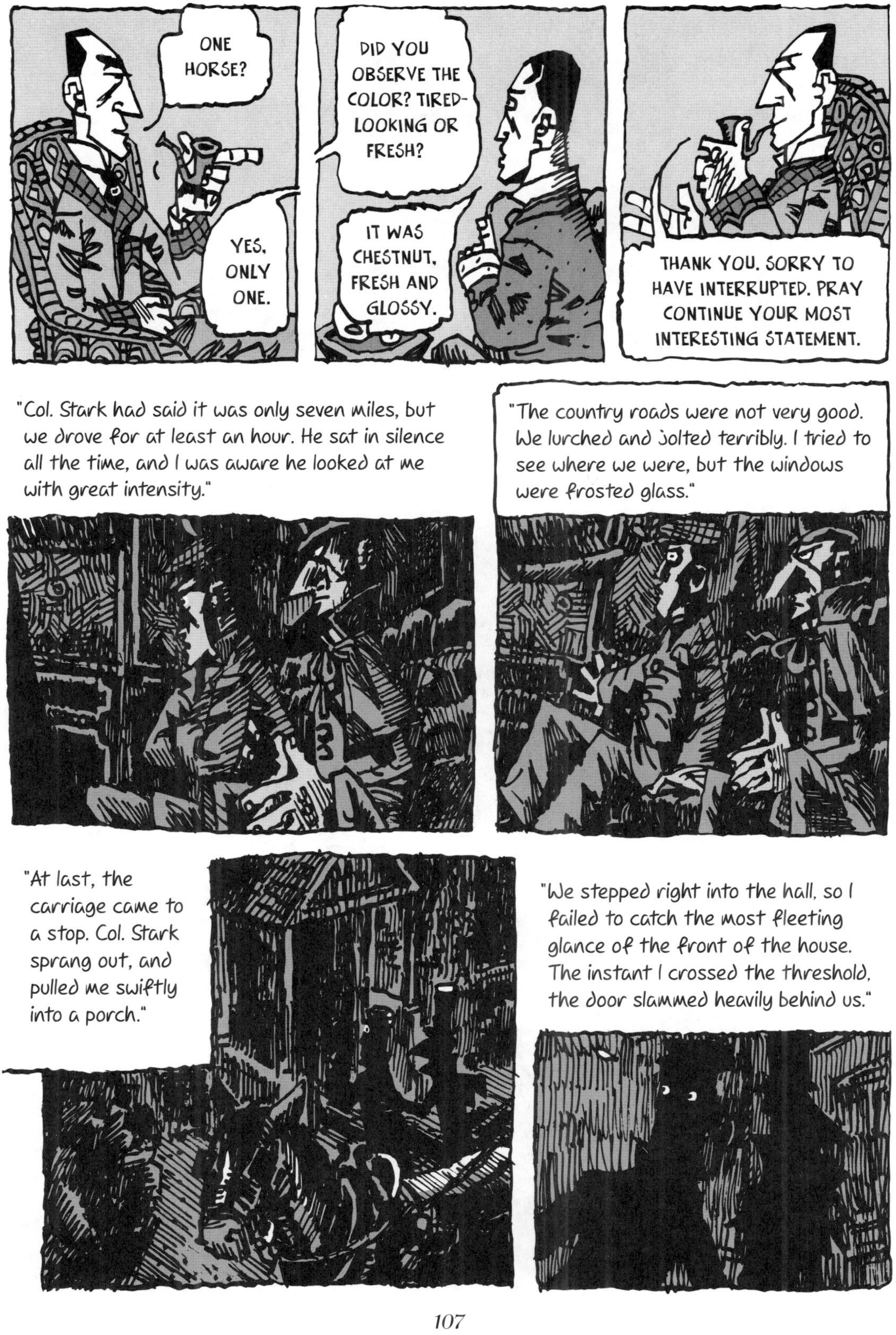
ONE HORSE?
YES, ONLY ONE.
DID YOU OBSERVE THE COLOR? TIRED-LOOKING OR FRESH?
IT WAS CHESTNUT. FRESH AND GLOSSY.
THANK YOU. SORRY TO HAVE INTERRUPTED. PRAY CONTINUE YOUR MOST INTERESTING STATEMENT.
"Col. Stark had said it was only seven miles, but we drove for at least an hour. He sat in silence all the time, and I was aware he looked at me with great intensity."
"The country roads were not very good. We lurched and jolted terribly. I tried to see where we were, but the windows were frosted glass."
"At last, the carriage came to a stop. Col. Stark sprang out, and pulled me swiftly into a porch."
"We stepped right into the hall, so I failed to catch the most fleeting glance of the front of the house. The instant I crossed the threshold, the door slammed heavily behind us."

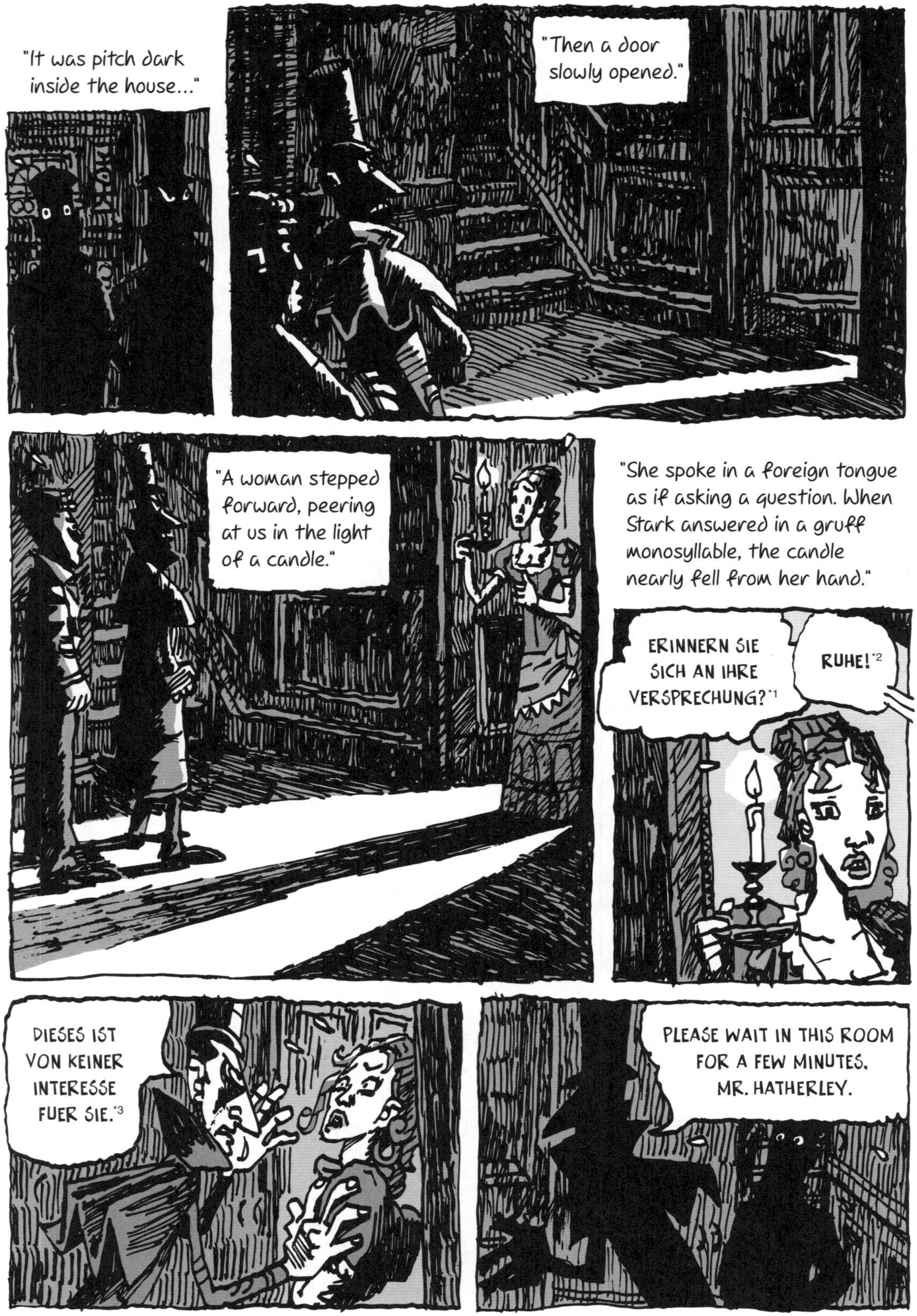
"It was pitch dark inside the house..."
"Then a door slowly opened."
"A woman stepped forward, peering at us in the light of a candle."
"She spoke in a foreign tongue as if asking a question. When Stark answered in a gruff monosyllable, the candle nearly fell from her hand."
ERINNERN SIE SICH AN IHRE VERSPRECHUNG?*1
RUHE!*2
DIESES IST VON KEINER INTERESSE FUER SIE.*3
PLEASE WAIT IN THIS ROOM FOR A FEW MINUTES, MR. HATHERLEY.

*1 – You remember your promise?
*2 – Quiet!
*3 – This is of no concern to you.

"It was a small, plainly furnished room, with a table on which several German books were scattered."

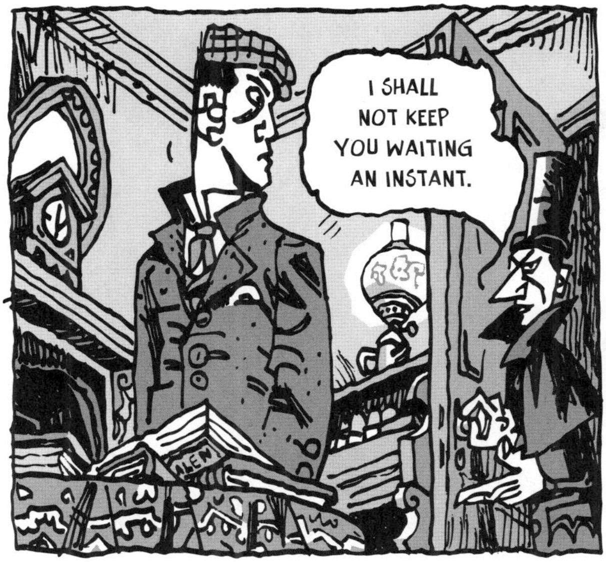
I SHALL NOT KEEP YOU WAITING AN INSTANT.

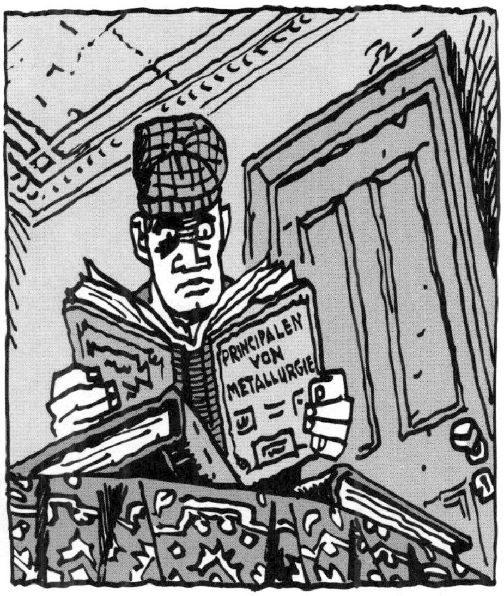
PRINCIPALEN VON METALLURGIE

"Two appeared to be treatises on science, and the others were volumes of poetry."

"A vague feeling of uneasiness began to steal over me."

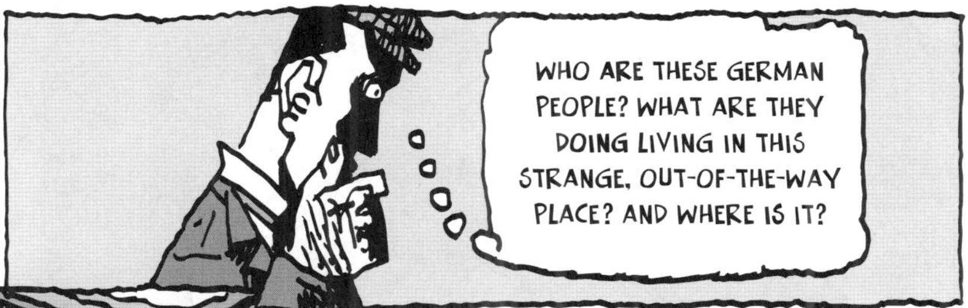
WHO ARE THESE GERMAN PEOPLE? WHAT ARE THEY DOING LIVING IN THIS STRANGE, OUT-OF-THE-WAY PLACE? AND WHERE IS IT?

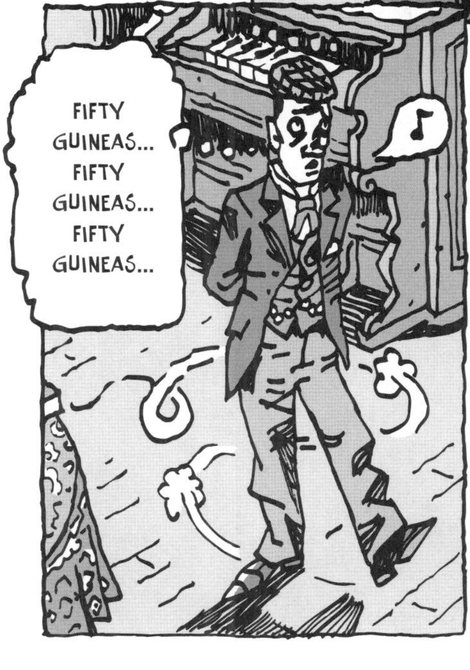
FIFTY GUINEAS... FIFTY GUINEAS... FIFTY GUINEAS...

"Suddenly, the door swung open. It was the woman. I could see she was sick with fear, and the sight sent a chill to my own heart."

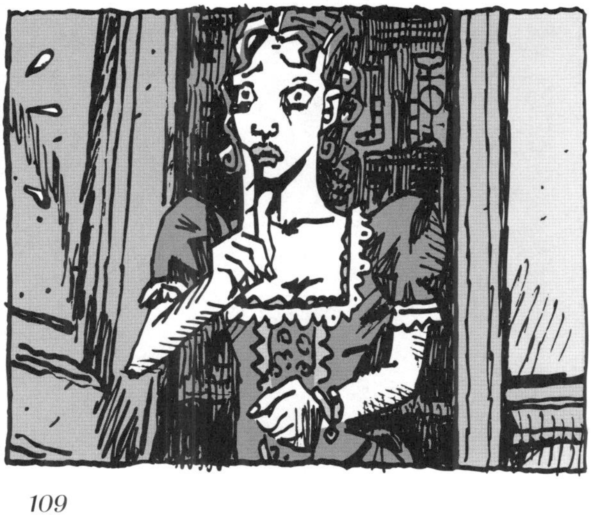

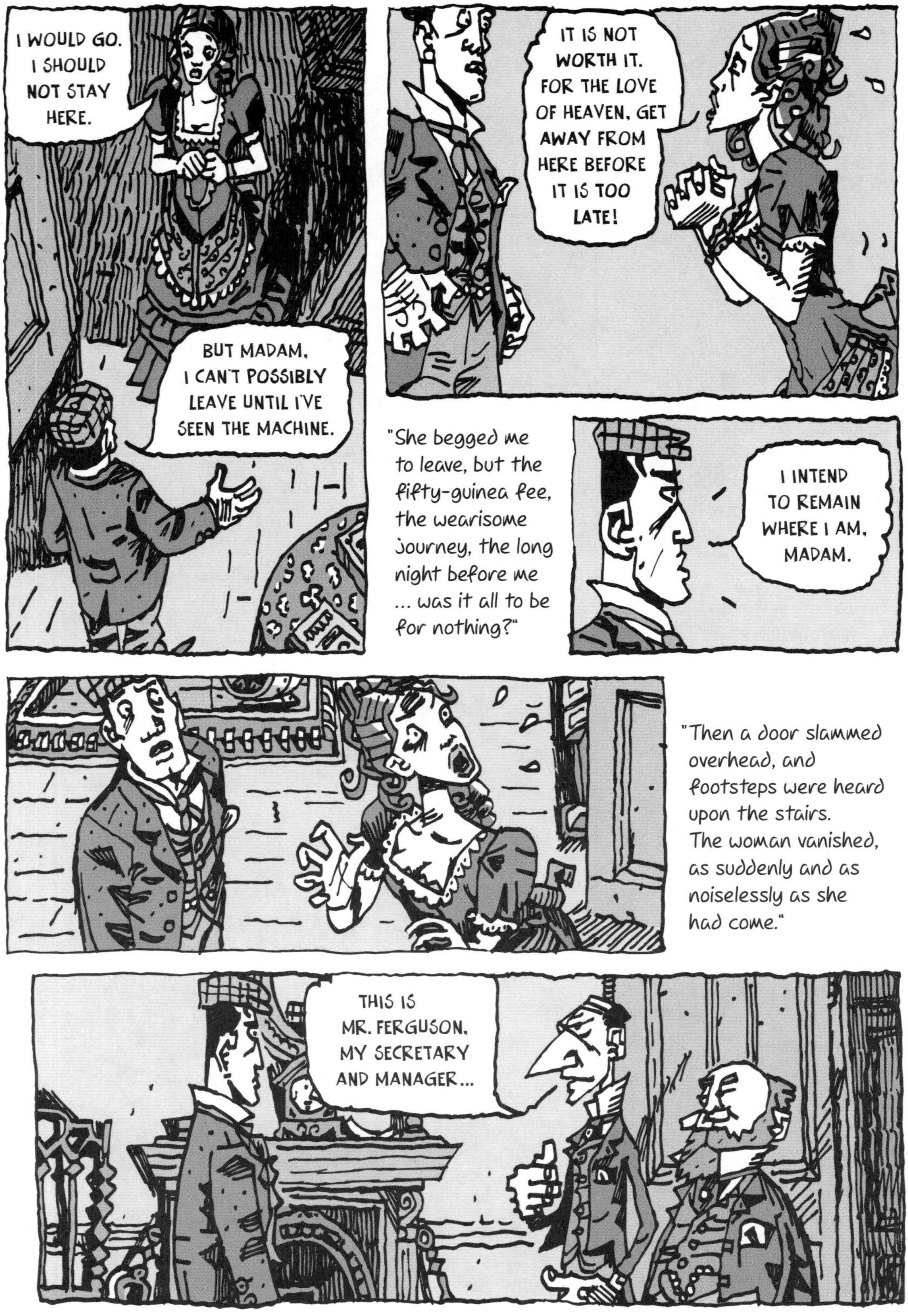
I WOULD GO. I SHOULD NOT STAY HERE.
BUT MADAM, I CAN'T POSSIBLY LEAVE UNTIL I'VE SEEN THE MACHINE.
IT IS NOT WORTH IT. FOR THE LOVE OF HEAVEN, GET AWAY FROM HERE BEFORE IT IS TOO LATE!
"She begged me to leave, but the fifty-guinea fee, the wearisome journey, the long night before me ... was it all to be for nothing?"
I INTEND TO REMAIN WHERE I AM, MADAM.
"Then a door slammed overhead, and footsteps were heard upon the stairs. The woman vanished, as suddenly and as noiselessly as she had come."
THIS IS MR. FERGUSON, MY SECRETARY AND MANAGER...

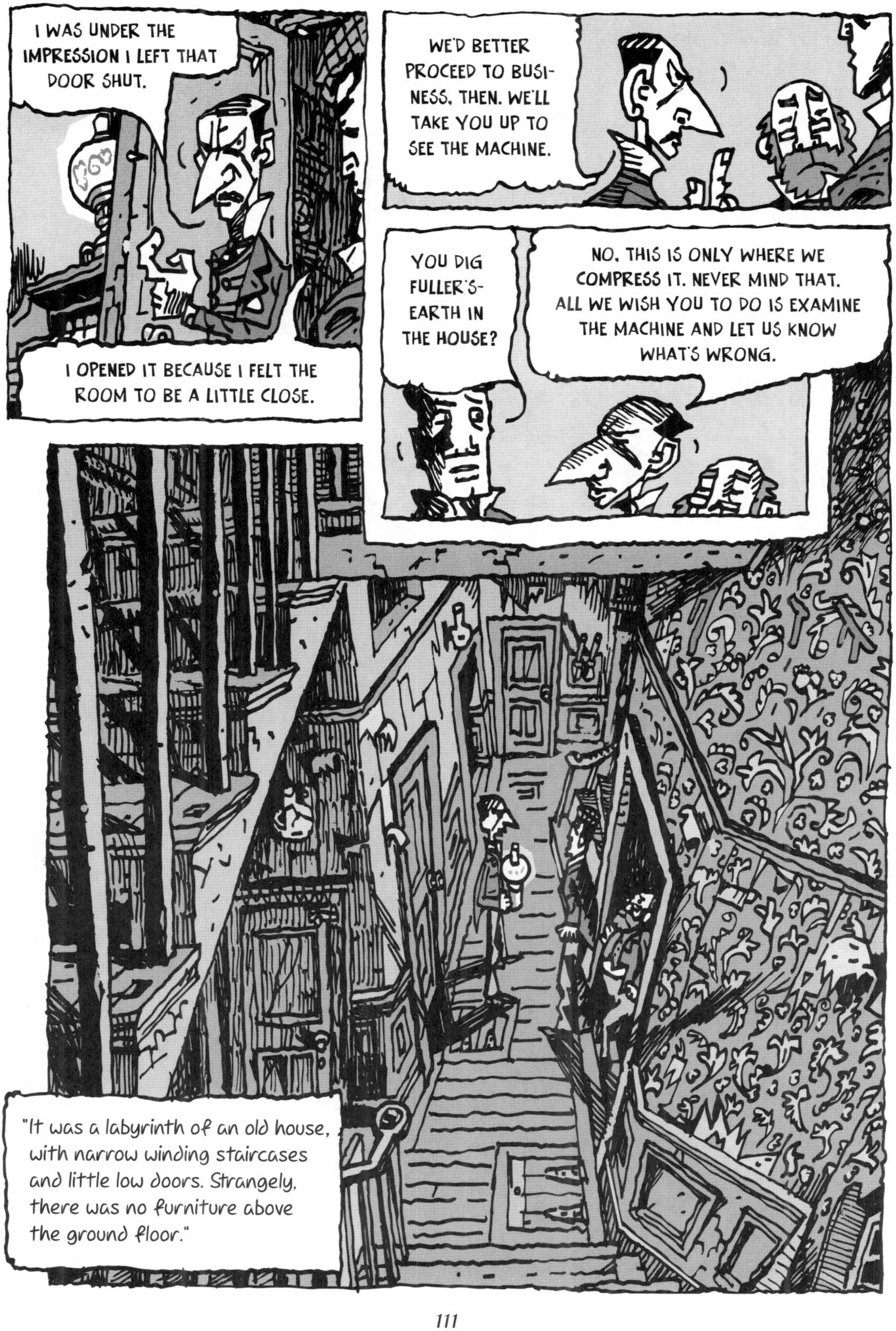
I WAS UNDER THE IMPRESSION I LEFT THAT DOOR SHUT.
I OPENED IT BECAUSE I FELT THE ROOM TO BE A LITTLE CLOSE.
WE'D BETTER PROCEED TO BUSINESS, THEN. WE'LL TAKE YOU UP TO SEE THE MACHINE.
YOU DIG FULLER'S-EARTH IN THE HOUSE?
NO, THIS IS ONLY WHERE WE COMPRESS IT. NEVER MIND THAT. ALL WE WISH YOU TO DO IS EXAMINE THE MACHINE AND LET US KNOW WHAT'S WRONG.
"It was a labyrinth of an old house, with narrow winding staircases and little low doors. Strangely, there was no furniture above the ground floor."

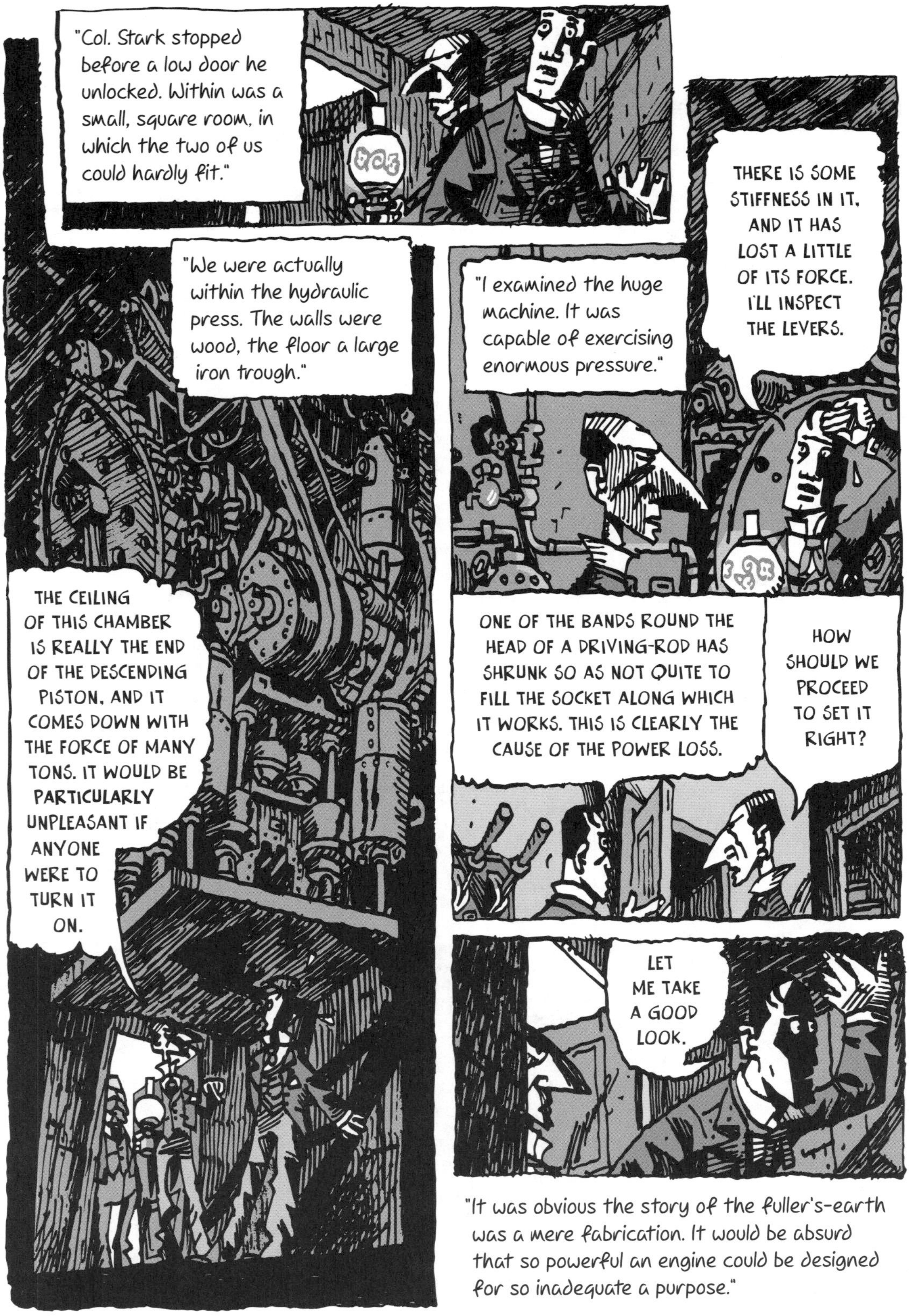
"Col. Stark stopped before a low door he unlocked. Within was a small, square room, in which the two of us could hardly fit."
THERE IS SOME STIFFNESS IN IT, AND IT HAS LOST A LITTLE OF ITS FORCE. I'LL INSPECT THE LEVERS.
"We were actually within the hydraulic press. The walls were wood, the floor a large iron trough."
"I examined the huge machine. It was capable of exercising enormous pressure."
THE CEILING OF THIS CHAMBER IS REALLY THE END OF THE DESCENDING PISTON, AND IT COMES DOWN WITH THE FORCE OF MANY TONS. IT WOULD BE PARTICULARLY UNPLEASANT IF ANYONE WERE TO TURN IT ON.
ONE OF THE BANDS ROUND THE HEAD OF A DRIVING-ROD HAS SHRUNK SO AS NOT QUITE TO FILL THE SOCKET ALONG WHICH IT WORKS. THIS IS CLEARLY THE CAUSE OF THE POWER LOSS.
HOW SHOULD WE PROCEED TO SET IT RIGHT?
LET ME TAKE A GOOD LOOK.

"It was obvious the story of the fuller's-earth was a mere fabrication. It would be absurd that so powerful an engine could be designed for so inadequate a purpose."

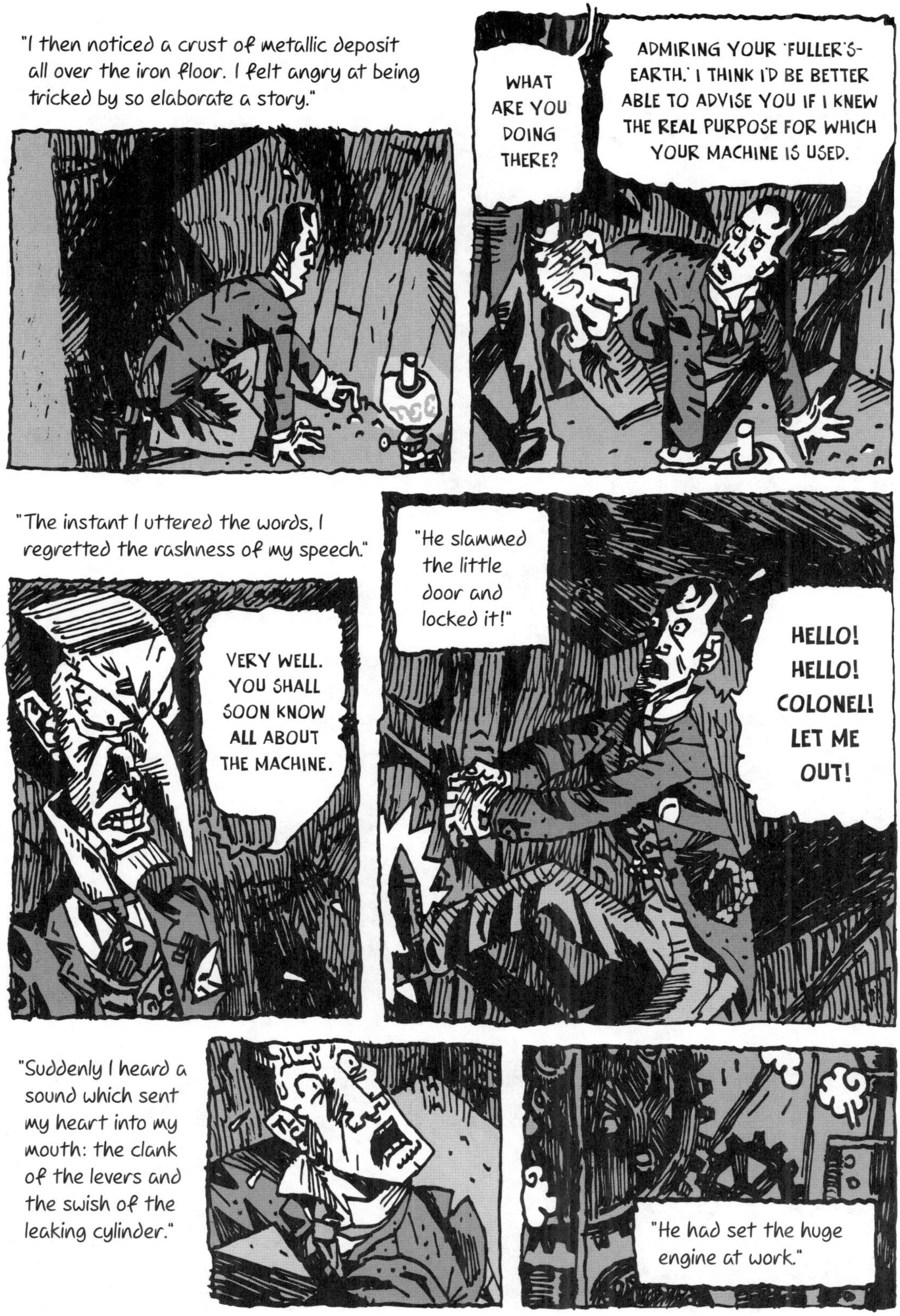
"I then noticed a crust of metallic deposit all over the iron floor. I felt angry at being tricked by so elaborate a story."
WHAT ARE YOU DOING THERE?
ADMIRING YOUR 'FULLER'S-EARTH.' I THINK I'D BE BETTER ABLE TO ADVISE YOU IF I KNEW THE REAL PURPOSE FOR WHICH YOUR MACHINE IS USED.
"The instant I uttered the words, I regretted the rashness of my speech."
VERY WELL. YOU SHALL SOON KNOW ALL ABOUT THE MACHINE.
"He slammed the little door and locked it!"
HELLO! HELLO! COLONEL! LET ME OUT!
"Suddenly I heard a sound which sent my heart into my mouth: the clank of the levers and the swish of the leaking cylinder."
"He had set the huge engine at work."

"The black ceiling was coming down slowly, but with a force to grind me into a shapeless pulp."

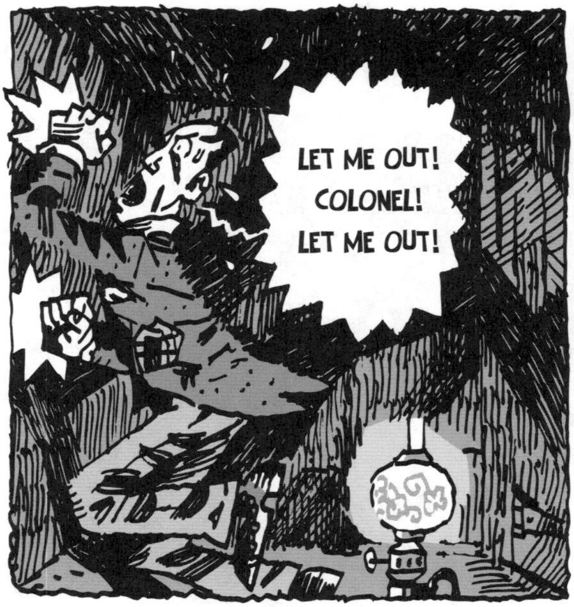
LET ME OUT! COLONEL! LET ME OUT!

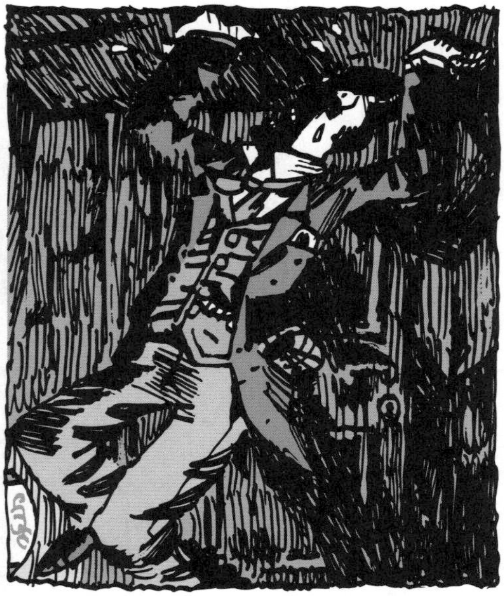

"Already I was unable to stand erect, when my eye caught something which brought a gush of hope to my heart."

"I saw a thin line of light between the boards, which broadened as a small panel was slowly opened."

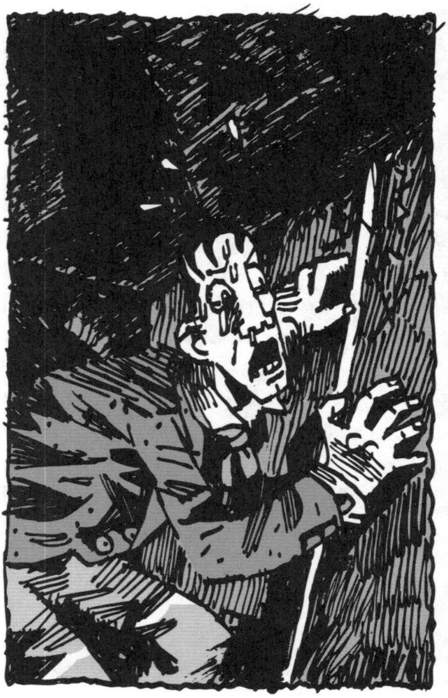

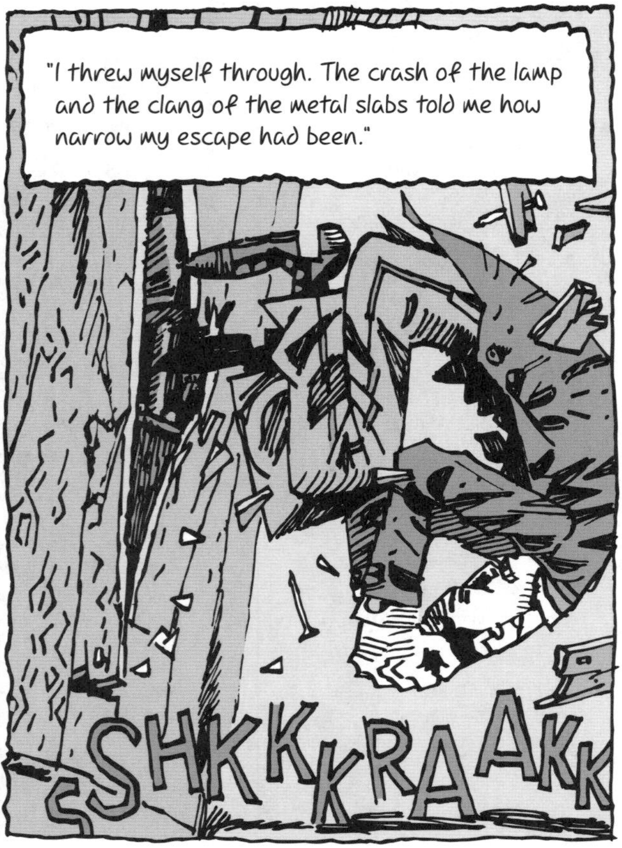
"I threw myself through. The crash of the lamp and the clang of the metal slabs told me how narrow my escape had been."
SHKKKRAAKK

"Half-fainted, I was recalled by a frantic plucking at my wrist. It was the woman whose warning I had so foolishly rejected."

COME! THEY WILL BE HERE IN A MOMENT. OH, DO NOT WASTE THE SO-PRECIOUS TIME, BUT COME!

"This time, I did not scorn her advice."

"Just as we reached another passage, we heard the sound of running feet and the shouting of two voices."

WO IST ER?*1

DIE TREPPE!*2

IT IS YOUR ONLY CHANCE! IT IS HIGH, BUT YOU CAN JUMP IT!

"A light sprang into view at the end of the passage, and I saw Col. Stark rushing forward with a butcher's cleaver."

*1 – Where is he?
*2 – The stairs!

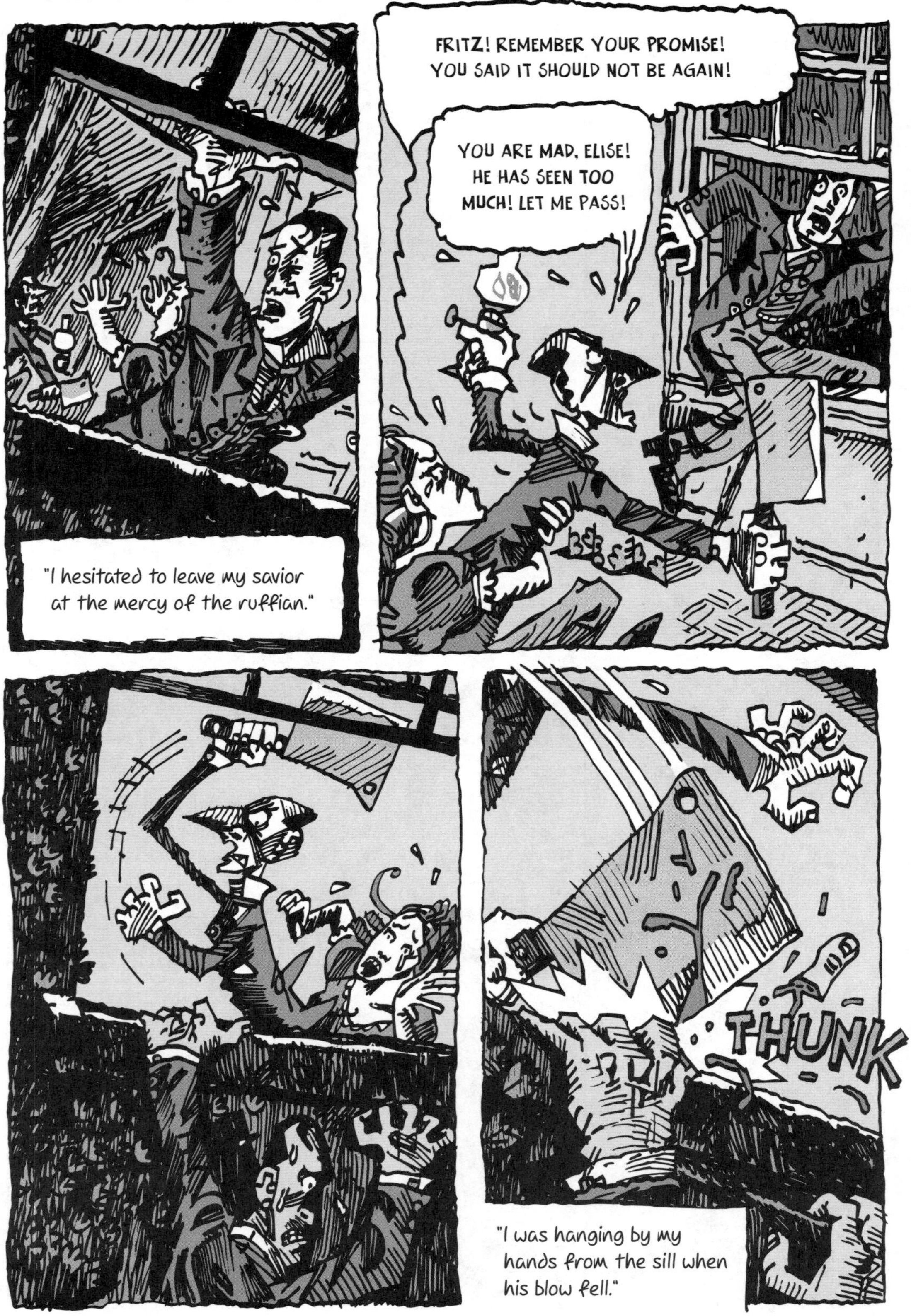
"I hesitated to leave my savior at the mercy of the ruffian."
FRITZ! REMEMBER YOUR PROMISE! YOU SAID IT SHOULD NOT BE AGAIN!
YOU ARE MAD, ELISE! HE HAS SEEN TOO MUCH! LET ME PASS!
THUNK
"I was hanging by my hands from the sill when his blow fell."

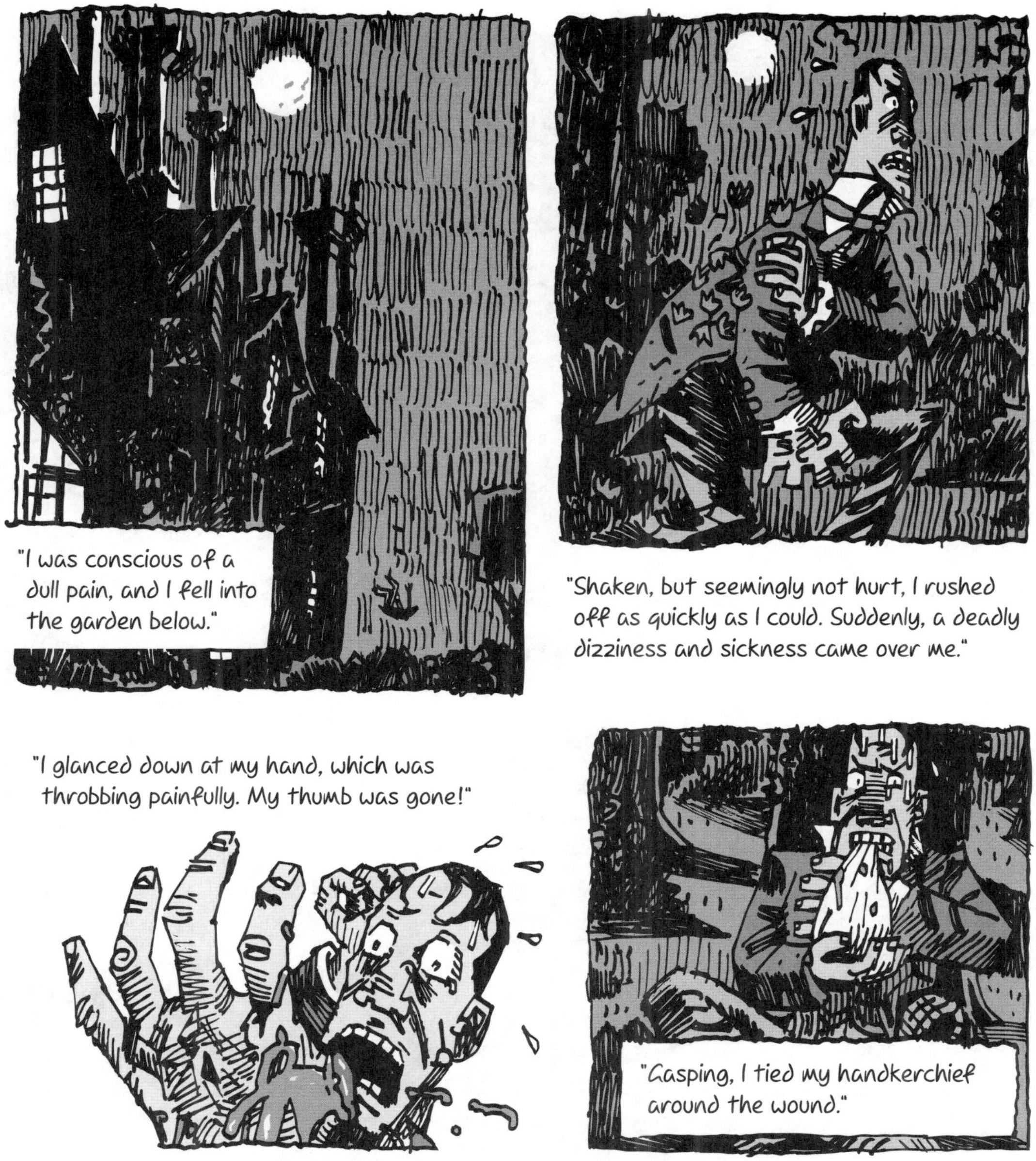
"I was conscious of a dull pain, and I fell into the garden below."
"Shaken, but seemingly not hurt, I rushed off as quickly as I could. Suddenly, a deadly dizziness and sickness came over me."
"I glanced down at my hand, which was throbbing painfully. My thumb was gone!"
"Gasping, I tied my handkerchief around the wound."
"I stumbled on, but there came a sudden buzzing in my ears, and I fell in a dead faint among the rose bushes."

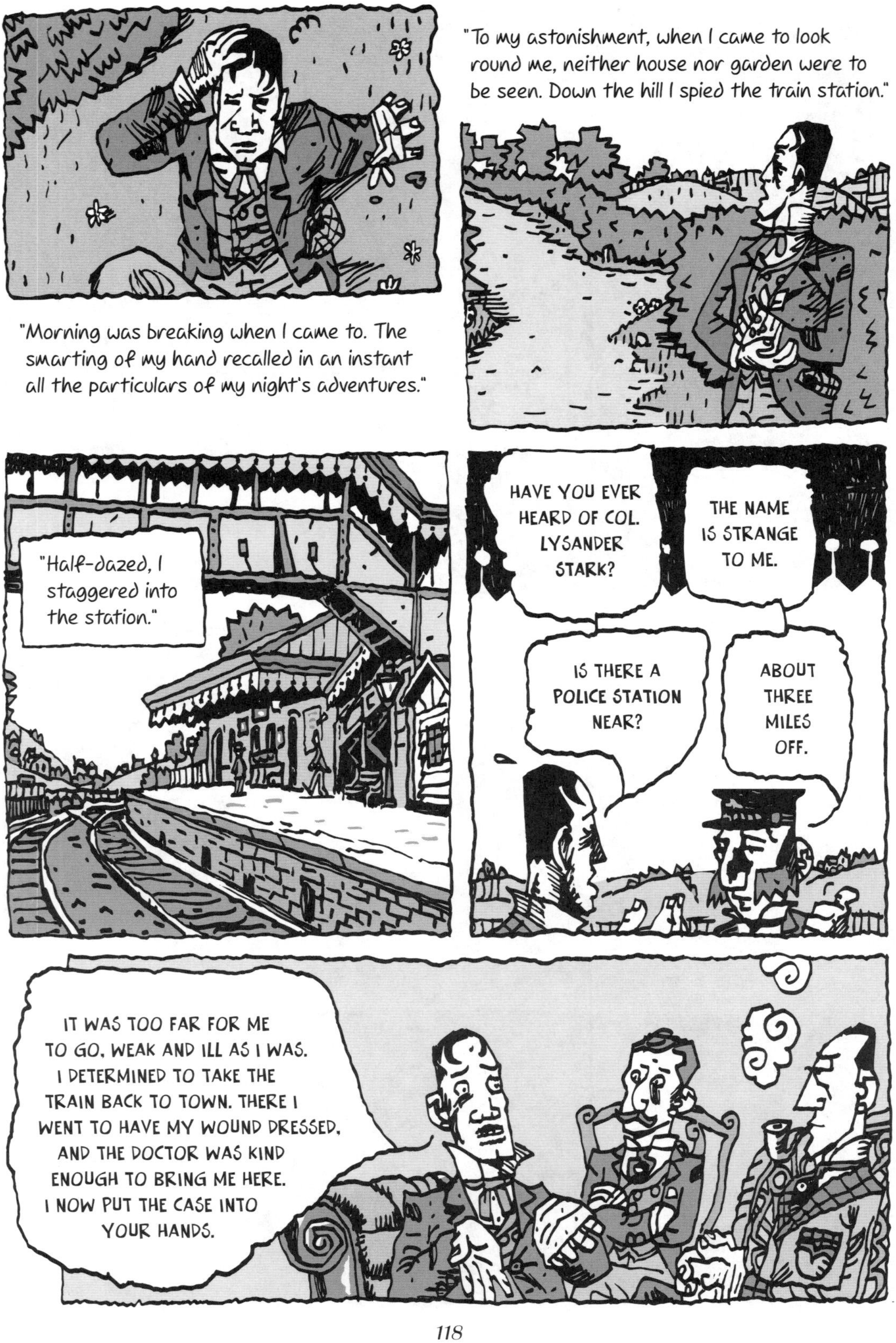
"Morning was breaking when I came to. The smarting of my hand recalled in an instant all the particulars of my night's adventures."
"To my astonishment, when I came to look round me, neither house nor garden were to be seen. Down the hill I spied the train station."
"Half-dazed, I staggered into the station."
HAVE YOU EVER HEARD OF COL. LYSANDER STARK?
THE NAME IS STRANGE TO ME.
IS THERE A POLICE STATION NEAR?
ABOUT THREE MILES OFF.
IT WAS TOO FAR FOR ME TO GO, WEAK AND ILL AS I WAS. I DETERMINED TO TAKE THE TRAIN BACK TO TOWN. THERE I WENT TO HAVE MY WOUND DRESSED, AND THE DOCTOR WAS KIND ENOUGH TO BRING ME HERE. I NOW PUT THE CASE INTO YOUR HANDS.

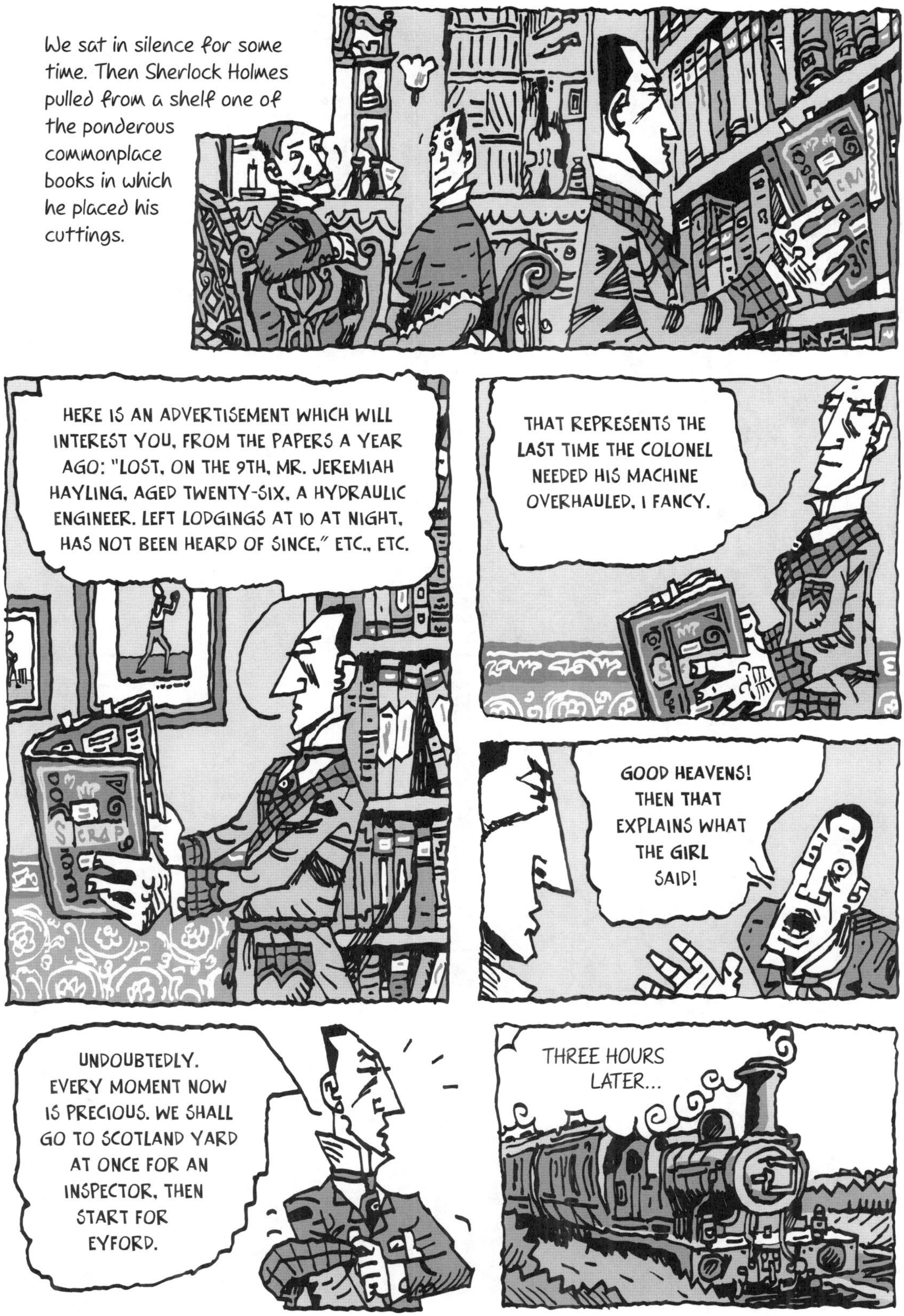
We sat in silence for some time. Then Sherlock Holmes pulled from a shelf one of the ponderous commonplace books in which he placed his cuttings.
HERE IS AN ADVERTISEMENT WHICH WILL INTEREST YOU, FROM THE PAPERS A YEAR AGO: "LOST, ON THE 9TH, MR. JEREMIAH HAYLING, AGED TWENTY-SIX, A HYDRAULIC ENGINEER. LEFT LODGINGS AT 10 AT NIGHT, HAS NOT BEEN HEARD OF SINCE," ETC., ETC.
THAT REPRESENTS THE LAST TIME THE COLONEL NEEDED HIS MACHINE OVERHAULED, I FANCY.
GOOD HEAVENS! THEN THAT EXPLAINS WHAT THE GIRL SAID!
UNDOUBTEDLY. EVERY MOMENT NOW IS PRECIOUS. WE SHALL GO TO SCOTLAND YARD AT ONCE FOR AN INSPECTOR, THEN START FOR EYFORD.
THREE HOURS LATER...

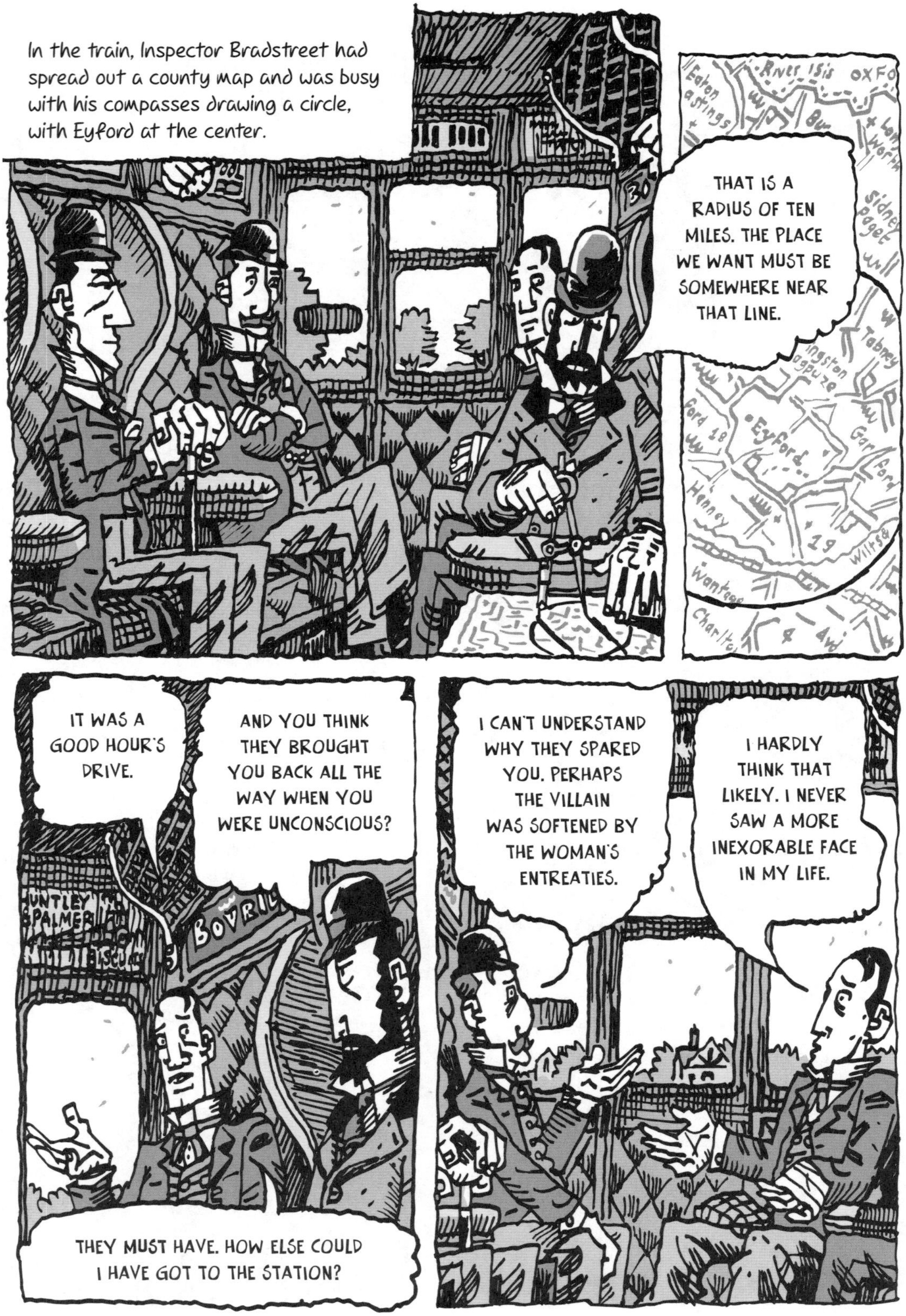
In the train, Inspector Bradstreet had spread out a county map and was busy with his compasses drawing a circle, with Eyford at the center.
THAT IS A RADIUS OF TEN MILES. THE PLACE WE WANT MUST BE SOMEWHERE NEAR THAT LINE.
Eyford
IT WAS A GOOD HOUR'S DRIVE.
AND YOU THINK THEY BROUGHT YOU BACK ALL THE WAY WHEN YOU WERE UNCONSCIOUS?
BOVRIL
THEY MUST HAVE. HOW ELSE COULD I HAVE GOT TO THE STATION?
I CAN'T UNDERSTAND WHY THEY SPARED YOU. PERHAPS THE VILLAIN WAS SOFTENED BY THE WOMAN'S ENTREATIES.
I HARDLY THINK THAT LIKELY. I NEVER SAW A MORE INEXORABLE FACE IN MY LIFE.

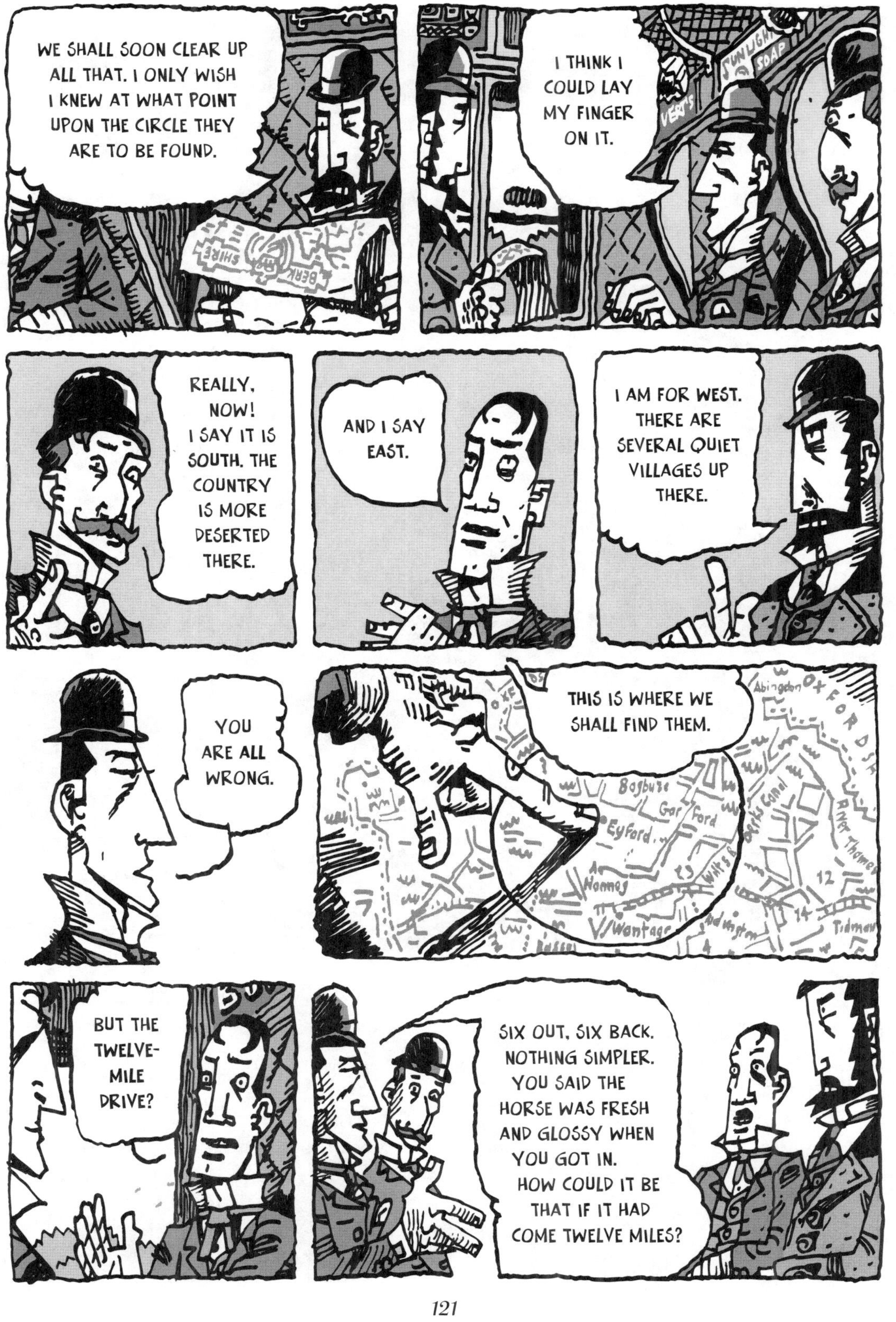
WE SHALL SOON CLEAR UP ALL THAT. I ONLY WISH I KNEW AT WHAT POINT UPON THE CIRCLE THEY ARE TO BE FOUND.
I THINK I COULD LAY MY FINGER ON IT.
REALLY, NOW! I SAY IT IS SOUTH. THE COUNTRY IS MORE DESERTED THERE.
AND I SAY EAST.
I AM FOR WEST. THERE ARE SEVERAL QUIET VILLAGES UP THERE.
YOU ARE ALL WRONG.
THIS IS WHERE WE SHALL FIND THEM.
Abingdon
Eyford
Wantage
BUT THE TWELVE-MILE DRIVE?
SIX OUT, SIX BACK. NOTHING SIMPLER. YOU SAID THE HORSE WAS FRESH AND GLOSSY WHEN YOU GOT IN. HOW COULD IT BE THAT IF IT HAD COME TWELVE MILES?

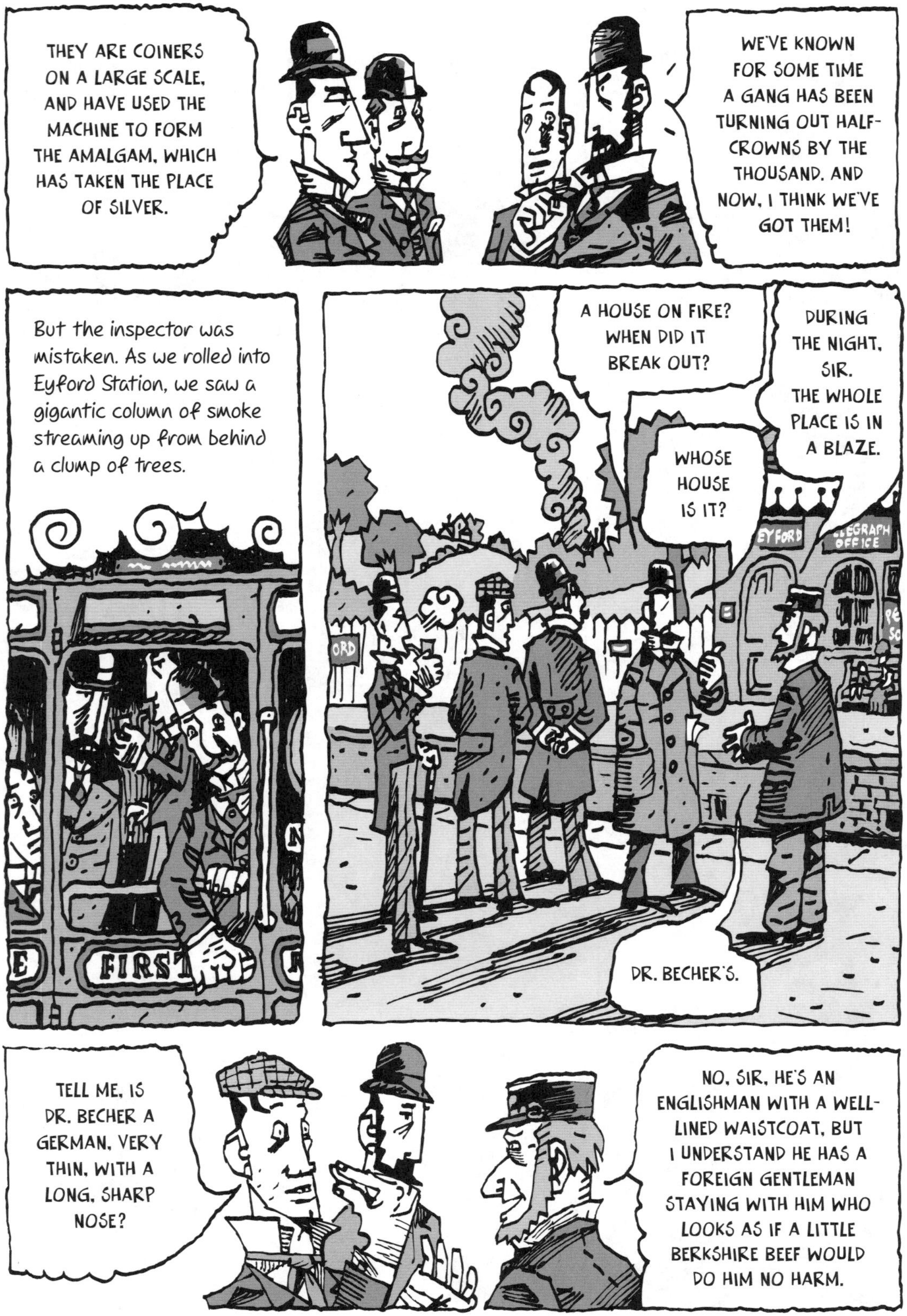
THEY ARE COINERS ON A LARGE SCALE, AND HAVE USED THE MACHINE TO FORM THE AMALGAM, WHICH HAS TAKEN THE PLACE OF SILVER.
WE'VE KNOWN FOR SOME TIME A GANG HAS BEEN TURNING OUT HALF-CROWNS BY THE THOUSAND. AND NOW, I THINK WE'VE GOT THEM!
But the inspector was mistaken. As we rolled into Eyford Station, we saw a gigantic column of smoke streaming up from behind a clump of trees.
FIRST
A HOUSE ON FIRE? WHEN DID IT BREAK OUT?
DURING THE NIGHT, SIR. THE WHOLE PLACE IS IN A BLAZE.
WHOSE HOUSE IS IT?
DR. BECHER'S.
EYFORD
TELEGRAPH OFFICE
TELL ME, IS DR. BECHER A GERMAN, VERY THIN, WITH A LONG, SHARP NOSE?
NO, SIR, HE'S AN ENGLISHMAN WITH A WELL-LINED WAISTCOAT, BUT I UNDERSTAND HE HAS A FOREIGN GENTLEMAN STAYING WITH HIM WHO LOOKS AS IF A LITTLE BERKSHIRE BEEF WOULD DO HIM NO HARM.

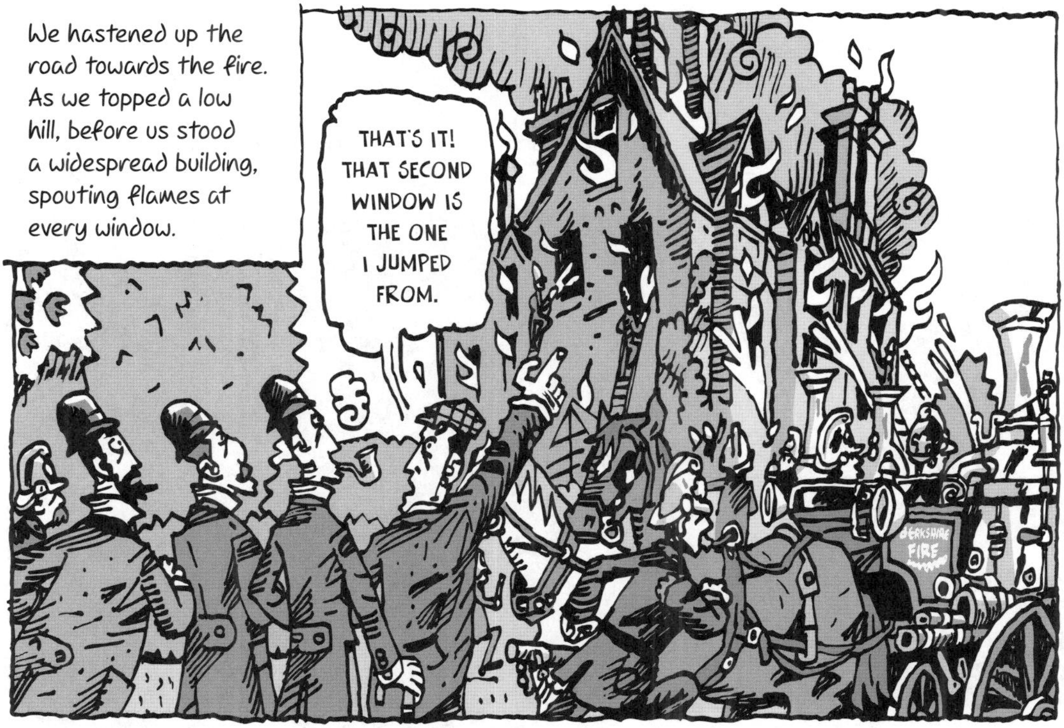
We hastened up the road towards the fire. As we topped a low hill, before us stood a widespread building, spouting flames at every window.
THAT'S IT! THAT SECOND WINDOW IS THE ONE I JUMPED FROM.

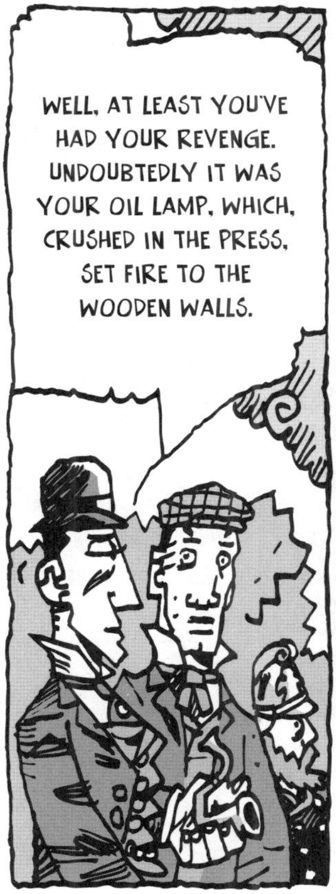
WELL, AT LEAST YOU'VE HAD YOUR REVENGE. UNDOUBTEDLY IT WAS YOUR OIL LAMP, WHICH, CRUSHED IN THE PRESS, SET FIRE TO THE WOODEN WALLS.

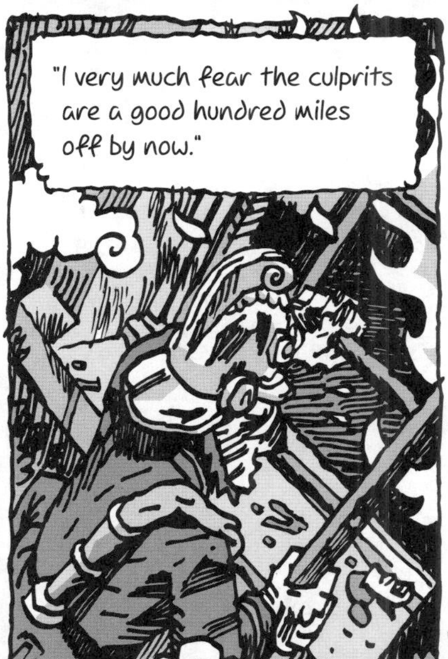
"I very much fear the culprits are a good hundred miles off by now."

Holmes' fears came to be realized, for no word has ever been heard of the mysterious woman, the sinister German, or the morose Englishman.

The whole place had been reduced to such absolute ruin that not a trace remained of the machine which had cost our unfortunate acquaintance so dearly. No coins were to be found.

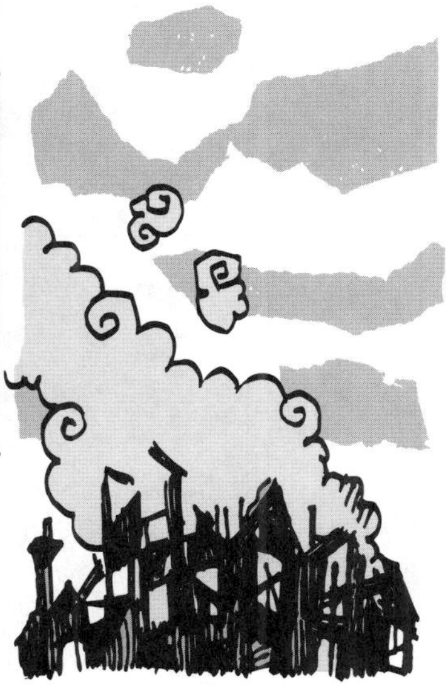

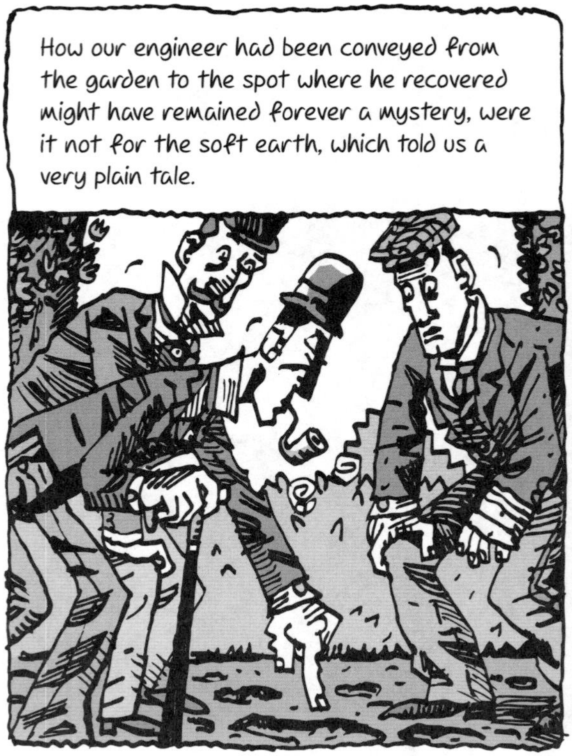
How our engineer had been conveyed from the garden to the spot where he recovered might have remained forever a mystery, were it not for the soft earth, which told us a very plain tale.

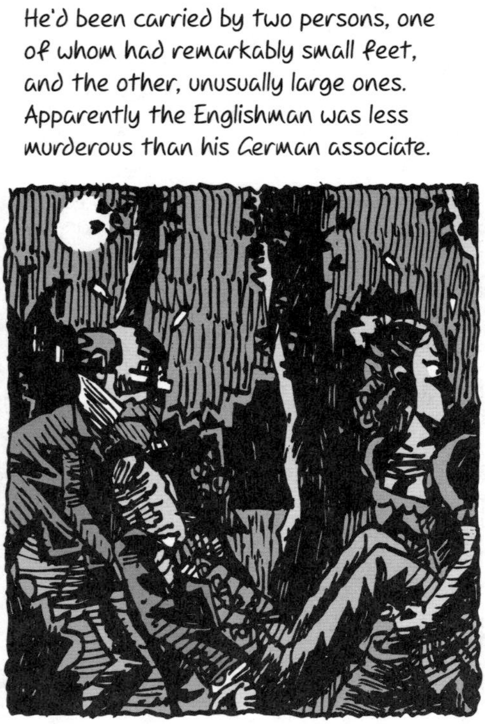
He'd been carried by two persons, one of whom had remarkably small feet, and the other, unusually large ones. Apparently the Englishman was less murderous than his German associate.

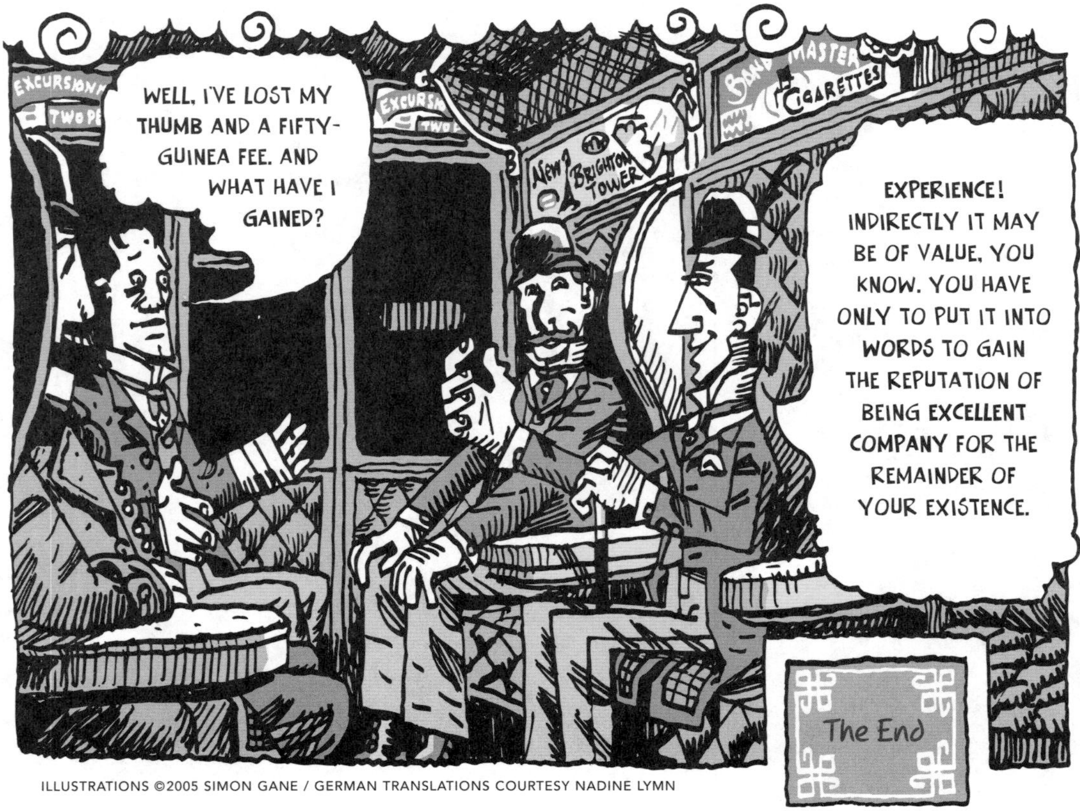
EXCURSION
TWO PE
EXCURSION
TWO
NEW BRIGHTON TOWER
BAND MASTER
CIGARETTES
WELL, I'VE LOST MY THUMB AND A FIFTY-GUINEA FEE. AND WHAT HAVE I GAINED?
EXPERIENCE! INDIRECTLY IT MAY BE OF VALUE, YOU KNOW. YOU HAVE ONLY TO PUT IT INTO WORDS TO GAIN THE REPUTATION OF BEING **EXCELLENT COMPANY** FOR THE REMAINDER OF YOUR EXISTENCE.
The End

ILLUSTRATIONS ©2005 SIMON GANE / GERMAN TRANSLATIONS COURTESY NADINE LYMN

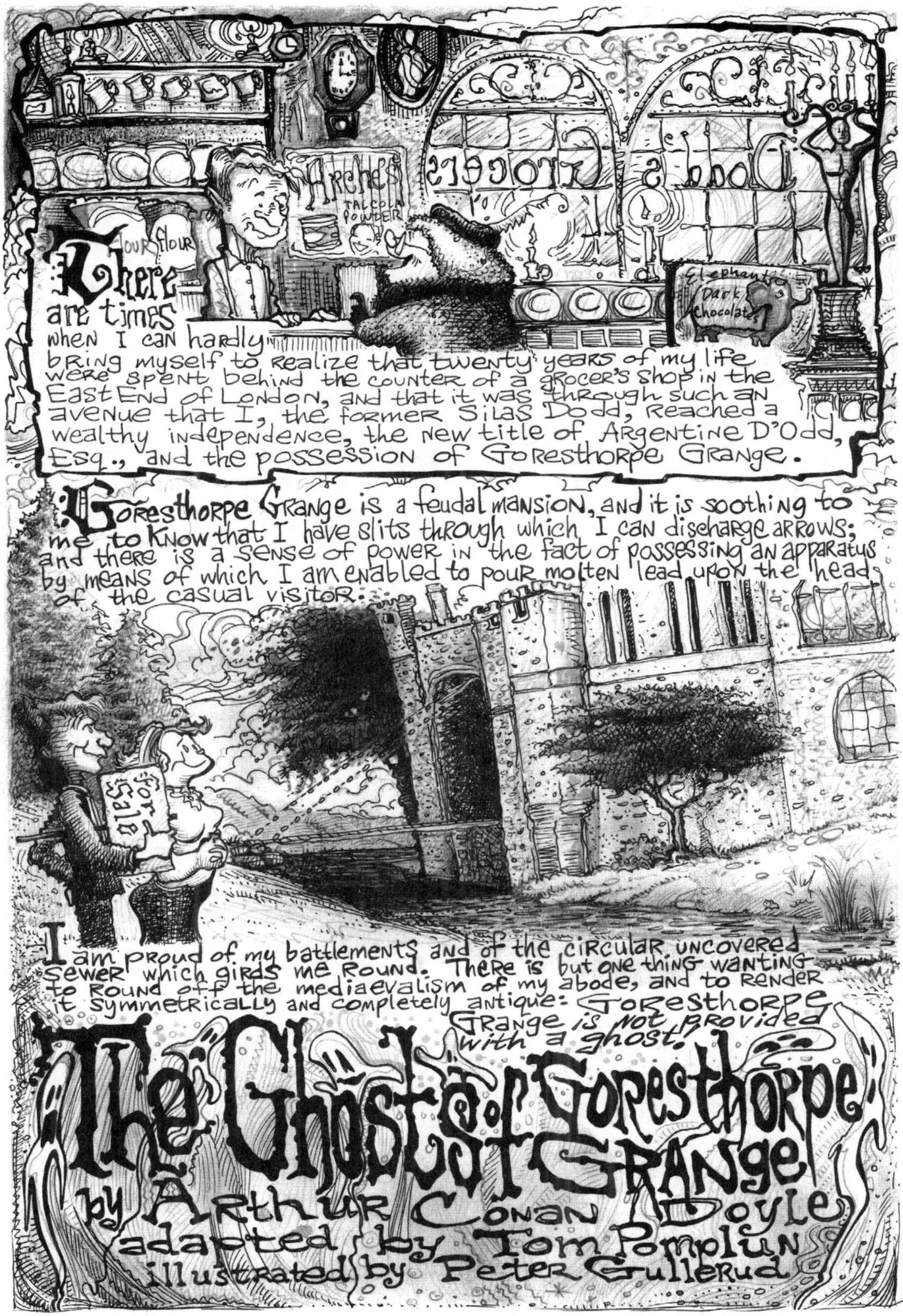
Flour Flour
Elephant Dark Chocolates
There are times when I can hardly bring myself to realize that twenty years of my life were spent behind the counter of a grocer's shop in the East End of London, and that it was through such an avenue that I, the former Silas Dodd, reached a wealthy independence, the new title of Argentine D'Odd, Esq., and the possession of Goresthorpe Grange.
Goresthorpe Grange is a feudal mansion, and it is soothing to me to know that I have slits through which I can discharge arrows; and there is a sense of power in the fact of possessing an apparatus by means of which I am enabled to pour molten lead upon the head of the casual visitor.
For Sale
I am proud of my battlements and of the circular uncovered sewer which girds me round. There is but one thing wanting to round off the mediaevalism of my abode, and to render it symmetrically and completely antique: Goresthorpe Grange is not provided with a ghost!
The Ghosts of Goresthorpe Grange
by Arthur Conan Doyle
adapted by Tom Pomplun
illustrated by Peter Gullerud

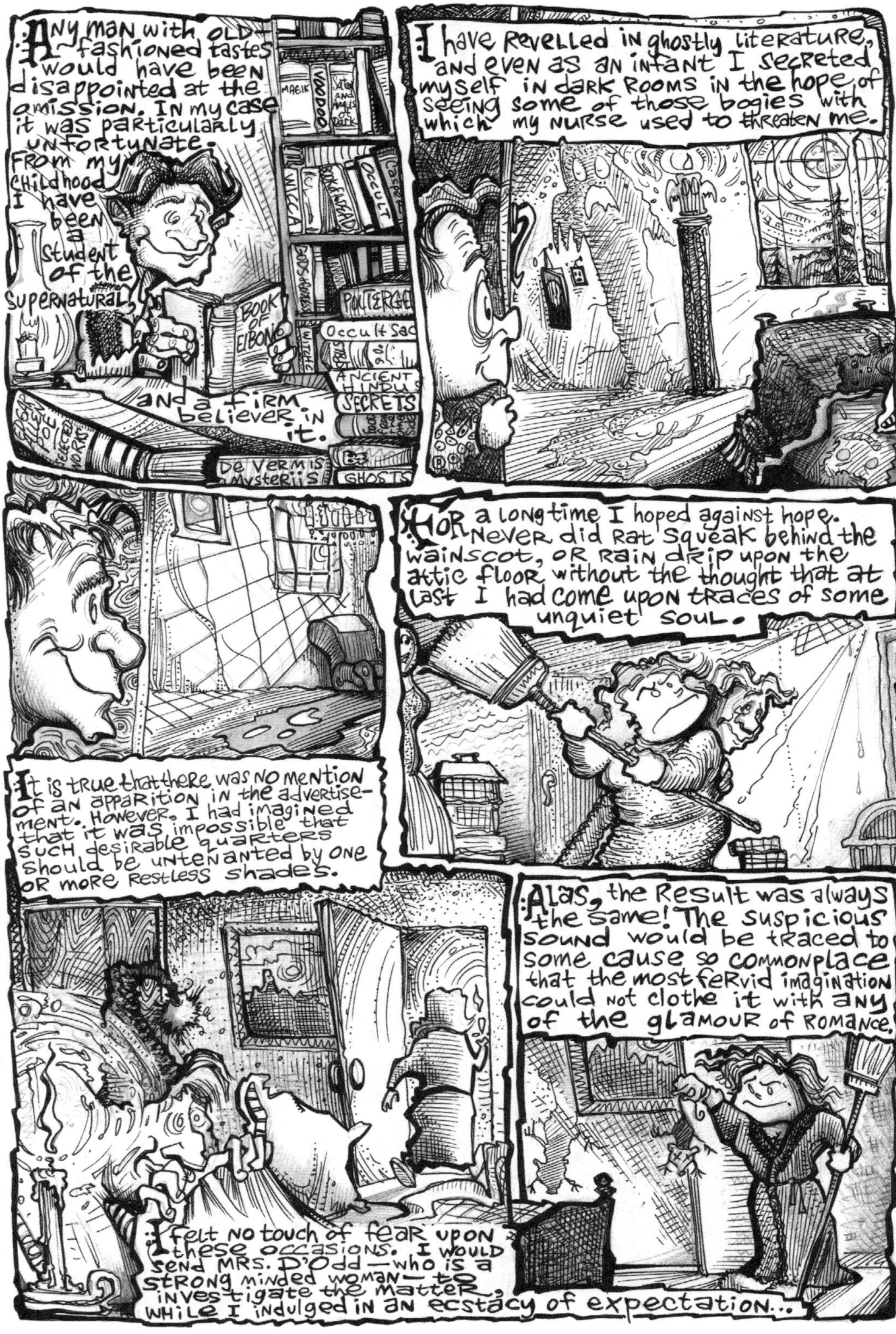
Any man with old-fashioned tastes would have been disappointed at the omission. In my case it was particularly unfortunate. From my childhood I have been a student of the supernatural,
and a firm believer in it.
MAGIK
VOODOO
WICCA
OCCULT
BOOK OF ELBON
POLTERGEIST
Occult Sac
ANCIENT HINDU SECRETS
De Vermis Mysteriis
GHOSTS
I have revelled in ghostly literature, and even as an infant I secreted myself in dark rooms in the hope of seeing some of those bogies with which my nurse used to threaten me.
It is true that there was no mention of an apparition in the advertisement. However, I had imagined that it was impossible that such desirable quarters should be untenanted by one or more restless shades.
For a long time I hoped against hope. Never did rat squeak behind the wainscot, or rain drip upon the attic floor without the thought that at last I had come upon traces of some unquiet soul.
I felt no touch of fear upon these occasions. I would send Mrs. D'Odd — who is a strong minded woman — to investigate the matter, while I indulged in an ecstacy of expectation...
Alas, the result was always the same! The suspicious sound would be traced to some cause so commonplace that the most fervid imagination could not clothe it with any of the glamour of romance.

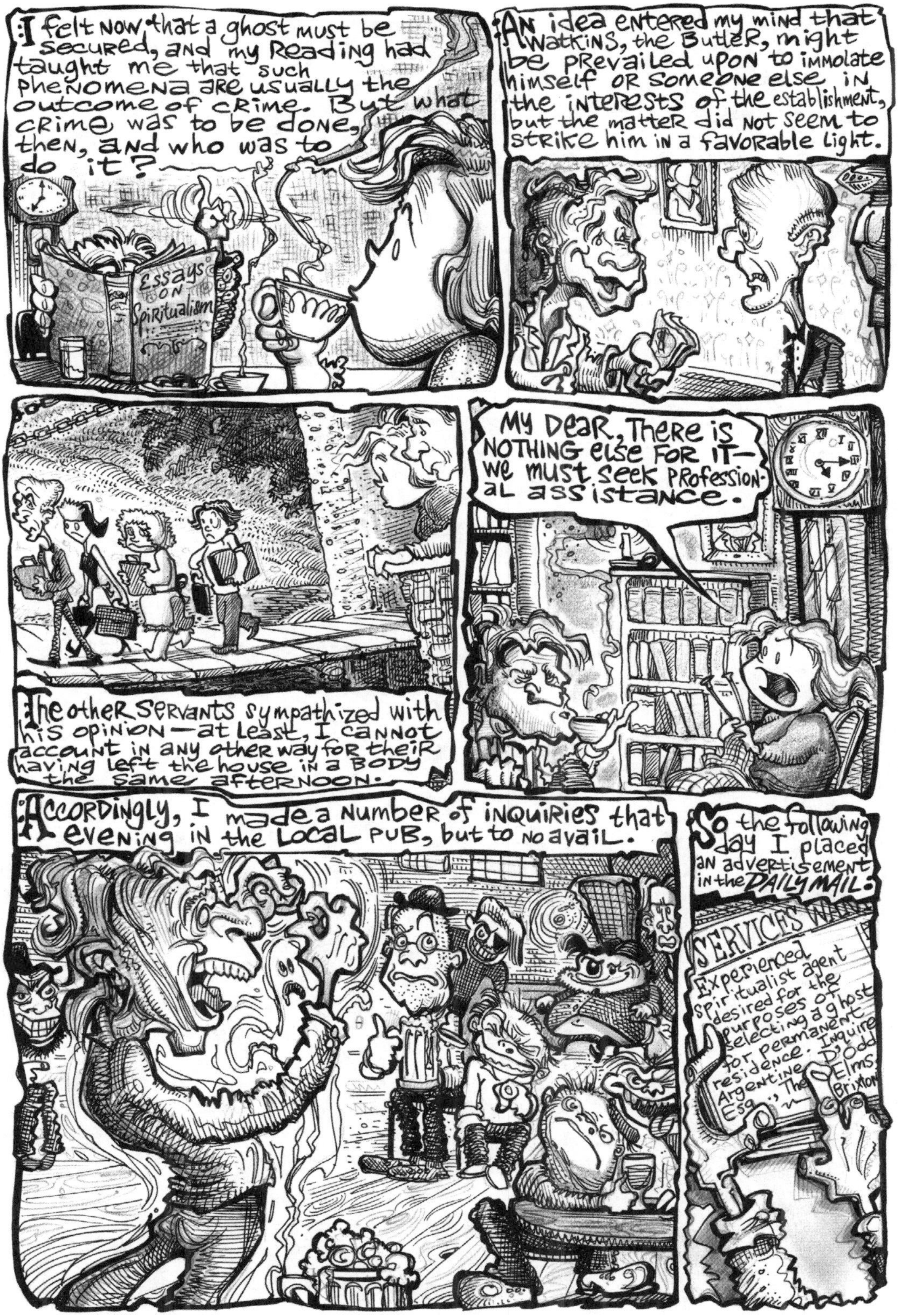
I felt now that a ghost must be secured, and my reading had taught me that such phenomena are usually the outcome of crime. But what crime was to be done, then, and who was to do it?
Essays on Spiritualism
An idea entered my mind that Watkins, the Butler, might be prevailed upon to immolate himself or someone else in the interests of the establishment, but the matter did not seem to strike him in a favorable light.
The other servants sympathized with his opinion—at least, I cannot account in any other way for their having left the house in a body the same afternoon.
My dear, there is nothing else for it—we must seek professional assistance.
Accordingly, I made a number of inquiries that evening in the local pub, but to no avail.
So the following day I placed an advertisement in the Daily Mail:
SERVICES W
Experienced spiritualist agent desired for the purposes of selecting a ghost for permanent residence. Inquire Argentine D'Odd Esq., The Elms, Brixton

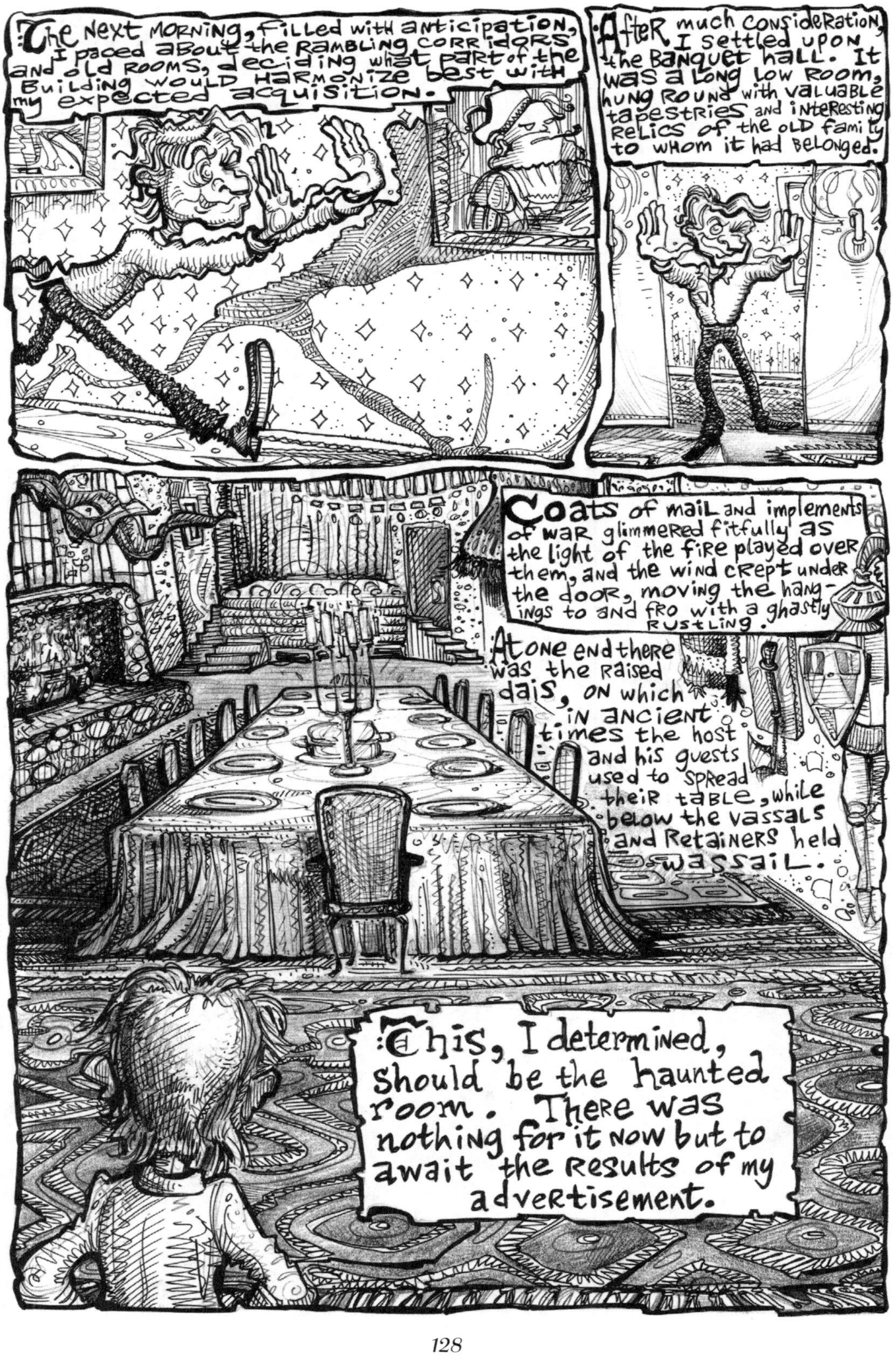
The next morning, filled with anticipation, I paced about the rambling corridors and old rooms, deciding what part of the building would harmonize best with my expected acquisition.
After much consideration, I settled upon the banquet hall. It was a long low room, hung round with valuable tapestries and interesting relics of the old family to whom it had belonged.
Coats of mail and implements of war glimmered fitfully as the light of the fire played over them, and the wind crept under the door, moving the hangings to and fro with a ghastly rustling.
At one end there was the raised dais, on which in ancient times the host and his guests used to spread their table, while below the vassals and retainers held wassail.
This, I determined, should be the haunted room. There was nothing for it now but to await the results of my advertisement.

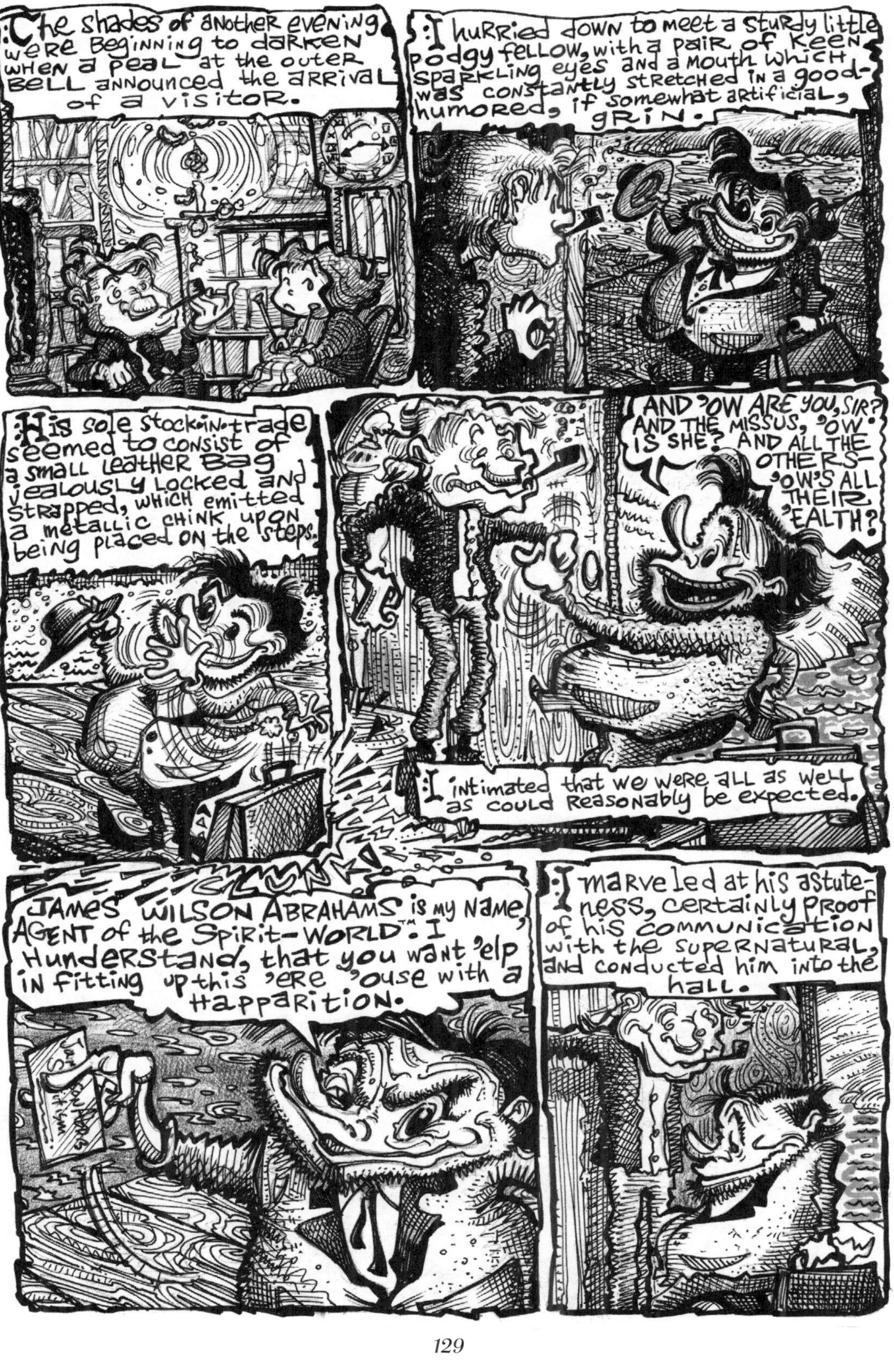
The shades of another evening were beginning to darken when a peal at the outer bell announced the arrival of a visitor.
I hurried down to meet a sturdy little podgy fellow, with a pair of keen sparkling eyes and a mouth which was constantly stretched in a good-humored, if somewhat artificial, grin.
His sole stock-in-trade seemed to consist of a small leather bag jealously locked and strapped, which emitted a metallic chink upon being placed on the steps.
AND 'OW ARE YOU, SIR? AND THE MISSUS, 'OW IS SHE? AND ALL THE OTHERS- 'OW'S ALL THEIR 'EALTH?
I intimated that we were all as well as could reasonably be expected.
CLUNK
JAMES WILSON ABRAHAMS is my name, AGENT of the Spirit-WORLD™. I Hunderstand, that you want 'elp in fitting up this 'ere 'ouse with a Happarition.
I marveled at his astuteness, certainly proof of his communication with the supernatural, and conducted him into the hall.

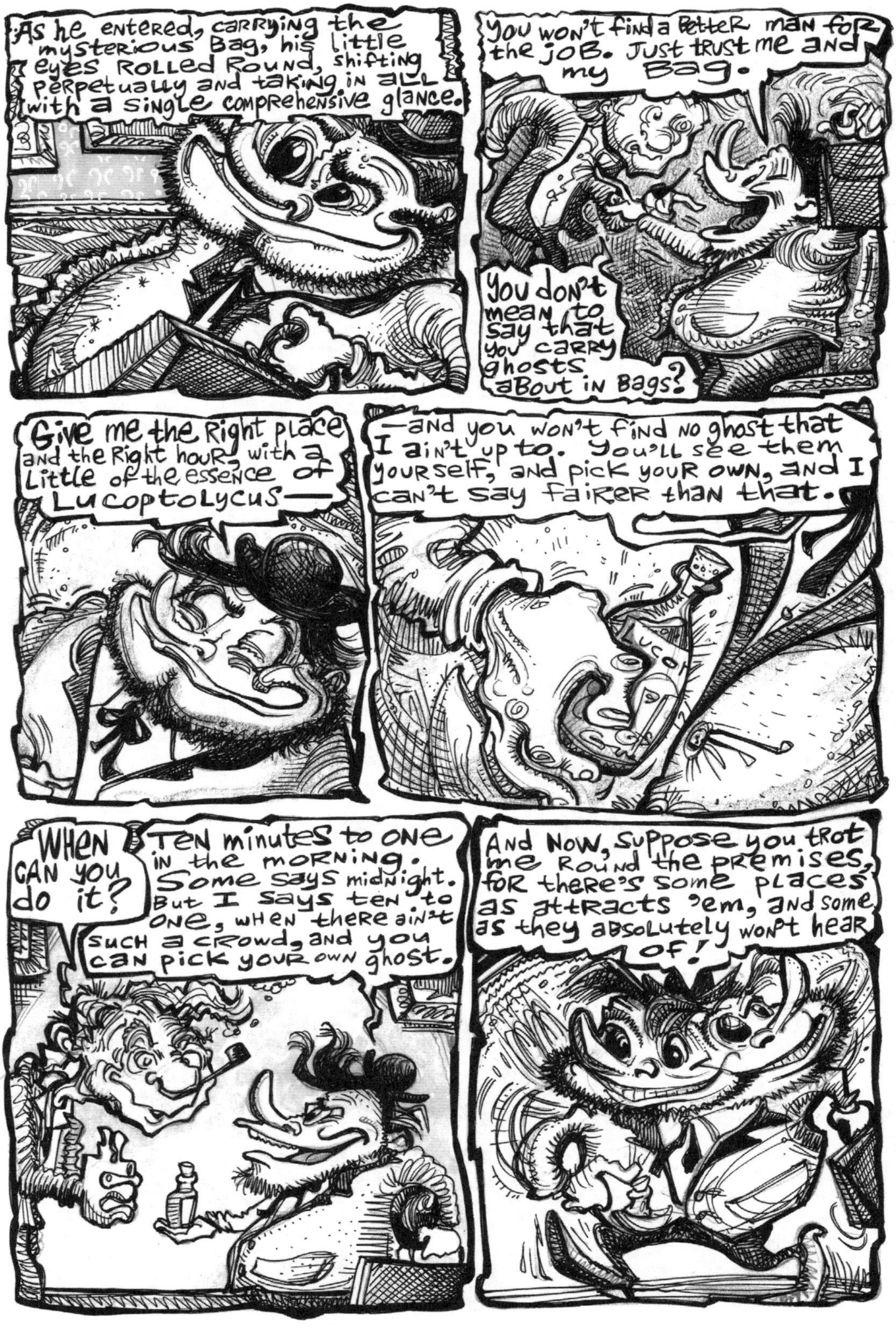
As he entered, carrying the mysterious Bag, his little eyes rolled round, shifting perpetually and taking in all with a single comprehensive glance.
You won't find a better man for the job. Just trust me and my Bag.
You don't mean to say that you carry ghosts about in bags?
Give me the right place and the right hour, with a little of the essence of Lucoptolycus—
—and you won't find no ghost that I ain't up to. You'll see them yourself, and pick your own, and I can't say fairer than that.
When can you do it?
Ten minutes to one in the morning. Some says midnight. But I says ten to one, when there ain't such a crowd, and you can pick your own ghost.
And now, suppose you trot me round the premises, for there's some places as attracts 'em, and some as they absolutely won't hear of!

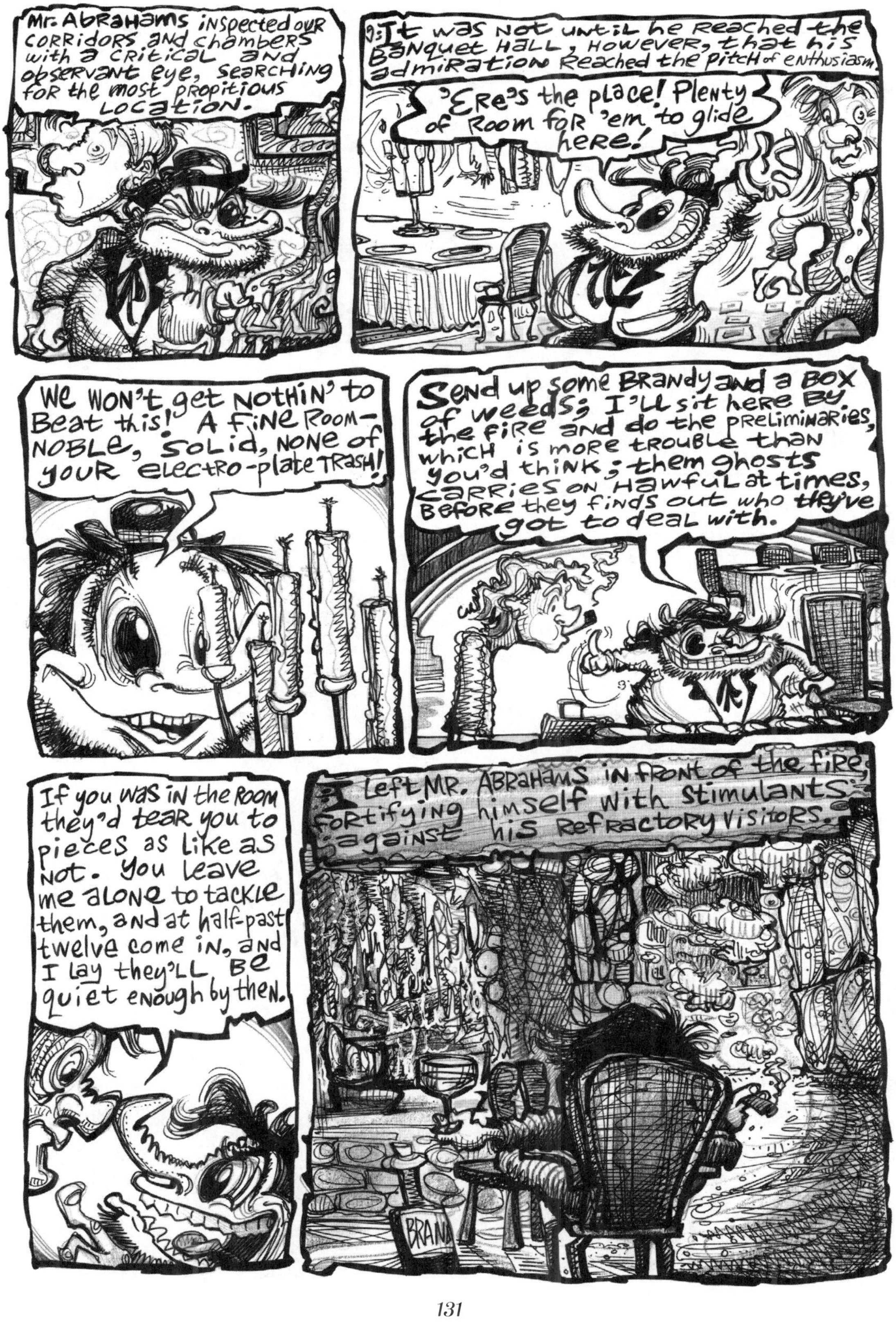
Mr. Abrahams inspected our corridors and chambers with a critical and observant eye, searching for the most propitious location.
It was not until he reached the banquet hall, however, that his admiration reached the pitch of enthusiasm.
'Ere's the place! Plenty of room for 'em to glide here!
We won't get nothin' to beat this! A fine room— noble, solid, none of your electro-plate trash!
Send up some brandy and a box of weeds; I'll sit here by the fire and do the preliminaries, which is more trouble than you'd think; them ghosts carries on hawful at times, before they finds out who they've got to deal with.
If you was in the room they'd tear you to pieces as like as not. You leave me alone to tackle them, and at half-past twelve come in, and I lay they'll be quiet enough by then.
I left Mr. Abrahams in front of the fire, fortifying himself with stimulants against his refractory visitors.

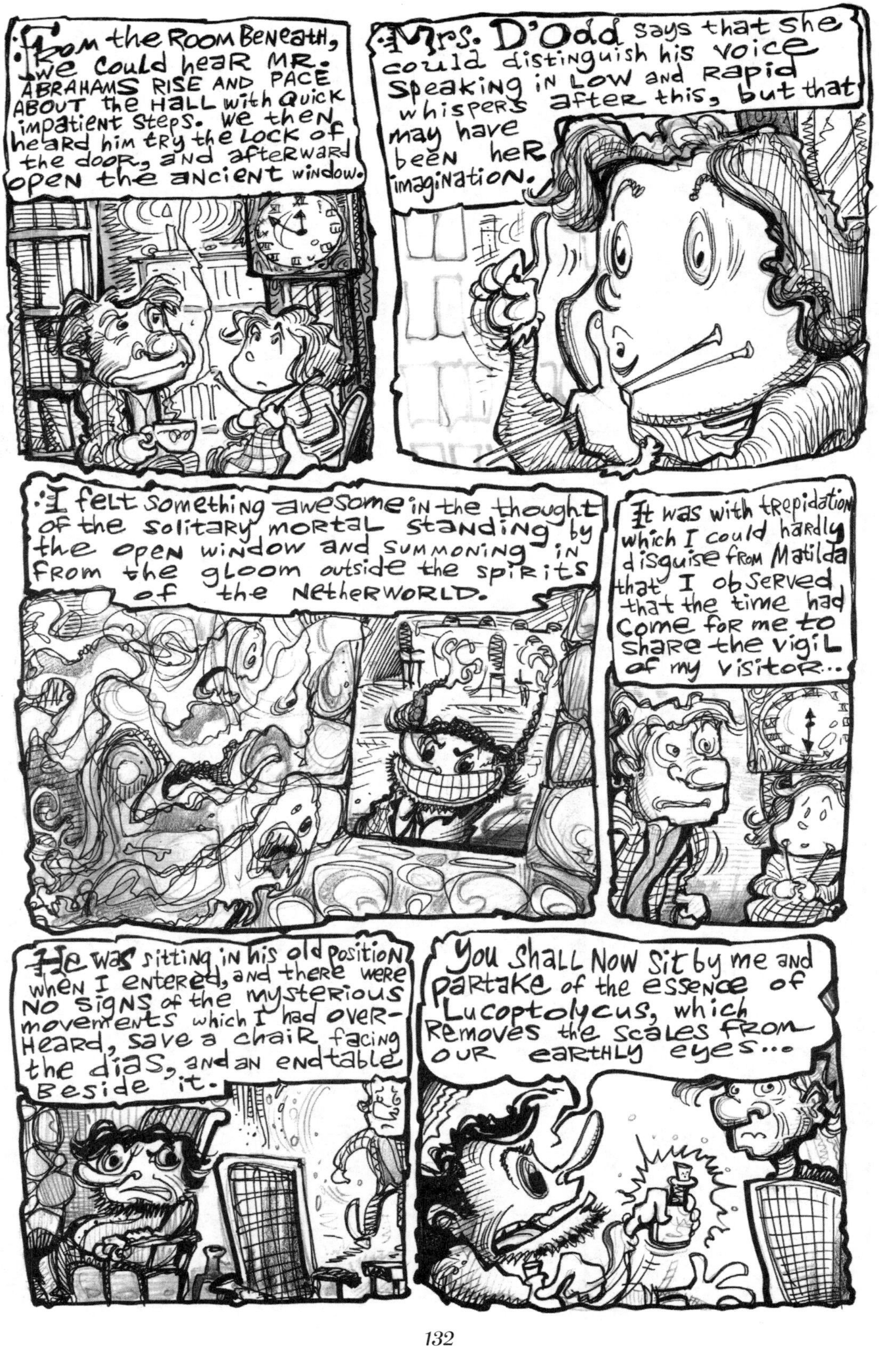
From the Room Beneath, we could hear Mr. Abrahams rise and pace about the hall with quick impatient steps. We then heard him try the lock of the door, and afterward open the ancient window.
Mrs. D'Odd says that she could distinguish his voice speaking in low and rapid whispers after this, but that may have been her imagination.
I felt something awesome in the thought of the solitary mortal standing by the open window and summoning in from the gloom outside the spirits of the Netherworld.
It was with trepidation which I could hardly disguise from Matilda that I observed that the time had come for me to share the vigil of my visitor...
He was sitting in his old position when I entered, and there were no signs of the mysterious movements which I had over-heard, save a chair facing the dias, and an endtable beside it.
You shall now sit by me and partake of the essence of Lucoptolycus, which removes the scales from our earthly eyes...

Whatever you may chance to see, speak not and make no movement, lest you BREAK the spell.

My companion then described a circle and mystic symbols upon the floor, while uttering a long invocation in some gutteral language...

zooboojaabboo scooboo ngoyoo doodoo

Having finished his preparations he poured a couple of teaspoons of fluid into the glass, which he handed to me with an intimation that I should drink it.

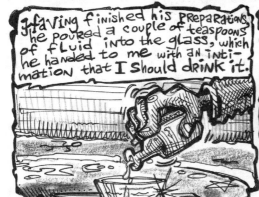

I hesitated for a moment before applying it to my lips, but an impatient gesture from my companion overcame my scruples, and I tossed it off.

A sense of delicious warmth and langour began gradually to steal over me. Everything in the room appeared to be reeling slowly round in a drowsy dance, of which I was the center.

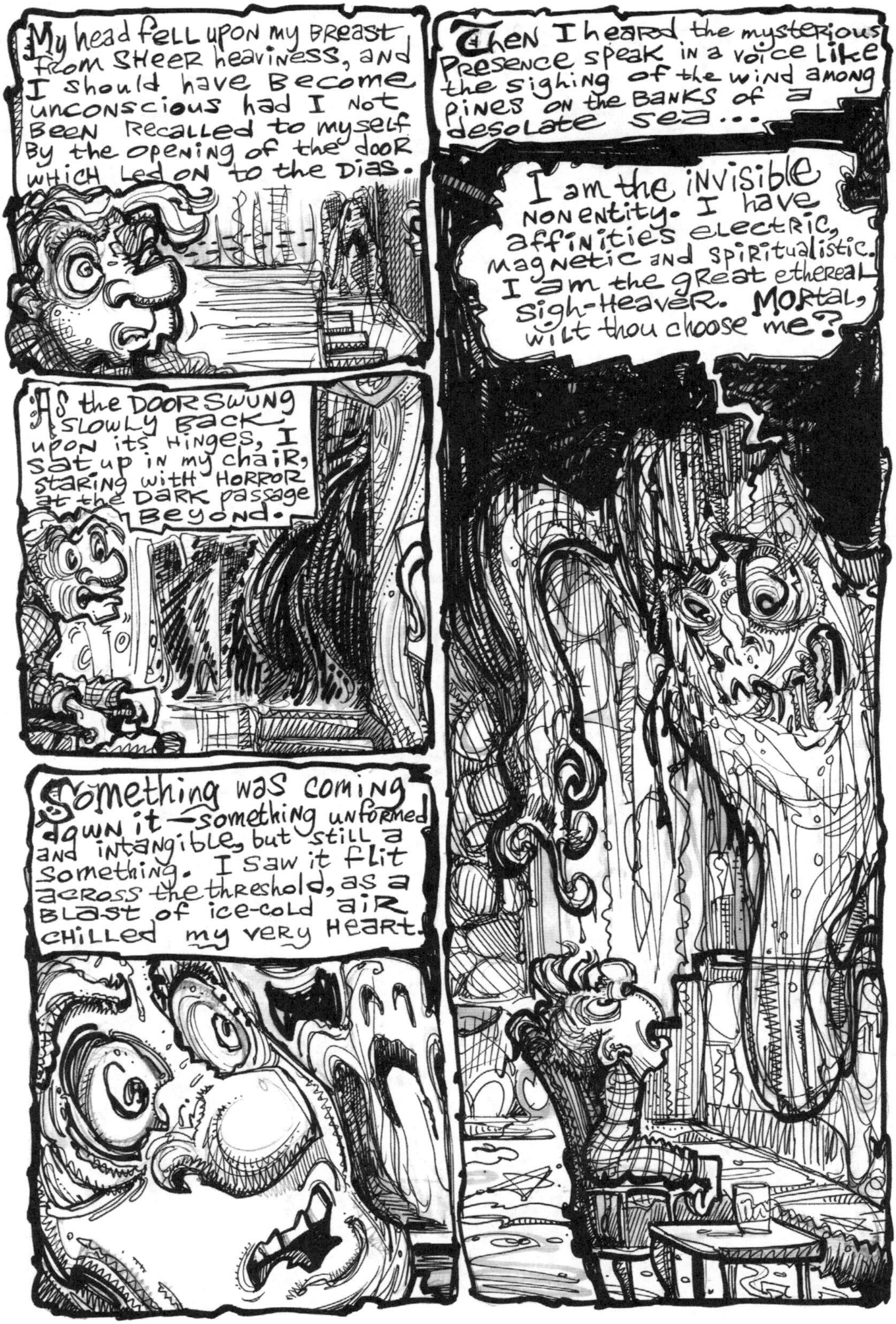
My head fell upon my breast from sheer heaviness, and I should have become unconscious had I not been recalled to myself by the opening of the door which led on to the dias.
As the door swung slowly back upon its hinges, I sat up in my chair, staring with horror at the dark passage beyond.
Something was coming down it—something unformed and intangible, but still a something. I saw it flit across the threshold, as a blast of ice-cold air chilled my very heart.
Then I heard the mysterious Presence speak in a voice like the sighing of the wind among pines on the banks of a desolate sea...
I am the invisible nonentity. I have affinities electric, magnetic and spiritualistic. I am the great ethereal sigh-heaver. Mortal, wilt thou choose me?

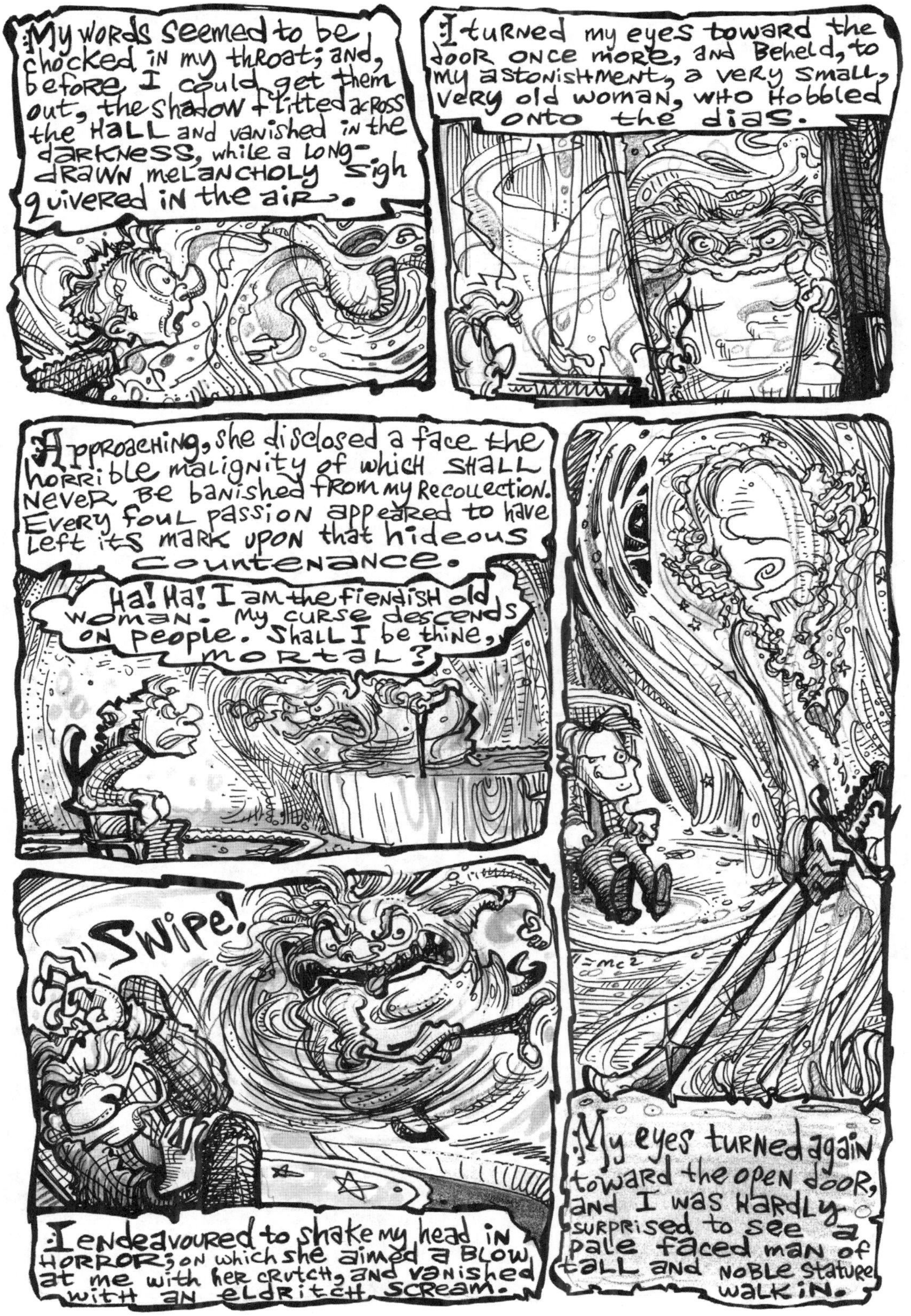
My words seemed to be chocked in my throat; and, before I could get them out, the shadow flitted across the hall and vanished in the darkness, while a long-drawn melancholy sigh quivered in the air.
I turned my eyes toward the door once more, and beheld, to my astonishment, a very small, very old woman, who hobbled onto the dias.
Approaching, she disclosed a face the horrible malignity of which shall never be banished from my recollection. Every foul passion appeared to have left its mark upon that hideous countenance.
Ha! Ha! I am the fiendish old woman. My curse descends on people. Shall I be thine, mortal?
Swipe!
I endeavoured to shake my head in horror; on which she aimed a blow at me with her crutch, and vanished with an eldritch scream.
My eyes turned again toward the open door, and I was hardly surprised to see a pale faced man of tall and noble stature walk in.

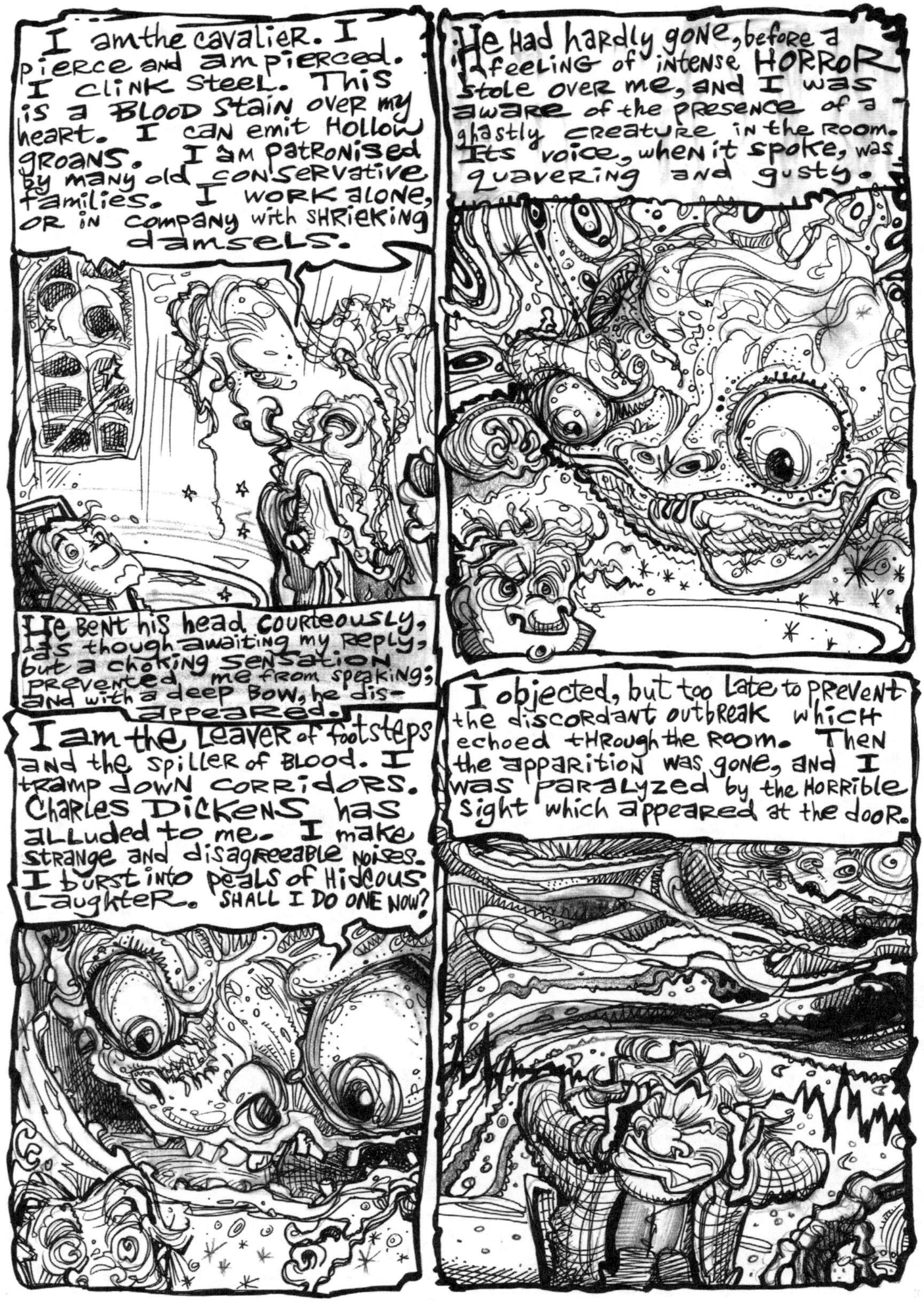
I am the cavalier. I pierce and am pierced. I clink steel. This is a blood stain over my heart. I can emit hollow groans. I am patronised by many old conservative families. I work alone, or in company with shrieking damsels.
He had hardly gone, before a feeling of intense HORROR stole over me, and I was aware of the presence of a ghastly creature in the room. Its voice, when it spoke, was quavering and gusty.
He bent his head courteously, as though awaiting my reply, but a choking sensation prevented me from speaking; and with a deep bow, he disappeared.
I am the leaver of footsteps and the spiller of blood. I tramp down corridors. Charles Dickens has alluded to me. I make strange and disagreeable noises. I burst into peals of hideous laughter. Shall I do one now?
I objected, but too late to prevent the discordant outbreak which echoed through the room. Then the apparition was gone, and I was paralyzed by the horrible sight which appeared at the door.

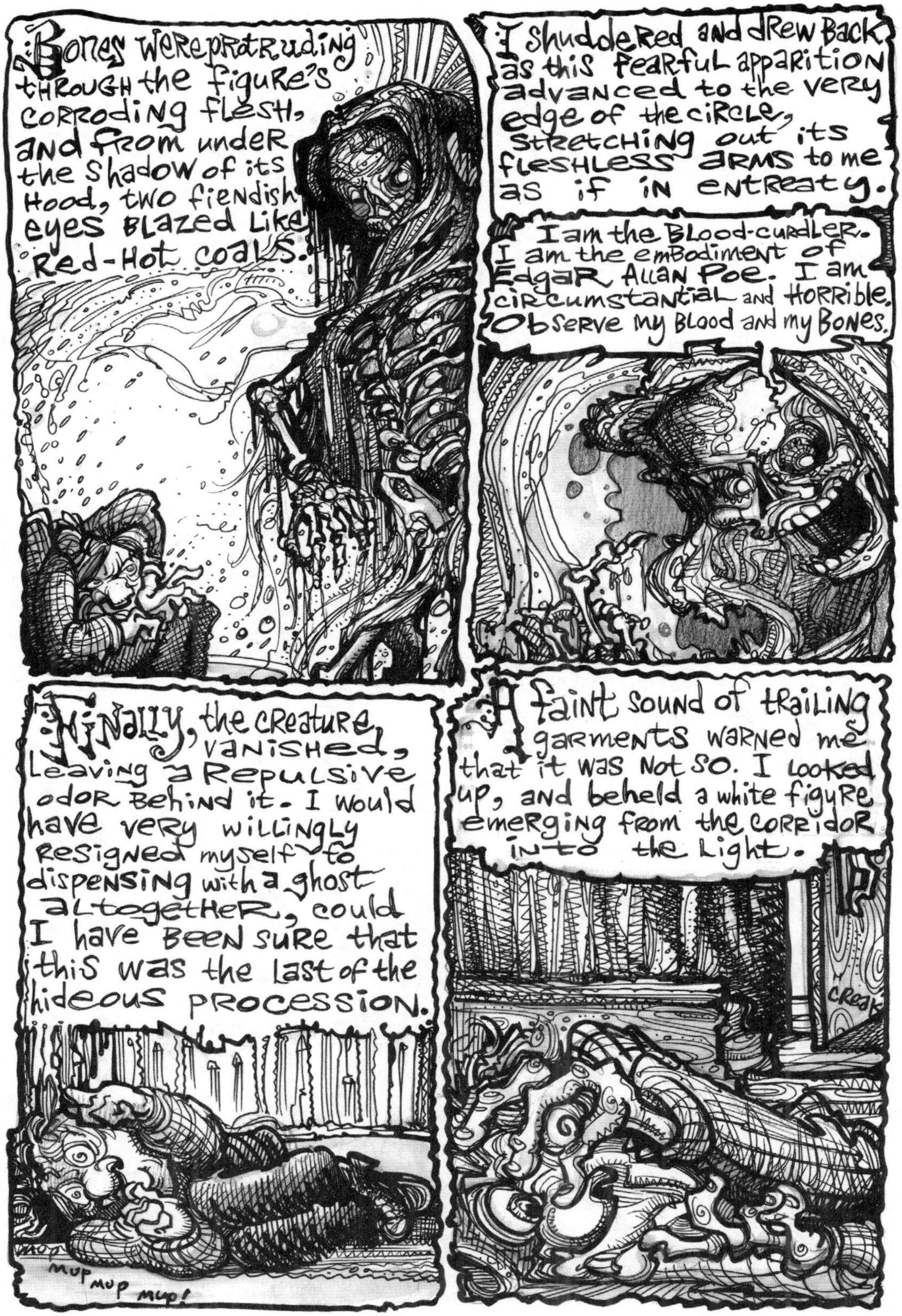
Bones were protruding through the figure's corroding flesh, and from under the shadow of its hood, two fiendish eyes blazed like red-hot coals.
I shuddered and drew back as this fearful apparition advanced to the very edge of the circle, stretching out its fleshless arms to me as if in entreaty.
I am the Blood-curdler. I am the embodiment of Edgar Allan Poe. I am circumstantial and horrible. Observe my blood and my bones.
Finally, the creature vanished, leaving a repulsive odor behind it. I would have very willingly resigned myself to dispensing with a ghost altogether, could I have been sure that this was the last of the hideous procession.
mup mup mup!
A faint sound of trailing garments warned me that it was not so. I looked up, and beheld a white figure emerging from the corridor into the light.
creak

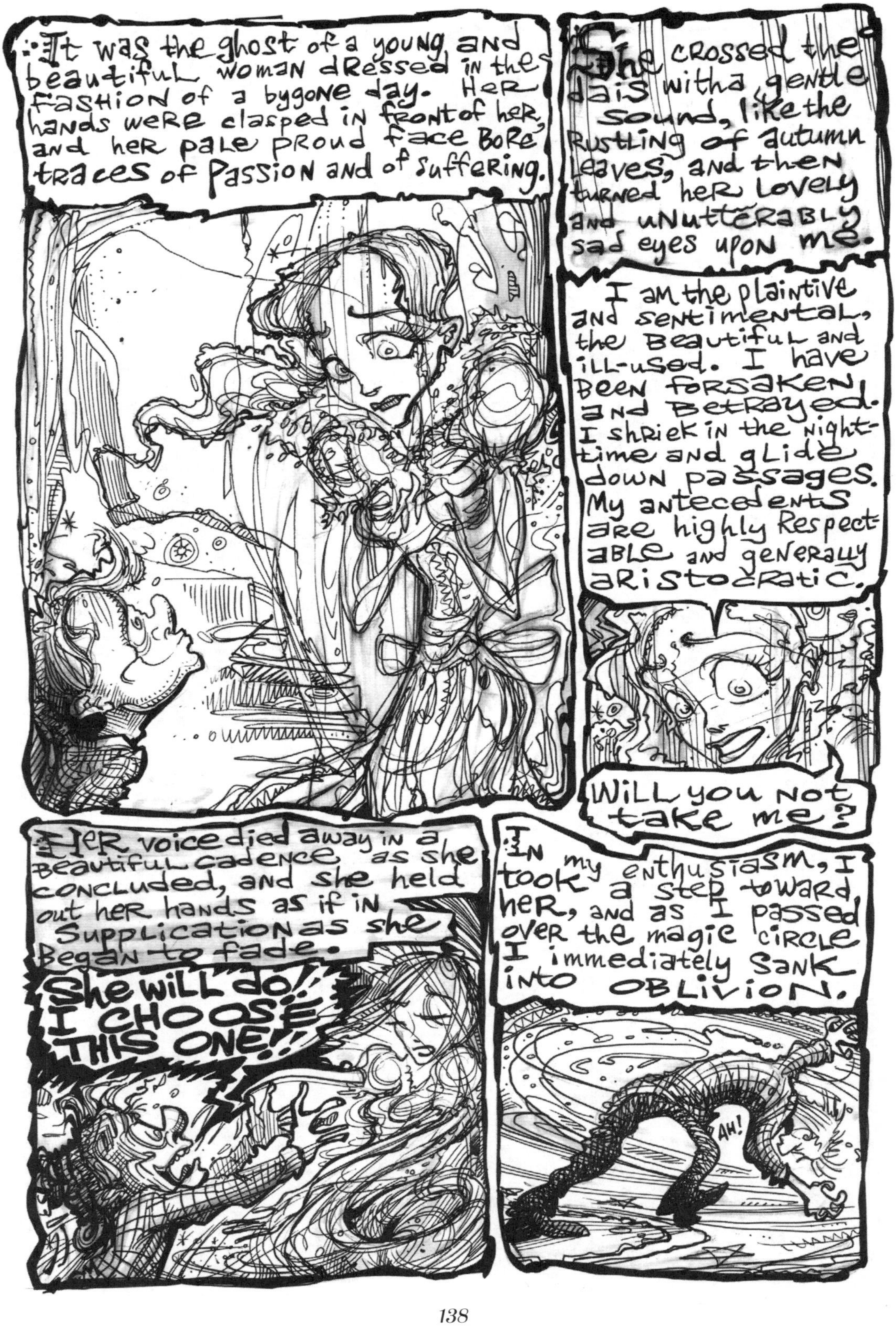
It was the ghost of a young and beautiful woman dressed in the fashion of a bygone day. Her hands were clasped in front of her, and her pale proud face bore traces of passion and of suffering.
She crossed the dais with a gentle sound, like the rustling of autumn leaves, and then turned her lovely and unutterably sad eyes upon me.
I am the plaintive and sentimental, the beautiful and ill-used. I have been forsaken and betrayed. I shriek in the night-time and glide down passages. My antecedents are highly respectable and generally aristocratic.
Will you not take me?
Her voice died away in a beautiful cadence as she concluded, and she held out her hands as if in supplication as she began to fade.
She will do!! I choose this one!!
In my enthusiasm, I took a step toward her, and as I passed over the magic circle I immediately sank into oblivion.
AH!

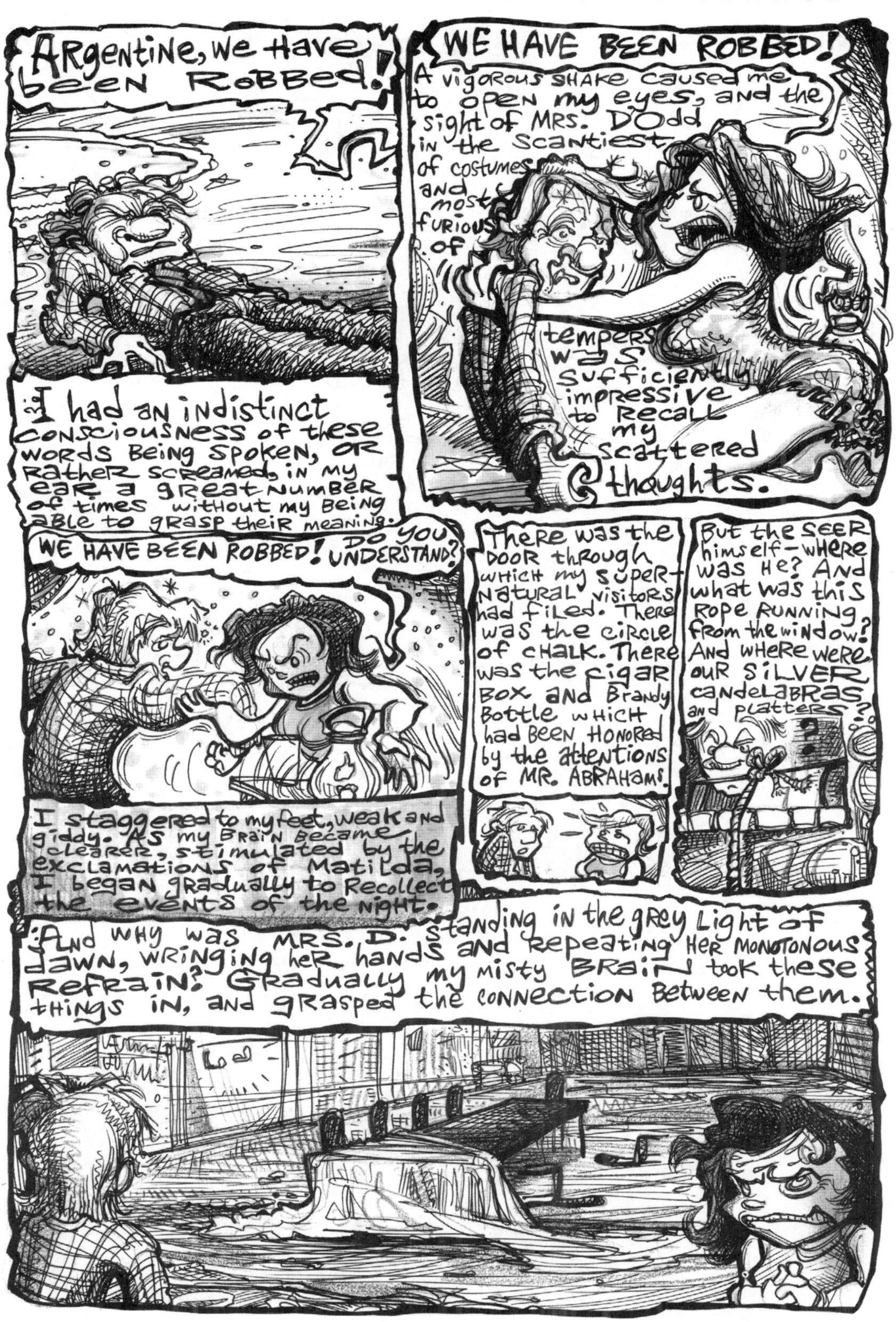
Argentine, we have been Robbed!
I had an indistinct consciousness of these words being spoken, or rather screamed, in my ear a great number of times without my being able to grasp their meaning.
WE HAVE BEEN ROBBED!
A vigorous shake caused me to open my eyes, and the sight of Mrs. Dodd in the scantiest of costumes and most furious of tempers was sufficiently impressive to recall my scattered thoughts.
WE HAVE BEEN ROBBED! DO YOU UNDERSTAND?
I staggered to my feet, weak and giddy. As my brain became clearer, stimulated by the exclamations of Matilda, I began gradually to recollect the events of the night.
There was the door through which my supernatural visitors had filed. There was the circle of chalk. There was the cigar box and brandy bottle which had been honored by the attentions of Mr. Abrahams.
But the seer himself—where was he? And what was this rope running from the window? And where were our silver candelabras and platters?
And why was Mrs. D. standing in the grey light of dawn, wringing her hands and repeating her monotonous refrain? Gradually my misty brain took these things in, and grasped the connection between them.

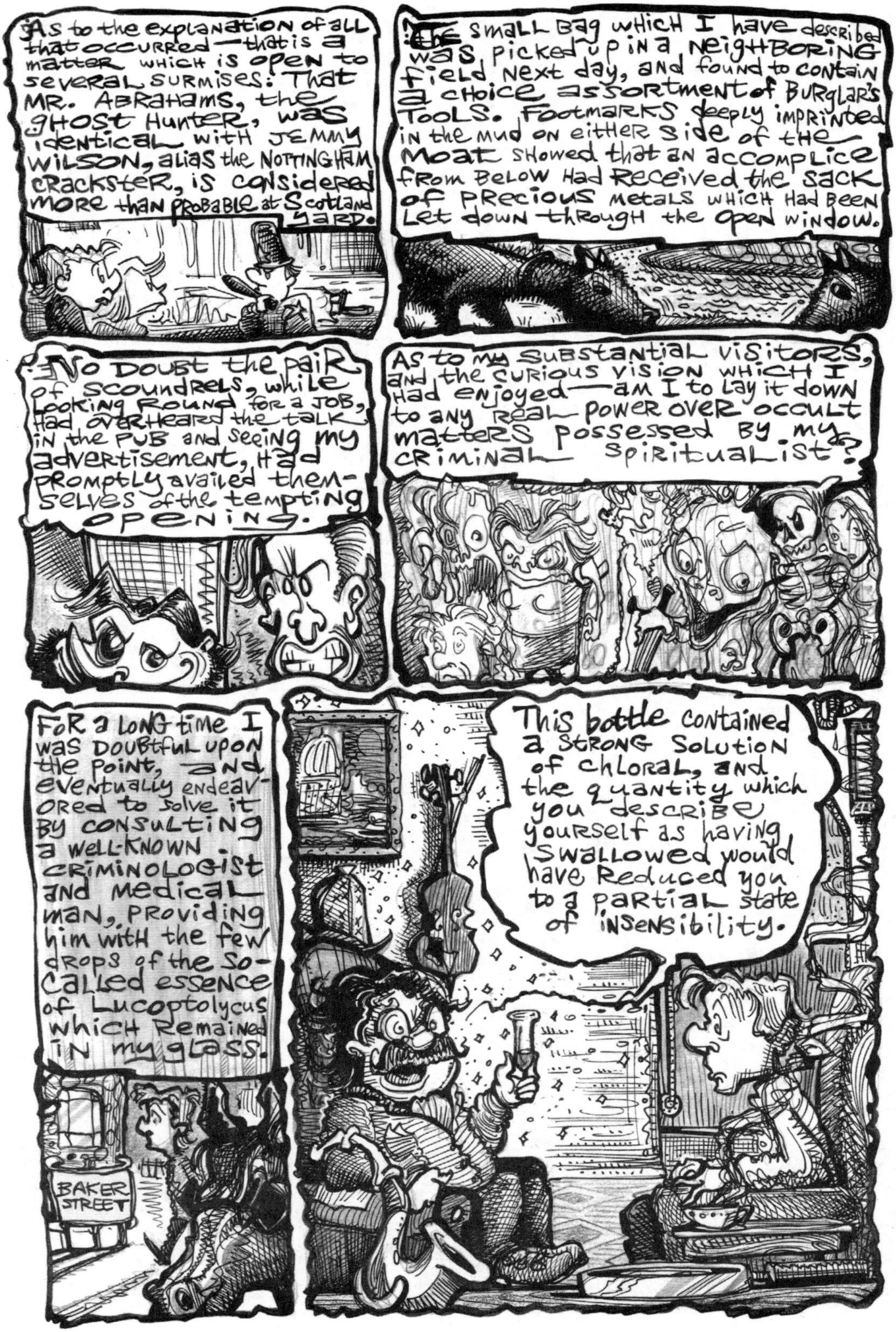
As to the explanation of all that occurred — that is a matter which is open to several surmises: That Mr. Abrahams, the ghost hunter, was identical with Jemmy Wilson, alias the Nottingham Crackster, is considered more than probable at Scotland Yard.
The small bag which I have described was picked up in a neighboring field next day, and found to contain a choice assortment of burglar's tools. Footmarks deeply imprinted in the mud on either side of the moat showed that an accomplice from below had received the sack of precious metals which had been let down through the open window.
No doubt the pair of scoundrels, while looking round for a job, had overheard the talk in the pub and seeing my advertisement, had promptly availed themselves of the tempting opening.
As to my substantial visitors, and the curious vision which I had enjoyed — am I to lay it down to any real power over occult matters possessed by my criminal spiritualist?
For a long time I was doubtful upon the point, and eventually endeavored to solve it by consulting a well-known criminologist and medical man, providing him with the few drops of the so-called essence of Lucoptolycus which remained in my glass.
Baker Street
This bottle contained a strong solution of chloral, and the quantity which you describe yourself as having swallowed would have reduced you to a partial state of insensibility.

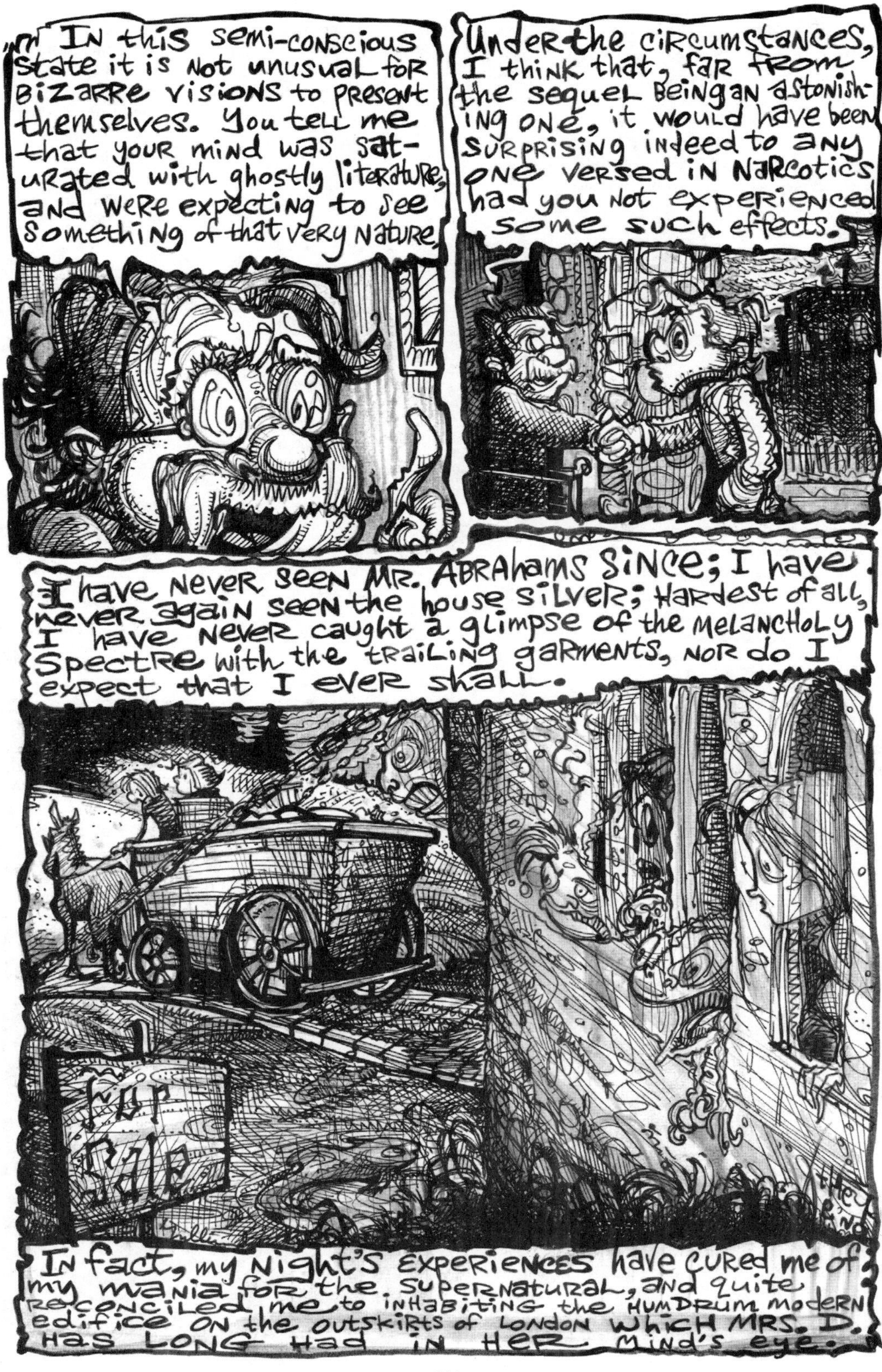
"...In this semi-conscious state it is not unusual for bizarre visions to present themselves. You tell me that your mind was saturated with ghostly literature, and were expecting to see something of that very nature.
Under the circumstances, I think that, far from the sequel being an astonishing one, it would have been surprising indeed to any one versed in narcotics had you not experienced some such effects.
I have never seen Mr. Abrahams since; I have never again seen the house silver; hardest of all, I have never caught a glimpse of the melancholy spectre with the trailing garments, nor do I expect that I ever shall.
For Sale
In fact, my night's experiences have cured me of my mania for the supernatural, and quite reconciled me to inhabiting the humdrum modern edifice on the outskirts of London which Mrs. D. has long had in her mind's eye.

ARTHUR CONAN DOYLE

Arthur Conan Doyle was born in 1859, studied in England and Germany and became a Doctor of Medicine at the University of Edinburgh. He built up a successful medical practice, but also wrote, and created his most famous character, Sherlock Holmes, in 1887. Following a less-successful practice as an oculist, Doyle concentrated on his writing career. He was proudest of his historical novels, such as *The White Company*, and in 1894 introduced his second popular character, Brigadier Gerard, and in 1912 a third, Professor Challenger. But Holmes continued to be his most famous creation. Doyle felt that Holmes was a distraction and kept him from writing the "better things" that would make him a "lasting name in English literature." He killed his detective in 1893 in *The Final Problem*, only to resurrect him in 1903 due to public demand. Doyle wrote an astonishing range of fiction including medical stories, sports stories, historical fiction, contemporary drama, and verse. He also wrote nonfiction, including the six-volume *The British Campaign in France and Flanders*. His defense of British colonialism in South Africa led to his being knighted in 1902. By 1916 Doyle's investigations into Spiritualism had convinced him that he should devote the rest of his life to the advancement of the belief. He wrote and lectured on the Spiritualist cause until his death in 1930.

RICK GEARY (cover, page 4)

Rick is best known for his thirteen years as a contributor to *The National Lampoon*. His work has also appeared in Marvel, DC, and Dark Horse comics, *Rolling Stone*, *Mad*, *Heavy Metal*, *Disney Adventures*, *The Los Angeles Times*, and *The New York Times Book Review*. He is a regular cartoonist in *Rosebud*. Rick has written and illustrated five children's books and published a collection of his comics, *Housebound with Rick Geary*. The seventh volume in his continuing book series *A Treasury of Victorian Murder* is *The Murder of Abraham Lincoln* (NBM Publishing, 2003). More of Rick's work has appeared in the *Graphic Classics* anthologies *Edgar Allan Poe*, *H.G. Wells*, *H.P. Lovecraft*, *Jack London*, *Ambrose Bierce*, *Mark Twain* and *O. Henry*. You can also view his art at www.rickgeary.com.

RICHARD SALA (page 1)

A master of gothic humor in the tradition of Charles Addams and Edward Gorey, Richard Sala creates stories filled with mystery, adventure, femmes fatales and homicidal maniacs. Richard is the artist and author of several collections, *Hypnotic Tales*, *Black Cat Crossing*, *Thirteen O'Clock*, *The Chuckling Whatsit*, plus an homage to Gorey titled *The Ghastly Ones*.

His work has appeared in *RAW*, *Blab!*, *Esquire*, *Playboy*, *The New York Times*, *Graphic Classics: Edgar Allan Poe*, *Graphic Classics: Bram Stoker* and his current, critically-acclaimed comic series, *Evil Eye*. Richard also created *Invisible Hands*, which ran on MTV's animation show, *Liquid Television*. Recent projects include the children's book *It Was a Dark and Silly Night* and illustrations for a previously unpublished screenplay by Jack Kerouac titled *Dr. Sax and the Great WorldSnake*. Visit Richard's website at www.richardsala.com for "lots of wonderfully creepy things to look at."

NEALE BLANDEN (page 2)

Neale lives in Melbourne, Australia and has been self-publishing comics since 1988. He has appeared in in various comics anthologies around the globe, and his artwork has been exhibited in galleries in Australia, Canada and Europe. He currently teaches cartooning, animation and storyboarding at a Melbourne college. Neale illustrated two of Bierce's fables in his unique style in *Graphic Classics: Ambrose Bierce*, a poem in *Graphic Classics: Robert Louis Stevenson*, and pictured a scene from *Dracula* in *Graphic Classics: Bram Stoker*.

NICK MILLER (pages 3, 76)

The son of two artists, Nick Miller learned to draw at an early age. After leaving college, he worked as a graphic designer before switching to cartooning full-time. Since then, his work has appeared in numerous adult and children's magazines as well as comics anthologies in Britain, Europe and the U.S. His weekly newspaper comics run in *The Planet on Sunday*. He shares his Lancaster, England house with two cats, a lodger and Antonella Caputo, his partner in Team Sputnik. Nick's stories have appeared in *Graphic Classics: Jack London*, *Graphic*

ILLUSTRATION ©1991 GEORGE SEARS

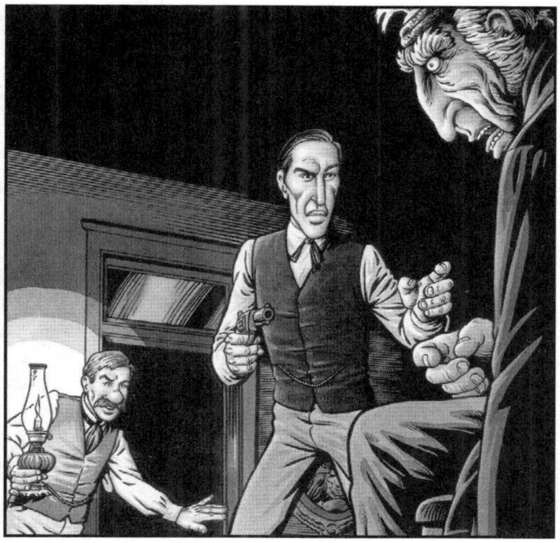

ILLUSTRATION ©1991 GEORGE SEARS

Classics: Ambrose Bierce, *Graphic Classics: Mark Twain* and *Horror Classics*. Contact Nick at sputnik@miller9090.freeserve.co.uk. A second tale of Brigadier Gerard adapted by Team Sputnik is featured in *Adventure Classics*.

JOHN W. PIERARD *(page 27)*

John Pierard has had a varied career in illustration. After leaving the bosom of his beloved Syracuse University for New York City, he immediately found work in publications such as *Screw* and *Velvet Touch Magazine*, where he illustrated stories like *Sex Junky*. In a major departure, he then graduated to illustrating children's fiction, including Mel Gilden's *P.S. 13* series, and various projects by noted children's author Bruce Coville. He has worked for Marvel Comics, *Asimov's Magazine* and Greenwich Press and has exhibited his art in New York galleries. John's comics adaptations are also featured in *Graphic Classics: Jack London*, *Graphic Classics: Bram Stoker* and *Horror Classics*.

J.B. BONIVERT *(page 46, back cover)*

Jeffrey Bonivert is a Bay Area native who has contributed to independent comics as both artist and writer, in such books as *The Funboys*, *Turtle Soup* and *Mister Monster*. His unique adaptation of *The Raven* originally appeared in 1979 in *Star*Reach*, and was revised for *Graphic Classics: Edgar Allan Poe*. Jeff's art is also published in *Graphic Classics: Ambrose Bierce*, *Graphic Classics: Jack London*, *Graphic Classics: Bram Stoker* and *Adventure Classics*, and he was part of the unique four-artist team on *Reanimator* in *Graphic Classics: H.P. Lovecraft*. Jeff's biography of artist Murphy Anderson appears in *Spark Generators*, and *Muscle and Faith*, his Casey Jones / Teenage Mutant Ninja Turtles epic, can be seen online at www.flyingcolorscomics.com.

ROGER LANGRIDGE *(page 58)*

New Zealand-born artist Roger Langridge is the creator of Fred the Clown, whose online comics appear every Monday at www.hotelfred.com. Fred also shows up in print three times a year in *Fred the Clown* comics. With his brother Andrew, Roger's first comics series was *Zoot!* published in 1988 and recently reissued as *Zoot Suite*. Other titles followed, including *Knuckles, The Malevolent Nun* and *Art d'Ecco*. Roger's work has also appeared in numerous magazines in Britain, the U.S., France and Japan, including *Deadline, Judge Dredd, Heavy Metal, Comic Afternoon, Gross Point* and *Batman: Legends of the Dark Knight*. He adapted a fable for *Graphic Classics: Robert Louis Stevenson*, *Eldorado* for *Graphic Classics: Edgar Allan Poe*, and collaborated with Mort Castle on a comics bio for *Graphic Classics: Jack London*. Roger now lives in London, where he divides his time between comics, children's books and commercial illustration.

MILTON KNIGHT *(page 60)*

Milton Knight claims he started drawing, painting and creating his own attempts at comic books and animation at age two. "I've never formed a barrier between fine art and cartooning," says Milt. "Growing up, I treasured Chinese watercolors, Breughel, Charlie Brown and Terrytoons equally." His work has appeared in magazines including *Heavy Metal, High Times, National Lampoon* and *Nickelodeon Magazine*, and he has illustrated record covers, posters, candy packaging and T-shirts, and occasionally exhibited his paintings. Labor on *Ninja Turtles* comics allowed him to get up a grubstake to move to the West Coast in 1991, where he became an animator and director on *Felix the Cat* cartoons. Milt's comics titles include *Midnite the Rebel Skunk, Slug and Ginger* and *Hugo*. He has contributed to the *Graphic Classics* volumes *Edgar Allan Poe, Jack London, Ambrose Bierce, Mark Twain, O. Henry, Horror Classics* and *Adventure Classics*. Check the latest news at www.miltonknight.net.

ANTONELLA CAPUTO *(page 76)*

Antonella Caputo was born and educated in Rome, and is now living in England. She has been an architect, archaeologist, art restorer, photographer, calligrapher, interior designer, theater designer, actress and theater director. Antonella's first published work was *Casa Montesi*, a weekly comic strip that appeared in *Il Journalino*. She has since written comedies for children and scripts for comics in Europe and the U.S., before joining Nick Miller as a partner in Sputnik Studios. Antonella has collaborated with Nick, as well as with artists Rick Geary, Mark A. Nelson and Francesca Ghermandi in *Graphic*

Classics: Jack London, *Graphic Classics: Ambrose Bierce*, *Graphic Classics: O. Henry*, *Graphic Classics: Mark Twain*, *Horror Classics* and *Adventure Classics*.

ROD LOTT (page 98)
Based in Oklahoma City, Rod Lott is a freelance writer and graphic designer in advertising and journalism. For twelve years, he has published and edited the more-or-less quarterly magazine *Hitch: The Journal of Pop Culture Absurdity* (www.hitchmagazine.com), and recently started *Bookgasm*, a daily book reviews and news website at www.bookgasm.com. Rod's humorous essays have been published in several anthologies, including *101 Damnations* and *May Contain Nuts*. Rod has scripted comics adaptations of stories by Edgar Allan Poe, Clark Ashton Smith, H.G. Wells, Sax Rohmer and O. Henry for *Graphic Classics*, and has just completed an adaptation of *Captain Blood* for the upcoming *Graphic Classics: Rafael Sabatini*. You can learn more about his work online at www.rodlott.com.

SIMON GANE (page 98)
British artist Simon Gane lives and works in Bath as a magazine and children's book illustrator and graphic designer. His first published strips appeared in the self-produced punk fanzine *Arnie*, and others followed in self-contained mini comics and eventually the collection *Punk Strips*. He recently completed *All Flee*, a comic about a "finishing school for monsters" and is working on a four-issue series set in the Paris and New York of the 1950s for Slave Labor Graphics. "I especially enjoyed drawing *The Policeman and the Citizen* in *Graphic Classics: Ambrose Bierce*," says Simon, "because it encompasses many of my favorite themes: alcohol, police aggression, a past-times setting and a sense that whilst largely forgotten now, comics remain a peerless medium for satire." For *Is He Living or Is He Dead?*, in *Graphic Classics: Mark Twain*, Simon spent time sketching in Menton, the setting of the story, which contributes to the rich backgrounds and detail that are also evident in his interpretations of *Dr. Jekyll and Mr. Hyde* for *Graphic Classics: Robert Louis Stevenson* and *The Invisible Man* for *Graphic Classics: H.G. Wells*.

PETER GULLERUD *(page 125)*
A self-taught artist, Peter went straight from one year of theological college to Disney Studios, where he worked his way up to the position of visual development artist on feature films including *Aladdin*. He later moved to Warner Brothers Studios, where he worked on *Space Jam* and *Iron Giant*. He eventually left animation behind to concentrate on his personal work, including wildlife art. His involvement with California's Mountain Lion Foundation led to a thirteen-month stay as nightwatchman at Tippi Hedren's Shambala nature preserve, caring for lions, tigers and elephants. Peter's paintings have been shown in galleries nationwide, his *Grootlore* comics (www.grootlore.com) have been collected by Fantagraphics, and his *Hueby* comic strip (www.hueby.us) has appeared in papers including the *Chicago Reader*. Peter's previous work for *Graphic Classics* appears in the *Robert Louis Stevenson* and *O. Henry* volumes.

GEORGE SEARS *(pages 142, 143)*
For over twenty years George has been doing illustrations and comics for children's magazines, including *Jack & Jill*, *Enid Blyton Mystery Magazine*, and *Blue Moon Magazine*. He has also done illustrations and cartoons for numerous businesses, organizations, and adult publications and a syndicated comic strip called *Senator Boondoggle*. He had collaborated with writer Tim Quinn on several children's magazine projects before creating with him a pair of Sherlock Holmes adaptations, *The Speckled Band & The Blue Carbuncle*, and *The Hound of the Baskervilles*, which were published in Britain by Collins Lions in 1991. George is an avid reader of Golden Age British detective stories, and boasts a collection of over 3,000 hardback mysteries.

TOM POMPLUN
The designer, editor and publisher of the *Graphic Classics* series, Tom previously designed and produced *Rosebud*, a journal of poetry, fiction and illustration, from 1993 to 2003. He is now working on the production of *Graphic Classics: Rafael Sabatini*, scheduled for release in February 2006. The book features the origin of Sabatini's famed gentleman pirate Captain Blood, plus six more tales of mystery, romance and adventure. You can find previews, sample art, and much more at www.graphicclassics.com.

GRAPHIC CLASSICS
GREAT TALES OF MYSTERY, PLUS SWASHBUCKLING ADVENTURE WITH CAPTAIN BLOOD!
RAFAEL SABATINI
ROGER LANGRIDGE · MILTON KNIGHT · RICH TOMMASO · CARLO VERGARA

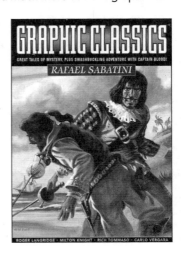